*A publication of the
Association of Governing Boards
of Universities and Colleges*

GOVERNING
PUBLIC
COLLEGES AND
UNIVERSITIES

*Richard T. Ingram
and Associates*

Foreword by Clark Kerr

GOVERNING PUBLIC COLLEGES AND UNIVERSITIES

*A Handbook for Trustees,
Chief Executives, and
Other Campus Leaders*

Jossey-Bass Publishers · San Francisco

For sales outside the United States, contact Maxwell Macmillan International Publishing Group, 866 Third Avenue, New York, New York 10022.

Manufactured in the United States of America

The paper used in this book is acid-free and meets the State of California requirements for recycled paper (50 percent recycled waste, including 10 percent postconsumer waste), which are the strictest guidelines for recycled paper currently in use in the United States.

10% POST CONSUMER WASTE

The ink in this book is either soy- or vegetable-based and during the printing process emits fewer than half the volatile organic compounds (VOCs) emitted by petroleum-based ink.

Library of Congress Cataloging-in-Publication Data

Ingram, Richard T., date.
    Governing public colleges and universities : a handbook for trustees, chief executives, and other campus leaders / Richard T. Ingram. — 1st ed.
        p.   cm. — (A joint publication in the Jossey-Bass higher and adult education series and the Jossey-Bass nonprofit sector series)
    Includes bibliographical references and index.
    ISBN 1-55542-566-6
    1. Public universities and colleges—United States—Administration—Handbooks, manuals, etc. 2. College trustees—United States—Handbooks, manuals, etc. 3. College presidents—United States—Handbooks, manuals, etc. 4. College administrators—United States—Handbooks, manuals, etc. I. Title. II. Series: Jossey-Bass higher and adult education series. III. Series: Jossey-Bass nonprofit sector series.
LB2341.I5325   1993
378.1′00973—dc20   93-19512
                                                        CIP

FIRST EDITION
HB Printing   10 9 8 7 6 5 4 3 2 1   *Code 9360*

A joint publication
in
The Jossey-Bass
Higher and Adult Education Series
and
The Jossey-Bass
Nonprofit Sector Series

Contents

Tables, Figures, and Exhibits

Tables

Figures

Exhibits

*This book is dedicated to the nearly ten thousand
trustees and chief executives of public higher education,
who are ultimately responsible for
the quality of the education of
80 percent of the nation's full-time and part-time students.*

Foreword

Central responsibility for the quality of higher education governance rests with voluntary citizen boards of trustees. This handbook is about how best to keep boards of trustees operating effectively. Doing so will not be easy, because the burdens on trustees are increasing, especially as presidents serve for shorter terms than in decades past and are surrounded as never before by the politics of special interest groups.

Four areas in which trustees have special duties are becoming more crucial:

- *Securing and deploying financial resources.* National productivity increases over the past thirty years have fallen precipitously. And there are more insistent competitors for our diminished new resources.
- *Managing the legal environment.* The growing number of legal cases in higher education over the past thirty years mirrors their proliferation elsewhere in society.
- *Encouraging public understanding and support.* Higher education is experiencing fiercer criticism, warranted or not, than ever before.

- *Defending institutional autonomy.* Federal and state controls have intensified over the past thirty years. Trustees are at the front line, protecting the independence of colleges and universities.

This handbook concentrates on public college and university trusteeship. Many of the same issues arise in independent institutions, but public trusteeship has its special problems: two-thirds of all public campuses are part of multicampus systems, an arrangement that carries additional complexities.

Trustees, whether elected or appointed, are chosen to one degree or another according to external political considerations. Thus, external concerns are also likely to affect board decision making:

- Fewer members of public boards than in the past have a prior devotion to the welfare of the institution, and they usually serve for shorter terms than their counterparts on private boards.
- Boards are also subject to more oversight by governors and legislators and greater scrutiny by the media in states with "sunshine" laws than in the past.

Trusteeship of public institutions, with its special problems, has responsibility for 80 percent of all students in higher education. Consequently, public trustees deserve a handbook of their own, and they are very well served by this one, which is well written and edited. The presentations, by authors with a deep knowledge of their subject, cover all the most essential issues. The best system of public higher education in the world now has the best handbook on trusteeship.

A word of caution, however. All the necessary information is here in a general sense, but each institution of higher education is in some ways unique. Thus, trustees not only should read the broadly applicable advice that follows but also should think of how it can best be adapted to their particular institutions. The authors have done their part. It is now up to the readers: what can each of us do better?

Tom Ingram has shown splendid leadership in creating this

handbook, which continues a series of publications on trusteeship undertaken by him and Bob Gale, president emeritus of the Association of Governing Boards of Universities and Colleges (AGB), with John Nason's definitive *The Nature of Trusteeship* (1982), originally published (under the title *The Future of Trusteeship*) nearly twenty years ago. Gale and Ingram and their colleagues at AGB have done a great deal to raise the expectations for and the performance of trusteeship.

Berkeley, California   Clark Kerr
August 1993   President Emeritus
                                     University of California

Preface

W. C. Fields was once asked to give his opinion about a novel he had read. His quip went something like this: "Well, I'd say, on the whole, it's a good book. The only trouble with it is—the covers are too far apart!" And so it may be with *Governing Public Colleges and Universities*. Its length is testimony, however, to the complex responsibilities that boards and trustees face in coping with difficult issues in difficult times. The book is meant to serve as a resource— to be pulled off the shelf when needed for any number of purposes, including in-service education programs at regular board meetings or retreats.

The first edition was published in 1980 for trustees, chief executives, and other leaders in the public *and* private sectors. It is time for a revision, and for a volume public sector leaders can call their own, one dedicated to the fascinating thicket of public trust-eeship. Although the responsibilities of governing boards are fundamentally the same in public and private higher education, the environments within which public and private boards meet their public trust are very different. Thus there is a clear need for two completely new books: this one and its companion volume for private college and university leaders.

Much can be said and done to strengthen the membership, organization, development, and performance of governing boards in public higher education. From one point of view, much—perhaps too much—is expected of too few by too many. The volunteer trustees and regents of the nation's diverse and expanding public higher education system are expected to function effectively in one of the most complex political, economic, and social environments ever created. They need all the help they can get.

Of the twenty-two contributors to this volume, eight are current trustees and six others are recent or current chief executives. All the contributors are longtime students of trusteeship who share the following convictions about a unique, if imperfect, institution that has served higher education and the nation with distinction:

- Volunteer trusteeship is currently undergoing the most stringent test of its viability and competence since the 1960s and the period of student unrest caused by the Vietnam War.
- Calls for the reform of trustee selection processes are likely to continue—and should, notwithstanding the committed and superb service of thousands of capable trustees.
- Boards, trustees, and chief executives must think and act more strategically than they have done or have had to do thus far.
- Boards and their most influential members must be much more assertive and effective advocates, first, for higher education generally, and second, for their institution or public system.
- Boards and trustees must more resolutely pursue their commitment to periodic self-study and third-party assessment to help ensure the highest possible performance standards.

Overview of the Contents

Governing Public Colleges and Universities is divided into four parts.

Part One will help the reader understand the context within which trustees must function—the swirl of financial, demographic, social, legal, and planning issues that keeps trustees and everyone who works with them on their toes. A brief look at the emergence of public sector higher education and the origins of citizen trusteeship, a tradition largely misunderstood and underappreciated by the general public and political leaders, is offered in Chapter One. Chapter Two describes the implications of the 1990 census and the demographic challenges affecting institutional missions, clientele, faculty, access, and equity. Chapter Three addresses the practical and philosophical issue of who should pay for public higher education in a decade of limited resources. How boards can reduce personal and institutional liability is the subject of Chapter Four, which emphasizes the duties of loyalty and care; use of legal counsel; immunity and indemnification; and insurance. Chapter Five illustrates how trustees can think and act more strategically to shape their institutions' future. The first five chapters are thus devoted to describing some of the many issues yet to be addressed in what will be an extended period of reassessment and change. Taken together, they describe a higher education system in transition.

Part Two is devoted to key responsibilities of governing boards. Following an overview in Chapter Six of the board's job description and some reminders of what is expected of individual trustees, the most visible of all board duties—selecting the chief executive—is discussed in all its nuances in Chapter Seven. Chapter Eight explains what has been learned about the tricky business of assessing the presidency, and in particular how boards should support their incumbent. Chapter Nine makes understandable the complex responsibility to oversee the financial condition and capital assets of the university or public system. And Chapter Ten offers useful information about public higher education's increasing dependence on private gift dollars—and about how to get donations.

Chapter Eleven covers the principles of board relationships with government agencies and political leaders. For trustees who serve on the boards of multicampus systems, Chapter Twelve describes sensible attitudes, policies, and practices that contribute to maintaining healthy communication with constituent universities and campuses. The principles and values that should guide institutional leaders as they wrestle with increasingly complex political, social, and ethical issues are the subject of Chapter Thirteen. Chapter Fourteen traces the origins and development of collective bargaining and gives practical advice on the negotiating process and trustees' role in it. Academic tenure and the importance of understanding the policies and practices that govern faculty members' employment and performance are described in Chapter Fifteen. The current obsession with quality and how trustees should be concerned with it are addressed in Chapter Sixteen. The eleven chapters in Part Two thus help the reader to cope with the inevitable ambiguities of academic trusteeship, by clarifying the distinction between board and executive responsibilities.

Part Three offers advice to those who recognize that *every* board can be better. Effective academic trusteeship is learned, not innate; education of trustees should begin with a substantive orientation and continue through in-service programs. Chapter Seventeen discusses orientation of new board members and board development. Chapter Eighteen is a provocative look at board meetings and how trustees behave in them. Chapter Nineteen clarifies for the chief executive and the board chair their mutual and distinctive responsibilities in leading the board. Chapter Twenty looks at what constitutes solid staff support, especially through the position of board staff secretary, an emerging professional position in the academy. And Chapter Twenty-One makes the case for periodic assessment of board performance and suggests strategies for meeting that responsibility.

The resources at the end of the book reinforce the concepts and advice offered throughout. Resource A answers these questions: What constitutes a good job description for the board and for the trustee? What qualifications should be sought in candidates for trusteeship? Resource B responds to the question How do some characteristics, policies, and practices of our board compare with those of other boards? Resource C provides performance standards for public multicampus and system governing boards, as an illustration of what the Association of Governing Boards of Universities and Colleges (AGB) makes available in survey form to other public (and private) institutions. Resource D recommends the best of the available literature as further background for each chapter.

The Association of Governing Boards is dedicated to helping trustees and chief executives make good decisions in these difficult times. It provides its members with the information and the tools to help them think and act strategically. As a continuing education resource, the AGB seeks to strengthen board performance and

The Authors

Richard T. Ingram is president of the Association of Governing Boards of Universities and Colleges. Before joining the association in 1971, he held positions in the Department of Student Life at the University of Maryland, served as admissions and personnel officer of the U.S. Military Academy Preparatory School, taught high school, and served as an adjunct faculty member at the University of Virginia and the University of Southern California.

Ingram was awarded his B.A. degree (1963) in social sciences education from Indiana University of Pennsylvania, his M.Ed. degree (1964) in secondary education from the University of Pittsburgh, and his Ed.D. degree (1969) in higher education from the University of Maryland. Ingram has been a teacher, researcher, consultant, and writer in the fields of higher education trusteeship, administration, and planning for more than twenty years. He has led some fifty workshops and retreats for trustees and chief executives in both the public and private sectors of higher education. He is a trustee of Connelly School in Potomac, Maryland, and a former trustee of the University of Charleston in West Virginia. Ingram serves as secretary and treasurer of the board of directors of United Educators Insurance Risk Retention Group and as an advisory commissioner of the Education Commission of the States.

E. Grady Bogue is professor in the Department of Educational Leadership at the University of Tennessee and chancellor emeritus of Louisiana State University in Shreveport. Bogue has written articles in journals such as the *Harvard Business Review, Educational Record, Journal of Higher Education,* and *Phi Delta Kappan* and four books, the most recent of which is *The Evidence for Quality* (1992). He has been a consultant on planning, evaluation, quality assurance, and leadership to colleges and universities and to state-level planning agencies and corporations. He holds three degrees from Memphis State University: a B.S. degree (1957) in mathematics, an M.S. degree (1965) in education, and an Ed.D. degree (1968).

Molly C. Broad is senior vice chancellor for administration and finance and chief operating officer of the California State University System, which is the largest four-year college and university system in the nation. She has responsibility for business and financial operations, human resources, collective bargaining, and physical planning and construction, among other areas, and also serves as the university's principal link with the state government in Sacramento. Previously, she served as executive director and chief executive officer for the Arizona Board of Regents.

Broad received her B.A. degree (1962) from Syracuse University and her M.A. degree (1963) from Ohio State University, both in economics. She is currently in the Ph.D. program in economics at Syracuse University.

Robert L. Carothers is president of the University of Rhode Island. Before assuming this position, Carothers served as chancellor of the Minnesota State University System and president of Southwest State University in Marshall, Minnesota. He received his B.S. degree (1965) in education from Edinboro University, his M.A. (1966) and Ph.D. (1969) degrees, both in English, from Kent State University, and his J.D. degree (1981) from the University of Akron.

Richard P. Chait is professor of higher education and management and director of the National Center for Postsecondary Governance at the University of Maryland. Previously, he served as Mandel Professor of Non-Profit Management at Case Western Reserve University, associate provost at Pennsylvania State University, and assistant professor at the Harvard Graduate School of Education. He earned both his B.A. degree (1966) from Rutgers University and his M.A. degree (1968) from the University of Wisconsin in American history and his Ph.D. degree (1972) in educational administration, also from the University of Wisconsin. He is coauthor of *The Effective Board of Trustees* (1991, with T. Holland and B. E. Taylor) and a trustee of Goucher College.

Frances Freeman has been program and financial development consultant to numerous colleges, universities, and professional associations, including the Association of Governing Boards of Universities and Colleges. For six years, she was a member of Gale Associates, an educational consulting firm. She has written extensively and has lived and worked overseas. Freeman has served on two nonprofit boards. She earned her B.A. degree (1958) in art from the College of New Rochelle.

Robert L. Gale is president emeritus of the Association of Governing Boards of Universities and Colleges. He served as president of the association from 1974 to 1992. A trustee of Carleton College in Minnesota since 1970, Gale serves on the boards of the National Executive Service Corps, CARE, the Alliance of Independent Colleges of Art, and the National Center for Nonprofit Boards. He is a frequent speaker before national organizations, governing boards, and foundation boards. He has served as president of Gale Associates, director of public affairs for the Equal Employment Opportunity Commission, director of recruiting and of public affairs for the Peace Corps, vice president of Carleton College, and editor-in-chief of Maco Magazine Corporation. He earned his B.A. degree (1948) in mathematics from Carleton College.

Harold L. Hodgkinson is currently conducting research on demographics and education for the Center for Demographic Policy. He serves as senior adviser for the American Council on Education, trustee at Hartwick College, and member of the board of overseers, Regents College, New York. Hodgkinson has directed eight major research projects for the Carnegie Commission, the U.S. Office of

Education, the Exxon Foundation, the Ford Foundation, and the Atlantic Richfield Foundation. He has written twelve books and more than two hundred articles. He earned his B.A. degree (1953) in literature and philosophy from the University of Minnesota, his M.A. degree (1955) in teaching from Wesleyan University, and his Ed.D. degree (1959) in education from Harvard University.

Sandra L. Johnson is a manager in the National Higher Education/ Nonprofit Group at Coopers & Lybrand. Johnson edits Coopers & Lybrand's *Higher Education Management Newsletter* as well as the *Nonprofit Management Newsletter.* She also writes articles for higher education publications. Johnson coauthored *The Decaying American Campus, a Ticking Time Bomb* (1989, with S. C. Rush). She holds a B.S. degree (1974) in public communication from Boston University and an M.B.A. degree (1986) from Simmons College. She is a certified public accountant in Massachusetts.

Joseph F. Kauffman is professor emeritus of educational administration at the University of Wisconsin, Madison. He is also executive vice president emeritus of the University of Wisconsin System and president emeritus of Rhode Island College. Kauffman has served as president of the Association for the Study of Higher Education and as chair of the board of directors of the American Association for Higher Education. He is the author of *At the Pleasure of the Board: The Service of the College and University President* (1980). He earned his B.A. degree (1948) in sociology from the University of Denver, his M.A. degree (1951), also in sociology, from Northwestern University, and his Ed.D. degree (1958) from Boston University.

George David Kieffer is a partner in the national law firm of Manatt, Phelps & Phillips. Kieffer is a former member of the board of governors of the California Community Colleges and has served on a number of other boards and commissions. He is the author of *The Strategy of Meetings* (1988). Kieffer received his B.A. degree (1969) in history from the University of California, Santa Barbara, and his J.D. degree (1973) from the University of California, Los Angeles.

David M. Lascell is partner in the law firm of Hallanbeck, Lascell & Pineo in Rochester, New York. He earned a law degree (1966) from Cornell University. He has served as chairman of the board of trustees of Wells College for more than ten years. Lascell has also been director of the American Council on Education, trustee of Rochester Area Colleges, and member of the board of directors of the Association of Governing Boards of Universities and Colleges (1980–1991). He is a director of the Common Fund, chairman of the board of the National Center for Nonprofit Boards, and trustee of Mount Vernon College.

Sanford H. Levine is university counsel and vice chancellor for legal affairs of the State University of New York. He received both his A.B. degree (1959) in political science and his J.D. degree (1961) from Syracuse University. Active in the practice of higher education law for more than twenty years, he served as president of the National Association of College and University Attorneys in 1986–87.

David A. Longanecker is Assistant Secretary for Postsecondary Education, U.S. Department of Education. He has extensive experience in higher education policy development at the institutional, state, and federal levels. He served as executive director of the Colorado Commission on Higher Education from 1988 to 1993. Previously, he served the Minnesota Higher Education Coordinating Board, the Congressional Budget Office, Stanford University, and George Washington University in various administrative and policy-making roles. His many publications focus on the economics and financing of higher education. Longanecker earned his B.A. degree (1968) in sociology from Washington State University, his M.A. degree (1971) in education from George Washington University, and his Ed.D. degree (1978) from Stanford University.

Aims C. McGuinness, Jr., is director for higher education policy at the Denver-based Education Commission of the States. He received his B.A. degree (1965) in political science from the University of Pennsylvania, his M.B.A. degree (1970) from George Washington University, and his Ph.D. degree (1979) in social science from the Maxwell School of Citizenship and Public Affairs, Syracuse University. McGuinness is member of the board of trustees for the State Colleges in Colorado and elected member and president of the board of education of the Littleton, Colorado, public schools. He wrote a basic reference guide on higher education coordination and governance in the fifty states, the *State Postsecondary Education Structures Handbook* (1985).

Judith Block McLaughlin is educational chair of the Harvard Seminar for New Presidents, lecturer at the Harvard Graduate School of Education, and research associate in Harvard's Department of Sociology. She has published journal articles on presidential searches and higher education governance and is coauthor of *Choosing a College President* (1990, with D. Riesman) and *An Education of Value* (1985, with M. Lazerson and B. McPherson). She earned an A.B. degree (1970) in sociology from the University of North Carolina, Chapel Hill, and M.A.T. (1971) and Ed.D. (1983) degrees from Harvard University.

Joel W. Meyerson is director of AGB's Strategic Policy Institute. He is also co-director of the Stanford Forum for Higher Education Futures. Previously, he was partner and director of the higher education and nonprofit practice of Coopers & Lybrand. He was a faculty member at the Harvard Institute for Educational Management and serves on several advisory panels, including the Massachusetts Board of Regents task forces on capital maintenance and tuition policy. Meyerson is author or coauthor of many publications, including *Strategy and Finance in Higher Education* (1992), *Productivity and Higher Education* (1991), and *Strategic Analysis: Using Comparative Data to Understand Your Institution* (1990). He received his A.B. degree (1973) in history from Vassar College, his A.M. degree (1980) in American studies from Brown University, and his M.B.A. degree (1978) from Columbia University.

Kenneth P. Mortimer is president of the University of Hawaii. He is former president of Western Washington University and former vice president and vice provost of Pennsylvania State University, where he also directed the Center for the Study of Higher Education from 1976 to 1981. He has written extensively about academic governance and management and about policy development in higher education. From 1983 to 1985, he chaired the Study Group on the Conditions of Excellence, which produced the highly acclaimed report *Involvement in Learning: Realizing the Potential of American Higher Education* (1984). He holds an A.B. degree (1960) in English from the University of Pennsylvania, an M.B.A. degree (1962) from the Wharton School of Finance and Commerce, and a Ph.D. degree (1969) in higher education from the University of California, Berkeley.

Curtis R. Simic is president of the Indiana University Foundation. He received his B.S. degree (1963) in physical education from Indiana University. Before returning to Indiana University, Simic served as vice chancellor for development at the University of California, Berkeley, and president of the foundation of that university. He also served as vice president for university relations at the University of Oregon, assistant vice president for educational development at the University of Alabama, director of development of the School of Medicine at Yale University, and director of development of the University of Tennessee Health Sciences Center. He is a contributor to publications of the Council for the Advancement and Support of Education and the Association of Governing Boards of Universities and Colleges.

Bonnie M. Smotony is secretary of the regents of the University of California. Formerly, she was assistant to the chancellor and secretary of the board of regents of the University of Nevada. Since the early seventies, she has collaborated with the Association of Governing Boards of Universities and Colleges in developing annual workshops for professional staff members and board secretaries of higher education governing boards and has conducted three surveys examining the role of the board secretary.

Barbara E. Taylor is vice president for programs and research at the Association of Governing Boards of Universities and Colleges, where she directs a variety of workshops and seminars and designs and conducts research projects exploring board responsibilities and performance. She is the author of *Working Effectively with Trustees*

(1987) and coauthor of *The Effective Board of Trustees* (1991), with R. P. Chait and T. P. Holland) and has written numerous articles, book chapters, and case studies concerning the governance and financing of higher education. She is a trustee of Wittenberg University in Ohio. Taylor received her B.A. degree (1968) in English from the State University of New York, Potsdam, her M.S. degree (1969) in counseling from Miami University, and her D.Ed. degree (1982) from Pennsylvania State University.

Paul N. Ylvisaker was dean emeritus and Charles William Eliot Professor at the Harvard Graduate School of Education at the time of his death in early 1992. He taught at Bethany Lutheran Junior College, Swarthmore College, Princeton University, the University of Pennsylvania, and Yale University. He also served as New Jersey commissioner of community affairs, as chairman of the Task Force on Cities under President Johnson, and as member of a United Nations technical assistance mission to Japan. Ylvisaker was chairman of the Association of Governing Board's Higher Education Issues Panel and senior consultant to the Council on Foundations. He earned his A.A. degree (1940) from Bethany Lutheran Junior College, his B.S. degree (1942) from Mankato State University, and his M.P.A. (1945) and Ph.D. (1948) degrees from Harvard University.

GOVERNING
PUBLIC
COLLEGES AND
UNIVERSITIES

PART ONE

Understanding
the Environment
of Public
Higher Education

Institutional and multicampus governing boards find themselves in the midst of a gigantic kaleidoscope of conflicting values and ideologies that, in the end, only they can successfully negotiate themselves and their colleges and universities through. Serving as a trustee is increasingly a high-wire act in a complex and demanding society that expects flawless performance from all its institutions. Trustees and governing boards need to reconsider nearly all conventional wisdom about public higher education, including how it is and should be financed in a period of limited resources and how its essential mission must be protected in the most litigious environment in the world.

Part One is devoted to helping the reader understand the intricate environment within which the volunteer trustee and academic governing board function. Its five chapters highlight the roots, traditions, and ambiguities of academic trusteeship within the context of the current decade, which is so markedly different from the last one. And it addresses the profound demographic changes that will determine how change is finally shaped in and by the academy, which in the past has been bound by tradition and very resistant to change. This section describes a higher education system in transition, in which strategic thinking and acting by trustees and chief executives have never been more important to the nation.

1

CHAPTER 1

Exercising Stewardship
in Times of Transition

Richard T. Ingram

Citizen trusteeship in U.S. higher education has been variously described as a "gift of history" (Kerr and Gade, 1989, p. 17), as having done "more injury than Benedict Arnold" (Wayland, in Rudolph, 1965, p. 172), as being "a barrier to rational progress" (Galbraith, 1967, p. 37), and as being "the keeper of the social conscience" and "protector of the public interest" (Millett, 1962, p. 183). For decades, college and university trusteeship has been criticized by leaders in academia, business, and government more often than it has been praised.

But there can be no doubt that trusteeship is here to stay. It will not become the harmless anachronism predicted by Galbraith (1967). As imperfect as they are, governing boards have proven their value in the U.S. version of participatory democracy, which is averse to monopoly of power and which provides systems of checks and balances. William F. Buckley (*AGB Notes*, 1971, p. 1) once quipped that he "would sooner be governed by the first 2,000 names in the Boston telephone directory than by the 2,000 members of the faculty of Harvard University." Higher education trusteeship is an extension of the American ethos that dates back to Harvard in 1636, although its roots are found in Western Europe some four centuries before.

3

The university was always and continues to be one of the most complex organizations ever created by human beings. It has always been a major source of tension within the societies that support it, as well as their source of hope for the future. And citizen boards of trustees find themselves squarely in the middle of these tensions and hopes—between the academy and its many constituencies.

The continuing challenge for members of governing boards is to more effectively meet the purposes and expectations so ambiguously held for them by a demanding and troubled society. The thesis of this chapter, indeed of this book, is simply that the citizen board of trustees is our best hope for sustaining the one institution among precious few that has maintained a strong competitive edge. The citizen board has emerged as the best alternative to governmental or exclusive faculty control of higher education. But citizen trusteeship needs to be much better understood and nourished than it is currently—by the trustees themselves and by those who criticize its shortcomings without offering a viable alternative.

Ironically, the general public, including many of the nation's elected political leaders and some corporate executives, do not fully understand or appreciate what trustees and governing boards do and do not—indeed should not—do. The existence of trustees and governing boards has contributed to spirited competition between institutions that has kept U.S. higher education the envy of the world.

Some opinion makers do not seem to understand that the majority of volunteer trustees devote very significant time to their responsibilities but cannot and need not know the institution's or system's every nuance, nook, and cranny. Some people are not aware of how different and fragile the culture of the academy is compared with that of virtually all other types of organizations. Misunderstanding of this point may have inconsequential outcomes or outcomes that are very harmful to the essential role that academic institutions have in a free society. Of course, faculty members, administrators, or trustees should not be above criticism. Indeed they all make mistakes—some of them big ones. And the university *is* slow to respond to the needs of the society that supports it financially. It always has been, for many complex reasons.

It should not surprise us that faculty members, students, and alumni are equally mystified by what goes on in the boardroom. Trustees have the obligation to be clear about their responsibilities and the broader context for their stewardship, that is, to help educate others, to correct misunderstandings, to interpret the academy to its many publics, and to help the community of scholars know when and what changes are legitimate, indeed essential, to meet society's needs.

Robert Ulich writes in his anthology of the ideas of the great thinkers on education that "we are fumbling around in education because we know so little about the future and do not bother to know enough about the past" (1959, p. v). This chapter offers a glimpse of trusteeship's past, present, and likely future as an important and evolving part of U.S. higher education. It includes a section on the dimensions of public sector trusteeship and makes the case that, in this decade, competent trusteeship will become even more important to public higher education and to the nation's future than previously. Six persistent myths about governing boards are addressed along the way.

A Gift of History

The idea that nonacademics should oversee the academy, to hold it accountable to the public as well as to protect it from capricious political entanglements, has a very long and distinguished history. Virtually all organizations in both the for-profit and tax-exempt sectors of U.S. society have governing boards, but the link between the two sectors in academic trusteeship is both real and exaggerated. It is true, for example, that about one-third of the nation's some fifty thousand trustees in private and public higher education are executives in business and industry, but academic trusteeship has evolved into an institution unique in form and substance to set it apart from the governance or dominance of for-profit enterprises.

Myth one: the origin of the lay governing board is found in the American corporation. This myth is apparent in a statement by the Assembly on University Goals and Governance (1971, p. 52): "For too long, colleges and universities have borrowed their governance models from business and public administration. Neither is appropriate for most functions of academic institutions." Actually, the roots of boards of lay (volunteer) trustees are not found in the corporation. They are found in the Protestant Reformation, especially in Calvinist institutions of higher education.

Kerr and Gade (1989, p. 17) offer a brief and superbly written history that tracks public governing boards as far back as the mid-fourteenth century in Italy and Germany, when student universities on the Bologna model "were placed under public control in response to perceived excesses against both the professorate and the townspeople." John Calvin's Academy, founded in Geneva in 1559, was the first of the Reformation colleges to embody the theory of lay (nonclergy and nonacademic) control. Spain had "social councils" of prominent local citizens for each of its universities as early as the twelfth century. They helped to ensure proper student discipline and use of public funds. Other countries of Western Europe followed suit and have their own fascinating stories.

In colonial America, the first governing board for Harvard was established in 1642. The Board of Overseers was made up of "leading men" from throughout the colony, but President Dunster persuaded the overseers to seek a charter from the colonial government to permit the formation of a second board, internal to the college. The subsequent group, consisting of the president and fellows of Harvard College, was intended to help address the overseers' problem of traveling great distances to attend meetings. The relative youth of the internal board members and the rapid turnover of the board ensured, however, that the external overseers retained authority. Some local ministers were eventually added to the second board, thus bringing the concept of the lay board to Harvard and the colonies.

The College of William and Mary in Virginia was the second colonial college with two boards (1693), and Brown College in Rhode Island became the third. The dual board model did not hold up, however, perhaps because of role conflicts. The governing board of Yale College (1701) served as a model for those that followed for quite some time: a single self-perpetuating board consisting originally of all clergy members.

Until six of the original thirteen states chartered public universities, the notion of public and private education as we know it today did not exist; the provincial college was established for public purposes and was thought of as a community institution. When the idea of the public university began to emerge after 1785, state charters incorporated self-perpetuating boards of trustees, often dominated by religious groups. Thus they followed the model of a single board and, eventually, moved to appointed or elected boards without clergy representation.

Kerr and Gade's history of governing boards (1989) should be read by all trustees, as should a superb chapter on the same subject in Cowley (1980). The concept and practice of citizen trusteeship in higher education preceded corporate boards by many, many years. Indeed, the corporate board of directors was more likely influenced by the college and university experience than the other way around. Undoubtedly, many lessons are still to be learned and shared between the academy and the business community, but there is no evidence that the corporate sector ever dominated higher education in the powerful ways alleged by social critics such as Upton Sinclair and Thorstein Veblen.

The Emergence of Public Higher Education

Until about 1940, more students were enrolled in private colleges and universities than public ones. The emergence of the community college, the regional state university, and especially systems of public higher education is really *the* story of the past fifty years. It is an astonishing story of success in capacity building, of the state-by-state search for the ideal governing structure (ultimately from the perspectives of governors and legislators), and of the continuing concern about whether consolidation and control is preferable to autonomy and competition (Kerr and Gade, 1989).

Myth two: the vast majority of students in public higher education are enrolled in institutions that have their own governing boards. More than 14 million people are enrolled full- or part-time in higher education. Nearly 80 percent are on campuses of public colleges and universities and of these more than 10.5 million students, about 70 percent—close to 7.4 million students—are on campuses within multicampus systems that do not have their own local governing boards.

According to Kerr and Gade (1989, p. 116), "The freestanding public campus headed by a board of trustees fully under its own authority is now the exception (500 out of 1,500 public campuses). It once was virtually the universal situation, until change began about 1960. What we now see is the result of a revolutionary transformation over the past 30 years." It is estimated that fewer than ten thousand trustees and regents in the public sector of higher education serve on nine hundred boards, whose institutions educate in excess of eleven million students. This contrasts sharply with the private sector of higher education, where some forty thousand trustees serve on fifteen hundred boards, whose institutions educate fewer than three million students (Anderson, 1985, pp. 34–35).

Public and private sector trustees conduct themselves in dramatically different ways in their boardrooms and between board meetings. Working within a political environment, meeting frequently, and consuming masses of information and data are among the challenges faced by public sector trustees. These and other constraints require extraordinary commitment, time, and judgment.

Public two-year and four-year multicampus systems are an important and pervasive part of U.S. higher education, and more research and study of the leadership styles, structures, policies, and practices that distinguish the most effective systems is urgently needed. Are public systems that employ institutional advisory boards more effective than those do not? What is the proper balance between consolidation and competition among institutions?

No one predicts a reversal of the trend toward centralization and control, nor any acknowledgment by political leaders that giving students a high-quality education may require more competition between institutions (as having more institutional autonomy through local governing boards would provide). Nor does anyone predict a lessening of the sometimes shrill calls for more efficiency, accountability, productivity, and trustee control of resource allocation.

Multicampus systems and boards are here to stay, and most are justifiably proud of their accomplishments. The tremendous growth of higher education facilities and programs following World War II and the expansion of access were made possible in large measure by the growth of public multicampus systems and the community college movement.

But tensions between elected political leaders and the academy remain high. Unfortunately, many more skirmishes are likely. The dangers attendant to preoccupations with political party affiliations in the boardroom are also very real—an unfortunate phenomenon more commonly found in elected boards than appointed boards.

Myth three: given the sustained preoccupation of state public policymakers with centralizing authority in multicampus systems and their success in doing so, governors and legislatures of most states are generally pleased with the resulting performance of their institutions and governing boards. Unfortunately, there is no evidence to support such a conclusion and much to refute it (Newman, 1987). This statement from a publication of the National Conference of State Legislatures (1992, p. 37) makes the point: "As the cost of education increases, students and parents may raise new questions about the accountability of institutions of higher education. Constituents will voice their concerns to legislators about access to the faculty, the quality of the faculty, access to courses and the size of classes. Where once legislators were careful not to intrude in these areas, the demands for higher education accountability may force their involvement. The result is likely to be a tense relationship in the decade ahead between legislators and the higher education community."

One of trustees and board members' most pressing concerns is the increased politicization of public higher education in the name of strengthening accountability and improving academic quality. Greater effort by board members to improve communication with political leaders, vigilance, and resistance to intrusion are necessary.

But reform of the processes by which trustees and regents are selected is also necessary in many or most states to ensure that the most qualified citizens are appointed or elected. Even most incumbent trustees may not believe that appointing authorities generally place the most able people on public boards of higher education (Association of Governing Boards of Universities and Colleges, 1973).

In most states in which public university and system board members are nominated by governors, options for making the process more objective and businesslike are available. An excellent example is the Regents Candidate Advisory Council, established in 1988 by the Minnesota legislature, which selects the University of Minnesota regents. This carefully selected group of twenty-four Minnesotans has established a clear job description for regents and qualifications sought in candidates, and it recruits, interviews, and nominates citizens for subsequent selection by the legislature (see Resource A).

The majority of state and local governing boards for public two-year community colleges have elected members. One or more of the major university boards in at least five states also have elected members. Trustees and leaders of alumni associations can demonstrate leadership by actively encouraging the most qualified citizens in their state or district to run for board positions—a prospect unfortunately shunned by too many qualified people. Political party leaders need to be consistently encouraged by every responsible group to welcome rather than resist consultation with those people who best understand and care deeply about the college, university, or system—the trustees, the chief executive, and alumni association leaders. These people know best how the board's effectiveness can be strengthened with new talent. The importance and appropriateness of consulting with boards and chief executives is difficult to convey to appointing authorities, but a public education program whose purpose is to enlighten the public and opinion makers about the functions of citizen trusteeship and the importance of competent institutional governance is a good place to start.

Motivations of Trustees

The boardrooms of many public colleges, universities, and multi-campus and state systems seem to have more than their fair share of tensions—tensions that often reflect these typical circumstances: single-issue board members who push their own agenda or who see themselves as representing a particular constituency, campus, or cause; open meeting laws whose provisions are so strict that reflective thinking and honest discourse are discouraged; factions within the board that are based on politics or personality rather than honest differences on issues; overreaction by trustees to criticism or to political pressure; changing student demographics that produce campus tensions that spill into the boardroom; and so forth. The boards of private institutions face some of these tensions, too, but the small size of public boards and the political nature of trustee selection often exacerbate the problem.

Why are people willing to serve on boards of public higher education in the midst of such tension and conflict, especially in this period of declining resources (which often adds yet another layer of stress)? There are as many reasons as there are board members, but the following are some of the best:

- *They were asked to serve (or to run for the position).* People are flattered to be asked to serve on a board by someone they respect or admire, and they instinctively want to please that person by saying yes. The reality of the commitment comes later; rarely are trustees honestly told what serving on a board requires of them.
- *They have a deep and abiding conviction that a college or university or public system of higher education is more consequential to future generations than virtually any other type of institution.* They feel they can make a difference and contribute something to an enterprise that will outlive them.
- *They want to give something back to society.* People often attribute their personal success to the education they received and find tremendous satisfaction in working with others who share the same values.
- *They feel that board membership is a great honor and promises to be intellectually stimulating.* Interpreting a complex social institution to those who often misunderstand it, addressing very perplexing social issues of the day with other thoughtful people, and conveying society's needs to the academic community are challenges that bring their own rewards. Higher education trusteeship is considered by most Americans to be the crown jewel of volunteerism because of the people and issues connected with the enterprise. For every five thousand citizens, only one is a current member of a board of trustees or regents in public or private higher education.

There are other good motivations for serving on a board, to be sure, but there are also some inappropriate and even dangerous motivations. Unfortunately, some trustees mistakenly believe that they as individuals possess special authority and are entitled to certain prerogatives. In fact only the board as a corporate body has legal power. Some trustees bring personal causes or agendas to boardrooms before they fully understand the university or their responsibilities. Some people misuse their trusteeship to strive for higher political office, encourage their boards to micromanage, insist on the use of friends' law firms, encourage factions and cliques within their boards, criticize their chief executives in public meetings (sometimes followed by private apology), and fail to listen to and learn from others—a particularly ironic shortcoming in academic institutions.

The best trustees are those who are open-minded, understand the vital importance of helping to build consensus, and are willing to learn how to be effective team members. Trusteeship is hard work that requires tempered egos, a good measure of humility, and a willingness to help keep the board's house in order.

Distinguishing Challenges of the 1990s

The mettle of trustees and boards in the public sector will be tested through the remainder of this decade as never before. The real value of governing boards as an alternative to direct governmental or faculty control will either become more apparent to the general public, elected political leaders, and opinion makers or a new round of severe criticism (which will rival that of the 1960s, when students discovered trustees and removed their veil of anonymity) is in store.

Why is one of these outcomes likely? What are the crosscurrents that promise to make trustee service more challenging than ever?

Some of these crosscurrents are not new but are extensions of those experienced in the past. One primary trend is shrinking resources coupled with rising public expectations for high-quality programs, more productivity, more obvious impact on economic development, and ever-better facilities. Doing more with less will be a central theme for quite some time.

The stresses and strains within systems brought about by institutions competing for fewer dollars among themselves and especially with the flagship institution will surely continue. Boards will need to provide more help to presidents and chancellors by taking more of the criticism for unpopular decisions. It is time to stand by the chief executive to ensure the integrity of the institution or system and the governing board.

Myth four: the issues concerning them and the practices of trustees and regents in public higher education will look very much the same as those of the past two decades. Actually, new pressures and developments are likely to be high on board agendas and, therefore, on the agenda of the Association of Governing Boards of Universities and Colleges (AGB). Higher education will no longer receive favored status although, among all the institutions supported by modern society, it has earned and is likely to retain the respect and confidence of the majority of U.S. citizens. But public confidence in institutions of higher education has been severely shaken, and the case for a larger share of limited tax dollars will be difficult to make. Furthermore, the flagship, or research, university—whether public or private—is under the microscope as never before. Its mistakes will produce adverse public opinion about all other colleges and universities. Investigative reporting about academe is on the rise. All institutions will be affected by one another's improprieties or faulty judgments, reminding trustees and chief executives how interdependent higher education really is.

Calls for Relevance

Higher education cannot continue to give the impression that it is aloof from the urban problems and other ills of U.S. society. It must demonstrate a willingness to help search for solutions to real and pressing social and economic problems. Hundreds of colleges and universities have reached out to K-12 education in their communities to establish cooperative programs that strengthen curricula, prepare and develop teachers, and encourage minority youths to continue their education. The knowledge and research of faculty members and other institutional resources must be extended to other endeavors, for example, to the administration of justice and the problems of homelessness, crime, drug abuse, and economic development. Governing boards can encourage faculty leadership in these directions by urging administrative and academic leaders to provide incentives for new initiatives.

From a traditional point of view, these social issues may seem to be beyond higher education's primary mission and scope of teaching and research. But public service, the hallmark of the land-grant and comprehensive universities and the community college, should be renewed as a major commitment in all public institutions. This renewal will not be easy. Entrepreneurial faculty members have become accustomed to being paid for their consulting work. The press of increasing teaching loads, expectations within disciplines for more and better research and publishing, and other duties expected by their departments and institution often preclude faculty members from new public service initiatives.

At the same time, however, trustees should be mindful that there are limits to the search for social relevance in the academy. The university cannot be, indeed must not be, as relevant as the morning news, lest its basic mission and purposes be compromised. Helping institutional officers and faculty members cope with the inevitable tension between the demands for change and the need for continuity is a critical responsibility of a governing board.

Trustee Responsibility for Fund Raising

Trustees of public institutions and systems easily accept their responsibility to ensure good fiscal management. They understand their responsibility to do the best they can to secure adequate state appropriations and are aware of the increasingly important role of the college or university foundation in soliciting private financial support. They also understand that decreasing state support for higher education may remain the norm and tuition pricing is likely to become even more political as governors and legislators insist on low tuition while cutting funding. Tuition pricing will be a major public policy issue for the next several years. In addition, for many public colleges and universities, state tax revenues are not the largest source of financial support. The distinction between public and private institutions of higher education is increasingly arbitrary.

Myth five: trustees of public higher education should not feel any responsibility to give and to help raise private dollars. It can be reasoned that raising funds is not part of the trustee's job description; public sector trustees are never told of any such expectation when they are appointed to a board or run for election. It can also be argued that the ability to give and to raise money is an inappropriate criterion for a trustee of a public college or university, where personal wealth or personal influence on others should have no bearing whatsoever on candidacy for trusteeship. These points are all well and good—as far as they go.

However, financial support from individuals, corporations, and foundations has become vitally important to public colleges and universities. Private dollars will increasingly distinguish excellent institutions from marginal ones. Trustees will be expected to give what they can and, more important, to become active partners in the search for private support. If the trustees and regents do not demonstrate their belief in the value of their institution or system by actively participating in fund raising, why should anyone else do so? This concept is new and controversial for most trustees in the public sector, but it should be addressed forthrightly and often by all boards. Board members may be tempted to rationalize and discard this responsibility by pointing to the foundation board, but the responsibility is unlikely to go away.

Need for Restructuring

Economists report that the decade of the eighties was good to higher education, with a real growth rate of about 2 to 3 percent per year. Administrative rather than academic staffs grew significantly, especially the number of middle managers. In fact, organizational charts of the late 1970s, when compared with those of the early 1990s, confirm the exponential growth in the size of administrative units in most institutions—a consequence in part of increased government requirements. Staff cutbacks will force universities to find new ways to do more work, more creatively, with fewer people, and with better use of technology. Thus, it is time for change—an opportunity that can come more easily in adversity than in prosperity.

The U.S. economy is unlikely to be strong for some time— at least not strong enough to produce real and sustained growth in personal discretionary income and the tax revenues with which

higher education is intimately linked. It is time to reconsider institutional missions, time for colleges and universities to do what they
do best, time to "right size," to become more productive and efficient, and to "grow by substitution." Although there is considerable
skepticism about whether institutions of higher education will
really look much different in five or ten more years, trustees must
prepare to be active partners in the debates about restructuring yet
to come. It is time for a different kind of strategic vision in the
boardroom.

Calls for Strategic Vision

Trustees are often criticized for their inability to think and act strategically. Their meeting agendas do not focus on long-term issues
but rather on short-term managerial and governance issues. It is
probably a fair criticism, one that also applies to presidents and
chancellors, who generally shape board agendas and the information to support them.

   If trustees and governing boards are to be helpful in reshap-
ing their institutions and management structures, they and their
chief executives will need information and strategic options that are
not available to them now. They will need encouragement to think
more strategically and the kind of useful data and analytical information that suggest viable courses of action.

Preparation for Diversity

Demographers tell us what we should already know: a much more
diverse population is not on its way—it is already here! Trustees in
Arizona, California, New Mexico, Texas, Florida, and New York
understand the implications of providing access to diverse student
populations in the traditional college, university, or public system
of higher education. The mainstream of higher education has become more aware of what needs to be done; there is less rhetoric and
more study. But action is still often lacking, especially in meeting
self-imposed goals in hiring minority faculty and staff members,
recruiting and retaining minority students, or diversifying board
membership. Governing boards in public sector colleges and uni-

versities are more diverse, however, than those of private sector institutions (see Resource B).

The makeup of student bodies will be changing dramatically over the remainder of the decade and well into the next. And so will teaching methods, campus cultures, and how academicians think about their work and their responsibilities to their institutions and society. In hundreds of communities blessed with a college or university, the typical student is no longer Caucasian and between the ages of eighteen and twenty-four. These demographic changes force the academic community to address stereotypes about how an American is supposed to look and act.

Some big problems loom in the foreseeable future. Precisely at a time when the philosophy and practice of open student access is taking on new and urgent significance, the weakening economy is causing many public institutions to cap enrollment or even to downsize. A weakened economy is no friend of access and diversity—tuition and fees rise, institutional student aid is capped, and the federal government contributes loans rather than grants. Many people from the new pool of students are reluctant to encumber themselves with loans. Trustees should be concerned about the increasingly large numbers of students who graduate with the burden of significant debt. The role of the board and the chief executive in this complex area is both simple and clear: staff and faculty members will not act on institutional priorities in this area unless there is consistent and persistent leadership from the top.

Concern for the Presidency

The academic presidency may be in jeopardy. The average annual presidential tenure is seven years in both the public and private sectors (Association of Governing Boards, 1992a). In this tumultuous period of change, continuity of effective presidential leadership is critical.

There is need for further study, but many people believe— rightly or wrongly—that this decline in average tenure, as compared with past decades, surely results from increasing tensions in the public sector coupled with the failure of boards to actively and visibly support their chancellors and presidents when difficult decisions must be made. Presidents and chancellors are surely no more perfect than their boards, but the only place they can look for support is their boards.

Now is the time to reassess how trustees stand up under pressure in full partnership with the president or chancellor. Chief executives must not have doubts about whether their trustees and boards will stand behind them (better yet, in front of them) when faced with criticism—often as a consequence of decisions that the boards ultimately make. All boards must be concerned about the integrity of the presidency. The job is difficult enough without the board being perceived as adding to the tension with which the president or chancellor contends. The relationship between a board and chief executive will affect the public's perceptions of the board's integrity as well as the reputation of the system or institution and their ability to attract and keep strong executive leaders.

Need for Proactive Public Policy

Many trustees and regents bring significant personal influence with elected public officials to their trusteeship, and many institutions and systems use this resource selectively and to good advantage. Chief executives are usually very astute in reading the tea leaves of state politics, especially when their institution or system is directly involved. This type of influence by board members is a simple extension of their advocacy role. But the prospects for more governmental regulation and inappropriate intrusion are likely to require a more proactive networking of trustees within the public sector and within states or even nationally. This networking may extend to the private sector as well, depending on the issues that emerge within the next few years.

Much more may be at stake than recurrent initiatives at the state or federal level that threaten the essential autonomy of institutions and systems of higher education and possibly academic freedom as it is broadly understood and accepted. There is the very real prospect, especially at the state level, that governors and legislators may propose harmful, even dangerous, public policy in one form or another on almost any issue—for reasons perfectly pure from their own perspectives. This possibility has always been present, of course, but the probability seems higher now than ever before, because the confidence of many state political leaders in higher education has been shaken. Will trustees and presidents be prepared to respond? Will presidents and chancellors really welcome more help from their boards and individual trustees than has been the case thus far?

A former governor who is currently president of a private university makes the point: "Many of the very people whom higher education should rely upon to press its cause are already on their boards of regents and trustees. Given the resources that are available to them in terms of the trustees, faculty members, alumni and others, the higher education community has never really unified. As a result, higher education is frequently the first thing cut and the last thing restored" (Cage, 1992, p. A23).

Understandably, chief executives worry about the wrong trustee inadvertently saying or doing the wrong thing at the wrong time with the wrong legislator or governor. And they are concerned that any serious trustee involvement in public policy at the state or federal level may inadvertently politicize their boards. Many presidents and chancellors consider public policy at the federal level to be their exclusive domain, one best coordinated by their associations in Washington, D.C.

At the same time, however, chief executives may not be the effective lobbyists they once were, at either the state or federal level. The end of sanctuary is very real, and presidents and chancellors and their representatives, unfortunately for everyone, are increasingly seen by political leaders as protecting the status quo.

All of this needs more thought and study, of course, but we know at least three things. First, some trustees can be very effective spokespersons on behalf of their institutions and systems and for higher education as a whole, especially at the state level and perhaps at the federal level as well. Second, lobbying requires careful coordination between the chief executive and trustees when it is possible or desirable for trustees to help. Third, great care must be taken to avoid conflict within the higher education community.

Chief executives and trustees should make clear their convictions that the nation needs strong systems of both public and private higher education. Leaders from each sector should seize opportunities to support each other. Unfortunately, the two sectors may be confronting one another while lobbying some state governments. This confrontation can only result in a lose-lose situation. Now is the time for academic leaders to take some risks by building new coalitions with trustees who can make the right difference.

Ambiguities of College and University Governance

Professor Burton Clark offers a helpful perspective on the ambiguities of academic governance: "Anyone who seriously and intensively probes the authority structure of his own college . . . and presents his observations for public consumption, is likely to make enemies and may have occasion to travel. . . . Academic authority is a peculiarly subtle and complex matter, a murky business that has caused highly intelligent men to veer away and throw up their hands" (Clark, 1961, p. 293).

Myth six: there is now a reasonably clear and generally accepted understanding of how policy decisions are made in the academic institution or system and the roles and responsibilities governing boards properly assume as part of the process. Not so. It remains ambiguous how governing boards should exercise or delegate their authority and otherwise meet their responsibilities. Mason (1972) says that the board is supreme and sovereign in a legal sense only, that in reality its primary and most legitimate functions are twofold: to represent the public interest and to ensure basic fiscal integrity. He concludes that the board's responsibilities are to remind the university that it is part of "ordinary" human society, to shield the university from dysfunctional public pressure, to tell the university what extremes of academic freedom cannot be tolerated, and to champion the university, especially when it is threatened by ignorance or ill will.

Mason also argues from the faculty perspective of the 1970s that boards do not "own" or "manage" the university, legal provisions in charters and enabling legislation notwithstanding. He says (1972, p. 29) that they must "forget about" legal provisions that, for example, authorize a board to hire faculty members and approve educational programs. He argues that the concepts of fiscal integrity and the public interest cause most of the ambiguities in academic trusteeship.

But how can trustees be expected to shield the university from dysfunctional public pressures and to ensure fiscal integrity when they are also expected to stay at arm's length from the institution, particularly with respect to its academic programs? How can trustees be expected to be champions in the midst of grave crises unless they are an integral part of institutional decision making, with a real sense of institutional ownership? How can able citizens be asked to defend the institution, to be where it counts when they are really needed, without having a continuing and thorough knowledge of their institution or helping to determine what it is and does? We cannot have it both ways.

Trustees and regents are under scrutiny and will be for many years to come—kept there by the law and a litigious society, elected political leaders, a demanding public that expects quality at the lowest possible price, and a society that expects help from its academic institutions with very pressing social and economic problems. Board members must realize that they are a vitally important part of institutional governance and remember that real change within an academic institution comes from building consensus.

Institutions cannot afford to have passive trustees or ones who feel that they are so much window dressing. People who volunteer their time to serve on governing boards expect it to be used well. Their ultimate commitment to their institutions or systems, in good and bad times, will depend on whether they are being taken seriously by their administrations, especially by their chief executives, and by their faculty members. But trustees and boards should seek to stand neither too close nor too far from the institution. Rather, they should constantly seek to find the balance between the exercise of authority and the exercise of restraint.

Academic governance in the United States is built on the principle that governing boards exercise their functions *with and through the chief executive*. This principle distinguishes our system from those of most other nations, where either faculty or government ministries or both dominate university decision making. Without citizen boards who reserve the ultimate right to select their own chief executives, presidents and chancellors would be controlled either by faculty members or the government. Thus chief executives and boards must understand that their effectiveness is interdependent—one can be little better than the other.

These issues and others raised throughout this book must be addressed in the context of finding better ways to communicate with everyone who has a stake in higher education, building new coalitions and more trust to accomplish what must be done, and avoiding the "we-they" syndrome so seemingly prevalent in contemporary society and in higher education. But how to let everyone participate and still accomplish goals is very perplexing. In the end, judgments must be made in the boardroom. The buck will always stop with the chief executive and the board.

There has never been a more exhilarating time to serve on the board of a public college, university, or system of higher education. Nor has there been a time when citizen boards of the nation's most capable individuals were needed more than they are today. We need board members who have an exceptionally high tolerance for ambiguity, a genuine love of higher education and its role in a free society, the strength of deep convictions, respect for the presidency, and values that will hold them, and higher education, in good stead in the face of what is yet to come.

CHAPTER 2

The New Demography

Harold L. Hodgkinson

The United States has changed enormously since the G.I. Bill and the National Defense Education Act of 1958 expressed our aspirations for Americans to attain as much higher education as they could master. During the Eisenhower and Kennedy years, not much was done to expand student aid based on need or academic merit. But in 1965, the Higher Education Act signaled an explicit commitment on the part of the federal government to support needy and able young people who wished to pursue a college education. In addition to loans and grants, the TRIO, Upward Bound, and Talent Search programs were designed to provide needy students access to and the opportunity to complete programs of higher education. The 1972 reauthorization of the Higher Education Act expanded student aid and rejected other forms of direct and unrestricted institutional support, and the 1978 Congress authorized assistance for middle-income students. During the Reagan years, appropriations leveled off, but the thirteen titles of the act still represent a solid commitment to a basic policy of student assistance, along with Title III for "developing institutions" and a few other nonaid measures. In 1991, $13 billion was earmarked for student aid under the Higher Education Act.

One of the major catalysts for the act was changing demographics in the United States, particularly the 70 million babies born during 1946 to 1964. This baby boom resulted in the enormous expansion in enrollment in colleges and universities from about 1964 to 1982. Along with enrollment, institutional mission expanded as well. State teachers colleges became comprehensive state colleges, with a variety of degree programs. State colleges and non-flagship universities clamored for more doctoral programs, in order to become comprehensive universities. And higher education leaders assumed that the expansion would continue forever. By encouraging more high school seniors to go to college, by working hard to retain more college students through graduation, and by enlarging adult and continuing education programs, colleges were even able (with about ten years' warning) to maintain and increase enrollment during the 1980s, when the actual number of eighteen-year-olds was in decline. However, 1990 to 2010 will present an entirely new demographic challenge for institutional mission, clientele, faculty, access, and equity.

What We Can Learn from the 1990 Census

According to the U.S. Bureau of the Census (1990), U.S. population grew to 249.8 million in 1990, up 23 million from 1980. However, 90 percent of the growth occurred in the South and West, where white populations are comparatively small. In 1990, half of the U.S. population lived in only nine states, and half of the nation's growth occurred in the three megastates of California, Texas, and Florida. Never before in the two hundred years of census taking have three states captured half of the nation's growth, picking up fourteen seats in the House of Representatives in the process.

More than half of the U.S. population now lives in the fifty largest metropolitan areas. In the 1980s, over half of all new jobs were created in suburban areas, making suburban residency a major advantage in finding a good job. Minorities moved to the suburbs during the 1980s, and black and Hispanic middle-class populations increased in many areas. In many metropolitan areas, most minority group members were living in suburbs.

The move to the suburbs is a move to the middle class for many minority groups. The analysis of Landry (1987) shows that black and Hispanic households are about 36–40 percent middle income, about 25–30 percent "at the margin," and about 25 percent in poverty. Black, Asian, and Hispanic middle classes are often living in the suburbs and planning to send their children not just to college but to Princeton or Harvard. I conclude, therefore, that if one were looking for a single criterion that would predict success in college, the best would not be Scholastic Aptitude Test scores or high school grades but whether or not the student's parents were college graduates. Today, an increasing percentage of college applications from minority students are from students whose parents are college graduates.

While the nation's population as a whole grew by 9.8 percent from 1980 to 1990, the number of whites increased 6.0 percent, blacks 13.2 percent, Native Americans 37.9 percent, Hispanics 52.8 percent, and Asian Americans an incredible 107.8 percent. At these rates, in 2010, the U.S. population will include 38 million blacks, the same number of Hispanics, 10 to 12 million Asian Americans, and as many as 3 million Native Americans. Today, there are 1.6 million Native Americans and more than 5 million people with "Indian ancestry." If it becomes even more desirable to claim Native American ancestry, the number of Native Americans could move to 4 or 5 million since ethnicity is defined by self-report in the census. It is difficult to project the increase in Americans from the Middle East. This population is now about 3 million and has a major potential for growth through immigration. There are now more Muslims in the United States than Episcopalians.

The 1990 census data on households show that during the 1980s, nontraditional households grew at a rate twice as fast as that of traditional married-couple households (Table 2.1). About 25 percent of all households were people living alone, an arrangement guaranteed to lower fertility rates over time, especially as the number of families with children actually declines. The number of married-couple households with children declined, while the number of married couples without children grew 17 percent, the highest growth rate among the traditional households containing a married couple. Currently, 52 million households in the United States include a married couple, and 40.9 million households do not.

The traditional portrait of the U.S. family, consisting of a working father, a homemaking mother, and two children of public

Table 2.1. Traditional and Nontraditional Households, 1980-1990.

	1980	1990	Change (%)
All households	80,467,000	93,920,000	+ 16.7
Family households	59,190,000	66,652,000	+ 12.4
Married couples	48,990,000	52,837,000	+ 7.0
Married couples with children	24,780,000	24,522,000	− 1.0
Married couples without children	24,210,000	28,315,000	+ 17.0
Single-female head	8,205,000	11,120,000	+ 35.6
Single-male head	1,995,000	2,575,000	+ 29.1
Living alone	18,202,000	22,879,000	+ 25.7
Living with nonrelated person	3,075,000	4,500,000	+ 46.3

Source: Data abstracted from U.S. Bureau of the Census, 1990, p. 26.

school age, now constitutes about 6 percent of America's households. Only 25 percent of all households have a child in public school. The baby boomlet created since 1985 should decline by 1992, as the number of women moving into the childbearing years goes down.

The 1990 census shows that poverty rates are much higher for children raised in single-parent families, than in two-parent families (Hodgkinson, 1992b). Single women, raising fifteen million children, had an average household income of $11,400 during 1988. The average income of a two-adult family with children was $33,000. Given the connection between household income, school performance, and dropout rates, it seems likely that an increasing number of children will be at risk of school failure and may not be candidates for a college education. Thus the boomlet may not guarantee more enrollments for higher education.

We can now project the number of children in the future U.S. population with considerable accuracy. From 1990 to 2000, the total number of children is likely to increase from 64 to 65 million, then drop suddenly to 62.6 million by 2010. Additionally, Table 2.2 shows that the number of white children in the United States will

Table 2.2. Projected U.S. Population, Age Seventeen or Under, 1990–2010.[a]

	1990	2010	Change
White	45.2	41.4	–3.8
Hispanic	7.2	9.8	+2.6
Black	10.2	11.4	+1.2
Other	2.2	2.8	+ .6
Total[b]	64.4	64.9	+ .5
Nonwhite total			+4.4

[a]Figures in millions.
[b]May not add exactly because of rounding.
Source: Data abstracted from Hodgkinson, 1992a, p. 26.

probably drop by 3.8 million by 2010 while the number of nonwhite children will probably increase by 4.4 million.

By 2010, thirteen states will contain 30 million of the nation's total population of 62.6 million children and will show a marked increase in the percentage of nonwhite children (Table 2.3). In these and many other states, we will have to rethink the definition of the term *minority group*, when more than half of our children are nonwhite. The issue is a serious one, with major implications for higher education—in which the current student body is about 19 percent minority. Today's public school enrollment is 30 percent minority and preschool enrollment is 35 percent minority (Hodgkinson, 1992a, p. 17).

About 10 percent of today's faculty members in higher education are from minority groups. The number of doctorates awarded to blacks has dropped almost 50 percent, from 1,116 in 1977 to 820 in 1986. Students in colleges and universities are becoming much more ethnically diverse, while the faculty members are not. About 14 percent of the recipients of the 34,319 doctoral degrees conferred in 1989 were nonwhite, but a majority of these were minorities who were not U.S. citizens (Hodgkinson, 1992a, p. 17). The major strategy of diversification for U.S. higher education is trying to recruit every well-trained minority academic. This is a reasonable short-term strategy but a long-term recipe for disaster. Higher education needs to become involved in the current effort to enlarge the

**Table 2.3. Projected Percentage of
Nonwhite Children by States and Areas, 2010.**

Washington, D.C.	93.2	Louisiana	50.3
Hawaii	79.5	Mississippi	49.9
New Mexico	76.5	New Jersey	45.7
Texas	56.9	Maryland	42.7
California	56.9	Illinois	41.7
Florida	53.4	South Carolina	40.1
New York	52.8	U.S. total	38.7

Source: Data abstracted from U.S. Bureau of the Census, 1990.

pool of well-trained students and faculty members from impoverished and minority backgrounds. This effort will take some time to succeed, but there is no other solution.

During the 1980s, colleges and universities managed to maintain and even increase enrollments by encouraging more high school graduates to go to college, helping more freshmen to stay in college and graduate, and expanding adult and continuing education programs. The 1990s will show a different trend.

About 50 percent of the children born in the baby boomlet of 1985 to 1992 live in the three megastates of Florida, Texas, and California. Each of these states will have no ethnic majority among its children by 2010. Note also that the other big, highly diverse states of New York, New Jersey, Maryland, and Illinois have no boomlet. Other big but less diverse states, like Michigan, Ohio, Pennsylvania, and Massachusetts, will find themselves trying to lure minority students and faculty members from other states, a battle that has already begun. Figure 2.1 shows projected changes in the number of high school graduates in each state.

States will become more diverse during the 1990s. California, Florida, and Texas will grow in number and diversity of student body at a great rate, while their legislatures are trying to cap and even reduce appropriations. A number of states east of the Mississippi, such as New York and Illinois, will be trying to retain current numbers of enrollments in the face of massive state budget short-

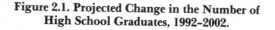

Figure 2.1. Projected Change in the Number of High School Graduates, 1992–2002.

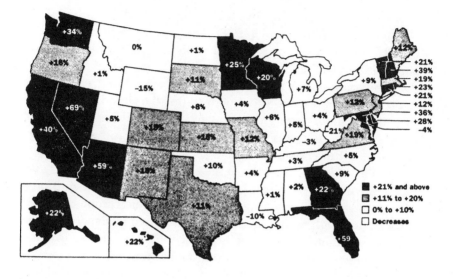

Source: Chronicle of Higher Education Almanac, 1992, p. 4. Reprinted by permission.

ages. So will most of the states in the Southeast, except Georgia and Virginia, which will face increased enrollments and decreased budgets. The Southwest, with comparatively small totals of students, will see large increases in enrollments, or at least in students seeking admissions.

As young people (increasingly minority) concentrate in the South and West, leaving much of the central part of the nation with declining or steady youth populations, we see the area in which the conflict between generations is most likely to occur. Although Florida has the population with the highest average age, the second oldest in average age is Iowa, not because older people are retiring there but because young people are moving out. Older citizens are not as concerned about educational issues as they are about research on arthritis and Meals on Wheels. And as one gets older, one is likely to vote more often. It is easy to imagine an erosion of public support for higher education in heartland states with aging populations.

A massive redistribution of wealth occurred in the United States during the 1980s. Kevin Phillips documented the shift in *The Politics of Rich and Poor* (1990). The richest 20 percent of the population saw a real income gain of 45 percent during the 1980s and ended up with a lower tax rate, while the poorest 20 percent of the population saw an income *decline* of 3 percent and an increase in tax rate of 16 percent. If one adds to this the abundant evidence that the middle-income groups are declining while rich and poor are increasing, it seems that the United States is resegregating around class rather than race.

The educational system in the United States is feeding a two-pronged work force. College graduates are trained for the millions of high-paying jobs emerging in technology, finance, and business services, and high school dropouts are employed in the areas with the largest numbers of new jobs in the 1991 work force, that is, minimum-wage positions for janitors, maids, waitresses, and clerks, which afford little opportunity for movement into the middle class. This trend will add to the approximately eight million workers in the United States who are eligible for poverty benefits as members of America's working poor.

Colleges are reporting a marked decline in applications from very bright, hardworking lower-middle-class students who need a great deal of financial aid and a big increase in applications from not very bright, not very energetic students from the upper-middle class, whose ability to pay most or all of the tuition cost makes them desirable. The institutions most committed to moving people into the middle class through postsecondary education—the community and state colleges, the "invisible" independent colleges, and the usually forgotten proprietary and vocational institutions—are most at risk financially during the 1990s, even as community colleges have moved toward having almost half of all higher education's new enrollments. Because these institutions do not have the financial flexibility of the flagship public and private universities and the truly selective liberal arts colleges, they are at risk of financial disaster, even as they strive to carry out the mission that inspired the Higher Education Act.

Implications of the Census for Higher Education

Analysis of the census of 1990 has sobering implications for higher education and for government. Should the federal government expand Title III's focus on academic institutions that serve impoverished and minority students, to include other than traditionally black institutions? Should grant and loan programs be reshaped? Should the delivery system of teaching and learning be radically changed? Do we need greater institutional diversity to more effectively serve an increasingly diverse clientele?

Title III

Title III was organized to support the approximately 114 "traditionally black institutions" (TBIs). Today, there are more than 60 institutions in the Association of Hispanic Universities, which possess the same expertise in working with Hispanic students that the TBIs have demonstrated so successfully with black students. And the tribal colleges serving Native American populations have moved to much more successful ways of serving their students.

Given that these institutions have special expertise in educating those groups that will increase as a percentage of higher education students in the United States, should Title III focus on all institutions that demonstrate special skills in working with impoverished and minority students? Asian students may warrant similar consideration, but there are few institutions established to meet the special needs of Asian students.

Grants and Loans

The conversion of many grant programs to loans is related to the decreasing success of minority students in higher education, as illustrated by the 50 percent decline in the 1980s of the number of doctorates awarded to blacks (National Research Council, 1990). Perhaps the issue of grants and loans needs to be reconsidered, particularly loan forgiveness provisions for minorities who elect to enter careers in which their skills are desperately needed—teaching, social work, and health care, for example. The current confusion over federal policy on scholarships restricted by race seems to send the signal that if you are poor or a minority member, higher education is not for you.

As a nation, we need to send very clear signals that we need and actively encourage the participation of minority and impoverished students in higher education. The TRIO, Upward Bound, and Talent Search programs all send these signals and are demonstrable successes in their areas, as is Head Start. Now the signals must pervade the educational pipeline. Incentives for keeping the educational pipeline open for impoverished and minority students from kindergarten through graduate school, treating the whole pipeline as a continuum, and coordinating services where necessary could become a vital thrust of the Higher Education Act.

Delivery System

Higher education is, in part, a service delivered to clients. The basic delivery mechanism, some 3,300 institutions, has a publications requirement for the faculty, tenure provisions, and an adversarial relationship between the faculty senate, the administration, and the board. Regional accrediting is intended to ensure quality, and learning is measured through the acquisition of time-based units, called credit hours. These institutions spend many times more on seniors in small seminars on pre-Raphaelite poetry than on freshmen in lecture halls in Introduction to Psychology, which is taught by teaching assistants. Students are encouraged to compete with each other for a scarce resource (A's) and are punished for most forms of collaborative learning.

As active vehicles for learning and teaching, our institutions may need some revisions as we look to the clients of 1990–2010. All of higher education could work to make the wonderful diversity of our system even more functional for the actual people served—40 percent part-time students and over twenty-four years old, almost 50 percent in community colleges, increasingly minority, and varied among states (*Chronicle of Higher Education Almanac*, 1992).

Entering freshmen at some institutions of higher education know more than graduating seniors from other campuses. Is that variation inherent in a nation of nations like the United States? If not, are we ready for a single set of exams that will define the bachelor's degree for all institutions? Would such exams be democratic? Useful? Equitable? While designing such exams may seem impossible, the nationalization of public school curricula and standards currently under way has an obvious upward extension.

Diversity

Today, we can make institutions of postsecondary education more alike, through national standards or more functionally different because of differences in clientele. We often debate the pluralism of individuals but rarely the pluralism of institutions. Perhaps community colleges should not only look different from flagship research universities but also from each other. If this kind of diversity prevails in the 1990s, how could one tell a "good" community college from a "bad" one when they are so dissimilar? One agenda behind the reauthorization debate in 1991 was the issue of *e pluribus unum* (one out of many), that is, the two great forces of individual and collective values. The issue and the debate are unresolved. How much of a national system of higher education do we want? Or, at the institutional level, how much autonomy of mission, strategy, and outcomes would be ideal? Do we need more institutional diversity to serve a more diverse clientele?

Part of the answer depends on the function we wish higher education to serve. Many people think that the purpose of higher education is to pick winners. Not much institutional diversity is needed for this function. Others think that higher education should also create winners, which requires much more institutional diversity. Institutional diversity will, to some extent, be altered by the nation's philosophy on student financial assistance as seen in the new incarnation of the Higher Education Act. Institutional diversity is a crucial unintended consequence of student financial assistance.

As we look at the youth population in 1990 and compare it with that of 2010, the galvanizing fact is the decline of 3.8 million in numbers of white children and the increase of 4.4 million in numbers of nonwhite children. There is no point in bewailing the loss of 3.8 million white children; in demography, if you were not born, you do not count. Anyone, including the people responsible for higher education, who believes that we can run the government, businesses, families, and cities thinking only about the loss of 3.8 million white children and ignoring the needs, talents, aspirations, and energy of the 4.4 million additional minority children needs some kind of special therapy.

Issues for Trustees

No matter how much money trustees raise, no matter how many research grants the faculty members get, it is hard to imagine a college without students. Because of the projected decline of white high school graduates after the year 2000, colleges will either have to become much more multicultural in faculty and student body, accept students of lesser ability, or get smaller. As a nation, we need to encourage enlargement of the educational pipeline—from the successes of Head Start, a program for three-year-olds, to TRIO, designed to enable more minorities and impoverished students to graduate from college. Trustees can carry out this mission in many ways, not only for their own colleges but at the state and national level as well.

Although the data are not precise, it would appear that trustees are one of the least ethnically diverse groups in higher education (see Resource B, Table B.3). A call to a prestigious black or Hispanic leader who might join a board is likely to be a call to a person who is already overcommitted. Trustees need to enlarge the pool of talented leaders and potential board members from minority and impoverished backgrounds. Otherwise they are merely overextending the time and energy of the few minority individuals that everyone always thinks of for board service. One distinguished Hispanic leader observed to me that he was on twenty boards and commissions, and on each one he was the only Hispanic. Little has been done at the institutional level to find and develop board members within minority communities.

Although financial concerns will continue to play a heavy role in trustee decision making, it is important that trustees get involved in the current debate on the nature of a multicultural campus and of "politically correct" ideological positions that may influence educational decisions. Both civility and academic freedom are suffering on many campuses—incidents of anti-Semitism, racism, and sexism seem rampant on some campuses while campus debate is being stifled on a variety of fronts. Is a multicultural campus a percentage or a frame of mind? Can a black or Asian person be a racist? Does equitable treatment mean identical treatment? How does an all white board respond to a legitimate claim for more student and faculty diversity without being hypocritical? How can this diversity be achieved in an environment of academic freedom and tolerance for dissent?

Discussion of issues like these can assist institutions of higher education in defining their own operational convictions. They are often the issues that influence the ethical and personal convictions of students. Although trustees do not usually make decisions on these issues, they can play a major role in determining the structure of participation in the discourse. The Emersonian view of the American scholar is to admit that thinking leads to action and that actions have consequences.

The 1990s are likely to be turbulent times on many campuses, as the financial and cultural winds shift with increasing speed. If trustees can represent the best of U.S. pluralism, they can assist their institutions in moving to a new interpretation of *e pluribus unum*, as an increasingly diverse student body strives to succeed in institutions not noted for their quickness in adapting to change. The process whereby individuals become participants in institutions represents the yin and yang of our democracy at its best. Trustees will and should be in the middle of it.

CHAPTER 3

The Economics and Financing of Public Higher Education

David A. Longanecker

What does it cost the public to provide public higher education in the United States, and what does it cost individuals to secure such an education? What economic issues face public higher education in the 1990s?

No simple way exists to explain the economics and finance of U.S. public higher education because higher education is not one activity; it is many, differing substantially from one sector to another. The cost of providing higher education varies from the modest amount required in community colleges to the much higher cost of educating within research universities. How the public ensures that higher education is provided also varies greatly. State and local governments often subsidize a large share of the costs at community colleges and other broad-access institutions. Thus, students often pay a lower price at these institutions than at others. The basic nature of the educational services provided from one sector of higher education to another also differs. Lower-cost institutions generally focus more heavily on teaching, while higher-cost institutions focus more on nonteaching activities, such as research and service.

States also differ substantially in their philosophical and practical approaches to financing higher education. They differ considerably in how well they finance higher education and how hard they try to finance it. Some states rely almost exclusively on public subsidies, while others expect consumers to pay a greater share of costs through higher tuition. Other states have found ways of obtaining support through gifts and contracts.

Different levels of government also approach the economics and finance of higher education from different perspectives. Local governments, if involved in higher education at all, are generally interested only in providing services to sustain local economic vitality. States have the principal responsibility for providing educational services and thus devote the greatest attention to financing higher education through programs that support both institutions and citizens. The federal government's current involvement in higher education reflects two distinct interests. First, the government wants to expand educational opportunity in accord with the federal constitutional mandate to ensure equal opportunity. This goal is addressed principally through federal student financial aid. Second, the government seeks to improve the nation's economic competitiveness, as reflected in substantial federal research and efforts to develop the U.S. work force.

The desired results of the disparate philosophical and practical approaches at the local, state, and federal levels, however, do not differ substantially. Citizens and government alike expect public higher education to provide broad access to high-quality education, excellence in research, and service to society in meeting general economic and social needs. Obviously, the capacity to achieve these results varies greatly from state to state and from institution to institution, depending upon the resources available.

The economics of higher education encompasses much more than simply the resources needed to provide this education; it also involves what higher education gives back to the U.S. economy. Higher education is a good investment for the individual securing the education and for the community providing it. A young man with one to three years of postsecondary education will initially earn 9 percent more annually than a male high school graduate with no postsecondary schooling. For a young woman with an equivalent level of postsecondary education, the returns are much more substantial. She will initially earn 26 percent more annually than a female high school graduate without such training. The returns are even more substantial for people with four or more years of college. Men with this level of education initially reap 43 percent more annually than male high school graduates without it, and women initially reap 68 percent more than female high school graduates. For both men and women, the difference in earnings increases as they move through the work force (*The Condition of Education, 1990,* 1990, p. 52).

Despite the clear value of this investment, higher education is not a dominant sector of the U.S. economy. The United States spends only about 2.4 percent of its gross national product on higher education (Andersen, 1991). This level of spending has remained virtually unchanged over the past twenty-five years (*Digest of Education Statistics 1990,* 1991, p. 32) and presents a mixed picture with respect to maintaining the economic competitiveness of the United States.

In many respects, U.S. higher education remains the envy of the world. No other country invests as large a share of its total resources in higher education as the United States does. As a result, no other nation boasts the quality, diversity of opportunity, or access that exists within U.S. higher education.

In other respects, however, the United States compares much less favorably with other countries. Although other nations spend less in total on higher education, most other industrialized nations, particularly those with which the United States competes most directly, invest more public funds in higher education. Only the United States and Japan rely substantially on private funding of higher education to supplement public resources. Less than 50 percent of the funds expended for higher education in the United States come from public sources. Most other industrialized countries, except Japan, fund higher education almost entirely from public resources (Andersen, 1991). This private investment, via tuition, gifts, and other sources, enables the United States to provide high-quality education with higher participation rates than exist in any other country. It is within this complicated context that the economics and finance of U.S. higher education must be considered.

Cost of Providing Public Higher Education

An overview of the four general types of public institutions—community colleges, four-year undergraduate colleges, regional universities, and research universities—illustrates the substantial differences in how public higher education is financed. The reader should keep in mind that wide differences sometimes also exist among states in how each type of college or university is supported by tax dollars and other sources.

Community Colleges

Traditionally, community colleges have provided the least expensive form of postsecondary education. Because they focus on teaching, the public does not implicitly subsidize much faculty research or service activity at these institutions. Even among community colleges, however, the cost of providing educational services varies greatly, depending upon the type of education and the size of the institution. Highly technical vocational education, which represents a substantial and growing component of most comprehensive community colleges, costs substantially more to provide than does the lower-division undergraduate education also offered within community colleges.

The size of a community college affects the cost of serving each student. Small colleges cost substantially more per student to operate than do large ones. John Millet (1980) has suggested that a community college needs a critical mass of at least twenty faculty members to provide an adequate two-year general education curriculum, aside from instructors that may be needed for specific vocational programs. Obviously, a small institution that is interested in maintaining a viable curriculum works at a greater financial disadvantage than a large institution, which can spread the fixed costs of a core faculty among a large number of students. As a result, the more than fifty two-year colleges in this country that enroll fewer than five hundred full-time equivalent (FTE) students face an unusual funding challenge.

Data about costs per student and productivity levels within

very large community colleges are sketchy. But institutions that serve large numbers of students (such as Miami Dade Community College, which with forty-one thousand students is the largest community college in the country) face a uniquely difficult challenge to sustain a sense of community and curricular integrity. This challenge may actually require more resources per student than required in institutions of more moderate size. Both very large and very small community colleges, therefore, face distinct financial problems.

Nationally, nearly 50 percent of all higher education students enroll in community colleges. Enrollment in different states varies substantially, however. For example, more than 66 percent of all California students enroll in public community colleges, but no students attend community college in South Dakota (*Digest of Education Statistics 1990,* 1991, p. 189).

Public financial support for community colleges also varies greatly. Community colleges emerged as local school districts began to appreciate the need within their communities for some education beyond high school. Because of the connection of these colleges with local school districts, financial support for community colleges initially came principally from local taxes and modest tuition charges. As the demand for community colleges expanded in the 1950s and 1960s, and as these institutions became more widely accepted as an integral component of higher education, the source of funding shifted in most cases from the local tax base to the state. In 1987, revenues provided by state and local governments per FTE community college student averaged $3,068 but ranged from a high of $5,073 in Alaska to a low of $1,604 in Vermont (U.S. Department of Education, 1987, p. 48).

Community colleges rely more heavily on public support than any other sector of higher education, with nearly 70 percent of their resources coming from state and local appropriations. But tuition still is an important source of revenue, although it too varies substantially from state to state. In 1987, the average annual tuition and fees per FTE community college student nationwide were $829, but ranged from a low of $283 in California to a high of $2,112 in Pennsylvania (U.S. Department of Education, 1987, p. 45).

In general, where states provide the bulk of support, community colleges receive more substantial funding. Community colleges are generally perceived as a very cost-effective means to provide lower-division education. Their instructional expenditures per student average only slightly more than 50 percent of the average of public four-year colleges and universities. In addition, community colleges provide an effective bridge to other schools for many students who might have difficulty academically or culturally if they entered a four-year college immediately after high school (U.S. Department of Education, 1987, p. 45).

Although community colleges certainly deliver their services efficiently, various factors suggest caution in comparing them with the rest of higher education. First, four-year colleges tend to spend appreciably more on upper-division students than lower-division students. Thus, the difference in the costs of providing lower-division education between two- and four-year institutions is not as pronounced as it might appear to be from aggregate statistics. Second, student retention rates, while alarmingly low for all of public higher education, are substantially lower for most two-year colleges than for most four-year colleges and universities. Retention rates affect the relative cost effectiveness of community colleges. Third, the difficulty some community college students have in transferring academic credits toward their degree can lengthen the time required to complete a degree or program. Thus, it is clearly in the states' financial interest to assure that students can and do make a comfortable transition from one level of higher education to another.

Four-Year Undergraduate Colleges

With the trend over the past twenty years to expand many undergraduate colleges into regional universities, the number of public institutions focusing totally on baccalaureate education has diminished appreciably. Although about twenty-five states continue to have one or two baccalaureate colleges, only Colorado maintains several public institutions that offer the baccalaureate as the highest degree. As public colleges evolve into more comprehensive universities, higher education loses one of its most efficient ways of delivering undergraduate education. In 1987, baccalaureate colleges spent an average of $3,077 per student per year, almost the same as the average instructional expenditure per community college student. This figure was 27 percent less than instructional expenditures in regional comprehensive universities and 35 percent less than in research universities (U.S. Department of Education, 1987, p. 48).

Four-year undergraduate colleges vary greatly in size, from Charter Oak College in Connecticut with eight hundred students to Metropolitan State College of Denver with sixteen thousand students. As with community colleges, economies of scale make large undergraduate colleges more cost-effective than small ones. John Millett's work (1982) indicates that a four-year college needs about ninety to one hundred faculty members to offer a comprehensive general education curriculum. Thus, any institution with fewer than about two thousand FTE students will need exceptional financial support to sustain a viable educational program.

As do community colleges, four-year undergraduate colleges generally rely almost entirely on state appropriations and tuition revenues for financial resources. Increasingly, these institutions are seeking private gifts to supplement their traditional base of support. They often find it difficult to generate substantial funds, however, because they lack the prestige and alumni support necessary to attract private financial support.

Regional Universities

The rapid growth in both the number and size of regional comprehensive universities over the past twenty-five years is the result of several influences. Their increasing size speaks to the substantial increase in the demand for higher education, particularly for baccalaureate degrees. The expansion of their role and mission, however, reflects more the desire of faculty members and communities to expand these institutions to serve graduate and research missions.

Although many of these institutions were established with the role and mission of a regional comprehensive university, large numbers evolved from normal schools or regional colleges. A few such universities still focus almost entirely on offering bachelor's degrees, but most offer master's degrees and many offer or aspire to offer doctorates.

These institutions vary tremendously in size and therefore in cost effectiveness. For example, Mayville State University in North Dakota has 650 students, and San Diego State University has 35,000 students. The cost of providing education in this type of institution depends upon the size of the faculty and the balance in faculty load between teaching, research, and service. As these institutions focus more on graduate education, they tend to reduce teaching loads to allow faculty members to focus more on research or other scholarly activities. Relatively little of the research and scholarly activity in these institutions, however, is funded by outside research support. Rather, it is generally funded by the institution. As a result of the emphasis on research and other scholarly activity, teaching productivity declines, ostensibly offset by an increase in research productivity. William Massy (1990) contends that the trend toward research accounts for much of the increase in higher education costs in recent years.

Research Universities

Every state has one or more flagship state universities that focus as much on research and graduate education as they do on undergraduate education. These institutions, however, also differ greatly from one another. They range in size from South Dakota's two research universities, with fewer than seven thousand students each, to Ohio State University, with sixty seven thousand students at its main campus. This category of institutions includes some of the world's most prestigious universities, such as the University of California and the University of Michigan.

Although these institutions generally receive the largest amount of state support per student of any sector of public higher education, state funding generally represents a much smaller share of total available resources than in any other sector. State funding for these institutions ranges from a high of 70 percent in New York to a low of 18 percent in Vermont, with most states providing about 50 percent of the funding. Research universities garner most research grants provided within the public sector, although this too varies greatly from institution to institution.

Considerable differences among research universities seem to have little effect on cost patterns. Many of the largest institutions have the highest expenditures per student, no doubt in part because they have the most significant research efforts as well. As in other sectors of public higher education, the total resources available to these institutions vary greatly. In 1987, for example, instructional expenditures per student for public doctoral universities without medical schools averaged $3,519 per year, but it ranged from a low of $2,151 in Louisiana to a high of $6,727 in Alaska (U.S. Department of Education, 1987, p. 57).

This chapter covers only the funding of operating expenses for public institutions of higher education. It does not discuss capital financing for facilities. Most facilities for these institutions are funded through separate legislative appropriations or bonding authority. In contrast to private higher education, relatively little capital construction in the public sector is funded through operating funds. Higher education now faces a serious issue of how to finance its aging physical infrastructure in the years ahead. In 1986, the physical plants in public higher education were valued at $82.9 billion, an amount that had been increasing by 7 to 8 percent annually (*Digest of Education Statistics 1990*, 1991, p. 315). Many reports suggest that higher education is falling further and further behind in keeping pace with the facilities and equipment needed to remain on the cutting edge of knowledge acquisition and transmission.

General Financing Trends and Funding Strategies

State support for higher education has varied substantially over the last twenty years, peaking in 1982 at 8.3 percent of state dollars and declining gradually to 6.9 percent in 1991 (Halstead, 1990, p. 148). The decline has occurred as demands from other state services, such as corrections, elementary and secondary education, and social services, increased.

Federal support has paralleled state trends, showing growth in the 1970s, reduction in the early and mid 1980s, and some recovery in the late 1980s. This pattern has been true of funding for both student financial aid and contract research. But within both areas, substantial shifts have occurred in the types of programs being funded. Federal funding for student financial assistance has shifted substantially from grants, targeted to the most needy students, to loan subsidies, which traditionally have helped students from middle-income families but increasingly are focused on impoverished students as well. Research funding has shifted somewhat from medicine and health sciences to defense and space-related science. No doubt, further shifts will occur in the 1990s as the Higher Education Act is reauthorized and as federal priorities shift. How these shifts will affect institutions depends on areas an individual institution emphasizes.

States use various strategies for determining how much support to provide higher education and for allocating these resources. *Incremental budgeting,* which consists of providing incremental annual increases in support based on inflation and enrollment growth, is perhaps the most common feature of statewide budgeting. Some states provide *core funding* for basic services, based on an assessment of what resources are needed to sustain adequate levels of quality. Core funding is most often used to sustain small institutions or institutions with unique roles and missions. With the emerging focus on outcomes assessment and on providing incentives for pursuing new directions, more and more states are developing *strategic funding initiatives* designed to provide performance-based financial incentives and rewards.

Cost of Purchasing Public Higher Education—
The Consumer's Perspective

The relationship between tuition pricing and financial aid is changing and likely to continue to change significantly over the next few years; the dynamic varies greatly from state to state and from one type of public institution to another. Tuition and financial aid policies, the sometimes forgotten "other" costs attendant on the pursuit of a degree, and the way students and parents meet those costs are the subjects of the next section.

Tuition and Fees

Both the amount of tuition charged and the rationale behind tuition charges vary greatly from state to state. In the mid-nineteenth century, when public higher education emerged in the United States, tuition charges were modest. Some states initially charged no tuition. It was presumed that the social benefit of higher education justified a substantial public subsidy.

This tradition of modest tuition within public higher education has begun to break down over the last twenty-five years. In part, the change has occurred because many public policymakers have begun to question the philosophical soundness of the case for low tuition. Beginning with the work of Hansen and Weisbrod (1969), research has made it increasingly clear that charging low tuition increases benefits to the most advantaged in society, who participate more often in higher education, at the expense of the least advantaged, who pay taxes but do not participate in higher education as much or as often.

This critique of the philosophical basis for providing low tuition to all citizens has occurred, perhaps not coincidentally, at the same time that such a policy has become difficult to afford. As participation in public higher education has increased without commensurate increases in public support, many states have found it necessary to increase their reliance on tuition as a source of revenue. Low tuition has turned out *not* to be an effective strategy for ensuring broad access because it fails to recognize the full costs of going to college and because it spreads limited public funds very broadly. More and more states, therefore, have found that they can better protect the goal of assuring broad access by more carefully targeting limited public subsidies through a combination of higher tuition and focused financial aid.

A number of states and institutions have developed explicit, interrelated tuition and financial aid policies. They expect or require that tuition revenues represent a specified percentage of instructional costs, generally ranging from 25 to 40 percent. The rationale for this approach to tuition policy has been to assure that all students share proportionately in the costs of the valuable service they receive. This policy recognizes the substantial social benefit of higher education but also recognizes the substantial private benefit to the consumer. In most cases, this approach has led to an increase in the share of cost borne by students through tuition. Increasingly, state tuition policy is also being tied to state financial aid policy to ensure that the increased price does not erode access for those students who come from families that do not have the capacity to pay.

In states that have explicit tuition policies, institutions often have some latitude in setting specific tuition rates, within general statewide parameters. Although most institutions charge one tuition rate to all students, a number of institutions have moved toward charging differential tuition, based on the variable costs of different programs. The University of Minnesota has perhaps the most elaborate differential tuition plan, but many research institutions now charge different amounts for students in areas such as engineering, business, and law. Traditionally, graduate and undergraduate students have been charged different amounts. Although graduate students generally pay higher tuition than undergraduates, their tuition charges usually represent a smaller percentage of instructional costs than the percentage borne by undergraduates because of the substantially higher costs of providing graduate education.

In addition to tuition, public institutions generally charge fees to cover all or part of the costs of noninstructional activities. In California and a few other states, charges for instruction-related activities are actually referred to as fees to avoid conflict with constitutional prohibitions against charging tuition.

Recently, increases in fees have become an issue in many states for three reasons. First, many students have begun to complain about mandatory fees for services that they do not use. For example, many nontraditional students who are only casually involved in campus life have begun to question whether or not they should have to pay for activities in which they do not participate or facilities that they do not use. Second, an increasing number of institutions have begun to follow the California model of charging fees in lieu of tuition to circumvent statewide tuition policies. Both students and statewide policymakers have begun to question whether this practice represents good public policy. Third, some students have simply begun to complain about the increasing size of fees. Often the fees students pay are the legacy of debt-financing activities approved by previous generations of students and governing boards but for which current students carry the burden of repayment.

Actual amounts charged for tuition vary substantially, both within and between the various sectors of higher education. California community colleges charged $115 per year for resident tuition and fees in 1990-91, compared to $3,491 at Vermont Technical College. At the other end of the continuum, major research universities ranged in price from $955 per year for resident tuition and fees at the University of Texas, Austin, to $3,463 at the University of Michigan, Ann Arbor (Rodenhouse, 1990).

Virtually all states charge nonresident students much higher tuition rates than they charge residents. But again, there is tremendous variance around the country, from the extremely modest $30 increase per year in tuition for nonresident students at most Nebraska community colleges to the $6,512 extra charged by the University of Colorado or the additional $7,730 charged at Wisconsin technical colleges ("Fact File . . . ," 1990, pp. A22–A25). In general, states charge out-of-state students 50 to 100 percent more than residents on the principle that residents have earned a greater subsidy through prior tax payments. Some states, most notably California and Colorado, have explicit policies to provide virtually no subsidy to out-of-state students.

Other Costs

From the student's perspective, going to college costs much more than just tuition and fees. The real cost of college also includes the cost of books and supplies, room and board, transportation, and other living and miscellaneous expenses. For many students, attending college also involves a substantial opportunity cost, that is, the earnings forgone from being in school rather than in the work force. Tuition represents only about 20 to 30 percent of the actual cost for a resident student to attend a public institution—a fact that the general public often seems unaware of or chooses to ignore in public policy debates about tuition.

The cost of books and traditional supplies has increased much more rapidly than inflation in recent years, principally because of the substantial increase in the cost of publications. It is not uncommon for a student to pay in excess of $50 per course for books and supplies. Furthermore, a student today often needs to purchase other ancillary equipment that simply was not available or necessary in the past. For example, the slide rule has been replaced by the hand-held multifunction calculator. Some institutions or programs even recommend or require that students purchase their own personal computers. These costs place an additional burden on students.

Other expenses, such as room and board and transportation, vary greatly, depending upon the costs for these services in the community and the student's choice of life-style. For students not living with their families, a frugal budget in 1991 can require as little as $5,500 for nine months in a low-cost community but could would run as much as $8,000 in a higher-cost community. Most students, however, chose a life-style that requires $2,000 to $5,000 more annually than the frugal budget identified above.

Obviously, the cost of attending college differs for students living with their families, but the difference is not nearly as great as many people believe. Although the student living at home avoids room and board expenses, he or she generally faces substantially higher transportation costs. All else being equal, a student living at home can generally attend college for $1,000 to $2,000 less than a student living away from home.

Older students, often with families of their own, view college costs much differently than do younger students who are still dependent on their parents. These nontraditional students face real costs that traditional students do not. Many, for example, must arrange child care for when they are in class or studying. They also see the opportunity costs of attending college in a different light. Forgone income is a significant factor in whether an adult chooses to return to or remain in college, particularly if he or she is responsible for supporting a family. Time also can be a significant factor for older students as they attempt to balance a larger number of responsibilities and personal needs than do traditional students.

How Students Meet These Costs

Historically, families have been expected to contribute to their children's education. In recent years, however, studies have begun to detect a trend toward families helping less. Three factors appear to account for this trend. First, student aid policies, which generously benefit independent students, have encouraged many students to emancipate themselves financially from their families. Recent changes in student aid policy, however, have made it much more difficult to claim independence from one's family. Second, many families are less able to help their children. In the 1980s, 70 percent of all wage earners suffered a loss in purchasing power (National Center on Education and the Economy, 1990). Family income did not deteriorate substantially for most families only because more families began to rely on an increased number of wage earners. Third, many families appear less willing to accept the responsibility for financing their children's education. Americans are saving less and spending less of what they earn on education.

Students themselves also contribute to the cost of an education from a combination of work, borrowing, and savings. About 80 percent of all students work. Much of this work is provided through campus employment, often funded through federal or state college work-study programs, although most students are actually employed in the private sector (National Center for Education Statistics, 1988).

Between 20 and 25 percent of all students who attend public institutions of higher education borrow to finance a portion of their education. Most borrow relatively modest amounts. In 1988, the median debt of borrowers who attended public institutions, according to the National Postsecondary Student Assistance Study, was $5,052 (National Center . . . , 1988). Not surprisingly, students attending four-year institutions are more likely to borrow and to borrow more than students attending community colleges. Relatively few students borrow excessive amounts, but an increasing number are borrowing amounts that will create a significant debt burden upon leaving school.

In fiscal year 1990, the federal government, through its array of federal programs, provided more than $13 billion in student loans. About 33 percent of this federal money was borrowed by students attending public institutions (National Center . . . , 1988). Some states have also created novel supplemental loan programs. Minnesota has a state student loan program that provides more than

$20 million annually at attractive borrowing rates. Minnesota also has developed a graduated repayment program that provides an income-sensitive repayment plan for students in medical fields. The Education Resources Institute provides parents in New England with market-rate loans to help alleviate temporary cash-flow problems when their children choose to attend high-cost institutions.

Students and their families also receive substantial assistance through a wide variety of federal, state, institutional, and private financial aid programs. In addition to student loans, students received more than $15 billion in other forms of student aid in fiscal year 1990, about half of which went to students attending public institutions (National Center . . . , 1990). The amount of aid available varies considerably from state to state. An increasing number of states provide substantial funding to ensure access, although many states continue to rely on low tuition, rather than financial aid, as the primary vehicle for promoting educational opportunity.

Issues for Governing Boards in
a Decade of Limited Resources

The following five issues will help shape the economic agenda for higher education in the 1990s: tradeoffs between access and quality, cost containment, appropriate sharing of costs, efforts to increase productivity, and new ways to deliver higher education.

Tradeoffs Between Access and Quality

For a variety of reasons, the demand for higher education will continue to increase in the 1990s. In many states, the number of high school graduates will begin to rise again. Efforts to reduce high school dropout rates, as they become successful, will increase the potential pool of college and postsecondary vocational students. The relatively new Montgomery GI Bill, which it is believed will attract more than 2 million participants by the end of the 1990s, will soon begin to funnel many students into postsecondary education. States with historically low participation in postsecondary education, particularly for minority and economically disadvantaged students, will begin to reap the benefits of increased participation as a result of the numerous initiatives in recent years to increase the involvement of underrepresented groups. And it is likely that large numbers of adults will be returning to colleges and vocational programs at an increasing rate to retrain for new careers and to secure the new job and living skills needed to succeed in the twenty-first century.

The demands for enhancing the quality of higher education will also increase. States are mandating greater accountability measures to ensure that the public sector of higher education is providing high-quality education, research, and service. At both the national and local levels, increasing attention is being focused on the need to reform undergraduate education. Many educators and policymakers have become vocal in their concern that U.S. higher education has lost its way. They believe that as an industry, higher education is losing sight of what its customers need and want and focusing too much on what the faculty members and administrators want to provide. Strong support exists for increasing standards throughout higher education so that students will be well educated enough to compete effectively in an increasingly competitive world. This increasing support for higher standards is particularly apparent in the frustration many public policymakers express about the increasing need for remedial education. In an era of limited resources, which the 1990s certainly will be for public higher education, some conflict will almost certainly arise between the goal of access and the goal of quality.

Cost Containment

As the financial demands of higher education continue to increase, one response will be to explore more rigorous ways of containing costs. One must be careful when talking of containing costs not to confuse the *cost* of educating students with the *price* charged for this education. Although price and cost are closely related, they remain very different.

Controlling costs is not a new concept to public higher education. Historically, effective institutions have had to manage within limits. The 1990s will differ, however, in the degree to which public attention focuses on containing costs. Many states have increased the pressure to contain costs by mandating studies of administrative costs and by requiring that administrative costs be reduced. An increasing number of scholars of higher education finance are building a body of literature and research on the factors behind escalating costs and on strategies for controlling these costs. Arthur Hauptman (1989), a consultant to the American Council on Education, has identified four factors that account for much of the rise in costs for public postsecondary education during the 1980s.

- Inflation, which tends to run somewhat higher than the consumer price index for institutions of higher education because of the goods and services that colleges and universities buy
- Real growth in expenditures of about 1 percent per year to cover increases in administrative expenses, student services, sponsored research, and student financial aid
- Leveling of enrollments at many institutions, which precludes averaging increasing costs over increasing enrollments as was done through prior years of growth
- Tuition growth beyond inflation to compensate for reductions in state support

Some institutions, including Stanford, Washington University, Dartmouth, Yale, and the University of Minnesota, have begun substantial and visible efforts to reduce costs and redirect activities. This focus on cost containment will almost certainly require that educators and administrators shift the way they judge what constitutes adequate funding. Today, many people in higher education judge the adequacy of funding based on comparisons with other states or institutions. In doing so, the most expensive producers in higher education are considered the most successful. This type of assessment stands in stark contrast to the way in which other industries use comparative data, where it would never be considered exemplary to have the highest cost per unit unless you could clearly prove that the increased costs translated into a higher-quality product.

Appropriate Sharing of Costs

As public resources become tight, more states and institutions will look to garner additional money from sources other than the state. Almost certainly, tuition revenue will become more of a focus, as perhaps it should. Issues of equity and the efficient targeting of limited resources present arguments for shifting a greater share of the burden to those who can pay, including individuals and firms investing in their employees. Reliance on tuition, however, also has its limits. Although access can be protected through increased targeting of public subsidies via hefty increases in financial aid, increasing tuition to the point where most students would have to rely on financial aid could produce the third-party payment dilemma that currently plagues the health care industry. If virtually no one pays full price for education, then price may no longer work effectively as one of the levers for containing costs.

Tuition increases for public institutions are also limited by what the citizens will bear. Low tuition not only buys access, albeit in an inefficient fashion, it also buys public support. And tuition cannot be raised to the point where public higher education is no longer perceived and appreciated as a public service.

Efforts to Increase Productivity

Because of the desire to increase both access and quality, and to do so in an era of limits, pressure is building to increase the productivity and efficiency of higher education institutions. As reflected in a report from the Aspen Institute's Program for a Changing Society, titled *Closing the Disconnect in American Higher Education* (O'Keefe and Timpane, 1990), these efforts are also driven by the disenchantment of many citizens and consumers who believe that higher education is gradually losing touch with its reason for being.

Efforts to increase productivity in the 1990s will translate into initiatives at the program, institutional, state, and national levels. Much of the effort will focus on measuring and funding the achievement of identifiable outcomes, rather than simply rewarding effort. We will see a more critical assessment of whether the graduates of higher education, as the products, are adequately prepared for all the roles they face as educated adults and whether higher education is underproducing or overproducing graduates in fields where they are needed and can succeed.

New Ways to Deliver Higher Education

To increase their productivity, higher education institutions will have to not only do better what they have already been doing but also do things differently. Fiscal constraints will make it virtually impossible to rely on the past practice of building a new campus every time the need arises. Rather, higher education, if it is to be effective, must be delivered in new ways. The use of new technologies within public higher education must be expanded, particularly the use of telecommunications and computing for distance learning. New types of campuses, such as leased facilities that allow greater long-term flexibility, must be considered. One such option, now being called the *distributive university,* would provide distinct integral components of an institution in various locations.

The public sector must also examine the cost effectiveness of expanding the use of contracting with nonpublic institutions to provide publicly subsidized services. This could involve contracting with nonprofit or for-profit independent institutions of higher education, much as many states currently contract for care in private mental health and correctional facilities. And reciprocal arrangements between states and institutions continue to provide a tremendous opportunity to achieve efficiency in the delivery of services.

Role of Board Members

The five issues just discussed will stretch the imagination and patience of public governing and coordinating boards in the 1990s. The ability and willingness of these boards to tackle these tough problems will, to a great extent, determine how well public higher education responds to society's needs in this decade. The inevitable difficulties facing this enterprise we call higher education will force effective board members to take on many different roles.

One role board members must assume is that of being advocates for higher education, that is, helping other important stakeholders better appreciate the value of higher education. The precipitous decline in the share of public resources devoted to higher education over the past decade suggests that past boards have not made a convincing case for investing public funds in higher education. And as the 1990s begin, relatively few states can boast of strong, demonstrated state financial support for public higher education.

Without doubt, board members will find this advocacy role difficult, and the worn rhetoric of the past clearly is not enough. Simple cheerleading will not suffice. Boards will need to provide governors, legislatures, and the citizenry at large with a convincing and documented case for investing in higher education, including a clear appreciation for the long-term consequences of not making this investment.

Publicly making the case for higher education, however, is only part of the board members' responsibility. Despite the best efforts of governors, legislatures, and citizens, the weak national economy of the United States going into the 1990s will create severe financial constraints for many states throughout the decade. As a result, board members must take on another role, that of Solomon, the wise counsel who balances difficult, sometimes seemingly impossible, choices. If funding is insufficient to respond to the increasing demands for access and also to sustain and enhance the quality of services provided, governing and coordinating boards will face tough decisions about which goals will be preserved and which will be sacrificed and precisely how this will occur.

Board members will have to weigh the advantages and disadvantages of different funding strategies. Does it make sense, for example, to continue to provide similar substantial subsidies to all students through low tuition, or should access be preserved by targeting limited public subsidies on the most needy students through high tuition and high financial aid? Struggling with such questions will be part of the balancing role of public higher education boards in the 1990s. Some of the decisions will be painful. Almost all will be difficult to explain to the public because promoting change from the status quo is always difficult to sell, even to those who ostensibly demand change.

A third role that board members must play in the years ahead, perhaps more so than in the past, will be that of "loving critic." Board members have a responsibility to promote the reform that will be imperative if higher education is to flourish in the austere years ahead. However, boards should not meddle in the management of the enterprise; management is the job of administrators and faculty members. But it is not meddling for boards to ask what efforts are under way to increase the productivity of higher education in the institutions under their charge. Nor is it meddling to demand evidence about whether these efforts to improve performance are working. The budget provides a powerful tool; boards can choose to fund the status quo or to fund improvement.

Understanding the economics and finance of higher education is critical for board members to be effective stewards of the public trust. Whether recognized or not, boards' decisions about the pursuit and allocation of funds will determine the future viability of higher education. In many respects, higher education is like other industries. Whether it remains a healthy and vital service will, to a great extent, depend on how well boards respond to the tough financial challenges ahead. And as in so many sectors of the economy, following past practices will not serve well the needs of the future.

CHAPTER 4

Coping with
a Litigious
Environment

David M. Lascell
Sanford H. Levine

We live in a litigious society. Colleges and universities are involved in litigation over a wide range of matters. Trustees in both the public and private sectors of higher education have a responsibility to reduce their personal and institutional vulnerability to lawsuits through enlightened policies and practices. To meet this responsibility, trustees must understand the nature of institutional and personal liability and their fiduciary duties of loyalty and care to their institution.

The Present Environment

Trustees should know the major sources of lawsuits against the academy and ask themselves whether they should insist on much greater use of alternative dispute resolution techniques and expertise, such as mediation and arbitration. And insisting that their college or university take measures to reduce its exposure and risk is especially important.

Note: We gratefully acknowledge the assistance of Michael J. Cooney of Nixon, Hargrave, Devans and Doyle, Rochester, New York, in the preparation of this chapter.

Growth of Litigation

The increasing institutional exposure to legal liability does not come as a surprise. The increase in the number of lawsuits filed and in the number and size of awards made supports the perception that U.S. society as a whole, particularly since the 1960s, has become more litigious (Helms, 1987). Furthermore, higher education institutions appear to be less insulated from these developments than in the past, in part because of the major increase in federal regulation of activities in institutions receiving any federal funds. Disaffected constituents (particularly faculty members and students) and outside parties are no longer hesitant to bring their claims into the courtroom (Zirkel, 1989; Helms, 1990). Legal challenges, once rare in connection with colleges and universities, now play a prominent role in the business of higher education (Kaplin, 1985).

Higher education institutions have activities and interests broad enough to expose them to an enormous array of legal claims, ranging from employment termination and discrimination to consumer fair practice and trade complaints to environmental liability and First Amendment charges. As corporate entities with a distinct educational mission, they provide fertile ground for controversy.

Colleges and universities face many of the same problems that confront any business enterprise. For example, institutions must respond to routine claims of negligence and contract liability. Breach of contract claims involving construction, employment, and services, to name a few, continue to arise, as do negligence actions. If the institution operates a teaching hospital, medical malpractice claims are another major source of litigation.

In contrast to the for-profit corporation, the academy faces some unique exposure to lawsuits. For example, faculty tenure matters continue to provoke a considerable number of lawsuits. These suits often involve claims of discrimination under federal or state law or deprivation of a constitutional right. Similarly, the number of academic and disciplinary actions involving students continues to grow. Students contest institutional decisions (mainly on constitutional and contract grounds) in hope of securing judicial reversal of those decisions.

In 1990, United Educators Insurance Risk Retention Group,

a major liability insurer of private and public institutions, found that more than 70 percent of its claims were employment related, of which 25 percent alleged some form of prohibited discrimination (personal telephone conversation with Sandra H. McMullan, general counsel and director of risk management, United Educators Insurance Risk Retention Group, July 1991). Almost 60 percent of the claims made for excess legal liability alleged serious bodily injury. United Educators has also found that, despite the concerns of the commercial market, there was a low rate of university claims arising from child care facilities, campus security, host liquor liability, and product liability.

New issues, however, continue to emerge in the law of higher education, reflecting "a dynamism and ferment that show no signs of abating" (Dutile, 1990, p. 151). Several significant problems for colleges and universities in the 1990s have already arisen. For example, has higher education entered an extended period of austerity that will sharpen the issues of faculty member and student "rights" in the event of program and campus closures? How will institutions adapt to a rapid increase in ethnic diversity on campuses? Can the regulation of offensive conduct be balanced with the constitutional protection of free speech? Will institutions improve their self-regulation of scientific integrity in research programs? Will higher education continue to be subject to new and expanded governmental oversight and regulation? Do antitrust laws extend to all cooperative and collegial efforts among competing colleges and universities? Will courts become more assertive in settling intrainstitutional controversies, setting aside traditional judicial deference to the expertise of the academy itself? Should institutions utilize alternatives to judicial litigation, such as mediation and arbitration, to promote earlier resolution of disputes?

Reduction of the Exposure to Lawsuits

The increased litigiousness of society must not deter trustees from carrying out the educational missions of their institutions. Although it may be virtually impossible to eliminate the threat of legal challenge or, indeed, to stop a lawsuit, trustees can take steps that will reduce the institution's exposure to liability. Periodically, they should critically examine all major policies and procedures to ensure consistency with legal requirements and to see that policies and procedures are not applied arbitrarily or capriciously. This role is an integral part of trustees' responsibility for fundamental institutional decisions and policy setting.

Legal Role of Trustees

The college or university trustee's experience with our litigious society is in many ways unique. Consider, for example, the different ways in which a trustee may become involved in litigation. Most often, trustees will be sued in their representative capacity as trustees for the actions or omissions of the institution. Such actions rarely arise from the activities of the board directly. Today's trustees may be held to answer for a policy put in place decades before or an action committed by an employee of whom the trustees have no personal knowledge.

On a very few occasions, trustees have been sued individually, putting their personal assets as well as their reputations and those of their institutions in jeopardy (Porth, 1975; Peat Marwick, Main & Company, 1987). The trustee's personal resources may attract an action, or the plaintiff may wish to place pressure on the board by bringing a dispute with the institution to the foreground. Virtually any lawsuit can become a harrowing experience and take a significant toll on all parties involved, even if the institution or its trustees are satisfied with the outcome (LaNoue and Lee, 1987). *Happily, however, to the best of our knowledge, no college or university trustee has had personal assets attached in final settlement of a claim.* But it could happen, and it is this threat, however remote, that calls for individual and collective diligence by board members.

The fiduciary duties and obligations of trustees encompass the entire institution, not just a part of it. Only the board and chief executive are in a position to take such an institutionwide perspective, which is why in the final analysis it is they who are held legally responsible for the institution (Hadden and Blaire, 1987). Yet in many circumstances, the trustee may have to choose between various interests within the institution. The trustee's job becomes especially difficult in circumstances that cause conflicts between competing special-interest groups, whether they are students, faculty members, administrators, or groups external to the university, including alumni. Even in determining the proper extent of trustee indemnification or insurance, the trustee is faced with the conflict, at least conceptually, between his or her personal interests and those of the institution. Knowledgeable trustees recognize that they will sometimes be placed in this unenviable position and prepare to meet conflicts and ambiguities before a crisis occurs.

Even if trustees are not named in litigation personally, they still have a responsibility to the institution to minimize legal liability. This responsibility usually involves addressing potential areas of liability before they exist. Trustees are always concerned with legal questions; the only issue is at what point trustees should become involved in resolving them. The same tools that serve trustees so well with regard to other decisions affecting the institution (for example, use of committees and experts and well-developed policies) should be used when approaching legal questions. The most important requirement of trustees is that they be aware and informed of the possible legal ramifications of the institution's practices and policies.

Duty of Loyalty

There has been a move away from viewing the responsibilities of the college or university trustee in a limited, strictly defined manner to seeing the trustee's role as more like that of a corporate director. However, in many cases, the duty of loyalty remains absolute. Trustees must place the interests of the college or university they serve first and foremost. This duty sometimes places trustees in a difficult position with respect to demands from faculty members, students, alumni, the community, and outside business interests. Divining where the best interests of the institution end and those of these constituents begin is not easy.

The most obvious occasion on which the trustee must avoid breaching the duty of loyalty is in transactions involving the trustee personally. Financial dealings with trustees involving compensation, benefits, or other perquisites or profit provide clear situations in which a trustee may be held personally liable. These situations may present direct conflicts of interest between the trustee and the institution.

"Indirect dealing," or situations involving third parties related in some way to the trustee, may be prohibited as well. To avoid direct or indirect conflicts of interest, trustees must be alert to personal situations that may cause conflicts and to how the college or university may be affected by these situations. A trustee may fulfill the duty of loyalty if he or she avoids or mitigates situations in which there is a direct or indirect conflict between the interests of the institution and those of the trustee. If a board identifies a conflict of interest between a trustee and the institution, its options are often quite limited, sometimes by the state's nonprofit or corporate law. The duty of loyalty might be best described as "doing no wrong."

The first step in avoiding conflicts of interest is recognizing that a conflict may exist. Some trustees are quite aware of the potential for conflict, while others may need to be helped to see it. Trustees' relationships with family members and other nonprofit and for-profit institutions for which they are a trustee, director, manager, officer, partner, shareholder, or key employee *must* be disclosed at the outset. Then the relationships must be regularly reexamined to assure that a change in circumstances will not put the college or university at a disadvantage. Distilled to its most useful form, the standard is not whether the trustee is receiving a benefit but whether the institution's interests are or could be adversely affected by a conflict or the *perception* that one exists.

Although there is no absolute bar on financial dealings between the trustee or officer and the institution, these dealings are often subject to the closest scrutiny. State laws governing nonprofit institutions commonly cover instances in which the personal interests of the trustee may come into conflict with those of the institution. These laws often necessitate full disclosure of the possible conflict, a vote by disinterested trustees, or both. Almost all states forbid payment for work as a trustee or director. In some situations, such as those in which a trustee's business interests are involved, an absolute prohibition on possible self-dealing transactions may also be advisable. All trustees must be aware of any state law that governs such a situation and should educate themselves before the need becomes pressing or before they accept appointment or election to the board.

Furthermore, the institution should have its own policy about conflicts of interest, not only at the board level but also throughout the organization. Such policies may be modified to address specifically the conflicts different groups at the institution may encounter. Admissions personnel, purchasing agents, and faculty members may all face different situations, and the institutional policy should be broad and yet detailed enough to speak to each group.

Duty of Care

The standard of care for a college or university trustee is a matter of state law. Willful or wanton misconduct or illegal acts are, without exception, violations of the standard of care, but less blatant acts or omissions may also violate the standard. The standard of care has a dual function: it defines the trustee's personal liability and institutional liability for suits brought against the institution. If trustees meet their duties with respect to the standard of care, they and the institution are free from liability.

The standard against which trustees' conduct is measured is the same as the *business-judgment rule* in for-profit corporations. Trustees coming from the corporate environment will be familiar with this rule. In general, the rule essentially states that a court, or anyone else, will not sit in judgment of a board's action in the absence of bad faith or a conflict situation. The party questioning the board's actions has the burden of showing why the board's judgment should not be respected. The rule arises out of the expectation that corporate directors (or university trustees) are better equipped to evaluate institutional matters than are outsiders.

Following the business-judgment rule will not necessarily prevent liability in actions brought against the institution by members of the public at large. Even if the board properly exercises business judgment, the institution may be liable for actions affecting the public, regardless of whether procedural requirements were satisfied. For example, the adoption of a campus public safety plan may be good business judgment, but a person who is assaulted on campus may still win a lawsuit against the institution.

Identifying and meeting challenges arising from the trustee's duty of care is difficult. The duty of care will apply to many more matters than will the duty of loyalty. Statutes and case law make quite clear that the duty of care is met through *active* participation in the affairs of the institution. The trustee who expects to satisfy the standard of care by "doing no wrong" will be gravely disappointed. The duty of care requires that all trustees do what is right.

Fulfilling the duty of care is not impossible, however. By acting in a responsible, prudent manner, trustees can adequately counter any future challenge to the sufficiency of their actions. Diligently attending meetings, including committee meetings, reading and reviewing reports, and actively participating in the conduct of board affairs by inquiring into matters at issue largely meet the requisite standard.

Sometimes, of course, trustees must rely upon the opinion of others whose expertise uniquely qualifies them to respond to a particular inquiry. Trustees rely on committees of the board in fulfilling specified functions, such as finance or fund raising. The board regularly relies upon reports from institutional officers in matters such as admissions, finances, risk management, physical plant, and campus safety. The opinions of outside authorities are also helpful. In meeting the challenges of today's litigious society, reliance upon legal counsel before and during any actual litigation gives the board the opportunity to use expert advice in tackling difficult problems. A good board learns from its mistakes or those of others and does not repeat them.

Although advice from experts may assist the board in achieving its objectives, questions still arise about the extent to which a board can rely upon the advice of outside experts without making a direct inquiry of its own. The standard permitting such reliance varies under different state laws, from no specific provision on the point to an approved reliance upon financial statements (as in New York) to a broad safe harbor with regard to expert opinions (as in California). Trustees should be aware of the standard that applies in their state. Also, it is important that the decision to delegate duties encompass the same considerations of prudence and care that the board's decisions do generally. The choice of what duties to delegate and to whom should be made with the same measured, thoughtful consideration as are all decisions of the board.

Setting Good Policies

Ensuring the soundness of the policies and practices in place requires ongoing review of their adequacy, appropriateness, practicality, and fairness. The board may need to serve as a court of appeal under certain very limited circumstances.

Importance of Continuing Review

Although a governing board can substantially minimize the incidence and impact of adverse litigation by properly crafting, implementing, and reviewing policies and procedures, the process must be a continuing one (Marks, 1987). The ultimate responsibility for the activities of the institution rests in the board, and the bylaws of the board form the nucleus for all other institutional policies. Although the bylaws may allow the delegation of authority to committees, officers, administrators, faculty members, and others, the board may never abdicate institutional responsibility. As the working document for the conduct of board affairs, the bylaws should reflect contemporary policy and practice, consonant with the requirements of state law (Moots, 1991). Good institutions review their bylaws regularly, and good board members are familiar with the contents of the bylaws.

Dealing with faculty members presents an increasing challenge to college and university trustees, especially with regard to employment discrimination charges involving race, sex, age, and disability. Such allegations not only involve great legal and administrative expense but also harm the reputation of the institution and its ongoing relationship with faculty members or other employees. One of the most reliable ways to avoid such allegations is through maintaining a thorough faculty and employee handbook that clearly addresses all policy matters with regard to faculty, including tenure, promotion, salary, sabbatical, retirement, and so on. In unionized institutions, these policies may also be subject to the requirements of collective bargaining under federal or state law.

Employee policies require a great deal of thought. For example, dismissal or termination of a faculty member is commonly preceded by the opportunity for a hearing or "due process." The exact parameters of this hearing should be set forth in the employee handbook, including the notice to the faculty member about the hearing, the faculty member's access to evidence, the ability to open the hearing at the faculty member's request, and the protection from unwanted publicity afforded the faculty member. The faculty member's right to representation must also be explicitly set forth, including whether that right includes active representation by an attorney. By setting these ground rules, the administrator lessens the possibility that the personnel decision will be unfair and, therefore, successfully challenged.

Three guides to institutional policymaking should always be considered. First, policies should be put in place only after the board has considered the different options and the risks attending each policy. Second, policies must be monitored to assess changes in risks and the ability to address these changes. Third, policies may actually place the institution at a disadvantage if the administrator is not willing or capable of applying them correctly and evenhandedly. The board must consider the practical application of the institution's policies.

Board as Court of Appeal

A college or university board will sometimes act as a court of appeal for conflicts within the institution. Although the role of arbiter is seldom a desirable one, especially where the judgments of the trustees may later be subject to court scrutiny, arbitration is a necessary but rare function of trustees. Those situations and conditions under which the board will be required to arbitrate conflicts must be clearly defined and include guidelines for the board's exact role. The board should normally be confined to satisfying itself that established policies and rules of procedure were followed.

Conflicts that the board is asked to arbitrate arise most often from the sensitive relationships between the chief executive of the institution, his or her staff, and the faculty. Generally, however, appeal processes, including those involving tenure disputes, should be confined within administrative or academic departments.

The perceptible rise in the number of lawsuits concerning faculty grievances may result in more appeals to the board if the president or other administrative body cannot deal with faculty complaints effectively. Established procedures are especially important in these cases to ensure that only those matters the board has already decided it will consider come before it. A periodic legal review of the faculty handbook is also helpful for trustees.

Comparison of Public and Private Institutions

Although the fundamental legal concerns of trustees—identifying risks and minimizing the exposure to them at the lowest cost—are the same whether the institution is public or private, there are some significant differences. Constitutional claims, for example, are rarely pressed against private institutions.

Conversely, public institutions may enjoy immunity from some lawsuits through the Eleventh Amendment, which prevents private citizens from filing suit in federal court against state governments. State-run educational institutions are therefore immune from some kinds of suits in federal court.

State laws may also provide immunity to the state and its constituent institutions. Educational institutions are seen as an extension of state government, and unless immunity is waived, the college or university will be immune from certain types of suits. State sovereign immunity, however, is riddled with exceptions as a result of judicial decisions and legislative action. The activities in which the institution is involved may also be proprietary or private in nature and thus afforded no more protection than the activities of a private institution.

State-run colleges and universities also have a responsibility under the Fourteenth Amendment to protect the rights of citizens. Private institutions do not share this responsibility unless they are acting as agents of the state or involved in state action. By accepting governmental funding, a private institution may become a state instrumentality, subject to the Fourteenth Amendment or perhaps other regulation. Recent legislation, such as the Drug-Free Schools and Communities Act, is specifically written with the intent of tying compliance to the receipt of any federal funds. The reach of federal regulation even into private institutions has become pervasive, and institutions must be alert to this new legal landscape.

Immunity, Indemnification, and Insurance

The changing concept of charitable immunity, the applicability of indemnification, and the importance of adequate liability insurance are subjects for trustee concern. How should state boards address them?

Charitable Immunity

In the past, many states insulated educational institutions from lawsuits by providing immunity on account of their charitable activities. This once venerable doctrine has been all but abolished in most states. Recent cases demonstrate that the doctrine is viewed unfavorably, even where it is still in force.

Charitable immunity for trustees has become more common, however. Recognizing that charitable organizations have been increasingly subject to lawsuits and that worthy individuals might not be willing to serve as directors or officers if their personal assets were exposed, many states have enacted some form of statutory immunity for those people serving nonprofit organizations, including colleges and universities. Many states have passed "volunteer protection" laws with varying degrees of immunity.

Delaware, for example, allows a corporation to eliminate or limit personal liability of directors to the corporation for violations of the duty of care by adding a provision to this effect to the corporate charter. The statutory protection covers only actions by the institution. Not surprisingly, transgressions against the duty of loyalty (improper benefit), intentional misconduct, or knowing violations of the law are not covered.

Tennessee and Arizona have simply provided that trustees are immune from suit. Such protection does not apply, however, in cases of intentional misconduct or, sometimes, in cases of grossly negligent conduct. Virginia allows corporations to limit the personal liability of trustees to the amount of their compensation. Texas limits a trustee's liability to prescribed monetary limits if, among other things, the organization has liability insurance covering the remaining exposure. The protection of these statutes is very specific to each state, so trustees are urged to consult the law of their institution's state for changes that may affect them.

Indemnification

Indemnification is an agreement by the institution to prepay or reimburse expenses incurred by an officer or director in defense of an action. The amount paid may include not only the costs of defense but also settlements, fines, or penalties as well. Most state laws permit indemnification by the institution of its trustees and officers acting in furtherance of the institution's purposes. These laws are often very specific as to what costs will be covered by the corporation and under what circumstances. As a general rule, willful, wanton, or illegal misconduct is not covered.

In some states, indemnification is mandatory in certain situations. For example, in California and Delaware, indemnification is mandatory if the director or trustee successfully refutes the merits of the claim. In those instances, if the institution refuses to indemnify, a trustee may bring a court action demanding that the institution indemnify him or her. In other situations, indemnification depends upon the provisions in the organization's certificate, charter, or bylaws.

Trustees should ask their institution the following questions about indemnification policies: Does indemnification cover derivative suits on behalf of the entity, that is, those by the corporation or another acting in its stead, such as the state attorney general? Does it cover third-party actions by an outsider? Is the legal standard the same in both cases? Does indemnification cover the cost of any judgment, attorneys' fees, or settlements with or without court approval? Is a board finding as to the propriety of an action required before the organization can indemnify a trustee? Is advancement of legal costs covered and on what terms? The answers to each of these questions should be clear to trustees so that they know precisely what is covered and when.

Insurance

Insurance is used to spread risk, reduce costs to an acceptable level, and provide funds for payment of losses. For trustees personally, liability insurance provides a vehicle for indemnification (United Way of America, 1988; Tremper and Babcock, 1990).

Insurance carriers classify risks in discrete categories, not necessarily along the same lines that the trustee or the institution would identify. The institution does not usually find coverage for all its insurance. As a result, the institution must piece together different policies and may end up with gaps or needless overlaps in coverage (Singsen, 1988). An increasing number of institutions use a combination of commercial insurance policies and self-insurance to meet their needs. Self-insurance has been most frequently used for workers' compensation and as a "deductible," or a self-insured retention, in a general liability policy.

Reading the insurance policies is an important first step toward identifying where the institution is needlessly exposed. But most policies, with numerous riders and addenda, are not written with ease of reading in mind. Access to an insurance broker, an attorney skilled in insurance matters, or an insurance adviser is invaluable in sorting through the coverage (Stone and North, 1989). The board should seek an adviser other than the broker who sells the policy.

Delivery of Legal Services

Governing boards have the responsibility to ensure that their institutions have adequate legal counsel. They also have responsibility for seeing that it is used effectively and that its effectiveness is asessed periodically.

Needs Assessment

In a litigious environment, the question of whether or not to retain or employ legal counsel is rhetorical. All colleges and universities, whether public or private, secular or religious, large or small, need legal advice or representation. Before trustees choose a lawyer or law firm for a particular service or on general retainer, they must recognize the potential functions counsel can perform and clarify what is appropriate for their particular institution and needs.

Although attorneys can play many possible roles for institutions of higher learning, from adviser to litigator (Daane, 1985), most institutions expect a legal counsel to

- Advise trustees of the laws and regulations applicable to the institution
- Apprise trustees of new legal developments and their impact
- Defend the institution in litigation and initiate actions, where appropriate
- Negotiate agreements on behalf of institutional interests
- Prepare and review documents
- Review policies and procedures relating to faculty, staff, and students

Options

Colleges and universities have a range of options in seeking legal advice or representation. The most widely accepted choices are in-house counsel, outside counsel, or state attorney general, if the institutions are tax-supported. In deciding upon representation, trustees must consider the following questions: Will counsel be retained solely for litigation? Will counsel be needed on a daily basis or intermittently? Is a legal specialty required? What level of funding is available for legal assistance? How many lawyers are needed? Trustees should assess the relative advantages and limitations of each option.

Some states require by law that a public college or university be represented by the office of the state's attorney general. (For a locally sponsored community college, this role may be assigned to a county or school district attorney or other municipal law officer.) There are certain advantages to this type of legal assistance (Beale, 1974). The attorney general is usually highly respected by both the courts and the community. Furthermore, the attorney general's office exercises considerable authority and its opinions will be given due deference.

On the other hand, this type of counsel has some potentially serious disadvantages. The attorney general will not have close contact with the institution and thus will not be as sensitive to its needs. Additionally, lawyers within an attorney general's office are not likely to be very experienced in dealing with the legal issues, culture, or environment of higher education. The practice of law in higher education has become a specialty in the past three decades, and state attorneys general rarely have expertise in the field.

In-House Counsel

In most cases, full-time attorneys are desirable as university counsel or general counsel, particularly for large private or public institutions. The number of full-time in-house attorneys at universities and colleges has more than doubled since the early seventies (National Association of College and University Attorneys, 1984). These attorneys are immediately available to provide regular assistance to trustees and administrators in managing university business. Performing much the same function as corporate counsel in the business community, in-house attorneys can not only aid colleges or universities when legal controversies materialize but also assist in adapting institutional policies and procedures to avoid lawsuits. The benefits of in-house counsel include:

- Immediate availability for consultation
- Sensitivity to the collegial nature of the institution
- Knowledge of higher education law and an understanding of the educational mission of the college or university
- Generally lower costs than attorneys who charge by the hour
- Familiarity with members of the college or university community and knowledge of current institutional concerns
- Practice of the principles of "preventive law," which can help to reduce short- and long-term exposure to lawsuits

On the other hand, in-house attorneys may lack certain highly specialized knowledge and skills in fields such as patents or taxation (National Association of College and University Business Officers, 1982). Some institutions employ separate attorneys in these fields, just as they employ risk managers who may or may not be legal counsel.

Outside Counsel

Small institutions or those without frequent need for legal services may prefer to hire outside counsel. A private law firm may provide legal guidance as the need arises and thus be more economical. Using outside attorneys can have several advantages. Specialists can be selected to handle precise needs. Outside attorneys will have experience with local court practices. And access to expertise and legal networking can be obtained.

However, the services of outside counsel may become expensive, because fees are billed at hourly rates. Furthermore, the institution will be one of many clients and may not receive immediate attention. With only intermittent contact with the institution, outside counsel may not have the opportunity to practice preventive law.

Is there a happy medium? Instead of retaining either in-house counsel or outside counsel exclusively, trustees may wish to combine both types of legal assistance. For instance, they may find that using in-house counsel for institutional matters and outside counsel for litigation and other special issues can be the most effective form of representation. Similarly, in public institutions represented by a state attorney general for some or all trial and appellate work, trustees may wish to consider the retention or employment of in-house counsel for nonlitigation issues.

Trustees who are practicing attorneys and law professors have in the past provided legal services as an adjunct to their other responsibilities, with or without compensation. Today, however, there are major disadvantages to this practice. Aside from doubts about the adequacy of service, there is usually a conflict of interest per se in such practices. It is important for trustees to maintain independent judgment to be effective, and any attempt to serve as both attorney and trustee severely compromises this independence.

Although opinion may vary on this subject, as a general matter, the practice is to be discouraged.

Role and Use of Counsel

Who should be considered the actual client of the institution's attorney? After all, a number of possible clients exist within a college or university: the institution as a whole, the governing board, the administration, the faculty, the student body, the alumni, and others. Trustees and administrators must recognize that counsel's primary loyalty is to the college or university itself.

Because counsel works chiefly with trustees and administrators, however, these constituents generally perceive themselves as the clients. As a consequence, legal counsel may be placed in awkward or inappropriate situations that pose an ethical problem or conflict of interest. In these situations, separate counsel may be required.

When a board is considering whether to terminate or dismiss the institution's chief executive, counsel would normally serve the governing board as client. In this case, indeed in most cases, the board *is* the institution in a legal sense.

Should attorneys play a policy-making role? Some trustees believe that an attorney should ordinarily assume a passive role in the decision-making process; that is, counsel should be called upon only to facilitate, explain, or defend policies promulgated by the board. Confining attorneys solely to this reactive role, however, may be too rigid.

Trustees should consider using counsel in a preventive capacity (Weeks, 1980). If attorneys are consulted early in a decision-making process, they will be able to advise trustees about any potential exposure to legal challenge. In this manner, the counsel can assist the administration and board in achieving the objective of an intended policy within legally appropriate options. However, a fine line exists between having an attorney *apprise* trustees of legal ramifications of a policy and having an attorney *make* policy. It is not the function of the counsel to choose alternatives or decide policies. These prerogatives must remain with the board and chief executive.

Evaluation of Counsel

How do trustees evaluate their attorneys? Trustees employ specific criteria in evaluating other aspects of institutional policies and practices, and legal counsel should not be immune from such evaluation. As with all methods of evaluation, the parameters should be clear, concise, and communicated to those who are being evaluated.

The grounds on which the counsel is judged will, of course, be quite specific to the relationship between the attorney and the institution. No list can be exhaustive, but some matters that the board may wish to consider include:

- What does the institution need? The choice whether or not and how to involve legal counsel, whatever the form, belongs to the board. A needs assessment, often in conjunction with counsel, is the first step to any evaluation.
- Has counsel achieved the board's objectives? If not, why not? The outcome of a particular case cannot be guaranteed, but the trustees should expect thorough preparation and effective advocacy. For example, is the attorney prompt in responding to inquiries from the trustees or administration? Is the attorney responsive to these inquiries? Does the attorney present the institution with an evaluation of alternatives?
- Has counsel achieved the board's objectives within established time and budgetary constraints? Counsel should have clear guidelines as to these and other limitations. Legal costs, like other institutional costs, should be monitored.
- What is the relationship of the counsel to the institution? The board's expectations will be quite different depending on the task at hand and who is called to address it. In general, in-house or outside counsel are expected to keep the interests of the institution foremost in mind, alerting the trustees and administrators to possible changes in the law and taking a long-term view of the legal solutions available. Counsel hired to address specific issues, such as development and fund raising, on the other hand, would be expected to achieve more limited goals.

CHAPTER 5

Planning for Strategic Decision Making

Joel W. Meyerson
Sandra L. Johnson

Strategic planning is the process of continuous adaptation to a changing environment. It involves periods of analysis, creativity, negotiation, and implementation. Although the process may vary—and in fact should be tailored to the needs of each institution—its ultimate goal is effective action.

There are many approaches to strategic planning. Our objective is to present a multiple-perspective model that borrows significantly from the literature on planning in the higher education, nonprofit, and corporate sectors. Although strategic planning by business organizations falls in and out of favor, it is critical to the future health of higher education, where few commonly accepted performance measures are set by the market. Instead, trustees and executives must rely on self-analysis, noting the satisfaction of key constituents within the institution, its financial stability, and its external public image.

Role of Trustees in Strategic Planning

Making strategic decisions about the future direction of an institution is one of the key roles of its trustees. Strategic planning promotes an institution's goals and objectives. It requires knowledge about the current environment as well as a vision for the future. Trustees can provide a perspective often unavailable elsewhere in the institution.

Trustees may be more objective about an institution's internal strengths and weaknesses than anyone else in the institution and have the widest exposure to the external environment. Such a vantage point enables them to help management establish a clear mission and then evaluate the accomplishment of the mission. Trustees also represent the public's interest. Although they must respond to political mandates, the trustees must also be mindful of the future as well as the current political situation. Trustees act as guardians of the institution for the present and the future generations. The long-term outlook and objectivity of trustees and the working knowledge of higher education administrators make a valuable combination.

Active participation of the trustees in the strategic process is crucial. However, the most successful outcome is likely to result from an informed partnership of the board, key administrators, and faculty members. No one group can form a strategic vision and inspire the institution to realize it without the active cooperation of the others.

Key Issues

Strategic thinking has never been more important to the future success of U.S. colleges and universities. They face significant management and academic challenges that will require difficult decisions about resource allocation. The funding of operating and capital needs is likely to be one of the most challenging management issues that institutions of higher education face. State appropriations constitute *an average* of 50 percent of revenue for public institutions. The availability of these funds is affected by the strength of the local economy and the political climate for higher education. In addition, public institutions attract most of their students from their own geographical area, making local demographics and families' ability to pay for education particular concerns.

To compensate for revenue constraints, institutions will need to control costs for utilities, equipment, supplies for research and operating facilities, and other capital items. Salaries and benefits will also be a major concern in the 1990s, especially given predicted shortages of faculty in many disciplines and the size of the staff needed to administer institutions of higher learning. Another concern will be managing aging facilities and finding ways to fund their renewal and replacement.

Certain academic issues are also likely to assume greater strategic importance in the 1990s than in earlier decades. These issues include serving a diverse student body, improving academic productivity, encouraging more students to pursue doctoral degrees to ensure an adequate supply of qualified faculty members, renewing institutions' commitment to teaching, and continuing to enhance the curricula to prepare students for life in the twenty-first century.

Given the significance of these management and academic issues, strategic planning will be an increasingly important tool on U.S. campuses. Although such planning cannot change political or economic realities, it can help an institution anticipate and prepare for periods of adversity. Strategic planning also can help focus an institution's resources on the areas in which it has the greatest comparative advantage, instead of diffusing them broadly. Thus, quality can be maintained or even improved while costs are reduced.

Strategic Planning Process

Theorists and practitioners disagree about the best approach for developing and implementing strategy. Some people favor a formal process that relies on analytical tools and methodologies. Others favor a behavioral approach that takes organizational politics into account and uses negotiation. Debate also centers on whether strategy should be a deliberate, active management process or a learned experience that emerges from past actions.

Planning groups may want to tailor the twelve-step process we describe in this section to their own institutions. Or they may want to choose a different method from among those in the literature on strategic planning. According to Henry Mintzberg (1987, p. 70), "Effective strategies show up in the strangest places and develop through the most unexpected means. There is no one best way to make strategy."

1. *Initiate and plan the project.* The first step in strategic planning is to form a planning group composed of board members, administrators, and faculty members. The group's task is to prepare a detailed work plan, assign responsibilities, and establish a time-table for the project.

2. *Develop a preliminary mission statement.* The mission statement describes an institution's purpose. Developing a mission statement is the starting point as well as the product of the strategic planning process. According to John Carver, author of *Boards That Make a Difference,* "The most important work of any governing board is to create and re-create the reason for organizational exis-tence. . . . It is a perpetual obligation, deserving of the majority of board time and energy" (1990, p. 56).

Defining the mission of an institution of higher learning may appear deceptively obvious: colleges and universities educate students, perform public service, and may also conduct research. However, preparing a good mission statement requires extensive discussion and analysis of the institution's values and traditions; unique characteristics; geographical market; relationships with and obligations to stakeholders; and relative emphasis on teaching, re-search, and service.

3. *Develop preliminary plans for academic and administra-tive units.* Planning groups from each major academic and admin-istrative unit should be formed to frame strategies and identify resource requirements for each area, based on the preliminary stra-tegic vision for the institution developed in step two. The prelimi-nary plans may include the purpose, goals, priorities, and relative market position of each unit.

4. *Assess the external environment.* Political, economic, so-cial, and technological trends increasingly affect the competitive position and financial health of U.S. colleges and universities. Given the diverse backgrounds of trustees and their broad exposure to the external market, their talents can be used very effectively to monitor changes in the external environment and interpret data in the following four areas:

Area	*Considerations*
Political	State and federal support for research, education, and financial aid
Economic	Inflation, family incomes, and the local and national economy
Social	Public values, local and national demographics, supply of faculty members, and immigration and migration trends
Technological	Information technology, telecommunications, improvements in machinery and equipment, innovations in physical plant operations, and control of toxic waste

The planning group should not overlook the increasing globalization of the world's economies when they consider political, economic, social, and technological trends. Some global influences on U.S. higher education include foreign students, foreign-trained faculty members, international study programs, overseas research partners, and foreign investment opportunities.

Planners may also want to consider the higher education "industry" as part of their assessment of the external environment. According to Michael Porter (1985, p. 1), "Competitive strategy is the search for a competitive position in an industry, the fundamental arena in which competition occurs." Porter describes the following five forces that shape an industry, and we have added some considerations for colleges and universities:

- *Intensity of rivalry among competitors:* Colleges and universities operate in a highly competitive market.
- *Threat of new entrants:* Higher education is a mature industry. It may be more difficult to establish new institutions than it was several decades ago.
- *Threat of substitutes:* Public institutions could be substitutes for

private colleges and universities. Foreign institutions of higher learning may be substitutes for U.S. colleges and universities.

- *Bargaining power of buyers:* Determinants of the bargaining power of buyers include the price sensitivity of consumers (usually students and their families) given perceived differences in quality between institutions.

- *Bargaining power of suppliers:* Determinants of the bargaining power of supplies include the concentration of suppliers, including faculty members. Faculty members, especially those in the hard-to-hire fields and superstars, may be able to command a premium given the inadequate supply.

In relating to the external environment, colleges and universities may choose to pursue one of the three strategies that Porter has described in his book *Competitive Advantage* (1985). One strategy is *price leadership.* Public institutions can offer lower tuition prices than private universities and often compete on this basis. Private institutions may function as price leaders within their peer group.

Organizations that compete by offering unique products or services follow the *differentiation* strategy. Although these organizations cannot ignore price, they may charge a premium because of the perceived uniqueness of their service, means of delivery, marketing, or other factors. Many institutions of higher learning pursue this strategy, either for the entire institution or for particular academic programs. For example, an institution that has a leading economics program, a renowned biology department, or an eminent law school is pursuing a differentiation strategy.

In the *focus* strategy, organizations select a segment of the market and tailor their products or services to fit their niche. For example, schools with strong religious affiliations or those that historically serve a black student body are following a focus strategy.

5. *Assess the internal environment.* Every organization has areas of excellence and mediocrity. The objective of an institutional assessment is to identify strengths—the core competencies of the institution—to build upon and weaknesses to minimize. Appropriate areas for investigation will vary from institution to institution.

Taylor, Meyerson, Morrell, and Park (1991) suggest internal assessments and comparative analysis of the student body, faculty and administration, academic programs, research, facilities, tuition and fees, other unrestricted resources, and results of operations.

Area	*Considerations*
Student body	Applications, acceptances, selectivity, matriculation, retention rates, diversity, geographical representation, alumni profile
Faculty and administration	Composition, growth, diversity, tenure, salaries and benefits, morale, ratio of faculty and staff to students
Academic programs	Expenditures; quality of faculty, library holdings, computing resources, facilities and equipment; demand; comparative advantage; scope of offerings
Research	Funding sources; quality of researchers, facilities, and equipment
Facilities	Operating expenditures, deferred maintenance, planned construction, constraints of building usages
Tuition and fees	Annual increases, internal and external financial aid
Other unrestricted resources	Levels of past giving, size and number of gifts, sources of contributions, planned capital campaigns, level of endowment income, investment mix and return, size of endowment and quasi endowment

Results of operations   Performance results, sources of
                               revenue, cash-flow require-
                               ments, expenditures by cate-
                               gory, overall financial
                               flexibility

Satisfying customers or stakeholders is becoming increasingly important as more colleges and universities institute cost-
containment and productivity programs. Many of these programs
also focus on improving quality as it is perceived by an institution's
stakeholders. A stakeholder is any person or group that competes for
an institution's attention, services, and resources or is affected by its
output (Bryson, 1989). The stakeholders of a public institution of
higher education include students, alumni, faculty, staff, unions,
trustees, grantors, suppliers, lenders, taxpayers, interest groups, citizens, the state government, the local community, and other institutions of higher learning.

Different stakeholders often judge an organization's performance using very different criteria. For example, students may be
interested in the quality of campus life, small classes, the cost of
their education, and the marketability of their degree. On the other
hand, faculty members may want sufficient time for research, capable assistants, and adequate compensation. An important part of
the assessment of the environment is determining how well the
institution is performing according to the criteria of its various
stakeholders. This analysis may reveal valuable information about
an institution's internal strengths and weaknesses.

One model that the planning group may want to use to
evaluate their academic programs is the grid that was originally
devised by the Boston Consulting Group and then adapted for
higher education by George Keller (1983, p. 155). Keller's model
includes four categories:

- Stars—high quality and high student demand
- Cows—high quality and low student demand
- Question marks—low quality and high student
  demand
- Dogs—low quality and low student demand

Institutions may chose to nourish their "stars," phase out their "dogs," retain their "cows," and improve the quality of their "question marks." One limitation of this model is that quality and demand are very subjective and difficult to measure.

6. *Develop a vision of success for the institution.* A vision of success describes what an institution would look like if it were to achieve its full potential. The vision statement should be challenging and inspire everyone to work toward a common goal. Most important, it should be communicated widely in the organization.

Many successful organizations formulate a vision, which is sometimes called *strategic intent.* According to Hamel and Prahalad (1989, p. 67), "Strategic intent implies a sizable stretch for an organization. Current capabilities and resources will not suffice. This forces the organization to be inventive, to make the most of limited resources. Whereas the traditional view of strategy focuses on the degree of fit between existing resources and current opportunities, strategic intent creates an extreme misfit between resources and ambitions. Top management then challenges the organization to close the gap by systematically building new advantages."

The planning group may want to consider the following questions posed by Keller (1983, p. 121) to help them determine the vision of success for their institution: "What special role do we play in America's higher education network? . . . What comparative advantages do we have over approximately similar places? . . . What academic fields and college services will be most needed by the country and our region in the next decade? With our traditions, endowment, location, and collection of faculty and administrators . . . what should our college aspire to be 10 years from now?"

7. *Review preliminary plans for academic and administrative units.* The planning groups from each major academic and administrative unit should reconvene to review their preliminary plans, based on the analysis of the internal and external environment as well as on the vision of success identified in step six. These groups should reaffirm their sense of strategic intent (step six), especially in light of their environmental analyses.

8. *Identify strategic alternatives and determine the institution's strategic plan.* Strategic alternatives—challenges about which planners must make fundamental choices—often emerge from a

review of the internal and external environment. Step eight may reveal potential changes in the market or the possibility of some event that will present threats or opportunities and affect an institution's ability to achieve its mission.

One good approach for identifying strategic alternatives is to hold a brainstorming session for the planning group. The most important ground rule for this session is that participants should be encouraged to suggest all ideas that come to mind without analyzing them, no matter how improbable some of them may seem. A facilitator to lead the discussion and write down the ideas that emerge can be particularly useful.

The planning group may then want to narrow the list of ideas to between ten and twenty-five, reaching general consensus if possible about which ideas should be included. Next, the costs and benefits of implementing each alternative should be weighed. This analysis will help to focus the planning group on the most important ideas. Few institutions have enough resources to fully support all deserving activities. It may be better to concentrate resources in the areas deemed to be most strategically important to the institution.

After this analysis, the list of strategic alternatives should be reviewed once more to consolidate it to a more manageable number of items. The final list of strategic alternatives will form the basis for the institution's strategic plan. The planning group also may want to reconsider the institution's preliminary mission statement, which may need to be revised to reflect the new strategic plan.

Identifying strategic alternatives and formulating the institution's strategic plan can be a difficult as well as an exciting part of the planning process. It involves conflicts about what should be done, how it should be done, and who will do it. Open discussion, negotiation skills, and strong leadership are critical.

9. *Move the strategic plan into action.* In step nine, action plans are developed that link the institution's strategic plan with its budget. To implement the strategic plan, the institution may, for example, need to restructure its organization or renovate facilities. Budget cuts in some areas may be necessary to free up funds for new initiatives. The importance of linking the budget and the strategic plan should not be underestimated. A college or university may

have carefully crafted a strategic plan, but it is the allocation of resources that determines the course the institution takes.

10. *Develop detailed implementation plans for each academic and administrative unit.* Step ten is to develop action plans and measurable goals for the institution as a whole as well as for individual schools, academic departments, and administrative functions. Setting such goals in each academic program as well as in finance, technology, student support, admissions, development, and so forth contributes to an institution's success.

11. *Introduce the strategic plan and build consensus.* The planning group may want to hold sessions with key constituents to present the plan to the university community. Strategic planning will not work unless its goals are widely communicated and accepted by trustees, administrators, and faculty. According to Keller (1983, p. 149), "Politically, most of the key people need to be on board the strategy train when it leaves the station." The planning group should communicate—and build commitment to—the themes of strategic plans at critical points in their development. Frequent, informal discussions between key campus leaders may be more effective than formal planning meetings and documents (Schmidtlein and Milton, 1988–89).

12. *Review the planning process and monitor performance.* The planning group should develop measurable goals—benchmarks—for all major areas, including financial position, campus facilities, curriculum, faculty and staff salaries and benefits, student life, enrollment, and so forth. Although quantitative measures may be harder to develop in the academic world than in the for-profit world, "performance is the ultimate test of any institution" (Drucker, 1990, p. 139).

Trustees should regularly monitor the institution's performance against the established benchmarks and also ask whether the action plan and allocation of resources are helping the institution achieve its long-term goals? Planning is an ongoing process that does not stop with the development of a single strategic plan. Rather, the plan needs to be retooled as new strengths and weaknesses as well as threats and opportunities present themselves.

Impediments to Planning

Higher education is not an easy environment in which to implement strategic planning successfully. Departments operate autonomously, different campuses may have very different needs and characters, decision making is often very political, and institutions are loosely organized and resistant to change. Many colleges and universities have tried strategic planning, but not all have been successful. For example, one study of planning in higher education indicated that few participants could describe specific benefits that resulted from their planning processes (Schmidtlein and Milton, 1988–89). The study showed that many institutions did not have good data on external trends or internal capabilities. Faculty members thought they were ineffectively involved, while administrators thought that faculty members were only interested in protecting their own interests. Planning documents provided limited operational guidance. Some public institutions in the study initiated planning because of state mandates. Campuses resented this intrusion and often ignored the planning documents that were produced to satisfy the external agency.

One authority on strategic planning and management studied two hundred companies and identified ten major mistakes to avoid in the planning process (Koteen, 1989, pp. 93–94). Although this list was developed for corporations, it could apply to colleges and universities as well.

1. Assuming that planning can be delegated to a planner
2. Focusing on current problems to the exclusion of long- range plans
3. Developing goals that were not suitable for formulating long-range plans
4. Not involving major line personnel in the planning process
5. Not using plans as standards for evaluating performance
6. Fostering an internal environment resistant to planning

7. Failing to integrate planning with the management process
8. Emphasizing formality rather than simplicity, flexibility, and creativity
9. Failing to review long-range plans with departmental and divisional heads
10. Consistent rejecting of the planning process by top management through making intuitive decisions that conflict with the formal plan.

Strategic planning is not a panacea. Answers to difficult problems do not always arise and when solutions can be found, they are never perfect. Sometimes, big payoffs do occur. More often, however, strategic planning may help an organization avoid major mistakes or make incremental changes that benefit it over the long term.

Critical Success Factors

At least three factors are critical to the success of strategic decision making in the academic community: consensus, leadership, and management of the process of change. Effectively used, these factors will help institutions successfully overcome the impediments described above.

Faculty members, trustees, and administrators share power on college campuses. Drucker (1990, p. 171) says that "we need to think of the management of schools . . . as a partnership between the board and the professional staff. I use a side-by-side organizational chart, with the board of trustees in one column and the faculty in another column, and the president's office and various members of the administrative team in between. All three are centers of power, and centers of authority."

The most successful approach to strategic decision making may be a blend of centralized and decentralized planning and leadership. Trustees are often in the best position to identify and address changes in the external environment. Trustees and senior managers will need to work together to identify institutionwide issues, allocate resources according to strategic priorities, initiate broad changes, and make decisions about eliminating or expanding aca-

demic or administrative programs. Faculty members also have a
vision for the school. In addition, they are most knowledgeable
about developments in their fields and are closest to students. They
are in the best position to develop departmental plans, budgets, and
curriculum changes.

Leadership also is a critical success factor in any strategic
planning process. A champion can provide the energy, momentum,
and commitment necessary to carry the process through. Leadership
is particularly critical if the institution must change to achieve its
goals or if its external environment is unstable. Often, this leadership can come from the board. Managing change is the subject of
much thought, discussion, and writing, since most organizations
and individuals resist change. "A fundamental dilemma of strategy
making is the need to reconcile the forces for stability and for
change—to focus efforts and gain operating efficiencies on the one
hand, yet adapt and maintain currency with a changing external
environment on the other" (Mintzberg, 1987, p. 71).

If the institution must change to succeed, the "seven-S framework" can help trustees conceptualize the process. This framework
consists of three technical "hard S's"—strategy, structure, and systems—and four behavioral "soft S's"—skills, staff, style of management, and shared values. Leaders must use all seven S's to produce
constructive change in an organization (Koteen, 1989).

One benefit of a clearly defined and communicated strategic
plan is that it can inspire internal and external constituents to
achieve common goals. Public disillusionment with higher education set in during the 1980s, and leaders will need to work hard to
win support during the 1990s. Creating a strategic vision for the
future as well as action plans to implement the vision, and communicating the plans and the vision widely, can help foster support
for an institution.

Trustees can play a critical leadership role in strategic decision making by setting the tone and direction of the institution's
plan. Quality is the watchword here, as in other areas of institutional management. "For in the long run, as surely as excellence
ends with clients, patients, students, or other customers, it begins
with governance" (Carver, 1990, p. 211).

PART TWO

Fulfilling Board Functions

Serving on a board of trustees or regents of an academic institution or multicampus system is the most revered of all volunteer positions in U.S. society. Unfortunately, most people probably accept this calling without any sense of what is expected or how difficult and challenging the job will prove to be. Conscientious trusteeship is stimulating and enormously rewarding, but it requires a deep and abiding commitment and a willingness to learn how to exercise trusteeship effectively.

The eleven chapters in Part Two are devoted to most of the key responsibilities of governing boards. Each chapter explores the boundaries between the responsibilities of governing board and chief executive—where these responsibilities are shared and where they should be distinguished from one another. The line between the board's role in setting policy and the administration's role in implementing policy is often fuzzy and must be negotiated and renegotiated over time. These chapters provide helpful guideposts along the way.

One of the most difficult concepts for new trustees and re-gents to grasp is that of *shared governance,* a concept unique to academic trusteeship. Defining when and how the many internal and external constituencies of the institution can and should be

91

consulted and on what issues surely constitutes one of the board's most challenging responsibilities—if effective leadership and a clear sense of institutional direction are to prevail. This is a particularly perplexing task for state and multicampus systems in a period of declining resources. Several chapters in this section address these particular matters, but the net contribution of all of the chapters is in their focus on how the inevitable ambiguities of academic governance can be reduced to reasonable clarity.

CHAPTER 6

Responsibilities of the Governing Board

Richard T. Ingram

This chapter clarifies the difference between the legal or corporate entity that is the governing board and the individual trustee, who has no legal authority but from whom much is expected. The responsibilities of the board and the individual trustee are quite different, yet they are complementary. As a critical part of a complex system of checks and balances in the governance of an academic institution or system of institutions, the governing board and its members must be clear about their respective job descriptions—about what is and is not expected of them. What goes on in the boardroom is as important to a college or university as what goes on in the classroom.

The concept of shared governance is a distinctive feature of U.S. higher education, one that is often difficult for the new trustee to grasp—especially those trustees who have the illusion that all major decisions are made unilaterally in the boardroom. As an alternative to direct governmental control, thousands of people from all walks of life assume trusteeships in higher education each year. They are not usually prepared for what is likely to be one of the most exhilarating, exasperating, rewarding, worrisome, and educational experiences of their life.

Unfortunately, enabling legislation, constitutional provisions, charters, and even board bylaws rarely help to clarify the fundamental responsibilities of the board or the trustee. Much legalese and bureaucratese must be overcome in reading such documents. And orientation programs often fail, too, in spite of sometimes herculean effort. It is easier to orient new board members to the institution or system and the board's structure and composition than to their responsibilities or to what is expected of them. But progress is being made here and there as statements of board authority are made explicit in bylaws and as separate statements of trustee responsibilities are adopted. There are enough challenges, ambiguities, contradictions, and ironies in academic trusteeship without confusion about the basic roles of board and trustee.

Trusteeship is a constant balancing act, a search for the middle ground between "standing up too close or back too far," knowing when to exercise legal authority and when to show restraint, making unilateral board decisions and consulting with other constituents, advocating institutional interests and serving the public good on behalf of all state citizens, accepting legitimate accountability to elected political leaders and guarding against inappropriate intrusion, standing up for one's principles and helping to build a consensus on complex issues, knowing when to lead and when to follow. The list could go on. It represents what makes being a trustee so stimulating, challenging, and important.

Trusteeship can also be extremely rewarding and even fun at times. The personal satisfaction that comes from helping a college, university, or system meet its purposes and goals is very gratifying. The intellectual stimulation that comes from associating with some of the brightest minds in the community and being part of the most complex of organizations ever created by human beings is compelling. The antics between board members can sometimes be entertaining and always are useful to an understanding of group behavior, human psychology, and leadership; the boardroom is real-life theater where everyone present is a player. It is not uncommon to find that "people behave differently in the boardroom than they do when they are not" there (Mueller, 1984, p. 189).

But perhaps most important of all, serving as a trustee of an academic institution can bring special meaning to one's life—

whether or not one is an alumnus of the institution. Given the academy's permanent place in society as perhaps its most important transmitter of culture and knowledge to future generations and the relative brevity of human life by comparison, what can be more compelling than giving something of oneself and even part of one's fortune to something that will surely outlive us and do good things for thousands of others?

We have John W. Nason (1982) to thank for our understanding of the governing board's primary functions. Although many other students of academic trusteeship have offered job descriptions of one sort or another, it is his seminal studies of higher education trusteeship in the early 1970s that have stood the test of time. The twelve board responsibilities addressed next, in the context of public higher education, are his contribution.

Setting Mission and Purposes

Virtually all policy decisions ultimately made or affirmed by the board should reflect what the institution or system of institutions is and strives to be. An articulate and compelling mission statement, in both strategic terms (the long view) and operational terms (a more immediate view), should guide everyone who has a decision-making role.

A kind of "mission mania" is currently sweeping the nation, and with good reason. The tremendous growth of public higher education, which requires more and more resources in a period of no or slow economic growth, inevitably causes policymakers at all levels to reassess what colleges and universities are doing and providing.

Although the governing board may not have unilateral authority to decide the ultimate shape of the mission statement and related statements of operational goals and objectives (and although trustees do not in any case write these statements), the board does have a pivotal role with the chief executive in their determination. It does so, however, through its prerogative of asking the right questions and its ability to persuade and lead—both internally, with its management team and faculty leaders, and externally, with legislators, governors, coordinating agencies, and state government bureaucrats.

The board's aim is to educate its many publics and internal constituents about the institution or the system (and each college or university within the system) in the most effective and compelling way possible. To do so, trustees and other leaders throughout the university or system must use good judgment in answering questions along these lines: What makes this university or campus distinctive among the other public institutions in the state? Whom does it serve and why? Whom does this system serve and how? Why does the university or the system deserve a significant investment of tax dollars? (See Chapter Eleven, especially pp. 206-207.)

Many governing boards of multicampus systems have found it useful to "carry the system's flag" to each of its constituent institutions by scheduling their meetings on campuses. Over time, the board should meet at all of its institutions to convey that it values each and every component of the system and their leaders.

This is hard work. But among the board's responsibilities, setting institutional missions and distinguishing between them are especially important. They and their operational goals guide the board and everyone else connected with the institution or system in fulfilling their functions. The mission statement should be reviewed periodically by appropriate representatives of those who have a stake in the process and adjusted as appropriate.

Appointing the President

As Clark Kerr (1984) emphasizes in his study of the academic presidency, the ultimate test of a board's effectiveness is its ability to attract and keep strong, competent executive leadership. The board plays a critical role in providing the kind of environment that attracts top talent to the university or system. No board decision is likely to have greater impact on the institution or system—or be more potentially political, more exciting and yet frustrating, more a test of its leadership and vision—than selection of the chief executive. This impact is no less for the selection of campus leaders within systems, even though the board may not be as involved in the selection process.

The selection of a president is made increasingly difficult by several factors jeopardizing the academic presidency. These include an average tenure of about seven years, for public independent college and university presidents, according to an analysis by the Association of Governing Boards of Universities and Colleges, (1992a, p. 2), the changing nature of the position (more political at the expense of opportunity or time to exercise academic leadership), and an apparently increasing reluctance on the part of academic vice presidents and deans to aspire to the presidency (the traditional route to the position). The lack of confidentiality in the search process, due in part to unreasonably restrictive open meeting laws in some states, also makes presidential selection difficult and sometimes disastrous. Too many careers have been ruined when names have been revealed prematurely, and too many institutions have missed outstanding leaders because superb would-be candidates did not trust the selection process.

Here again, the board must perform a delicate balancing act between assuming a difficult and important responsibility and consulting with the many groups that have a stake in the ultimate decision. The board must not abdicate this selection process, which is the least ambiguous of its duties.

Boards can learn from the successes and failures of other boards; the wheel need not be reinvented when the time comes to search for a new chief executive. Good literature is available, but there is no substitute for securing professional, objective help from an appropriate executive search firm throughout the process. Such help is nearly always worth the investment and should be retained early. The firm should have solid experience with the culture of higher education and have a strong capacity to network with individuals and organizations in the field; the best leaders must be identified and actively recruited. Chapter Seven addresses this board responsibility in detail and suggests a good set of standing policies and procedures.

Supporting the President

When a board is blessed with the kind of leader or set of campus leaders it can look to with pride and satisfaction, its job is made immensely easier. But effective leaders are increasingly difficult to find in all industries, for-profit and nonprofit. Our society is extremely demanding of those in positions of authority.

The only place a chief executive of an academic institution can look to for support is the board. But the relatively frequent turnover of trustees and especially board chairs, the increasingly politicized nature of the trustee selection process, described by Kerr and Gade (1989), and the demands of special-interest groups who claim a stake in what the university does or does not do present special problems in the public sector—along with opportunities.

The board has an opportunity to demonstrate its leadership by seizing and creating initiatives that these lessons from boardroom behavior have taught us:

- Remember that a chief executive's performance can be little better than that of his or her board (Kerr, 1984) and vice versa.
- Assess the chief executive's work in the context that, through this assessment, the board is also assessing its own effectiveness. The leadership of the president and that of the board, while distinctive and complementary, are inevitably interdependent.
- Distinguish between the president's personal style and professional competence. They are both important to a president's success, but be mindful of the difference when offering advice and counsel.
- Strive to be reasonably consistent and predictable. Both the president and the board should adhere to the dictum of "no surprises," or at least as few as possible.
- Recognize the unfortunate tendency for trustees to be more critical than complimentary. Acknowledge good work and express appreciation for exceptional initiative.
- Do not take an effective chief executive or his or her spouse for granted. Recognize their respective contributions, and demonstrate concern for their health and morale in tangible and intangible ways.

Even experienced presidents and trustees are imperfect, but they have learned that "the best thing to hold on to in the boardroom is each other" (Mueller, 1984, p. 3). Chapter Eight offers several practical ways for boards to support the chief executive, a responsibility that is shared by both the board and individual trustees.

Monitoring the President's Performance

Monitoring the president's performance is one of the more provocative responsibilities of the board, one that can produce as much harm as good. Although students of academic trusteeship universally agree that this is a vital board function, opinion differs widely on methods and whether and how the conclusions should be made public. There is, however, widespread agreement on the general principles discussed next.

Chief executives are public figures who are assessed by everyone with whom they associate every day. A distinction should be made between annual informal reviews and periodic formal comprehensive assessments. The latter are the most difficult to do well. The purpose of a formal assessment process is to *enable the incumbent to strengthen his or her performance.* The primary purpose should not be a decision to fire a president or renew a contract. Great care must be taken not to undermine the integrity of the chief executive or his or her office by inadvertently conveying to the system's or university's publics (when the process may extend beyond the board itself) anything but the clear and useful purpose of the review process.

Should standing policy require a periodic and comprehensive review beyond the board itself, it is best to identify competent third-party help from outside the organization to bring objectivity and professionalism to this delicate task. Furthermore, the chief executive should have a voice in the selection of such assistance and in the details of the process itself. The assessment process is more likely to be successful if the outside consultant is requested to look at the conduct of the presidency in the context of the institution's or system's governance; that is, he or she should be free to offer recommendations that may involve the board's performance and its policies and practices. External advice can ensure a healthy process for everyone, particularly in systems where relationships may be strained between the system executive and a campus executive who is up for review.

From the point of view of the successful president or chancellor, especially if he or she has been in the position for some time, there can be distinct advantages to a formal evaluation. The opportunity for a fresh start, a "clean bill of health" with a mandate to move ahead, can be very useful to everyone. But an assessment must be made with care and sensitivity. Presidential assessment should be thought of as one way the board can support the incumbent, a point that is elaborated in Chapter Eight.

Insisting on Long-Range Planning

The conventional and still-valid wisdom is that governing boards should insist that good planning be done, participate in the planning process, evaluate the quality of the process and its outcomes, formally adopt the results, and assume appropriate ownership of the strategic priorities and goals set in the process. All well and good, but how does a board fulfill this role?

Unfortunately more lip service than real attention is often given to this responsibility. However, the board should not *do* planning; the chief executive is delegated this responsibility, along with such leaders within the faculty, administration, and perhaps student body as he or she wisely involves. The trustees' role is to clarify what they expect the planning process to address, push for the kind of planning that needs to be done (there are several kinds of planning, as elaborated in Chapter Five), willingly participate in the process where appropriate, and ask good questions along the way. By participating in the process, the trustees are likely to assume ownership over the plan's priorities and goals when they formally adopt it—and work harder to help implement it.

A multicampus system will approach planning very differently from the community college that has its own board. A regional university will require a different approach from that of the major research university. And approach and timing will be affected by when and how successfully the last process was conducted.

Insisting on strategic planning is a significant board responsibility that is even more important in hard economic times. As boards must make more difficult decisions to husband limited resources among competing demands for these resources, they have new opportunities to demonstrate leadership by approving changes where they are necessary and desirable in the best interests of the institution or system and the citizens they serve. Chapter Five is a very helpful elaboration of this responsibility.

Reviewing Educational and Public Service Programs

Teaching and public service are two of the nearly universal functions of the public university and higher education. Research is a third function, but it is usually reserved for one or more of the largest or specialized institutions within each state. Until recently, the conventional wisdom was that these functions were the exclusive domains of the administration and faculty members. Trustees were expected to concentrate on fiscal, physical plant, and political matters. This emphasis has changed dramatically, although not without considerable ambiguity for administrators, faculty members, and trustees.

Approval of budget requests is one of the most significant policy decisions. Budgets support academic programs, public service, and research priorities. Therefore, how can a board exercise its fiduciary responsibilities without being reasonably knowledgeable about the relative strengths and weaknesses of programs and services? On the other hand, how can busy trustees, who already typically gather monthly, be expected to give more time to learn about and probe these areas? This conflict is a special problem for the board of a system with several constituent campuses. A philosophical problem can also be raised: how can trustees know when they are imposing their judgments about matters best left to others more qualified?

Boards must find the middle ground to fulfill this responsibility. To micromanage in this area would be as irresponsible as ignoring the area entirely. Over the course of several meetings, board members can get a good exposure to the goals, objectives, strengths, and needs of each of the major academic programs and services (system boards would likely focus on institutional missions and relevant performance indicators). Reports of accrediting agencies or of outside experts brought in periodically at the chief executive's request also can be helpful. Comparative data from similar institutional settings can be illuminating.

Boards should be more knowledgeable about academic and public service programs, including academic personnel matters, than they typically are. Trustees should be able to answer, for example, questions like these: Which of the system's institutions offers the best program in (subject)? Why is it the best? What are the university's weakest academic or public service programs and why? If, miracle of miracles, the legislature suddenly bestowed an increase of 25 percent over the asking budget in the annual appropriation, with only the stipulation that it be used to improve the quality of the academic programs, where should it be allocated?

For more perspectives on the board's responsibilities in this fascinating thicket, see Chapter Sixteen, on assessing and nurturing quality, and Chapter Fifteen, on academic personnel policies. The latter provides a useful explanation of the institution of academic tenure. Also, Chapter Fourteen addresses the board's role in collective bargaining.

Ensuring Adequate Resources

What a public college, university, or system can do is obviously limited by its resources. There is never enough money.

Faculty, staff, and students expect the governing board to be respected by and influential with the state's political leaders. The board is expected to ensure maximum access to tax funds but also, to see to it that the institution or institutions request no more than is seen as absolutely essential by the citizenry and their elected leaders. Rarely are the members of the academic community or the public pleased with the board's record on this score.

Explaining and defending budgets through the appropriations process is a challenging board responsibility. Appearing before appropriations committees of state legislatures or city or state councils is among the most daunting of experiences for any trustee or chief executive.

It is always difficult for a board or others to assess the board's effectiveness in meeting this responsibility because many circumstances affect outcomes. These circumstances include the relative

health of the local, state, and national economies; myriad competing needs for limited tax dollars; the relative standing of public
higher education in the minds of the general public and government leaders at any point in time; and so on. But one point should
prevail: The board has a duty to do its best to ensure that its institution or institutions are financed adequately to meet their missions. There is no room for passivity here, no room for rationalization for not having demonstrated good faith and diligent effort. (See
Chapter Eleven on the importance of building and maintaining
good relationships with government agencies and political leaders.)

Tax dollars and tuition and fees do not pay all of the bills,
of course, and this fact bears on a fundamental matter of philosophy
or purpose: is access to public higher education a right or a priv-
ilege? Should those parents who can afford to pay more of the cost
of educating their children be entitled to the same subsidization as
those parents who cannot? Tuition in public colleges and universities is likely to increase significantly in states whose economies are
weak, and this old issue will be debated anew. The debate continues
to rage in European systems of higher education. How the public
college and university in the United States should and will be financed in the future will be one of the major public policy issues
involving trustees for years to come.

In the meantime, the inevitable budget shortfalls between
funding levels and expenditures must be covered by private gifts and
grants from individuals, corporations, and philanthropic foundations. Since 1989, public higher education has received in the aggregate slightly more money in grants and gifts *from corporations
and corporate foundations* than has private higher education (Voluntary Support of Education, 1991). Business and industry now
consider giving to public colleges and universities perfectly appropriate and necessary. Virtually all tax-supported institutions now
have foundations to receive, account for, and spend gifts and grants.
In 1990, private giving *from all sources* totaled about $5 billion to
independent higher education and $3.1 billion to public colleges
and universities.

The governing board and trustees, therefore, should set an
example in private fund raising. The newly elected or appointed
trustee is typically not told that he or she should give an annual gift

to the foundation or a special program at the university and should help to open doors with individuals or organizations who can give. But this expectation is slowly but surely becoming a general practice—controversial though it may be among incumbent trustees. Some trustees argue that they already give unstintingly of their time and energy and even give up income by being away from their professions. Gifts and grants from loyal alumni and other individuals, corporations, and corporate and other foundations, however, will increasingly provide that margin of excellence that will distinguish one university or system from another—and trustees will lead the way in securing this money. (See Chapter Ten on the importance of building an effective fund-raising program and foundation.)

Ensuring Good Management

To paraphrase Robert Louis Stevenson, men and women do not live by bread alone, but by catchwords. And some of the current ones in the boardrooms and business offices of the academy are *productivity, growth by substitution, downsizing, cost containment,* and *reallocation.* In good and bad economic times, boards must closely monitor their institution's or system's financial condition and management, debt financing, deferred maintenance needs, auditing process, staffing structure, compensation policies and practices, capital construction and renovation priorities, foundation initiatives, and so on. Doing more with less is the slogan of the decade, and trustees must be knowledgeable about all aspects of their considerable fiduciary responsibilities if they are to influence future decisions.

In meeting its responsibility to ensure good management, the board places a great deal of trust in its chief executive and a competent staff. And they, in turn, depend on the board for guidance, leadership, and assertive public support when tough decisions are made to balance budgets. Indeed, how a board supports management's unpopular decisions in a financial crisis is another test of its effectiveness and reputation.

Trustees should insist that financial reports be demystified through better formats and that they, the trustees, be educated on fund accounting and balance sheets. Periodically, boards should ask that experts be commissioned to review any management area that may benefit from independent review and for comparative data from peer institutions or systems on such matters as faculty-staff ratios and per-student costs. Several other chapters in this volume will be helpful to the board in ensuring good management, including Chapters Three (economics), Four (litigation and risk management), Five (planning), Nine (financial and plant management), Ten (fund raising and the foundation), and Fourteen (collective bargaining).

Preserving Institutional Independence

Citizen boards provide an alternative to what is found in most other countries of the world, namely, direct governmental control of higher education through strong, bureaucratic ministries of education and strong faculty control at the institutional level through senior professors. Citizen boards are a time-honored feature of U.S. higher education that has reflected the nation's competitive spirit and participatory democracy for 350 years. In the public sector of higher education, especially, boards of trustees serve a vital buffer role.

Most institutions of higher education and their boards are usually the creatures of state legislation or occasionally of state constitutions. Public universities, colleges, and systems have never had and should not expect to have complete autonomy from the government or elected officials. But public institutions of higher learning do require relative independence from unreasonable intrusion into their affairs.

The public academic institution is different from other agencies of government because of its unique mission to transmit and advance knowledge. It has proven to be amazingly resilient in its ability to stay true to its mission in a democratic society, notwithstanding occasional attacks from the political left and right. It has survived the pursuit of communists in the McCarthy era, the election of a few governors who would have transformed the university in their own image, and the political power of some legislators who have sought line-item control over budgets. But it has done so because boards of trustees have had an excellent, if not perfect, record of defending the academy when necessary. And in doing so, trustees have met the mandate required of them in serving the public trust.

But the governing board must also maintain the government's trust. It must protect academic freedom while respecting the responsibility of elected representatives to interpret the needs of the larger society that pays the bills and expects a reasonable return on its investment. The governing board must earn the respect of those in political power and in special-interest groups that have a claim on the university without allowing the university to be exploited for any purpose. Such external influences can include the alumni, business interests, wealthy donors, athletic booster clubs, and even the federal government.

Again, trusteeship is a balancing act. But a willingness to take a strong stand in defense of academic freedom and institutional independence when it is necessary is the mark of an effective governing board.

Relating Campus to Community

Boards are "bridges" more often than they need to be "buffers." Trustees, in their collective and individual capacities, are often called upon to explain, defend, interpret, promote, or advocate for the institution or system. But it works the other way, too. They represent the public interest in, curiosity about, and expectations for the institution. Faculty and staff may isolate themselves from the public just as they often do from colleagues in other disciplines, schools, or departments. They need help in relating to the community, even though they do not seek or welcome that help.

Academic institutions make mistakes, sometimes big ones. Given the sometimes tens of thousands of people who converge into a finite space for protracted periods of time, it is surprising that the record of academic institutions is as good as it is. The ills of a modern urban society inevitably spill over to the campus; universities do not have walls. How the board manages crises with its administration and the media is yet another mark of its effectiveness.

Trustees who see themselves as representatives of any group cause harm to the institution or system, regardless of how or why they were selected. Single-issue trustees rarely earn the respect of (or effectively influence) their peers. All members of governing boards have an ethical and moral responsibility to serve all citizens of the state that financially supports the institution or system. However, female, minority, alumni, or student trustees have a responsibility, indeed a duty, to bring their special perspectives and experience to the boardroom. The difference may be subtle, but it should be clear.

I suggested earlier that universities, colleges, and systems of institutions are resistant to change. Their capacity to resist inappropriate intrusion, however, also enables them to effectively resist change that is appropriate. The United States is experiencing the most profound economic, political, social, and demographic changes in memory, and boards will be criticized as never before if their institutions and systems do not adjust to some dramatic new needs. The academy's record in recruiting and retaining minority students, faculty members, and staff members calls for much more improvement. The quality of undergraduate teaching has been criticized severely, even by friends of higher education, at a time when campuses should be preparing for enormous numbers of students who will need different and better teaching methods. Trustees can help meet evolving needs by keeping one eye on the past (preserving the best of the academic traditions they hold in trust) and one eye on the future (encouraging academic leaders to adjust what they do best—teaching, research, and public service—in a dramatically changing society).

Serving as a Court of Appeal

Governing boards hold the middle ground between the courts and judicial system and the internal due process policies and procedures of the institution or institutions they serve. The board, willingly or unwillingly, may be called upon to serve as a court of appeal on certain matters, usually involving personnel. It does so, however, only under exacting and carefully considered circumstances. The distinction between informal and formal involvement by the board is useful. At times, the chief executive will bring a delicate personnel matter to the trustees in closed session for information or informal advice and counsel. For example, the president may seek advice about a senior officer or faculty member whose behavior is of concern. The doctrine of no surprises may necessitate such consultation if a proposed personnel action may result in litigation or involve an individual the board considers to be beyond criticism.

The board may have formal responsibility on the rare occasions when a personnel issue has run its course through due process and internal appeals but doubt remains about whether policies and procedures were appropriately applied. Or the board may be asked to determine whether special circumstances were appropriately considered by those who have made or propose to make a personnel action involving tenure, promotion, hiring, or firing.

The board may be formally required by institutional policy to review certain cases or may do so according to its own independent judgment. Some general principles can help boards to walk through the minefield of formal judgments:

- Avoid substituting the board's judgment on academic personnel matters for those of others within the institution who have more competence.
- Handle personnel matters at the lowest possible administrative level.
- When a matter is deemed appropriate for board review, limit the process to the question of whether institutional policies and procedures were met in letter and spirit. If they were not, the case should be remanded to the appropriate administrative level for reconsideration.
- Ensure that due process and appeal policies and procedures meet contemporary legal standards in protecting both individual and institutional rights.
- Make explicit in institutional policy the requirements of gaining access to the board's appeal function. These requirements should be extremely stringent, with access to the board through an appropriate standing or ad hoc committee.

Given the complex legal environment within which academic institutions function, all trustees should read Chapter Four and be especially mindful of the individual's right to privacy and due process.

Assessing Board Performance

Assessment of board performance is the most contemporary of board responsibilities, one that John W. Nason and the Association of Governing Boards have advocated in various ways since 1974. Chapter Twenty-One elaborates the rationale and various options for meeting this responsibility.

A 1991 AGB survey reveals that only about one-third of public college and university boards had conducted a formal self-study within the preceding five years (Resource B). This is not good news. If boards accept their responsibility to assess presidential performance, they must also accept the responsibility to assess their own performance. For the reasons stated earlier, the performance of the board and president are interdependent and should be reviewed in that light. Boards should set an example and overcome any natural reluctance to subject themselves to scrutiny.

It is not easy for trustees to engage in serious introspection, especially to allow a third-party in their midst who can bring perspective, objectivity, and skill to the process. But boards will perform self-assessments more often when they realize that good tools and resource people are available to assist them; that self-study should be conducted when things are going well and not during crisis; that self-assessment signals strength and not weakness; and that many serendipitous benefits can accrue to the board, chief executive, and institution through such an assessment. Many boards have found that a self-assessment process every three or four years can be productive and even fun. This process is also one of the most effective ways for new board members to be oriented and for experienced members to renew their vows. Everyone wins, especially the college, university, or system.

Fulfilling Responsibilities as an Individual Trustee

The suggestion that the individual board member's responsibilities differ from, but are complementary to, those of the board was made earlier. Trustees have no special prerogatives, no special authority in their individual capacities, yet much is expected of them. They may have their own letterhead and business cards and even access to an office on campus, but these gestures of respect do not signal unilateral authority. Trustees are held to a very high standard of conduct. Those who are elected through statewide or local elections hold no more and no fewer responsibilities than appointed trustees do. All trustees are equals among equals in the boardroom.

Boards are finding it useful to adopt formal statements of responsibility to clarify some basic expectations that their members hold for one another. Although most of these expectations are obvious, others are more subtle and address some of the ambiguities surrounding the role. Basically, trustees are judged by their peers and others largely on their willingness to be team players and on knowing when to lead and when to follow in the boardroom. Trustees, like boards, are always performing balancing acts among competing behavioral options.

Faithfully attending meetings, reading materials sent in advance of meetings, being knowledgeable about the institution or system and its constituent campuses, asking good questions at meetings, and the like are obvious expectations. Trustees should also avoid the following situations: asking for special favors of the administration; making prejudiced judgments based on information from disgruntled faculty, staff, or state officials; giving even the appearance of a conflict of interest; and taking an inappropriate advocacy role for a system campus, academic department, or a favorite staff member.

Some areas can be very perplexing to the trustee who seeks to demonstrate commitment. Some guidelines for trustees follow:

- Speaking for the board or institution is ordinarily reserved for the board chair or chief executive. Beware rather than welcome the ambush interview by the local reporter.
- Serving the institution or system as a whole and not any one part of it is a responsibility of all trustees. Although you have every right and duty to bring your knowledge of any special group's interests to the board's discussions and to articulate personal principles to influence the judgments of others on any issue, you also have a responsibility to support the majority action, even if you disagree with it.
- Seeking opportunities to inform the public about your institu-

tion or system, about the many good things it is doing, and about why it deserves support are part of the fun of trusteeship. If trustees do not inform the public about the institution or system, who can or will?

- Enjoying relationships with other leaders in the community and on the board through your trusteeship is very rewarding, but be careful to avoid giving even the appearance of using the trusteeship for personal or political gain. College and university trusteeships should not be used as a stepping-stone to political office or for personal aggrandizement of any kind. Trustees who use their position in this way demean the institution and themselves.

Although expectations of trustees are very high and there is very little understanding of or appreciation for a trustee's contributions, the personal satisfaction, cerebral stimulation, and respect that accompany college and university trusteeship make it a worthy calling. But good exercise of responsible trusteeship is learned. The best trustees are taught and teach themselves largely through experience; they are not born with what they should know.

The most effective trustees are those who consistently exercise good judgement but are also careful listeners, those who are strong in their convictions but appreciate the value of others, those who seek advice as readily as they give it. They do not shy away from making difficult decisions in the boardroom and taking their share of criticism when necessary. But in their individual capacities outside of the boardroom, they also practice the behavior that was so eloquently described by Philadelphia Quaker Hannah Whitall Smith: "The true secret of giving advice is, after you have honestly given it, to be perfectly indifferent whether it is taken or not, and never persist in trying to set people right." Humility has its place, along with conviction and leadership.

CHAPTER 7

Selecting the
Chief Executive

Judith Block McLaughlin

Each year, trustees at three to four hundred colleges and universities select a new chief executive for their institutions. This decision is generally regarded as the single most important responsibility of a governing board. It is also probably the most visible manifestation of the board's leadership. With justification or not, boards of trustees are judged by the performance of the president they appoint.

But a search process succeeds or fails not only because of who is chosen at its conclusion. The search process itself is the object of great scrutiny by campus constituents. Unlike in the corporate world, where the choice of a chief executive is understood to be the sole responsibility of the board, often in close consultation with the outgoing executive, many constituencies within higher education believe they should be actively involved in the search for the new president. Long gone are the days when a college or university board of trustees could announce in a single breath the resignation of one president and the appointment of another. Today, constituents on most campuses expect that they will be informed about, if not directly participate in, the search for a new president. If a board fails to recognize this desire for participation, campus constituents may consider the search process illegitimate.

Thus, the question of how to conduct a presidential search is complicated. Not only must a governing board attempt to find the individual best suited for the institution at that particular point in its history but it must also do so in a manner viewed as legitimate by the members of the academic community. Even highly competent leaders will find it difficult, if not impossible, to succeed if the process by which they were selected has engendered distrust or dissension among constituent groups.

The successful presidential search, then, is one that identifies effective leadership for the college or university and does so in a manner that makes possible a successful entrée for the new chief executive. The successful search has one additional dimension. No other event in the life of an institution affords the same opportunity for institutional learning as does the search for a president. In the best cases, the search—and, indeed, the entire period of transition—offers the governing board and institutional constituents the chance to assess the institution's past, present, and future; listen to people inside and outside the institution; and gather different pieces of information about the institution and diverse perspectives on it. The successful presidential search, then, is also a process that heightens understanding of the institution by the board, the campus, and the new president.

This chapter will consider these three objectives of the successful search: selection of effective leadership, creation of a legitimate search process, and advancement of institutional learning. Although all three objectives are important, the search is complicated because the actions most appropriate for the attainment of one of these objectives, in many instances, are incompatible with those leading to the realization of another. Decisions that increase the likelihood of attracting the most qualified candidates, for example, may be antithetical to those that enhance that very candidate's legitimacy. This chapter discusses these dilemmas, looking especially at six phases of the search: the composition of the search committee, the definition of qualifications for the new president, the process of searching and courting, the policies and practices concerning confidentiality and disclosure, the decision about whether to use a search consultant, and the final stages of the search.

Composition of the Search Committee

Typically, the first issue that boards must confront during the search for a new president is who will be doing the searching. Many search processes become politicized and factionalized at their very outset over questions of committee structure and membership. Should one committee, two, or more be involved with the search and selection process? If more than one committee is involved, which committee will do what, and which will have the "real" power? Which constituencies will be represented and in what numbers?

The most common forms of committee structure are the single search and selection committee and the two-tiered process. Occasionally, multiple advisory committees will be employed, all reporting to a single search and selection committee. In the two-tiered process, the top tier generally consists of a selection committee chosen from the board of trustees or board of regents, while the second tier is a campus-based advisory committee that includes many campus constituents: faculty members, administrators, students, alumni, members of the local community, and so forth. The advisory committee is typically responsible for developing a large pool of candidates and then screening the long list to a smaller group who will be given further consideration. Sometimes, the advisory committee will also be responsible for interviewing candidates and forwarding an evaluation of them to the selection committee. In all cases, the selection committee retains the responsibility for the final selection.

The two-tiered model allows a large number of constituents to participate in the search process, which enhances support for the search. However, the two (or more) committees may prefer different candidates, a situation that will force a showdown at the last stages of the search process. Or the search can turn into a power struggle between the two committees. The advisory committee may be reluctant to relinquish the most exciting and significant part of the process—the actual selection of the president—to the selection committee. Advisory committees have been accused of "stacking the deck" so that the outcome is predetermined. Or the selection committee may be accused of already having made a decision, rendering the work of the advisory committee merely pro forma. At its best, the two-tiered structure permits campus constituents to participate in the search while preserving for the board the ultimate choice of the new chief executive.

The most popular committee structure is the single committee, which is charged by the board with all aspects of the search process, including the recommendation of a candidate or a slate of candidates for the board's final selection. At issue in the creation of this committee is what constituents should be represented on the committee. The tension between committee legitimacy and committee effectiveness is often evident. Many institutions establish large, broad-based search committees that include every conceivable constituency so that no important group will feel left out. On almost all campuses, faculty members are considered essential members of a presidential search committee. The concept of shared governance is widely accepted; to proceed through a search for a president without having faculty members on the search committee would render the outcome unacceptable at most institutions.

There is far less agreement on the question of which other constituents should be included on the committee. At some institutions, students are automatically included in the committee, but not at others. Some boards believe strongly that administrators should not be included on the search committee because they are, in effect, hiring their own boss. At other colleges and universities, administrators are a natural choice for the search committee. In some unionized institutions, a distinction is made between senior administrators, such as deans or directors, and other members of the professional staff, and this delineation carries over to the search committee. If someone from one group is included on the committee, someone from the other group must also be chosen. Nonprofessional staff members (for example, clerical, maintenance, and cafeteria workers) are occasionally appointed to the search committee, as well as individuals from off campus, such as alumni and local community leaders.

Given the number of groups that believe themselves to be important stakeholders in institutions of higher education, it is not surprising to find that many presidential search committees are large. But large committees, formed for representativeness, often hamper the effectiveness of the search process. With many people on the committee, there are multiple schedules to take into account in planning meetings, making full attendance at all committee sessions unlikely. In a small committee, all members are more likely to be present at all sessions to share in discussions and decisions. As search committee members work together to take stock of what leadership is most needed for their institution and what individual best exemplifies this leadership, all participants gain a greater appreciation of the complexities of issues and develop a deeper understanding of the institution.

If small committees are more desirable than large ones in terms of effectiveness and institutional learning, how can they be so constituted as to be considered legitimate by campus constituents? Individual institutional differences need to be taken into account. Each college or university must determine what is the appropriate committee structure and membership for its particular circumstances, keeping in mind that the committee must be deemed legitimate by the campus but must also be able to identify the best possible leadership for the institution. Committee members should bring to the search process multiple perspectives on the institution so that they can educate each other about the issues and circumstances facing new leadership. They should possess good judgment of people and be able to represent the institution well to prospective candidates. And they should be highly respected by their peers, so that their trustworthiness is above question.

Definition of Qualifications

The first order of business of most search committees is setting forth the list of qualifications for the job of president. In many searches, committee members are eager to get past what they see as a perfunctory task and get on with the more exciting work of evaluating people. They quickly draft a statement that tells prospective candidates and nominators little about what sort of person the institution is seeking, often because they have not thought hard themselves about what type of leader is needed.

When taken seriously, however, the process of defining the leadership needs of the institution not only produces a document that is informative for those who read it but also offers members of the search committee an opportunity to develop a better understanding of how others inside and outside view the institution—its strengths, weaknesses, issues, and opportunities. What at the college or university matters most to various individuals and groups? What are the diverse perceptions of the needs to which a new president must respond? How will the new president fit into the order of things, not only in the line of presidential succession but also in the array of problems and personalities currently at the institution? In what ways will the president serve as the symbol for the institution, and what are the important institutional symbols and myths that the president must recognize if he or she is going to be successful?

The answers to such questions are best discovered through extensive interviews with campus constituents by members of the search committee. This solicitation of diverse opinions enhances the committee's appreciation of the job facing a new president and helps it to define more clearly who is best suited for the job. It also increases the committee's interaction with campus constituents, thereby expanding the boundaries of communication and providing opportunities for many more people than can possibly join the search committee to have important input in the early stages of the search.

For the members of the search committee, the task of filtering through the diverse opinions and divergent agendas of institutional constituents is an opportunity to discover each other's interests, to go beyond initial preconceptions (for example, that trustees will want someone with extensive management experience, while faculty members will see scholarship as the top priority), and to negotiate differences and appreciate commonalities. Defining the qualities needed in a president is the first step in the committee's development of a mutual understanding of the institution and the profile of the person best suited to fill the post of president.

Process of Searching and Courting

Obviously, a search committee cannot select someone to be president who is not in their candidate pool. Nevertheless, many committees act more as selection committees than search committees. They spend far more of their time culling through the pages of applications and nominations that come to them as the result of advertisements than they do in active pursuit of people they might persuade to become candidates. In part, they do so because many members of search committees are not sure how to go about the work of searching.

The increasing use of consultants in the search process, discussed later in this chapter, is partially motivated by the hope that the consultant will expand the pool of applicants. Often, the process of courting is not done well because many committees prefer eager candidates; they want to be wanted. Indeed, candidates who campaign for the job can make members of the search committee feel good about their institution and about themselves for being connected with it. Whether candidates who most want the presidency, especially in the early stages of the search, are the most attractive people for the position remains an open question.

Occasionally, very strong candidates are actively job hunting, but usually the very best people are already well placed in jobs where they have considerable responsibility, are greatly respected, and are performing exceedingly well. Many such people will not have given much thought to leaving. Even those who may feel that a change of scenery or responsibility would be challenging are unlikely to have much time to pursue other options. Hence, the task of the search committee is to identify such individuals, talk with them about the presidency, encourage them to provide the search committee with preliminary information about themselves (for example, a curriculum vitae and papers presented at conferences), and studiously avoid forcing them to make a premature decision about their interest in becoming a candidate. The search committee should keep the conversation going to allow the prospective candidate and the committee to get to know each other better. During this period of discovery, both parties to the conversation act as buyer and seller; both are choosing and being chosen.

Policies of Confidentiality and Disclosure

Nowhere are the divergences between effectiveness and legitimacy more clearly evident than in the search committee's decisions about confidentiality and disclosure. Without exception, handbooks and consultants strongly urge that a policy of confidentiality be followed during the search process, that is, that the names of all candidates and all discussions about them remain the privileged information of the search committee. Confidentiality is considered important to attract and maintain a strong pool of candidates.

Many prospective candidates will not participate in a search unless they are assured of confidentiality because they do not want to jeopardize their effectiveness in their current positions. If they are seen by others as likely to leave, their ability to provide leadership in ongoing efforts may be seriously diminished. They are seen as lame-duck administrators, even if they (or a search committee) reach the decision not to continue in the search process. The higher placed the person, the likelier it is that he or she will suffer ill consequences from disclosure, and hence the less willing the person is to become a candidate in searches where disclosure is likely.

Additionally, prospective candidates often do not want it known that they are talking with members of a search committee because they are not at all certain they want to have their names considered for that presidency. Nothing curtails the process of mutual exploration faster than the disclosure of candidates' names! Premature disclosure of candidates' names also scares away candidates who do not want to harm their chances in future searches. They realize that their not having been selected president at one institution may be misread by others as a failure, as somehow indicating that they are not presidential material. Actually, many individuals who become presidents (and succeed admirably in the job) have been unsuccessful candidates at many institutions before they find a place that is a good match for their interests and talents. Attractive candidates realize that they have many options, and if they do not pursue one presidential possibility, another will come along.

In addition to limiting the pool of candidates, disclosure can negatively affect the search in other ways. It can lead to increased politicization of the search process. When candidates' names become public knowledge, search committee members often find themselves the objects of lobbying by supporters and detractors of the candidates. Candidates with strong political bases of support may proceed further in a search process than their qualifications would warrant because of the pressure brought to bear by important supporters of the candidate. Also, disclosure of candidates' names, committee deliberations, or ranking of candidates makes members of the search committee reluctant to talk candidly in committee meetings. Many opportunities for learning about the institution as well as for hearing others' honest assessments of prospective presidents are thus lost. The search committee that does not provide the conditions for a frank discussion of institutional needs and candidate qualifications is making its final decision on less than complete information.

The arguments in favor of confidentiality are persuasive, but the pressures for disclosure are also strong. Typically, people are curious about whom the search committee is considering, and many constituents believe they have a right to know this information. In public higher education, this "right to know" is often championed by representatives of the media in their efforts to bring presidential searches under the stipulations of open meeting and open records laws.

All states presently have open meeting and open records legislation (also known as sunshine laws) on their books, but the extent to which this legislation is applied to higher education searches varies greatly. In Florida, all aspects of the search must be made public, including the names of all candidates (both those who apply and those who are nominated by others), all letters of recommendation, all interviews, and all discussions and votes of the search committee. At the opposite end of the spectrum are searches at universities in Pennsylvania and Michigan, where all aspects of the search are conducted in executive session and no names of candidates are made public other than those of the new president. In these cases, state laws allow personnel evaluations to be conducted confidentially, and searches are considered to be personnel proceedings. The individual's right to privacy is considered alongside of the public's right to know.

At the outset of the search process, the trustees or regents, usually in consultation with board staff members, must determine their state's policy regarding confidentiality and disclosure and then decide accordingly the practices they will follow. Will the names of candidates and the discussions of committee members be shared beyond the membership of the search committee, and if so, with whom and with what likely consequences? If the committee decides to maintain confidentiality, how will it enforce this decision? What measures will be taken to prevent leaks? Many sincere pledges of confidentiality by search committees have been undermined by unanticipated disclosures, the result of successful sleuthing by investigative reporters or the consequence of carelessness or oversight.

Most search committees adopt a policy of confidentiality for most aspects of the search process. The difficulty arises in the last stages of the search as the committee confronts the issue of campus visits. Should the policy of confidentiality be waived so that campus constituents can meet a small group of finalists for the presidency? Or should confidentiality be maintained throughout the search? What is potentially gained and lost by involving more people in the final stages of the search?

The most obvious advantage of campus visits is the involvement of constituents and the legitimation of the search. Campus visits have become a tradition on some campuses, and their elimination might cause an outcry of protest from the campus. Faculty members, students, and administrators want to "see the merchandise," to participate, even if only minimally, in "comparative shopping." Campus visits also allow candidates to see the campus through eyes of others not on the search committee. Some candidates have become completely sold on an institution after the campus visit. Others have learned, during the many interview sessions of the campus visit, about institutional problems that made the presidency of that institution no longer appealing.

In some searches, the search committee is eager to elicit the reactions of campus constituents to finalists and welcomes input that will enable it to make its final decision. In other searches, however, the search committee has a clear preference for one candidate and holds campus visits only because they are expected. In such instances, the candidates and the campus are treated unfairly—the candidates, because some of them are risking the liabilities of disclosure when their chances to be chosen are negligible (but, of course, they are not told this, or they would not participate in the campus visit) and campus constituents, because they are led to believe their impressions will be taken into account when the visits are merely pro forma. Moreover, if campus constituents reach a different conclusion than the search committee on the basis of first impressions and limited information, the board of trustees—and, ultimately, the new president—is placed in a most difficult position.

The decision to hold campus visits may result in the loss of prospective candidates for the presidency. Many highly placed individuals, notably those who are presidents elsewhere, will not participate in a campus visit because of the publicity this brings their candidacy. For the reasons mentioned earlier, they do not want to jeopardize their effectiveness in their current position—or even their position itself. Boards have been known to fire presidents for looking at different positions, once this action becomes publicly known.

Aware of both the advantages and disadvantages of campus visits, some boards of trustees have decided in recent years to bring only the search committee's top choice to the campus for open meetings with faculty members, students, administrators, and staff members. The individual is presented as the candidate about whom the search committee is enthusiastic, although no binding decision has been made by the institution or the candidate. If the campus reaction is negative or if the candidate concludes after visiting the campus that the presidency is no longer attractive, the search committee can invite another finalist to the campus. Other search committees have decided to bring two or three finalists to the institution for meetings limited only to a small number of people beyond the membership of the search committee. These people are asked to take a pledge of confidentiality that they will not reveal the names of the finalists.

Whether to Use a Search Consultant

Ten years ago, search consultants were almost unheard of in many sectors of U.S. higher education. Today, an estimated 60 percent of presidential searches employ an outside consultant. This extraordinary increase in the use of consultants is due, in large measure, to the fact that searches have become such complicated affairs in recent years, for the reasons already discussed.

Search consultants can provide a board or search committee

with help in many areas, including deciding how to structure and manage the search process, defining qualifications for the presidency, identifying prospective nominators and candidates, interviewing candidates, conducting background investigations of finalists, and serving as an intermediary in negotiations with the top choice for president. The best search consultants are experienced navigators of the search process and are sensitive to the particular nuances and situation of each institution. They do not use a "cookie cutter" approach to the search process but rather appreciate the special needs and interests of each search committee and board with whom they work.

As soon as the *Chronicle of Higher Education* announces a search for a president or even before that, when word gets out on the grapevine that a president is stepping down, many consulting firms will write to express interest in assisting in the search process. The board of trustees or search committee then has a chance to look at these letters and accompanying brochures and decide whether to ask two, three, or sometimes more of the consultants to make presentations in person. Typically, members of the board or search committee will also contact people they know on other campuses who have held a presidential search recently to ask them about their experience with a consultant and whom they would recommend (or reject). If the search committee chooses a consultant on the basis of interviews, this process might be thought of as a trial run for the main task of choosing among finalists for the presidency.

What are some of the considerations on which the choice of a consultant should rest? Consultants differ enormously in terms of how much of the burden they carry and how long they carry it. Some consultants will spend a great deal of time in the early stages of the search, getting the process under way and helping the committee to determine what is required in a new president, and then will curtail their involvement, seeing their role primarily as advisers to the process. They do not attend search committee meetings and may not sit in on interviews with candidates. In contrast, other consultants will practically manage the entire process—screening resumes (either on their own or concurrently with screening by the search committee), interviewing candidates individually and providing the search committee with synopses of these sessions, conducting extensive background investigations, and so forth. A search committee should decide what sort of assistance it desires and make certain that the search consultant is prepared to offer this before reaching any agreement to proceed.

Search consultants differ, too, on their familiarity with higher education. Lack of experience with a college or university presidential search should not, per se, rule out a consultant. Several consultants have won high praise from the first committee they assisted. These consultants saw themselves almost as anthropologists: their first job was to size up the culture of the institution, to understand it from many different perspectives, before proceeding with the search. But the willingness of the consultant to put in the extra time to learn about the world of academe and to identify important resource people within it must be thoroughly examined by a search committee.

Ultimately, the quality of the work of the search consultant depends on the quality of the consultant's mind, that is, his or her judgment about people, perceptiveness and thoroughness. Additionally, the chemistry between search committee members (and especially the committee chair) and the consultant should be good for the relationship to work well during the search. As with candidates for the presidency, search firms (and particularly the individual consultant who will serve as adviser to the search) should be investigated thoroughly by a search committee.

Two caveats about the use of a search consultant deserve mention. First, a consultant's work should supplement, not replace, the work of a search committee and board of trustees. For institutional learning to occur, the committee and board must fully participate in the selection of the president, not delegate major chunks of the process to the consultant. But, second, the expertise of the consultant should be fully utilized. In many searches, the consultant pulls back or withdraws altogether at the time of negotiation with the candidate of choice. However, it is precisely at this time that the consultant can play a crucial role as go-between, a role that allows both presidential finalist and board of trustees to express their concerns openly and thereby to work out in considerable detail and to both parties' satisfaction the arrangements of the appointment.

Final Stages

Although search committee members are likely to heave a well-deserved sigh of relief when the selection of the new president is completed, their work should not be seen as fully done until they have evaluated the search process and drafted a summary of their findings, including the procedures they followed and their assessment of these procedures. The learning that has occurred during the search process should not be lost when the search committee disbands. Some committees will want to prepare two reports: a confidential report to the chairman of the board that documents the details of the search (to be retained as part of the archives of the institution) and a second report to the new president and the institutional community that describes what the search committee discovered about the institution through the search for new leadership.

The end of the search process is also a time for the board to consider the approach to be taken in the next presidential search. This search, it is hoped, will not occur for a long time, so specific requirements for search committee membership, search policies, and so forth should probably not be spelled out. But the board may want to establish a leadership transition committee that has responsibility for guiding the new president through his or her first year in office, serving as a sounding board for the president, and considering policies and procedures for future searches when these become necessary.

Participation in a presidential search process is a tremendously exhilarating and rewarding experience for the trustees involved. Search committee members are the most knowledgeable about their institution and, at least for some time, the most helpful to the new president and to the board in the transition to new leadership.

CHAPTER 8

Supporting
the President
and Assessing
the Presidency

Joseph F. Kauffman

Governing boards have many responsibilities, and several publications, including this book, identify and describe those responsibilities. In every description, the very highest priority is given to the board's responsibility for the selection of a president, the maintenance of an effective working relationship with that president, and the establishment of performance goals against which to assess presidential performance.

Nothing is more important to a college or university president than a successful relationship with that institution's governing board. Both the board and the president have a mutual responsibility to achieve this relationship. This chapter describes the ways a governing board can enhance the start of a new presidency, provide support for the president, and assess presidential performance.

Multicampus Universities and Systems

Most public universities today are part of a multicampus institution or system. As a result, most public campus heads do not report directly to a governing board but, instead, to a chief executive of a board or system. The administration of the system is the staff for the governing board in such cases, and campus officers are responsible to the board through that system office. As Kerr and Gade (1989, p. 116) have noted, "The freestanding public campus headed by a board of trustees fully under its own authority is now the exception." According to Kerr and Gade, only five hundred out of fifteen hundred campuses are freestanding.

For the public institution or multicampus system of institutions, the role of trustee is often complex, difficult to describe, and apparently contradictory. The faculty members' expectation of trustees as advocates competes with the legislators' expectation of trustees as watchdogs and defenders of the public interest. The conflict of expectations is especially apparent in the single boards of multi-institutional systems and consolidated state systems.

Only a general overview of the many different types of university systems is necessary here. At one end of a continuum is the flagship university that has developed branch campuses. At the opposite end of the continuum is a consolidated state system, in which all institutions in a state are incorporated under a single governing board. Ohio State University and the University of Minnesota are examples of the former. Wisconsin and North Carolina furnish examples of the consolidated state system. Between these two types are found segmental systems, in which homogeneous sets of institutions are grouped under single boards. Examples of segmental systems are the California State University System, the State System of Higher Education of Pennsylvania, and many community college systems.

The system executive is typically called chancellor or president. The title is based more on historical accident than anything else. For my purposes, I will call the system executive the president, as is the practice in the systems of Wisconsin and North Carolina, the University of California, and others. The campus chief executive will be referred to as the chancellor. One further complication needs to be mentioned. In a few states with consolidated state systems, individual campus boards or councils have been created, with limited authority delegated by their consolidated governing boards. This is the case in the state systems of New York, North Carolina, Massachusetts, and Utah. My own experience as a consultant in the first three states indicates that such campus boards have a significant voice and influence in the selection and assessment of the campus chancellor, often to the regret of the system chief executive.

The governance arrangements in public institutions affect how support for a campus executive is provided and how these executives will be assessed. In systems, governing boards may not have much direct knowledge of campus problems, and they will rely on the recommendations of their system executive. Therefore, president-chancellor relationships and expectations may loom larger than board-president relationships and expectations in such systems. This reality is reflected in my description of support and assessment activities.

System Administration and the President or Chancellor

As noted above, the majority of public institutions today are part of a system of institutions, and most campus chief executives not only do not have their own governing boards but also encounter an additional layer of administration between the campus and the board. There are considerable pressures for centralization of authority and decision making. A system head is inserted between board and campus, and it is the system head, here called president, who links the campus with both state government and the board. The system head enhances or inhibits the role of campus chancellor and assesses the chancellor's performance on behalf of the board.

I believe that the system presidency is the least stable of higher education presidencies and often the least satisfying chief executive position. System presidents get caught between the often ambiguous expectations of system boards and the tendency of the respective campuses to blame all ills on the system's administration. The board presses the system president to take charge, while the campus chancellors are pushed to defend maximum campus autonomy. Flagship campuses worry about having their institutions' special missions and prestige compromised by loss of revenue and recognition, while other campuses demand equity and fairness in teaching loads and salary levels. Given the political nature of seeking legislative appropriations, system heads are often disparaged as politicians rather than respected as educators. Elsewhere (Kauffman, 1980), I have written about the strong influence early incumbents in system presidencies have on the style and expectations of a system's administration.

A system's governing board should be aware of the need to clarify the system executive's role and authority and support its expectations. The governing board is, essentially, the only constituency a system president has, and its actual and symbolic support is vital. Campus chancellors have faculty members, students, alumni, and legislative representatives as constituencies. They have various ways of making their views known and heard. Without strong board support, the system president and staff members cannot be effective.

Campus chancellors in a system have many complaints. Many have less authority than they expected to and express discomfort with governance by a bureaucratic system. Weak chancellors want to send everything controversial to the system administration for review or decision. Strong chancellors resent the many system meetings, the emphasis on uniform procedures, and the reliance on second-level system intermediaries to interpret their concerns and needs. Finding a proper balance and division of labor is essential.

The administrators of a system must understand that campus chancellors are assessed by their constituencies on their success in obtaining resources in a competitive environment. Being considered a good team player by the system administration may win you high marks with the president and board, but on your campus, you may appear to be weak and a poor advocate. The form of organization or structure of a system is a means to an end, not an end in itself. Boards and system and campus executives must constantly renew their purpose and cooperate in achieving maximum effectiveness in delivering educational programs and services.

The New President: Preparation and Transition

The launch of a successful presidency starts with the search and selection process. If that process involves the appropriate constituencies of the institution; clarifies goals, objectives, and priorities; and enables the board to select a person all constituents can fully support, a foundation for success has been established. The rationale for the participation of constituent representatives in the search is that their perceptions and judgments are important and that these constituencies become stakeholders in the success of the new president. A botched search, resulting in angry faculty and staff members and students, can cripple the best efforts of a new president. It is crucial to invest adequate time and resources to ensure a respected presidential search.

The appointment discussions with the president-designee should clarify all financial matters—compensation, fringe benefits, moving expenses, housing allowance or expenses for the president's house, entertainment expenses, and so on. Financial agreements should be put in writing. If there is a president's house and it requires refurbishing, the work should be undertaken by the board and not left to the personal initiative and expense of the new president. Refurbishing should be finished before the new president moves in.

If the new president has a family, their needs should be considered as well. If the president is married, expectations for the role of the spouse should be clarified. Although the presidency of higher education institutions was once considered a two-person career, boards can no longer assume that a spouse is prepared to serve as an unpaid staff person. Many spouses will have their own careers and will expect adequate support for official entertainment activities.

The president-elect should also learn from the board what priorities board members hold and what performance objectives will serve as a basis for periodic assessment. Obviously, the many constituencies a president must serve will all have their own expectations—often contradictory ones. The board, however, must make clear what will be the basis of its assessment of success. In large state systems of institutions, campus chancellors spend a lot of time dealing with system officials and may be judged on their campus by how effective they are in such dealings. However, they may be judged by system administrators on how cooperative a team player they are.

A new president often learns during the transition period that his or her provost or vice president was the leading inside candidate for the presidency. How free he or she will be to replace inherited senior staff members and advisers must be made clear to the new president. Kerr, in *Presidents Make a Difference* (1984), refers to "untouchables," that is, senior staff members who have special relationships with governing board members and the employment security that accompanies such relationships. On the other hand, the board may consider some senior staff members unsatisfactory and in need of replacement. In such cases, terminations should be started before the new president takes office. Otherwise, a new president's tenure will begin with firing senior staff members, a situation that may jeopardize a successful beginning.

It is important to have a symbolic conferring of authority and legitimacy on the new president. Some institutions will have a substantial inauguration ceremony, with the participation of political leaders, alumni, and others. Whatever the scale or scope of such activity, I believe that it is important to launch the new president or chancellor with appropriate attention and introductions. When the search and selection ends, new presidents should not have to sneak into town and introduce themselves.

How a Board Can Support a President

The governing board obviously has a stake in the well-being and success of the new president or chancellor. He or she is the board's executive officer and agent. The board's authority is delegated to this newly selected person. A major investment of time, resources, and hope has been made.

There are several ways in which a board can help ensure the success and continuation of a president or chancellor. My suggestions range from offering understanding and encouragement to providing fair compensation to monitoring the conduct of the board at its meetings.

Because the board is the president's employer, it must assume responsibility for his or her working conditions. No one else will be able to respond to a president's need for staff members, adequate housing, encouragement, or a boost in morale. Presidents work hard and often endure lots of complaints and criticism. In carrying out board or system policy, they often encounter stress and controversy. Fisher (1991), in enumerating the many responsibilities of boards, speaks of the need for psychological as well as substantive support for the president. Simply caring about the welfare of the president goes a long way in expressing board support. Kerr (1984, p. 49) notes an obvious, but often overlooked, bit of advice to board members: "A word of encouragement at the end of a board meeting, at a commencement exercise, or after a dinner or other social occasion can go a long way."

Boards should also be concerned about adequate compensation, vacation time, and opportunities for professional development for presidents and chancellors. In some states, the presidencies of public institutions have salary caps, often statutory, which require that no officer receive more salary than the state's governor. As a result, professors and deans may receive higher salaries than presidents. When such restrictions cannot be changed, the board should increase housing allowances, expenses for travel by the spouse, retirement benefits, and other forms of compensation that would enable the board to retain effective and successful officers. It is useful to keep track of the compensation practices of peer institutions and to make every effort to be competitive in compensation and benefits.

Boards frequently overlook or take for granted the work and contributions of presidential spouses. This is especially the case if a university-owned house is provided for the president's family and for official entertaining. Traditionally, boards relied on a male president's spouse to volunteer for the duties associated with entertaining and managing the many social functions scheduled for the president's house. Although there are some male presidential spouses today, the many female spouses often resent the expectations that they will entertain and manage social functions for the institution. Boards need to clarify expectations and to recognize and support the spouse who is managing many university functions. Spouses, too, serve the institution.

Roberta Ostar (1991) has studied the representational role of presidents, with an emphasis on the concerns of presidential spouses. Her study highlights the experiences of spouses and makes many suggestions for boards to improve their practices, ranging from showing appreciation to providing compensation.

The Teachers Insurance Annuity Association (TIAA), mindful of the changed thinking about rewarding spouses, has created a new TIAA Special Service Retirement Annuity: Meaningful Recognition for the Spouse of the Campus Chief Executive. This annuity, created in 1990, was developed to provide tangible recognition for spouses. Former chairman and CEO of TIAA, Clifton R. Wharton, Jr., himself a former university president, said in announcing the new annuity program: "Nearly two decades of heading major universities, and observing many of the campuses of my colleagues, have left me with a profound respect and admiration for the contributions of the spouse of the chief executive. Spouses are full partners in a team effort, and as such they deserve tangible recognition" (Ostar, 1991, p. 93).

Nothing is more crucial to the president's effectiveness than the relationship of the board chairperson to the president. The board chair can be instrumental in seeing that board business is conducted in an orderly, rational manner. If board members' behavior appears to be arbitrary or capricious, it is difficult for the president to be an effective leader.

Most public institutions operate under some form of open meeting and open records laws. These laws affect communication between the president and the governing board and the style of discourse at meetings. Informal interactions are made difficult by these laws. Presidents may be reluctant to discuss sensitive issues or apprehensions about anticipated conditions, and board members may be constrained from sharply questioning a president's recommendations. Nevertheless, the board-president relationship must be one of respect, effective communication, and candor.

Purpose of Presidential Assessment

A performance review, assessment, or evaluation has many possible purposes. Ideally, the purpose is a totally constructive one, that is, to aid in the development of the president or chancellor and to improve performance and productivity. Assessment should contain elements of feedback and coaching within a mutual-benefit context. It should be useful to the chief executive and always viewed by the trustees as an extension of governing board support. Kerr (1984, p. 57) states the goal of assessment this way: "The intent of effective reviews is to identify obviously weak presidents sooner and then either give them help or replace them faster and to identify strong presidents sooner and encourage them to stay longer."

An effective assessment includes a fresh look at an institution's management and governance, not just the president's performance. It looks at institutional priorities and goals. It may even touch upon the performance of the governing board. After all, how the board and president work together may be the crucial determinant of presidential success.

Certainly, a board cannot remain effective if the chief executive does not function in a manner that wins the respect of key constituencies of the institution. By the same token, a president's performance is inevitably tied to perceptions of the board's competence, conduct, and performance. The board and president hold in common the burdens of stewardship. For this reason, a board may wish to examine its own performance at the same time that it reviews its president's performance. Kerr and Gade (1989, p. 94) have stated that "boards should realize that when they evaluate a president's performance they are also evaluating their own performance in selecting, advising, and supporting the president. Also, they should realize it is harder for a good president to survive a poor board than for a good board to survive a poor president."

In most cases, it is difficult and perhaps inappropriate to tie assessment to compensation. Usually, systems have considerable salary compression, with little difference between presidents of similar institutions. Further, market factors and statutory or political realities often preclude boards from making significant differences in salary increments. And neither should boards directly tie performance reviews to reappointment decisions. If the board has lost confidence in the president, it need not gather evidence to make charges. The board undermines its own authority by soliciting responses to the question of whether or not to let a president continue. The president serves at the pleasure of the board.

An evaluation of a presidential assessment process should include the following questions: Does the assessment process help attract and retain presidents of the highest quality? Does it help improve the presidents' performance, productivity, and job satisfaction? Does it aid in the retention of excellent presidents and assist in the rapid weeding out of those who are not suitable? Is it regarded as legitimate by those affected by it?

Politics of Assessment

Presidents and chancellors are often skeptical of formal assessment policies and procedures. It is not that they believe they perform some kind of mystical role that precludes the possibility of assessment. Rather, they realize that assessment may be conducted for political reasons and may be more symbolic than functional. They also have little confidence in the state of the art of assessment. For all these reasons, those who will be assessed need to be involved in the creation of a credible assessment process.

Some boards and systems institute assessment policies with fanfare to show that they will be tough managers and demonstrate accountability. Partisan politics may also be a factor in creating evaluation machinery in some systems. A board may preempt anticipated legislative action by creating its own administrative rule mandating presidential assessment, as occurred in Florida in 1974. Five years later, the former chancellor of the Florida system wrote a critical article on the evaluation process that was instituted as a result (Tucker and Mautz, 1979). The evaluation process of the Florida system has since been reformed and will be referred to in the section on current assessment methods. Kerr (1984, p. 58) has suggested that boards ought to follow academic practice: "Faculty members and students are evaluated in ways that do not unduly embarrass the person being evaluated or weaken the person's capacity to perform. The president deserves similar consideration."

The Criterion Problem

Assessment of performance presupposes some rational process in which there are criteria, objectives, or benchmarks against which performance can be measured. To determine how well someone is doing, some standard must exist for comparisons. But defining a standard for presidents and chancellors is complicated. Cohen and March (1974, p. 201), in their classic book on the presidency, spoke of the "ambiguity of success" in that role.

Most presidents acknowledge that the criteria for their roles are unclear. At institutions using an informal annual review, statements of mutually agreed upon goals and objectives may be submitted by campus heads to a board or system administration for use in reviewing performance. Goals may be stated in terms of specific outcomes or priorities of effort. Yet campus chancellors are well aware that system administrators will also judge them on whether or not they are cooperative team players, regardless of what else may be achieved. And system presidents know that they will be judged by the legislative appropriation they obtain, no matter what else they may do.

In an attempt to be objective, boards usually state performance goals in terms of outcomes or results. Yet we know that we assess performance on more than one dimension, including behavior. How results are achieved may become as important as or more important than the results achieved. Psychologist Harry Levinson (1976) has pointed out that the key elements in whether or not one succeeds in an organization are often political. Attitude, relationships established, respect for others, and similar factors are vital to success, and yet these rarely find their way into formal assessment systems. Performance appraisal should address both outcome goals and behavioral goals.

A board must set expectations before beginning an assessment program. Ideally, a statement of expectations that will serve as a basis of assessment will have been mutually agreed upon by the board and the president, or system president and campus chancellor, upon the appointment to office of the person being assessed, and updated in annual exchanges.

In formal assessment, my own approach to the problem of criteria is similar to that used in institutional accreditation. During an accreditation assessment, a team of external evaluators first examines the self-evaluation report of the institution, which provides information on how well the institution is reaching its own stated goals. The team seeks additional information in a campus visit by interviewing key staff, faculty members, and students. The focus is on discerning the strengths of the institution, its weaknesses or concerns, and suggestions for addressing those concerns. Similarly, in conducting a presidential assessment, I want to examine a president's self-evaluation and, then, through interviews with representatives of the faculty, staff, students, and others, discern accomplishments and areas of concern. Advice and suggestions are solicited as well, with improvement as the goal. The interviews are not mechanistic nor do they seek to affix grades or performance scores. Rather, they are seen as part of a consultative process to learn of concerns and ways in which improvements can be made.

Formal evaluations of presidents and chancellors should attempt to include constituents' views regarding overall leadership, representation of the institution or system; administration and management; handling of financial matters; relations with faculty and staff members and students; and personal qualities, including trust and integrity. Although perceptions about these factors are not the same as objective evaluation, the perceptions are important to learn from and act upon. Presidents and boards can benefit from this knowledge and reshape goals, priorities, and behaviors accordingly.

Assessment Methods and Procedures

Presidential reviews are typically either informal or formal. Presidents and chancellors point out that they are evaluated everyday in the decisions they make, their public statements, and so on. Although many institutions and systems may not have written policies and procedures for assessment, an increasing number do. I believe that assessment policies and practices should be institutionalized and exist in writing. An assessment is not carried out only in times of trouble. An assessment is a normal, recurring personnel practice aimed at continuing improvement.

Informal assessments are usually done on an annual basis and are private assessments by one's supervisor. System heads assess campus heads, and governing boards assess their chief executive. Typically, this informal assessment involves a self-evaluation report and a candid discussion that provides feedback and clarification of priorities and goals. Although perceptions of the views of constituents may be a part of the process, these views are not gathered systematically. The informal process is low key and the results are usually private.

Formal reviews are more structured and are usually scheduled for three- to five-year intervals. New presidents may be scheduled for a three-year review and incumbent presidents, for a five-year review. Some systems have linked such reviews to reappointment. Formal reviews are more public in nature than informal ones and include participation by subordinates and constituent representatives. Faculty, staff, student, and alumni representatives will be asked to provide their views on the performance of the president or chancellor. In some cases, surveys and other opinion-gathering techniques may be used. At the very least, formal evaluations will go beyond what governing boards feel and think about the president. Formal evaluations will often involve the use of an external consultant. A number of university systems have instituted formal assessment policies, some of which are discussed later in the chapter.

Presidents and chancellors tend to prefer informal assessment, although this is not uniformly so. Kerr (1984, pp. 53-55) has described six primary drawbacks to formal and public reviews: they can provide critics with an opportunity to coalesce accumulated grievances into a campaign against the incumbent; delay important, difficult, and unpopular presidential decisions during the review process (or encourage popular but unwise decisions just before it); occur during particularly advantageous or disadvantageous times or events, thus vitiating the process; reduce the board's flexibility of action by locking in commitment for another five-year period (dismissals rarely result from assessment processes); be used as a devastating weapon by unscrupulous system heads against campus heads; and unduly invade presidents' rights to privacy. In addition, confidentiality can be a major problem, especially in states that have strict and inflexible sunshine laws.

Perhaps the most comprehensive guide to the various assessment practices is John Nason's work, *Presidential Assessment* (1984), which contains descriptions of various informal and formal practices. Nason provides examples of actual assessments, with the identities of the individuals masked, and samples of rating scales and questionnaires used by various private and public institutions. Nason's book will not tell you what to do or how to do it, but it covers all the issues and techniques of assessment.

As a consultant in formal performance reviews, I have conducted more than a dozen formal assessments in the past three years, in addition to serving as an adviser to systems developing policies and procedures for periodic assessment. I strongly believe that assessments should include a confidentiality requirement. Personal interviews should be held with board members, administrators who report to the president or chancellor, faculty and student representatives, and others who may interact with the chief executive. These people may include alumni, community and legislative leaders, and so on. I am interested in identifying strengths and accomplishments as well as concerns and weaknesses. In addition, I ask for advice or suggestions for improvements that I can examine and pass on. I am opposed to anonymous communications and, for the most part, rating scales or other mechanistic devices.

The third-party consultant should provide the president or chancellor with an oral report of findings before reporting to the governing board or system president, to allow for corrections and a response to criticism. Sometimes the person being assessed will seek the advice of the consultant on how to deal with some aspects of the criticism. Some people will want to reflect on a continuation of their presidency or the intensity of some criticism. Consultants who have been presidents or chancellors (though such a background is not required) bring experience, credibility, and a certain detachment from the institution, thus making it easier for the incumbent to discuss career concerns. When reporting to the board, the consultant gives advice on how the board can help the president address any shortcomings. The end result of the assessment should always be a clear set of priorities for the next two to three years.

In some cases, what a president or chancellor likes to spend time on may not match what others believe to be the urgent needs of the university or system. Communicating those distinctions usually results in accommodation and consensus on both sides.

In formal reviews, the president or chancellor should write a self-evaluation that includes references to the state of the university. As with institutional accreditation self-studies, such a report should identify significant accomplishments since the last formal review. It should also identify goals not met and concerns or weaknesses needing attention. The report should conclude with plans and strategies for making corrections and improvements. Since the environment in which universities exist is not static, the report should identify new challenges and opportunities. This statement should be provided to the external consultant and shared with the board and others as appropriate.

Periodic self-assessment by the board is also of value and may be linked to a presidential review. The AGB has developed self-study instruments for boards that, with the help of a mentor or consultant, can strengthen the board's performance and aid in the performance of the board's chief executive.

Response to the Assessment

A president or chancellor views assessment with mixed feelings. How does one produce an adequate self-evaluation? And how can others really know all that goes into the extraordinary efforts of so many presidents? It is easy for boards to trivialize such feelings and concerns. Typical of the laments of many presidents I have interviewed is one from a senior president who described writing a self-assessment covering five years of effort and service. He wrote over sixty pages, making every effort to be forthcoming in his self-examination. He told me that the receipt of his self-assessment was never acknowledged, nor did he have an opportunity to present the assessment in any formal setting. Furthermore, he said he never received word of anyone's reaction to his effort, from either the system head or the governing board.

There should be a sense of closure when an assessment is completed. Something must be said and new understandings must be reached. Encouragement and suggestions must be conveyed, just as criticism must be communicated when necessary. Boards should be concerned with the status of the office of president, as well as with the incumbent. For most presidents, a presidency is probably only a temporary role and not a lifetime career. Thus, boards must not only select people to meet current situations but also must create graceful and dignified exits when the scene shifts and a new cast is required.

State Systems and Formal Evaluation

When I last wrote about this subject (Kauffman, 1980), I described three public university systems and their assessment procedures: the

State University of New York (SUNY), the State University System of Florida, and the state colleges of Pennsylvania, now called the State System of Higher Education of Pennsylvania. The descriptive material I gathered a decade later for this chapter reveals that all three state systems have altered their practices somewhat. In this section, I describe these three systems as well as the practices of state systems in Montana and Wisconsin.

State University of New York

When the presidential evaluation program at SUNY began in 1973, it was a formal process tied to reappointment. Campus executive officers, called presidents in that system, were appointed for a five-year term. If they wished to be reappointed, they had to undergo a formal evaluation process with input from faculty, staff, and student representatives and the campus council, comprising members similar to trustees with limited, delegated responsibilities. Presidents were given tenured faculty appointments in the system at the outset, so they always had the option of stepping down rather than seeking reappointment. The criteria for evaluation were essentially the description of the responsibilities of the president of each campus, approved by the governing board.

The evaluation process became excessively formal and detailed. Furthermore, with unionized faculty and staff members, it became overly political, and presidents and others were critical of the controversies that resulted. Over the years, the evaluation procedures have been modified and simplified.

The SUNY evaluation process places emphasis on the essential purpose of strengthening the president's role while providing for flexibility in his or her duties and acknowledging the need for accountability. The system head is expected to conduct the formal evaluation at "appropriate intervals" rather than at fixed times. Barring unusual circumstances, there is still a meeting with the campus council, including a representative of faculty and staff members and alumni. The campus president prepares a self-evaluation and campus assessment of five to ten pages in length.

The chancellor of SUNY has made it clear that he desires a constructive, low-key campus review and strongly discourages surveys and questionnaires. The cycle ends with a confidential report by the SUNY chancellor to the system governing board. The chancellor informs the president of the nature of that report and shares the major points of the evaluation with the campus council. The SUNY evaluation process has gradually changed from being a pass-fail evaluation that determined reappointment decisions to being a constructive performance-improvement process.

State University System of Florida

When I first described the Florida evaluation process (Kauffman, 1978), it was a formal process instituted by its governing board in the face of threats by the legislature to approve a statutory provision for formal evaluation of administrators. The review procedures called for all presidents in the system, in their fifth year of service, to express their desire to continue beyond the fifth year. Evaluation was tied to reappointment, and unlike in the SUNY system, presidential appointments did not automatically result in tenured professorships. Because of collective bargaining, input from faculty members and students, and a strong sunshine law, the evaluation process created continuing controversy among the presidents.

Florida seems to have moved to a less formal process now, with evaluations no longer tied to reappointment decisions. The administrative rule of the board of regents now states: "An evaluation of each president shall be done annually by the Board and the Chancellor. This evaluation shall be based on program goals that have been set jointly by the Board, the Chancellor and the President" (Florida Administrative Code, 1985, p. 6). Systems with the longest experience in formal evaluations seem to be moving to less complex, more flexible processes.

State System of Higher Education of Pennsylvania

The Pennsylvania system of fourteen institutions operates under a board of governors, with a chancellor as chief executive. Each of the fourteen institutions is headed by a president, and each institution has a council of trustees, with limited delegated responsibilities.

The councils have a significant role in both the selection and assessment of the presidents.

Prior to 1982, when the law was changed, presidents of these institutions were appointed by and served at the pleasure of the governor of Pennsylvania. In 1982, Pennsylvania Act 188 created the present state system of higher education and mandated annual evaluations of presidents, which are conducted by the local councils of trustees with the involvement of students, faculty members, and alumni. The chancellor and the board of governors now have final authority. The governor is not directly involved in either the selection or evaluation of presidents.

Informal reviews are conducted annually, and formal reviews are necessary every three years or as mandated by the chancellor. For formal and informal reviews, the president prepares a self-evaluation and a statement on the condition of the university. These are confidential documents, shared with the council of trustees, the chancellor, and the board of governors. The council arranges to receive information from faculty, student, and alumni representatives. Although such information may be held in confidence, all of it must be attributable (no surveys or anonymous input). The results are shared by the council chairperson with the president and conveyed in writing to the chancellor. The emphasis is on identifiable strengths and concerns, suggestions for remediating concerns and making changes in presidential leadership, and the council's commitments toward such improvements.

Montana University System

The consolidated state system of Montana consists of six institutions under a single governing board whose chief executive is the commissioner of higher education. Its evaluation procedures have changed over the years, becoming more formal and structured in the 1970s, then less formal for about a decade, and now tightened up again. The current procedure was approved by the governing board in September 1990.

The Montana plan now operates on a five-year cycle, with a formal evaluation at the end of the first and third years and a comprehensive external evaluation, conducted by the president of a peer institution, at the end of the fifth year.

The Montana presidential evaluation plan seeks to accomplish five objectives: (1) a comprehensive gathering of information that minimizes bias, innuendo, and hearsay; (2) the annual establishment of goals through an interactive process with the commissioner, regents, and president; (3) an evaluation based on performance in relation to those goals; (4) constructive guidance by the commissioner and regents to correct deficiencies and improve performance; and (5) an opportunity for public acknowledgment of the accomplishments of each president during the previous year.

University of Wisconsin System

The state higher education system in Wisconsin, one of the largest systems in the United States, consists of thirteen universities, thirteen two-year university centers, and an extension unit. It has a single board of regents, and the system is headed by a president. Each university is headed by a chancellor, as are the extension programs and the two-year centers. Altogether, there are fifteen chancellors.

Until recently, the system had no written policy concerning the evaluation of the chancellors or the president. In December 1986, the president and board instituted a policy that I would characterize as informal compared to that of SUNY or the Pennsylvania or Montana systems. The current policy in Wisconsin states that there shall be an annual evaluation of chancellors conducted by the president of the system. Each year, chancellors are to prepare a statement of goals for the upcoming year and an evaluation of the past year's efforts. This information is given to the president and shared with the board and becomes a matter of public record. The president meets with each chancellor for confidential discussions that review the information provided and cover ways to improve performance. There is no formal process of soliciting campus opinions, but system vice presidents are asked for their judgments of campus operations as well as their observations about the performance of each chancellor.

Lessons Learned

Assessment procedures should be tailored to the needs of the institution or system. History, political culture, and expectations will differ from state to state and institution to institution. In my own consulting work, I prefer to conclude with oral reports rather than written reports, where possible, because in states where written documents are matters of public record, it is difficult to be fully forthcoming without causing harm. A sanitized report will be attacked as a whitewash by the president's critics. A totally candid written report may well receive front-page newspaper attention and editorials, hampering a president's ability to make necessary improvements and to continue to serve.

I believe that informal evaluation must take place continually between a governing board and a president if both are to be successful in carrying out their responsibilities. This interchange requires open communication by both the board and the president and an effort to listen and consider seriously suggestions and criticism. The system executive and campus executive should similarly be focused on improving performance. Ideally, assessment should result in greater support and understanding of the party being assessed and the one doing the assessing . . . on the part of everyone.

Periodic formal evaluation can serve a useful purpose also, but only when it is done in a manner that does not undermine the office of the president. It is better not to do a formal assessment at all if it is not done right. The experience of the SUNY system is instructive in showing how SUNY improved its formal evaluations to remove the dysfunctional aspects of earlier practices. Above all, the evaluation process must not denigrate the office or person of the president. All too frequently, that is the outcome of some clumsy attempts at formal evaluation.

It is crucial that the president be willing to participate and to cooperate fully in any formal assessment. Formal evaluation should not be used as an excuse to terminate a president in whom the board has lost confidence. Such an abdication to others of the board's duties undermines both the board and future presidents. It also undermines the potential utility of formal assessment for the improvement of performance.

No one generic model of assessment suits every institution or system. However, at the very least, an institution or system needs some type of assessment and discussion of performance on a periodic basis. The absence of good communication between a board and president cannot be replaced by formal evaluation five years later.

An external consultant can be very helpful in the formal assessment process. Ideally, such a person should have experience as a president or chancellor and be fully acceptable to both the board and the president.

Assessment should contribute to improved leadership and heightened morale. It is in the governing board's interest to do it thoughtfully and right.

CHAPTER 9

Ensuring Sound
Financial and
Plant Management

Molly C. Broad

Fiscal stewardship for the capital assets and the operations of a public institution of higher education is one of the most important responsibilities of every governing board. Public boards carry out this stewardship on behalf of the constituent groups of higher education and the public at large. Individually and collectively, the board members bear the ultimate financial responsibility for their institution. It is important, therefore, that trustees understand financial matters and that they regularly receive an appropriate set of financial reports.

The majority of all higher education students in the United States are enrolled in institutions that are part of a public system. The specific governance arrangements of these systems vary significantly from state to state. Some public systems contain institutions with similar missions. Other systems are comprised of institutions with quite different missions; two-year and four-year colleges, comprehensive institutions, and research universities may be part of a single system. Some systems include only a few institutions, while others include many. This diversity makes it infeasible to draw distinctions with regard to financial stewardship, but the principles and the specific analytical approaches recommended here are applicable to any of these organizational arrangements.

Essential Reports

A relatively small number of reports can give trustees a sound basis for exercising fiscal stewardship as well as a better knowledge of the institution and its academic mission. It is the duty of both the board and the administration to ensure that trustees are provided with comprehensive and coherent reports that are clear and appropriate to their responsibilities. The reports used by financial administrators for day-to-day activities are not likely to serve the board's needs. Instead, a careful and systematic approach to presenting financial reports to a board is required.

Financial reports will be most helpful to trustees when they are presented in a summary form that will permit trustees to focus on the important measures and the key relationships. Other important dimensions of an appropriate set of financial reports include trend information, indicators of important interrelationships, and comparisons with peer institutions. A set of financial reports for the board might include:

- *A mission statement* that provides a description of the academic environment and the aspirations of the institution or system in comprehensive, long-range terms
- *A strategic plan* that establishes the major priorities and directions over a multiyear period, such as five years, with specific goals, performance measures, and deadlines
- *An annual operating budget* that sets forth the comprehensive financial plan for current operations across the entire institution
- *A capital plan and budget* that sets forth over a multiyear period, such as five years, the priorities for new capital construction, building renewal, building renovations, and major capital equipment acquisitions as well as the proposed means for financing capital outlay
- *Financial statements* that report all sources and uses of funds for current purposes (statement of current funds, revenues, expenditures and transfers), the overall financial position (balance sheet), and the flow of financial activity (statement of changes in fund balances)
- *Analytical reports on financial condition* that provide an anal-

ysis of financial health and spending priorities (ratio analysis), debt structure and capacity (ratio and debt capacity analysis), and capital investments, including endowments, land, buildings, and equipment (asset management)

Mission statements and strategic plans (see Chapter Five) are the cornerstone of effective trusteeship. The annual budget then becomes the means for linking the financial systems with the mission and the strategic directions for an institution or system. After all, money is the common denominator for reporting and measuring the full array of activities and the condition of an institution. Money serves as the indicator that can sharpen the focus for many issues, problems, and directions.

Annual Budget

The annual budget is a key instrument for carrying out the mission and for achieving institutional priorities. It is the financial plan for implementing goals and policies. In public institutions, the budget frequently has more than one part, such as the state budget and the local budget. The major sources of support for academic programs are state appropriations and student tuition. Frequently, other revenues contribute substantially to the total budget, including federal grants for research or other programs, private gifts and grants, and income from auxiliary operations. In public institutions, these revenues may be separated into subparts of the overall budget.

Trustees typically approve the complete and final budget after state appropriations are finalized, often shortly before the start of the new fiscal year. Periodic comparison by the board of actual spending against the budget plan will help identify potential problems early enough to take corrective action. Adjustments to the budget may be required if major change occurs to revenues or expenditures, such as a reduction in tuition income caused by declining enrollment.

Capital Plan and Budget

The development and regular review of a capital plan with a time line of five years or more are essential to effective board stewardship.

Frequently, a capital project is the earliest beacon of a change in an institution's direction, mission, or priorities. This project may be a new facility, a major building renovation, or the acquisition of new equipment (such as computers and telecommunications equipment). The capital plan identifies major projects and prioritizes them. The link between any new capital initiative and the institution's mission or strategic plan can be made clear in the capital plan.

The capital plan should be matched with a program to secure the necessary resources for the project. Unlike private business organizations, which finance capital expansion only through retained earnings or debt, a public higher education institution may secure capital from retained earnings, debt, or other sources, including state appropriations, fund raising, or federal grants. The means of financing capital development has both short-term and long-term ramifications. Using debt to finance new construction will require debt service to be budgeted for many years into the future. In addition to debt service, the annual operating budget must provide for building operations and any new programs initiated in the facility. A fully developed capital plan would include an update on the condition of existing facilities, a report on the utilization of space, and an assessment of building renewal and deferred maintenance.

Differences Between Higher Education Accounting and Business Accounting

Before turning to the key financial statements and analytical reports on financial condition, it is important to address the somewhat complicated conventions for accounting in higher education. Collier and Allen (1980b), point out that the conventions of higher education accounting can be quite imposing to trustees because they are different from those found in accounting for business and government. As a consequence, governing boards may have a difficult time understanding and interpreting the basic financial reports of their institution.

In higher education accounting, public disclosure of relevant financial data is intended to provide information about operations and financial conditions as well as to promote accountability. Because higher education exists to serve important public needs, its accounting and reporting procedures are focused on those needs. The business sector, by contrast, focuses upon financial reporting of profits or similar measures.

Another distinction between higher education and general business accounting is the absence of a direct connection between revenue source and expenditure in the former. The beneficiaries of the services of higher education are not always the same as the providers of the revenue. Furthermore, some revenue sources in higher education have use restrictions. Thus, an important emphasis has been placed upon fiduciary accounting in order to ensure that the restrictions have been met in the use of the funds.

Fund Accounting

Higher education accounting centers on the flow of revenues, such as tuition and state appropriations, through an institution to a specific use or purpose, such as instruction, research, or public service. The accounting concepts used in higher education derive from the stewardship role of trustees, that is, from the trustees' ensuring that funds provided by the legislature and by donors are used for the intended purposes. Thus, fund accounting is used to track each significant revenue source and link it to specific uses through a resource allocation process. Fund accounting permits separation of activity by fund type, category of restriction, source of revenue, and purpose of expenditure. For a more technical description of fund accounting, see Collier and Allen (1980b).

Current Fund Revenues

In fund accounting, revenues are categorized and reported by source and by type. The funds may be either restricted or unrestricted in their use. Categories of current fund revenues (resources to be expended in the near term for operating purposes) include government appropriations; tuition and fees; gifts, grants, and contracts; endowment income; and auxiliary enterprise sales and services.

Government Appropriations. Government appropriations are funds made available to an institution by enactment of a budget or other legislation. State appropriations are typically a primary source of revenue for educational and general purposes for public institutions of higher education.

Tuition and Fees. Tuition and fees include all money collected from students for current operating purposes. Tuition, although important as a source of revenue, is generally a smaller portion of total educational and general revenues for public institutions than for private institutions. Typically, fees are reported as tuition revenue.

Gifts, Grants, and Contracts. Gifts, grants, and contracts provide funds from government and private sources. These funds are typically made available for specific projects or programs and represent important additional sources of revenue to support current operations.

Endowment Income. Endowment income is return on endowment investments. This income may be a source of revenue for current operating purposes, either unrestricted or restricted.

Auxiliary Enterprise Sales and Services. Auxiliary enterprises bring in revenue through fees charged for providing essential services to students, faculty, and staff. Typical examples of auxiliary enterprises include residence halls, dining services, student unions, intercollegiate athletics, bookstores, hospital services, and other internal service departments. Each enterprise is operated as a separate business, and pricing is usually established to balance income against actual costs; thus, these enterprises are intended to be self-sufficient. By policy, however, some auxiliary enterprises are subsidized by other revenue sources.

Current Fund Expenditures

Expenditures are categorized and reported by uses or functions that derive from the mission and purpose of an institution of higher education. Ten fundamental expenditure categories describe the core functions of higher education and may be supplemented with several other categories.

Instruction. All funds expended for coursework and related activities conducted by faculty and staff members in academic departments fall under the category of instruction. If faculty research, scholarship, and public service activities are not funded as separate budget items, the costs of those activities will be reported as instruction for accounting purposes.

Research. The research category includes all expenditures for research activities that are specifically organized and budgeted for that purpose. Research expenditures may occur within a center or unit specifically organized to conduct research or may result from individual activities and research projects.

Public Service. Public service expenditures are expenditures for activities organized specifically to provide individuals, primarily outside the institution, with services other than instruction. Traditional examples of public service include cooperative extension programs (often agricultural in focus) and public television, but public service activities may also include a variety of community services and cultural activities.

Academic Support. All expenditures for indirect activities or related endeavors that support the academic mission of the institution fall into the category of academic support. Typical examples of academic support expenditures are expenditures for libraries, academic computing, curriculum development and media services, museums and galleries, and academic administration.

Student Services. Expenditures for student services include all expenditures for student-related activities that are supplementary to the curricular programs and are intended to support the social, cultural, and intellectual development of students. This category typically includes services such as admissions and student records, financial aid administration, counseling services and career placement, student health services, and the variety of programs and activities that support student life.

Institutional Support. Institutional support includes all expenditures for administration of the institution. This category covers day-to-day institutional operating activities, such as financial and personnel operations. But frequently physical plant operations are reported separately. It also includes activities that are strategic or long range, such as executive management, planning, and institutional advancement.

Plant Operation and Maintenance. All expenditures from the current funds for utilities, maintenance of facilities, custodial services, building and grounds activities, and repairs and renovations are included in the category of plant operations and maintenance. Expenditures for these purposes for auxiliary enterprises or independent organizations (such as hospitals) are charged directly to those organizations and excluded from this category. Expenditures for construction of facilities and major capital projects are also excluded from this category.

Auxiliary Enterprises. The category of auxiliary enterprises covers all expenditures associated with the costs of operations for independent enterprises established to provide goods and services to students, faculty members, and staff members. As mentioned earlier, auxiliary enterprises include residence halls, dining services, bookstores, student unions, intercollegiate athletics, and similar enterprises that are intended to be financially self-supporting.

Scholarships and Fellowships. All expenditures for student gift aid from institutional sources are covered in the category of scholarships and fellowships. These expenditures are for scholarships, graduate fellowships, and other grants awarded to students by the institution and financed from the current funds of the institution.

Mandatory Transfers. Mandatory transfers are all legally required transfers from the current funds to other funds such as plant funds or loan funds. These transfers cover debt service on capital plant and student loan matching requirements or similar binding commitments. Transfers from the current funds to other fund groups made by decision of the governing board are considered to be nonmandatory transfers.

Basic Financial Statements

Higher education governing boards will want to review carefully the three basic financial statements that are prepared annually: the statement of current funds, revenues, expenditures, and transfers; the balance sheet; and the statement of changes in fund balances. These documents are the most important financial reports of the institution. They represent the foundation from which other financial assessments can be made.

Statement of Current Funds, Revenues, Expenditures, and Transfers

Perhaps the single most important report to board members is the higher education version of the operating statement. As noted earlier, revenues within the current funds are classified by source and type, and expenditures are reported by use. Monitoring the rate of change in revenues and the distribution of revenues will provide important information for trustees. Diversification in revenue sources contributes to strength and overall financial stability, whereas excessive reliance on a given revenue source might indicate potential problems. Any rapid change in the revenue mix may also be a signal for special review. Similarly, reliance on nonrecurring revenues may cause financial vulnerability in an institution.

Public universities and higher education systems may find it useful to monitor the magnitude and distribution of revenues against those of a group of institutions with similar characteristics and missions. For example, a comparison of state appropriations per FTE student among a group of peer institutions over a period of time can reveal changes in state effort or support. Comparison of tuition, especially in relation to educational and general expenditures per student or to financial aid, is another indicator of market and financial positioning. Trends in these relationships may reveal underlying shifts in financial condition. Exhibit 9.1 is a sample year-end statement of revenues and expenditures.

Exhibit 9.1. Sample Statement of Current Funds, Revenues, Expenditures, and Transfers.

		Current Year		Prior
	Unrestricted	Restricted	Total	Year Total
Revenues:				
Tuition and fees	$2,600,000		2,600,000	2,300,000
Federal appropriations	500,000		500,000	500,000
State appropriations	700,000		700,000	700,000
Local appropriations	100,000		100,000	100,000
Federal grants and contracts	20,000	375,000	395,000	350,000
State grants and contracts	10,000	25,000	35,000	200,000
Local grants and contracts	5,000	25,000	30,000	45,000
Private gifts, grants, and contracts	850,000	380,000	1,230,000	1,190,000
Endowment income	325,000	209,000	534,000	500,000
Sales and services of educational departments	190,000		190,000	195,000
Sales and services of auxiliary enterprises	2,200,000		2,200,000	2,100,000
Expired term endowment	40,000		40,000	
Other sources (if any)				
Total current revenues	7,540,000	1,014,000	8,554,000	8,180,000
Expenditures and mandatory transfers:				
Educational and general:				
Instruction	2,960,000	489,000	3,449,000	3,300,000
Research	100,000	400,000	500,000	650,000
Public service	130,000	25,000	155,000	175,000
Academic support	250,000		250,000	225,000
Student services	200,000		200,000	195,000
Institutional support	450,000		450,000	445,000
Operation and maintenance of plant	220,000		220,000	200,000
Scholarships and fellowships	90,000	100,000	190,000	180,000
Educational and general expenditures	4,400,000	1,014,000	5,414,000	5,370,000

Mandatory transfers for:				
Principal and interest	90,000		90,000	50,000
Renewals and replacements	100,000		100,000	80,000
Loan fund matching grant	2,000		2,000	
Total educational and general	4,592,000	1,014,000	5,606,000	5,500,000
Auxiliary enterprises:				
Expenditures	1,830,000		1,880,000	1,730,000
Mandatory transfers for:				
Principal and interest	250,000		250,000	250,000
Renewals and replacements	70,000		70,000	70,000
Total auxiliary enterprises	2,150,000		2,150,000	2,050,000
Total expenditures and mandatory transfers	6,742,000	1,014,000	7,756,000	7,550,000
Other transfers and additions/(deductions):				
Excess of restricted receipts over transfers to revenues		45,000	45,000	40,000
Refunded to grantors		(20,000)	(20,000)	
Unrestricted gifts allocated to other funds	(650,000)		(650,000)	(510,000)
Portion of quasi endowment gains appropriated	40,000		40,000	
Net increase in fund balances	188,000	25,000	213,000	160,000

See accompanying Summary of Significant Accounting Policies and Notes to Financial Statements

Source: Copyright © 1975 by American Institute of Certified Public Accountants, Inc., pp. 114-115. Reprinted with permission.

Tracking expenditures and comparing relationships between expenditures can be quite helpful in monitoring an institution's pursuit of its mission as well as its overall financial situation. Here again, providing board members with comparisons of their institution and a set of peer institutions is an important way to help them track the marketplace. For example, major changes or trends in instructional expenditures as a percentage of total educational and general expenditures need to be explained. Tracking the other major expense categories (academic support, research, public service, student services, and institutional support) as a percentage of educational and general expenditures can be a simple way of monitoring the uses and functions being supported by the institutional budget. A comparison of the direct expenditures (instruction, research, and public service) with the indirect expenditures (academic support, student services, and institutional support) can likewise help trustees understand changes in the structure of costs and important trends.

During recent years, a substantial increase has occurred in expenditures within the categories of academic support, student services, and institutional support for many institutions. The causes of this growth are many but certainly include increased cost of governmental regulations, demands for service resulting from the increasing diversity of student bodies, and rapid changes in instructional and research technologies. Understanding the causes of this growth can bring better focus to the deliberations of governing boards.

Balance Sheet

While the statement of revenues and expenditures describes an institution's financial flow over a period of time, usually the fiscal year or the period of time since the beginning of the year, the balance sheet describes an institution's financial position at a given point in time, usually the last day of the fiscal year. It reveals the financial strengths and weaknesses of the institution and permits the board to assess the adequacy of the assets to fulfill the institution's mission.

Format. The format of the balance sheet for a college or university is derived from the concepts of fund accounting, described earlier. Because its many different sources of funds place differing fiduciary responsibilities on an institution, the format of the balance sheet reveals the financial condition of each of the fund types. The major fund types for higher education include the current funds, the loan funds, the endowment funds, and the plant funds.

The *current funds* include all revenues available for current operations of the institution for such expenditures as salaries, equipment, utilities, and so on. A very important distinction in the current funds is the distinction between unrestricted and restricted funds. As noted earlier, a significant characteristic of fund accounting is the separation of financial activity by category of restriction.

The *loan funds* include loans to students to help finance their education but may also include other loans made to faculty and staff members. The major source of revenue for the loan funds is likely to be the federal government, or it might be gifts or other institutional sources. The loan funds are a revolving resource for future borrowers and therefore must be reviewed by a board in that light. Funds will be available to lend to others only if loans are repaid.

The *endowment funds* include revenues that are invested to earn a return. The earnings from these investments are available for institutional use. Pure endowments are those gifts of principal for which the donor has stipulated that the gift will always remain intact and that only the earnings will be made available for expenditure. Other funds in this category may be quasi endowment funds, or funds functioning as endowment that do not have stipulations about use but that the governing board may have decided to invest with only the earnings available for expenditure. Of course, the board can alter its decision about these funds to permit the expenditure of principal. Governing boards face a constant dilemma in financial investment decisions of this sort, where present needs are juxtaposed against obligations to provide for the future.

The *plant funds* include the physical assets of the college or university as well as funds identified for new construction, acquisition of physical assets, debt service, and building renewal. The largest component of the plant funds is typically investment in plant, that is, the land, buildings, and capital equipment that are recorded at the cost of acquisition and remain at that value until demolition or disposition. Other significant and more flexible components of the plant funds include funds for retiring indebtedness and building renewal funds. Making adequate provision for retiring debt and renewing the physical plant are important financial responsibilities of the board. Protection of the physical plant of a college or university will require more than a review of the balance sheet. As noted previously, board stewardship, with its responsibility for the long-range well-being of the institution, must include the development of a capital plan for maintaining the condition of the institution's capital assets.

Each of these fund types, and sometimes others such as annuity and life funds or agency funds, is presented on the balance sheet as a self-balancing statement of its financial condition. Each fund type can be viewed separately so that any legal restrictions on the uses of resources can be clearly revealed. And since fund groups cannot be substituted for one another, issues of financial strength and flexibility can be more clearly discerned.

Assets, Liabilities, and Fund Balances. As on a balance sheet for a private corporation, assets of various liquidity and types (cash, receivables, financial instruments, and fixed capital) are enumerated on the balance sheet of a higher education institution. Similarly, liabilities of varying characteristics and durations are identified. What sets the balance sheet for a nonprofit or higher education institution apart from that of a private organization is the notion of *fund balance.* Like net worth, the fund balance represents the net accumulation of revenues (or resource inflows) over expenditures (or resource outflows).

Within each fund type, the fund balance is a key indicator of financial viability. The current fund balance in university accounting is the counterpart to "retained earnings" in private business accounting. It is equal to assets minus liabilities and thus reveals the amount available for future operations of the institution or for any use that a governing board may approve. It serves as working capital for the institution, with the restricted fund balance limited to specified purposes. The fund balance in the current funds is the most flexible reserve an institution will have. Within certain specified restrictions and within the approval authority of the governing board, funds may be transferred from the current fund balance into any of the other funds, such as endowment or plant funds.

The fund balances in endowment, loan, and plant funds are considered to be long-term capital. As noted above, resources may flow into these funds as transfers from the current fund or may flow directly from gifts and government appropriations. Comparing the various fund balances, or reserves, to the size of the current operating budget will give a board some indication of the financial health of the institution.

When viewed in total, the layers of balance sheets for each fund type provide the full picture of an institution's overall financial strengths and weaknesses. It is important for the board not only to see the distribution of assets, liabilities, and fund balances across the various funds but also to understand the restrictions placed on the use of the assets. In fulfilling its financial stewardship, the board should examine trends in balance sheet items and evaluate major changes. Since the balance sheet is a picture at a specific point in time, it is essential to review the component parts of this financial statement to see how they have changed over at least three to five years (for example, from 1991 to 1994). Exhibit 9.2 is a sample year-end balance sheet, with comparative figures from the previous fiscal year.

Ratio Analysis

For many years, private firms have used a variety of financial ratios to assist in evaluating their financial condition. A financial ratio is the relationship between two numbers drawn from an organization's balance sheet, current operating statement, or similar financial records. The analysis of ratios can provide a clearer perspective of financial health and of institutional spending priorities than the individual pieces of financial data standing alone can (see Chabotar, 1989; Peat, Marwick, Mitchell & Company, 1982; Dickmeyer and Hughes, 1980.) An advantage of ratios is that they can adjust for differences in size among institutions and, within limits, enable useful comparisons of relative financial condition between and

Exhibit 9.2. Sample Balance Sheet.

Assets	Current Year	Prior Year	Liabilities and Fund Balances	Current Year	Prior Year
Current Funds:			**Current funds:**		
Unrestricted:			Unrestricted:		
Cash	$ 210,000	110,000	Accounts payable	$ 125,000	100,000
Investments	450,000	360,000	Accrued liabilities	20,000	15,000
Accounts receivable, less allowance of $18,000 both years	228,000	175,000	Students' deposits	30,000	35,000
			Due to other funds	158,000	120,000
Inventories, at lower of cost (first-in, first-out basis) or market	90,000	80,000	Deferred credits	30,000	20,000
			Fund balance	643,000	455,000
Prepaid expenses and deferred charges	28,000	20,000			
Total unrestricted	1,006,000	745,000	Total unrestricted	1,006,000	745,000
Restricted:			Restricted:		
Cash	145,000	101,000	Accounts payable	14,000	5,000
Investments	175,000	165,000	Fund balances	446,000	421,000
Accounts receivable, less allowance of $8,000 for both years	68,000	160,000			
Unbilled charges	72,000	—			
Total restricted	460,000	426,000	Total restricted	460,000	426,000
Total current funds	1,466,000	1,171,000	Total current funds	1,466,000	1,171,000

	Current year	Prior year		Current year	Prior year
Loan funds:			**Loan funds:**		
Cash	30,000	20,000	Fund balances:		
Investments	100,000	100,000	U.S. government grants refundable	50,000	33,000
Loans to students, faculty, staff, less allowance of $10,000 current year and $9,000 prior year	550,000	382,000	University funds:		
			Restricted	483,000	369,000
Due from unrestricted funds	3,000	—	Unrestricted	150,000	100,000
Total loan funds	683,000	502,000	Total loan funds	683,000	502,000
Endowment and similar funds:			**Endowment and similar funds:**		
Cash	100,000	101,000	Fund balances:		
Investments	13,900,000	11,800,000	Endowment	7,800,000	6,740,000
			Term endowment	3,840,000	3,420,000
			Quasi endowment–unrestricted	1,000,000	800,000
			Quasi endowment–restricted	1,360,000	941,000
Total endowment and similar funds	14,000,000	11,901,000	Total endowment and similar funds	14,000,000	11,901,000
Annuity and life income funds:			**Annuity and life income funds:**		
Annuity funds:			Annuity funds:		
Cash	55,000	45,000	Annuities payable	2,150,000	2,300,000
Investments	3,260,000	3,010,000	Fund balances	1,165,000	755,000
Total annuity funds	3,315,000	3,055,000	Total annuity funds	3,315,000	3,055,000

Exhibit 9.2. Sample Balance Sheet, Cont'd.

Assets	Current Year	Prior Year
Life income funds:		
Cash	15,000	15,000
Investments	2,045,000	1,740,000
Total life income funds	2,060,000	1,755,000
Total annuity and life income funds	5,375,000	4,810,000
Plant funds:		
Unexpended:		
Cash	$ 275,000	410,000
Investments	1,285,000	1,590,000
Due from unrestricted current funds	150,000	120,000
Total unexpended	1,710,000	2,120,000
Renewals and replacements:		
Cash	5,000	4,000
Investments	150,000	286,000
Deposits with trustees	100,000	90,000
Due from unrestricted current funds	5,000	—
Total renewals and replacements	260,000	380,000

Liabilities and Fund Balances	Current Year	Prior Year
Life income funds:		
Income payable	5,000	5,000
Fund balances	2,055,000	1,750,000
Total life income funds	2,060,000	1,755,000
Total annuity and life income funds	5,375,000	4,810,000
Plant funds:		
Unexpended:		
Accounts payable	10,000	—
Notes payable	100,000	—
Bonds payable	400,000	—
Fund balances:		
Restricted	1,000,000	1,860,000
Unrestricted	200,000	260,000
Total unexpended	1,710,000	2,120,000
Renewals and replacements:		
Fund balances:		
Restricted	25,000	180,000
Unrestricted	235,000	200,000
Total renewals and replacements	260,000	380,000

Assets:

Retirement of indebtedness:		
Cash	50,000	40,000
Deposits with trustees	250,000	253,000
Total retirement of indebtedness	300,000	293,000
Investment in plant:		
Land	500,000	500,000
Land improvements	1,000,000	1,110,000
Buildings	25,000,000	24,060,000
Equipment	15,000,000	14,200,000
Library books	100,000	80,000
Total investment in plant	41,600,000	39,950,000
Total plant funds	43,870,000	42,743,000
Agency funds:		
Cash	50,000	70,000
Investments	60,000	20,000
Total agency funds	110,000	90,000

Liabilities and Fund Balances:

Retirement of indebtedness:		
Fund balances:		
Restricted	185,000	125,000
Unrestricted	115,000	168,000
Total retirement of indebtedness	300,000	293,000
Investment in plant:		
Notes payable	790,000	810,000
Bonds payable	2,200,000	2,400,000
Mortgages payable	400,000	200,000
Net investment in plant	38,210,000	36,540,000
Total investment in plant	41,600,000	39,950,000
Total plant funds	43,870,000	42,743,000
Agency funds:		
Deposits held in custody for others	110,000	90,000
Total agency funds	110,000	90,000

See accompanying Summary of Significant Accounting Policies and Notes to Financial Statements among institutions. Another important feature of ratios is their ability to control for shifts that occur over time. Thus ratio analysis may suggest changes in relative financial condition or highlight areas where deterioration or recovery have occurred. For these reasons, ratio analysis is most useful when five or more years of data are provided to reveal genuine trends and to minimize the influence of an extraordinary year.

By long-standing practice, private businesses have used ratio analysis to assess profitability, return on investment, cash flow, and financial stability. More recently, this type of analysis has been used in higher education, both by campus financial officers and by rating agencies and municipal bond firms, as part of an overall assessment of financial strength. Both investors and creditors are beginning to use ratio analysis on colleges and universities as part of meeting their fiduciary responsibilities.

Financial ratios can serve as a particularly useful means for governing boards to address issues of accountability and to exercise their stewardship. Indeed, it may be quite useful for institutions and systems of higher education to use ratio analysis as part of a strategic planning process. An institution might establish financial-ratio targets or performance objectives as part of its strategic plan, with a larger goal of improving the ratio of financial outcomes over time. Alternatively, ratios may be established as goals in relation to a set of peer or other institutions.

Ratios can provide important insights about a strategic plan and can be quite useful in communicating to board members the implications of that strategic plan for the institution. Properly understood, ratio analysis can assist both the administration and the board. It can reveal significant changes in the overall condition of an institution and serve as an early warning that some challenges lie ahead. Yet no ratio or set of ratios can reveal the entire picture. And while standards have begun to develop in the practice of financial-ratio analysis, the ratios should be viewed in the larger context of higher education finance.

Sources and Uses of Funds. Revenues and their rate of growth affect the ability of an institution to fulfill its mission in the face of inflation and enrollment growth. It is therefore useful to monitor each revenue source.

Revenue sources can be monitored through the *contribution ratio*. Diversification in fund sources contributes to financial health and the ability to withstand the adverse consequences of declines in a given source of revenue. The contribution ratio, when monitored over a period of years, can identify important trends and tradeoffs between available funds and restrictions imposed on the funds. The formula for the contribution ratio is

$$\frac{\text{Revenue (by source)}}{\text{Total educational and general expenditures and mandatory transfers}}$$

An escalating trend in the contribution ratio for tuition as a revenue source may signify increasing reliance on tuition as a source of support for the educational program. A declining trend in the state appropriations ratio suggests that either the state commitment is decreasing or that educational expenditures plus mandatory transfers are rising more rapidly than revenues from the state. Many states fund their public institutions on the basis of an enrollment-growth formula, which allows appropriations to rise and fall in proportion to enrollment. It is always easier for higher education institutions to adjust to increases in funding than to decreases because fixed costs are more difficult to reduce when enrollments decline. States suffering major fiscal problems may not fully fund these appropriation formulas, and the cumulative effects over a period of years can erode the budget base of an institution. An increasing trend in the amount of private gifts or grants as a percentage of expenditures (and especially on a per-student basis) will suggest the potential for enhancing academic programs as a result of improved fund raising.

In the analysis of expenditures, any major shift in the amount of funds being expended for a specific function or use may signal a change in institutional priorities. Expenditures can be monitored through the *allocation ratio*. This ratio and other expenditure ratios may provide a more accurate picture of strategic priorities than the language of the strategic plan or any other document. The formula for the allocation ratio is

$$\frac{\text{Expenditure (by function or program)}}{\text{Total educational and general expenditures and mandatory transfers}}$$

If mandatory transfers for the purpose of funding debt service are growing substantially as a ratio of total expenditures, the institution may have made an important shift in the tradeoff between short-run and long-run priorities. Changes in the relative share of expenditures for instruction, research, or institutional support (administrative overhead) are also indicators of potentially important shifts. For example, a university and its board may decide to expand the research mission of the institution and set a goal to increase the share of the total budget expended on organized research. Alternatively, a goal might be to limit or reduce the percentage of the institution's expenditures on administrative overhead.

A corollary to the allocation ratio, and one that is preferred by some accountants, is the *demand ratio* (see Peat, Marwick, Mitchell & Company, 1982), which uses revenues as the denominator rather than expenditures. Because educational and general revenues change independently of educational and general expenditures, the demand ratio may provide an even clearer picture of changing priorities than the allocation ratio does. The demand ratio may be especially useful in evaluating trends in the share of total available resources being devoted to a given expenditure category:

$$\frac{\text{Expenditures (by function or program)}}{\text{Total educational and general revenues}}$$

Another way of tracking expenditures, not a part of financial-ratio analysis, is based on expenditures per student or per student credit hour. Rising costs per student credit hour for instruction may be the result of smaller class size, increased emphasis on graduate enrollment, lower teaching loads of faculty members, or other factors. Alternatively, if expenditures per student for instruction decrease, the institution may have shifted strategic priorities to student support, recreation, counseling, health services, or programs related to student life. Because of increasing public concern about the costs of higher education and the perception that costs have been rising more rapidly than inflation, an analysis of this type can be quite helpful to boards.

Debt Structure. Another very important application of ratio analysis is in the evaluation of an institution's ability to repay its debt. In recent years, public institutions of higher education have turned increasingly to debt as a means of expanding physical facilities or renovating existing physical plants and infrastructure. This trend has occurred, in part, as a consequence of declining state appropriations for capital purposes and in some cases as a strategic choice that permits fund-raising proceeds from a capital campaign to be invested in endowment. This latter technique involves the classic debt-versus-equity decision between two alternatives for expanding physical facilities: (1) issuing debt and (2) raising funds for capital endowment. The differences between the alternatives can be discerned by examination of the institution's balance sheet and operating statements.

Over the past several decades, public monies for capital construction from federal or state governments have not kept pace with the need for expansion and renovation of facilities. Public institutions of higher education have turned to bonds, especially revenue bonds, to fill the gap. Under this means of financing, new auxiliary facilities (such as dormitories, recreation centers, and parking garages) are constructed by bonds or equivalent debt instruments, and the debt is serviced by the revenue stream from operations. Similarly, research buildings, equipment, and instrumentation are acquired by the sale of bonds and the indirect cost recovery on research grants and contracts is used to retire the debt. Even academic buildings at public institutions of higher education are now financed by revenue bonds, with tuition pledged to cover the debt service obligations, frequently over a period of twenty to thirty years. Several ratios will be helpful to trustees in evaluating debt structure. They should be reviewed individually as well as collectively.

The *debt service ratio* assesses the portion of annual operating revenues that must be set aside to pay for long-term debt. Because of the nature of restricted revenues in colleges and universities, the denominator of this ratio is expressed in terms of unrestricted current fund expenditures plus mandatory transfers:

$$\frac{\text{Debt service}}{\text{Unrestricted current funds expenditures and mandatory transfers}}$$

If this ratio remains stable over a period of time, it may be assumed that an institution has adequate resources to support its debt service needs. If this ratio increases, the budgeting flexibility of an institution will decrease. The threshold standard that has emerged from bond analysts and rating agencies is less than 10 percent; that is, when an institution is using 10 percent or more of its current unrestricted resources to pay for the retirement of long-term debt, creditors may become concerned. Institutions seeking to retain the highest credit rating will strive to keep this ratio low. However, such significant variability exists across public colleges and universities that this ratio must be interpreted within the full institutional context.

The *ratio of plant equity to plant debt* is one of the ratios that will test the institution's capacity to obtain more long-term financing. An institution's working capital, among other objectives, may be impaired if this ratio is inadequate.

$$\frac{\text{Plant equity (net investment in plant)}}{\text{Plant debt}}$$

The higher this ratio, the better off an institution's debt structure. A rapidly decreasing ratio would be a cause for alarm. A minimum standard of 300 percent for this ratio has emerged from the bond analysts and underwriters as a prerequisite for any institution with cash-flow problems.

The *ratio of expendable fund balances to debt* permits ready analysis for board members of whether the institution's financial capacity is growing stronger or weaker.

$$\frac{\text{Expendable fund balances}}{\text{Plant debt}}$$

A ratio of 100 percent would mean, of course, that a college or university has adequate unexpended fund balances to pay off its entire plant debt. For public institutions, such a circumstance is not commonplace. The trustees need to ascertain whether this ratio is declining over time, which would imply diminishing liquidity and perhaps diminishing financial capacity as well.

Other Ratios. A complete ratio analysis might also include other measures of institutional liquidity, such as the relationship of various assets to liabilities. A variety of such ratios exist, with labels such as "current" and "quick." The most conservative of these is the *available funds ratio* (that is, the availability of liquid assets sufficient to cover liabilities).

The relationship between expendable fund balances and unrestricted current funds expenditures is a ratio that will demonstrate ability to fund current programs from existing balances without depending upon current revenues. Such fund balances, as noted earlier, provide security against unforeseen events or economic hard times. As with other ratios, the trend of this one is important for trustees to monitor. A consistent pattern of decline in this ratio would signal deterioration of an institution's financial position.

Probably the best-known ratio is the *ratio of net revenues to total revenues* (with net total revenues comprising current funds revenues less current fund expenditures and mandatory transfers), which reveals whether there have been adequate revenues in the year to cover the annual costs of operations:

$$\frac{\text{Net total revenues}}{\text{Total revenues}}$$

The presence of surpluses is highly unlikely in a public institution, for both political and legal reasons. Occasional deficits would not be cause for undue alarm, but consecutively larger deficits would be.

Statement of Changes in Fund Balances

Of the three major financial statements, the least familiar is the statement of changes in fund balances. It shows the overall flow of financial activity into and out of the institution and across the various fund types. This report contributes to the total financial picture by revealing additional information about the sources and uses of funds. Unlike the balance sheet, which describes the financial "inventory" at a moment in time, the statement of changes in fund balances describes the financial flows or activities of the institution over the entire fiscal period. Exhibit 9.3 is a sample statement of changes in fund balances.

The statement of changes in fund balances describes the total "additions" to the institution, whether by means of revenues or other resource enhancements. It is important to note that in fund accounting, restricted revenues are recognized for accrual purposes only when they are expended. Thus, the statement of current funds, revenues, and expenditures records restricted revenue only to the extent that it is actually expended during the accounting period. For example, if a faculty member receives a multiyear grant from the federal government, only the amount actually expended in the fiscal year appears as restricted revenue. In the statement of changes in fund balances, the entire amount of the grant is recorded as part of the additions. For ease of understanding, the additions are arrayed across the table under each of the fund types. Thus, one can see in a single sweep of the eye all additions to the institution and their distribution across the fund types.

Similarly, the deductions include all funds that flow out of each fund type during the fiscal period, except for those transferred among the fund types. The section of the statement that lists expenditures and deductions includes, of course, expenditures for current operations for the year but also includes such disbursements as those for construction and new capital acquisitions.

The transfers section of the statement includes the flow of all funds among the various fund types over the fiscal period. The transfers are self-balancing, because each transaction creates an equal addition and subtraction, but from different fund types. Mandatory transfers include those transfers that result from a legally

Exhibit 9.3. Sample Statement of Changes in Fund Balances.

	Current Funds		Loan Funds	Endowment and Similar Funds	Annuity and Life Income Funds	Plant Funds			
	Unrestricted	Restricted				Unexpended	Renewal and Replacements	Retirement of Indebtedness	Investment in Plant
Revenues and other additions:									
Unrestricted current fund revenues	$7,540,000								
Expired term endowment—restricted						50,000			
State appropriations—restricted						50,000			
Federal grants and contracts—restricted		500,000							
Private gifts, grants, and contracts—restricted		370,000	100,000	1,500,000	800,000	115,000		65,000	15,000
Investment income—restricted		224,000	12,000	10,000		5,000	5,000	5,000	
Realized gains on investments—unrestricted				109,000					
Realized gains on investments—restricted			4,000	50,000		10,000	5,000	5,000	
Interest on loans receivable			7,000						
U.S. government advances			18,000						
Expended for plant facilities (including $100,000 charged to current funds expenditures)									1,550,000
Retirement of indebtedness									220,000
Accrued interest on sale of bonds								3,000	

Exhibit 9.3. Sample Statement of Changes in Fund Balances, Cont'd.

	Current Funds Unrestricted	Current Funds Restricted	Loan Funds	Endowment and Similar Funds	Annuity and Life Income Funds	Plant Funds Unexpended	Plant Funds Renewal and Replacements	Plant Funds Retirement of Indebtedness	Plant Funds Investment in Plant
Matured annuity and life income restricted to endowment				10,000					
Total revenues and other additions	7,540,000	1,094,000	141,000	1,679,000	800,000	230,000	10,000	78,000	1,785,000
Expenditures and other deductions:									
Educational and general expenditures	4,400,000	1,014,000							
Auxiliary enterprises expenditures	1,830,000								
Indirect costs recovered		35,000	10,000						
Refunded to grantors		20,000							
Loan cancellations and write-offs			1,000						
Administrative and collection costs			1,000					1,000	
Adjustment of actuarial liability for annuities payable					75,000				
Expended for plant facilities (including noncapitalized expenditures of $50,000)						1,200,000	300,000		
Retirement of indebtedness								220,000	
Interest on indebtedness								190,000	
Disposal of plant facilities									115,000

Expired term endowments ($40,000 unrestricted, $50,000 restricted to plant)				90,000					
Matured annuity and life income funds restricted to endowment					10,000				
Total expenditures and other deductions	6,230,000	1,069,000	12,000	90,000	85,000	1,200,000	300,000	411,000	115,000
Transfers among funds—additions/(deductions):									
Mandatory:									
Principal and interest	(340,000)							340,000	
Renewals and replacements	(170,000)						170,000		
Loan fund matching grant	(2,000)		2,000						
Unrestricted gifts allocated	(650,000)		50,000	550,000	50,000				
Portion of unrestricted quasi endowment funds investment gains appropriated	40,000			(40,000)					
Total transfers	(1,122,000)		52,000	510,000	50,000		170,000	340,000	
Net increase/(decrease) for the year	188,000	25,000	181,000	2,099,000	715,000		(120,000)	7,000	1,670,000
Fund balance at beginning of year	455,000	421,000	502,000	11,901,000	2,505,000		380,000	293,000	36,540,000
Fund balance at end of year	643,000	446,000	683,000	14,000,000	3,220,000		260,000	300,000	38,210,000

See accompanying Summary of Significant Accounting Policies and Notes to Financial Statements binding commitment. The most typical example of a mandatory transfer is debt service. Other examples include matching grants into the loan funds to meet federal matching requirements or mandatory building renewal requirements.

Other transfers are nonmandatory and may be among the most interesting pieces of information in the statement. Nonmandatory transfers can reflect the discretionary shifts of resources across funds, including, for example, transfer from the current funds into some form of capital accumulation such as the quasi endowment or the plant fund.

Financial Responsibility of Trustees in Context

This chapter has been devoted to a description of the most important responsibilities of a public board in its role as guardian of the financial health of the campus or system of campuses. A list of reports is identified as essential for carrying out the board's fiscal stewardship. It is important to emphasize, however, that ensuring the financial well-being of the institution and protecting the institution's investment in physical plant are but a part of the overall duties of good trusteeship. Financial reports must be reviewed in the larger context of an institution's academic mission. By themselves, financial reports will not capture all of the essential elements for good decision making by the board. They are not substitutes for strong institutional leadership with a clear vision. Sound decisions by the board must be based on a blend of the right reports, proper analysis, and good judgment exercised in partnership with institutional leadership.

The nineties are likely to be a decade of great financial stress for higher education. Changing demographics will have a profound effect upon enrollment. State officials may face the double bind of diminishing resources and accelerating competition for those resources. The trend toward increased accountability, especially for public institutions, is likely to persist.

Escalating costs and mounting concern about the quality of undergraduate education are contributing to the chorus of public criticism. If institutions and their governing boards do not demonstrate leadership in financial accountability, state officials may take matters into their own hands. Legislatures and state budget officials, faced with difficult choices in the allocation of the state's resources, may be tempted to intrude into the governance functions of public higher education. Loss of flexibility and long-term damage to academic autonomy and quality could be the result.

It is therefore exceedingly important that institutions of higher education lead the way in developing effective means of demonstrating accountability. To do so, fundamental changes in the institutional culture for both faculty members and administrators may be needed. Boards can play a pivotal role as the intermediary between the academy and the taxpayer. While prodding the institution to become more accountable for performance, the board must also protect the essential academic features that have made higher education in the United States the envy of the world. These mounting pressures on public governing boards are likely to make trusteeship ever more challenging and ever more important.

CHAPTER 10

Fund Raising and
the Development of
University Foundations

Curtis R. Simic

Take a walk across the campus of your university—the one that has
called upon your experience, expertise, and willingness to serve on
its governing board. Some of the students walking toward you are
here only because they received a scholarship made possible by donors to your institution. Some chose your university over another
school because they received a merit scholarship, again made possible by donors. Around you are buildings—the bones of the university—the places in which discoveries are made, music rings out,
and the words of the greatest minds of the centuries live. Some of
these buildings are named after donors whose generosity funded
construction of the buildings. Walk into the labs, the libraries, the
career centers, the reading rooms for students with visual impair-
ments. The computers, the books, the mass spectrometers may all
be gifts.

Welcome then to one of the most magical areas of responsibility that you will have as a governing board member: the voluntary giving to your institution by individuals, businesses, and
foundations. Contributions are becoming increasingly important to
public institutions, as they have always been to private ones. Although total amounts of money appropriated to higher education
by state legislators have gone up over the years to cover rising costs,

the percentage of the operating budgets that they cover is going down. At the same time, federal grants to both public and private institutions are declining. Auxiliary enterprises at colleges and universities, such as dormitories or hospitals, are not intended to make a profit. Tuition and fees can be increased only so much if higher education, especially public higher education, is to fulfill its mandate to be accessible to as many qualified students as possible. Therefore, more and more institutions look to gifts to make the critical difference.

Voluntary giving is a wonderful expression of the values and the will of individuals and organizations. Contributors come to understand which projects and programs are important to the quality and success of the institution, and they want to be a part of making them happen. These are the friends who share your school's vision. If they are alumni, they want to see the institution they love prosper and want others to share in the excitement they felt and the opportunities they had. They want to influence the present for the better and help shape the next century. They want to give something back to society.

Giving is evidence of the power of the human imagination. We can all imagine "more" and "better" and "what could be." We can all imagine a world in which all people realize their potential. Donors know that giving can make these dreams come closer to reality.

It is good to remind ourselves, after all, that "philanthropy and scholarship are each, separately, among the most powerful influences to shape the future of our society. In combination, they may be unsurpassed in their power to improve the human condition" (Boyd, 1989, p. 1). For all the problems detailed so minutely in the report *A Nation at Risk* (U.S. Department of Education, 1983) and in books like *The Closing of the American Mind* (Bloom, 1987) and *Cultural Literacy* (Hirsch, 1987), our colleges and universities are, as they have always been, a means for people to have access to a wider world and to broader opportunities. The opportunities offered by education are inextricably linked with the success of our society.

A former president of Indiana University, William Lowe Bryan, made the connection between education and a successful society clear many years ago: "What the people need and demand is that their children shall have a chance—as good a chance as any other children in the world—to make the most of themselves. . . . What the people want is open paths from every corner of the state, through the schools, to the highest and best things men can achieve. To make such paths, to make them open to the poorest and lead to the highest, is the mission of democracy" (Clark, 1973, p. 7). Even in the early 1900s, President Bryan, who launched the first fund-raising campaign at Indiana University, knew that donor dollars were essential to the quality and success of the educational enterprise. As a trustee of an educational institution, you have been invited to participate in this great effort of the imagination and to play a significant role in making your institution's dreams a reality.

Setting the Stage for Fund Raising

Like other important initiatives, successful fund raising begins at the top. It begins with the commitment of all members of the governing board—collectively and individually—to a comprehensive and farsighted program that reflects the viewpoints of their constituencies and is based on the long-range plan of the institution. No institution can maximize its fund-raising potential unless it knows who its prospects are and how it is perceived by its internal and external audiences. Within your institution, these audiences include administrators, faculty members, staff members, students, and the fund raisers.

These internal audiences should be afforded the same thoughtful consideration as the donors are. Often, they are not given such consideration. Each of these groups must be a full partner in the fund-raising office if the office is to succeed. The head of the fund-raising office should, for example, be a part of the top administrative team of the institution. In this way, the issues and the concerns of the administration are clear to the fund raisers.

Faculty members often supply the inspiration to prospective donors that the fund raisers can then bring to fruition. Regular meetings between your fund-raising staff and faculty representatives are a good way to keep the lines of communication open, especially if your fund-raising office is separate from your institution in the form of a nonprofit foundation.

The perceptions of students can affect your fund-raising efforts for years to come. Faculty and staff members must understand that every interaction they have with students—teaching in the classroom, counseling, even answering a question about where to find something—contributes to those students' overall impression of the quality and compassion of your institution. Years later, students' feelings about their experience at your school will profoundly influence what these former students contribute to the school.

You must also determine the sensibilities of groups outside your institution, including alumni, volunteers, corporations and foundations, legislators and local officials, donors, and friends. Perception is reality, of a sort, and what your constituents believe about your institution is the starting point for your institution's efforts to reinforce or change those perceptions. Whatever the perceptions are, you, as a governing board member, need to have ready and continuing access to information about and representatives of each constituency.

The perceptions of key constituent groups are essential information as part of the long-range academic and strategic planning process. Fund-raising priorities and strategies are determined on the basis of the institution's long-range plan, so it is essential that the institution have a long-range plan and that it is committed to implementation of the plan. The success of the plan depends on the willingness of all institutional offices and programs that deal with external constituents to work together. These offices deal with admissions, community or university relations, athletics, alumni, development, and grants and sponsored programs.

The plan should set out a vision for the future of the institution: what the institution wants to be and how it wants to be seen by others. Every organization should formulate or clarify its mission so that the members of the organization understand and agree on what functions and priorities are central. Once the vision for the institution's future is clear, you need to look carefully at where the institution is now.

An honest review of your institution's strengths and weaknesses will show what needs to be changed by making adjustments to policies, budgets, and priorities. You need to look outside the institution, too, both for the short and for the long term. After you have identified your constituencies and determined their perceptions, you need to go further and look at social, demographic, economic, and other changes affecting your state, the nation, and the world.

What happens outside your local area affects what happens in your institution. Early in an economic downturn, for example, you will hear key prospects say that they will wait awhile before contributing, or you will get a phone call from a donor who wants to accelerate her gift because of changes in the tax laws. People make the decision to give from the heart, but they consider that decision in light of all the realities of daily life.

Once you have considered all the factors described here, you are ready to set goals and priorities for your institution that will take you from where you are to where you want to be. What is important for the future of your institution? More minority students? More computers? State-of-the-art lab equipment? Better communications with constituencies? Whatever your goals and priorities, it is almost certain that they will cost you something. William Boyd (1989, p. 11) reminds us that "nothing can spare us the necessity for dealing with the intractable issue of the relationship between money and quality."

Setting Fund-Raising Priorities

It is the job of the governing board of an institution—not the fund-raising office or foundation—to set fund-raising priorities. The governing board must know this and insist on it.

In working through the strategic plan, you have determined where the institution is and where it wants to be. Again, your fund-raising priorities must be in concert with the long-range plan for the academic success of the institution. Of course, the long-range plan needs to be flexible, and goals and priorities should be periodically reviewed. But setting ad hoc fund-raising priorities in response to the demands of the moment will dilute your fund-raising resources and slow progress on the long-range plan as well as leave your decisions open to charges of favoritism.

The process of determining fund-raising priorities should be a careful series of steps, open to the examination of all constituencies.

1. During the first part of the process, input is solicited from all constituencies. Proposals for projects are forwarded from department or program heads to deans and then to chancellors or the equivalent officers. All proposed projects are reviewed by a committee that is appointed by the president of the institution. Committee members could be the president or chief academic officer and representatives from among the administration, deans, faculty members, the grants or sponsored programs office, the fund-raising office, and perhaps students. Projects that support the long-range plan are approved for further consideration.

2. The cost of each project is determined—a realistic cost, including inflation.

3. A grid is set up with the list of projects down the left-hand side and the possible funding sources across the top. Sources might include: state operating budget, state capital budget, state special project grants, federal grants and overhead, student tuition, special student fees, private support through annual gifts, and private support through capital gifts. Each project or program is assigned a tentative source or sources of revenue.

4. After the grid is completed, a list of programs requiring private support is turned over to a second committee that studies the feasibility of raising private funds to accomplish these purposes. This committee, also appointed by the president, is chaired by the president or chief academic officer and includes representatives of the administration, deans, faculty members, fund-raising office, and perhaps students.

5. The fund-raising office conducts an attitudinal assessment of the marketplace through conversations with key volunteers, donors, and other constituents to determine the feasibility of raising funds for the proposed project. The feasibility study asks these four questions:
    - What is the institution's overall potential for raising funds?
    - What is the institution's potential for raising funds for this particular project?

- What effect will a campaign for this project have on other ongoing fund-raising programs?
- What resources of the institution will be required to mount a successful fund-raising effort, and what will it cost to provide those resources?

6. To ensure proper planning and execution, the governing board assesses the appropriate unit's ability and readiness to manage its part of the campaign, if fund raising is decentralized. The board considers these questions:
   - How does the project goal compare to annual giving? The goal should not be more than ten times greater than the amount of annual giving.
   - How does the school, department, or program rate? What honors have faculty members won and what is their teaching, research, and service record?
   - How clearly defined, affluent, and influential is the constituency for this project? What is its giving record? Do donors include alumni, other individuals, corporations, and foundations?
   - Is the head of the school, department, or program willing to provide up to 20 percent of his or her time as well as resources and leadership?
   - How active are faculty members as donors, proposal writers, and solicitors?
   - If the project is to be self-funded, can enough unrestricted gift money be generated to cover the costs of the project? If not, what is an acceptable ratio of cost to dollars raised?
   - Can the school, department, or program support the fund-raising effort with clerical assistance, travel funds, office space, donor cultivation, and solicitation?
   - Can the project break even within two years (all costs matched by contributions) and return a minimum ratio of five to one of contributions to fund-raising costs within three to five years?

7. With the information derived from the questions above, the governing board can make decisions about the institution's readiness to undertake a campaign or a project and what should

happen to those proposed projects for which gift funds are not likely to be available at this time or ever.

8. From those projects evaluated as having "gift potential" and whose corresponding schools, departments, or programs are able to participate effectively in the process, the president of the institution chooses those that are to be designated priorities for the fundraising office, foundation board, campaign cabinet, or other group charged with responsibility for raising the funds.

Maximizing the Effectiveness of the Fund-Raising Organization

The goal of any fund-raising office is to serve the institution as effectively as possible. Whether the fund-raising office is a part of the institution or a separate foundation, it is a major contributor to success of the institution.

The fund-raising office must be organized and run to enhance giving to the institution and to fulfill the stewardship obligation to donors. Fund-raising offices do not, for example, just accept bequests. They have a planned giving staff that educates prospects about giving options and provides professional services to aid donors in their decisions. Fund-raising offices do not just deposit checks; they send acknowledgments and arrange events that thank and recognize donors. Fund-raising offices not only set up scholarship accounts but also inform donors about the students who hold those scholarships. Benefactors want the reporting, accounting, and stewardship functions that fund-raising offices provide, and your institution is better off when these services are in place.

Although these services can be performed equally well by a successful fund-raising office within an institution or a separate foundation, I believe that maximum effectiveness is achieved by setting up a separate fund-raising foundation. The external operation offers advantages that have major, long-term benefits for an institution.

Probably the first and most important advantage of a separate foundation is that it expands opportunities for "making insiders of outsiders." Expanding institutional ownership not only enables governing board members to have more time to devote to their primary responsibility—governing the educational institution—but it also offers substantive opportunities for involvement to another group: the directors of an institutionally related foundation devoted to fund raising and management of funds.

The directors of the foundation take responsibilities that involve them deeply in the life of the institution. In their committee work and individual contributions of time and expertise, they become allies of and advocates for the institution. As a result of their commitment, they increase the number of insiders who can represent the institution to its many publics. Unlike governing board members, who are often politically appointed or elected and who are usually few in number, the foundation directors can be elected according to their degree of affluence and their influence with groups specifically important to fund raising.

Through the foundation board structure, it is also possible to involve even more friends in service to your institution. Foundation boards benefit from having "consulting members" on their committees, people from inside and outside the institution whose expertise and concern will benefit the institution and give it more allies and advocates.

The governing board needs to choose foundation directors as carefully as it would choose board members. The old cliché that the most effective board members bring "work, wealth, and wisdom" applies to directors just as surely as to governing board members. Make sure that the mix of directors reflects the ethnic, geographical, and demographic diversity and gender balance of your alumni and your giving constituencies. Directors not only offer their expertise and make wise decisions but also participate in the fund-raising process, engage in public relations activities, and relate to the institution's key constituencies: alumni, corporations, foundations, parents, government officials, and the media, as well as donors. They will represent your institution best if they reflect the diversity of your institution as much as possible.

The governing board needs to be sure that the foundation directors are given substantive work to do. Certainly, there is no lack of important work that is of service to educational institutions. Give directors committee assignments and expect them to study, make decisions, evaluate progress, set policies, and so on. Your foundation directors are busy people; they must know that their time is spent on real work and not make-work to keep their respect and their attention.

A separate foundation also has other advantages. It provides a mechanism for keeping state funds separate from private funds, which is important for several reasons.

First, a separate foundation can benefit your institution by offering it flexibility in expenditures. Public institutions, including publicly assisted educational ones, are limited in the way that they can disburse funds. They are asked to budget one or two years in advance, and once the appropriation is made, they have little flexibility in determining how the money is spent. A certain amount of money is designated for salaries and wages, capital projects or improvements, maintenance of the physical plant, and so on. However, sometimes opportunities arise for the institution that cannot be predicted. For example, a used telescope may be offered to the institution by an observatory for a very reasonable price. When there is no money in the institution's budget to buy it, the separate foundation can arrange for and carry the financing until the institution can find the funds to buy the telescope. Or a building that the institution could use for a program may come on the market. The lengthy approval process required for such purchases almost certainly means that the building will be sold before the institution has approval for the purchase. The foundation can make the purchase, and the institution can have the use of the building until it gets official approval and financing and can pay the foundation back.

Certain kinds of expenditures, varying from state to state, simply cannot be funded with public money. For example, foreign travel for faculty members is often excluded even though faculty members are serving the institution by representing it abroad and are increasing their knowledge and thereby the institution's stature by studying in foreign countries. Faculty or staff relocation expenses are also often not covered by state funds, but such monies can help attract the best candidates to the institution. Automobiles for key officials may not be covered by state funds but can be a cost-efficient way to provide transportation to employees traveling on business.

Second, keeping gift funds separate offers an institution

more investment opportunities. Because of the restrictions imposed by some states on state institutions, publicly assisted agencies are often quite limited in the way that they can make investments. The difference between even a few percentage points on returns on thousands or millions of dollars in endowment can make a significant difference in the long-term health and growth of an institution.

For example, in 1989, Indiana University, which at that time was prohibited from investing in equities, earned an 8.3 percent return on its investments—its best year ever. The Indiana University Foundation earned an 18.8 percent return, enhancing considerably the value of the assets it held for the benefit of the university. Nonprofit corporations, such as foundations, are subject to a different set of laws and regulations than for-profit organizations, which allows them to invest more productively. While taking only a reasonable degree of risk, nonprofits can often realize better annualized returns than for-profit organizations. Since the fund-raising office is holding funds in trust for departments, schools, programs, and campuses, maximizing the value of gifts through prudent and productive investment strategies is a fiduciary responsibility.

Third, by having a separate fund-raising foundation, an institution can offer the donors confidentiality. More than half of the funds given to any institution usually come from relatively few major donors. These are the donors who will almost certainly want their privacy protected because they are most likely to have shared with staff members privileged and personal information about their families and finances in the course of making their gifts. Many donors will have made planned gift arrangements with an institution. No one wants his or her estate plans splashed all over the front page of the newspaper. By giving through a foundation, donors can protect their wills, trust agreements, and highly personal correspondence from public scrutiny.

Fourth, a separate foundation can be organized to be accountable to its most important external constituency—donors. The accounting systems, gift reporting, reporting of holders of scholarships and fellowships, gift agreements—all the service and consumer-oriented features—can be arranged so that the organization is responsive to donors and to the special requirements of fund raising.

For example, accounting systems used by states are not designed for use by fund raisers. An accounting system can be devised by a fund-raising organization that goes beyond the minimum accounting standards to answer questions from donors and account managers, report on investments, and return information to the staff about productivity. Such a system meets the special needs of the fund-raising office and still complies with all accounting and auditing standards for private sector corporations.

No matter whether your fund-raising office is within your institution or separate from it, the office can provide the specialized services and perform the functions necessary for successful fund raising. However, the separate foundation has so many advantages that I highly recommend it. Your goal, after all, is to maximize the benefit of the fund-raising operation for your school or college; a separate foundation can help you do so.

Balancing Foundation Rights and Responsibilities

The relative freedom that enables separate nonprofit foundations to better serve their institutions is a right that cannot be abused. There has been, and should be, an increasing awareness and concern on the part of the public, legislators, and colleges and universities about accountability, openness, and the responsible use of funds.

Higher education has attracted a great deal of negative publicity recently because of alleged misuses of overhead funds received from government agencies as part of research grants. At the same time, the public and the press are examining with a critical eye graduation rates, defaults on student loans, the emphasis (or lack of it) on good teaching, the availability of classes, and the pressures of "political correctness."

Separate, nonprofit foundations associated with colleges and universities are examined under the same glaring spotlight, as they should be. My arguments for a foundation separate from its institution are merely a prelude to my equally strong argument that foundations must be held to a very high standard; the regulations may be different from those that apply to state agencies, but they must be equally strict.

In fact, nonprofit corporations are carefully regulated. They are subject to state and federal laws and should have in place tight internal controls, just like any other corporation. Internal policies and procedures must ensure that gifts go into the correct account, expenditures from those accounts are made only for stated purposes and by authorized persons, the operating budget is closely monitored, and so on. Written fund descriptions, designated account managers, signature cards, external and internal audits, and numerous other checks and balances are necessary to assure that every transaction is documented and that the strictest accounting and reporting standards are met. At the same time, nonprofit organizations must be prepared to undergo audits by the Internal Revenue Service and federal and state agencies, as applicable. They must comply with laws and regulations relating to affirmative action, employee benefits, and many other matters.

Although I have pointed out the advantages of confidentiality, flexibility in expenditures, and broad investment powers that foundations have, I maintain that it is vital for an organization with these rights to be open and accountable to its many constituencies. Foundations have an obligation and a duty to inform those they serve.

I believe that foundations should routinely make accessible to their constituencies and the general public the following items:

- Financial audit, conducted by an outside auditor
- Annual report, including an honor roll of donors
- Operating budget, including funding sources
- Policies on disbursement of gift funds
- Investment policies, expenditure guidelines, and investment performance
- Report on the cost of fund raising
- Contract for service between the foundation and the institution it serves
- Policies regarding the establishment of fund-raising priorities
- Form 990, the annual tax return for nonprofit corporations

Foundations in some states have been challenged by the news media's or legislators' interpretation of open records laws, especially as they relate to prospect and donor records and expenditures.

Separate, nonprofit foundations that have a contractual relationship with their institutions are generally not, and should not be, subject to such laws.

Details of these records are confidential, and foundations are justified in refusing to release such information. It is proper for a foundation to release an honor roll that includes donors' names and ranges of giving (with the donors' permission). It is not ethical for a foundation to release details about a gift unless the donor has agreed to or asked for such publicity. In the same way, I believe it is proper for a foundation to refuse to release detailed information about account balances or expenditures from an account managed by a university dean. A bank would not release such information to a third party, nor would it be considered ethical to do so. Should the dean decide to release the information, however, the foundation should not object. The foundation can describe the checks and balances it has in place on expenditures and the purpose of an account, And it can announce, for example, that $1 million is required to establish an endowed chair. But it should not go further.

The best foundations are the ones that strike a balance between their responsibility to be open and accountable and their responsibilities to those they serve. Striking this balance does not always involve clear-cut or easy decisions, as some people might have you believe. Your responsibility as a governing board member is to be aware of these issues and to do what is fair, honest, open, and in the best interests of the institution that you and your foundation serve.

Monitoring the Process

The governing board does not abdicate its responsibility when it turns fund raising over to the foundation's directors. Board members can reasonably expect, however, that foundation directors will take the lead in fund raising. Whether the fund-raising operation is within your institution or a separate foundation and whether you or the members of another board are directly responsible for fund raising, you need to be sure that the fund-raising directors

- See to a process for identifying fund-raising priorities
- Identify the costs, including the indirect costs, of every project
- Determine the feasibility of proposed projects
- Take the initiative in developing plans to raise funds for the designated priority projects
- Measure the performance of the fund-raising organization against goals
- Understand the institution's requirements for current and endowed funds
- Develop policies and procedures concerning access to funds and information
- Evaluate whether investments are maximizing income while sustaining an acceptable degree of risk.
- Establish policies and procedures for setting up funds, disbursements, authorization, and reporting

When the foundation's directors are a separate group from the governing board, a special effort must be made to ensure that the two groups work well together. In addition to relationships between individuals, formal and structured interactions will help to foster closer cooperation and understanding and minimize the potential for conflict.

Members of the governing board may be included among the foundation's directors. Overlap is useful as long as the governing board members do not predominate. Governing board members may also serve on foundation board committees as consulting members, even if they are not directors. Directors may be governing board members or sit on committees. At a minimum, they can occasionally attend meetings of the board. Of course, foundation board members and governing board members should receive all the reports and information that I have suggested be made available to the public, but they should receive the materials before they are made generally available.

Supporting Fund Raising—The Individual's Role

Now that you have brought your institution to the point at which it can make a realistic evaluation of and commitment to its fund-raising effort, there are some matters you as an individual trustee need to attend to. Your own commitment to fund raising is as important as the institution's commitment.

Prospective donors look to the leaders of an institution to see if their personal commitments match their fund-raising rhetoric. Before your institution can ask others to give, you must make sure it looks to itself first. You need to set an example and encourage others to do so.

Some governing board members, and you may be among them, do not feel comfortable participating in fund raising. "I'll do anything but ask for money!" some new board members say. The process of fund raising is actually quite lengthy, with a number of steps. As an old saying goes, only 10 percent of getting a gift is asking for it, 90 percent is preparation.

You can participate in fund raising in several ways: suggesting prospective donors to your fund-raising office or foundation, evaluating the interest and giving potential of prospects, introducing a fund raiser to a prospect, hosting fund-raising events, accompanying a fund raiser on calls, inviting a prospect to a campus event, and following up with donors in person or by phone or mail to thank them for their gifts. Often, donors are especially pleased that a governing board member is associated with the fund-raising process. Your participation makes it clear that the institution places a high value on that particular prospect or donor and on private giving in general. As you become more familiar and more comfortable with the fund-raising process, you may eventually be ready to solicit donations, but keep in mind that your contributions to any part of the process are valuable.

Whether or not you become a solicitor, it is your responsibility to become well versed in the basics of fund raising and to understand the process. Effective fund raising requires long-range planning, solid institutional commitment, an adequate budget, talented leadership, enthusiastic volunteers, skillful management, and teamwork. Fund raising is a long-term, interactive process, and large gifts come only with long-term relationships and great attention to the concerns and dreams of the donors. Fund raising is not a "get rich quick" scheme, nor is it a one-shot deal or a big campaign.

In all your interactions with the institution's key constituencies, you can contribute to a positive climate for fund raising. Your interactions can take a number of forms with a number of different audiences.

You can be an example to donors in their concern for the welfare of the institution and should encourage donors' ongoing interest in the school. Expressions of appreciation from governing board members are especially meaningful to donors because of their prestige.

Alumni are important to any institution, and you should see that they are informed and involved in the institution's life as often as possible. Like other groups important to the fund-raising effort, alumni should be involved before they are asked to invest.

You should help parents obtain a clear idea of the institution's positive impact on their sons and daughters and an understanding of the institution's goals and plans. Parents are a large and often untapped potential donor base.

Corporations and foundations should know that your institution puts their gifts to good use and provides a good return on investment to donors. You, as a governing board member, can help build connections with businesses.

Governing board members can work closely with the institution to create and maintain relationships with federal and state legislators and public officials. Once the institution's needs have been determined, governing board members should fight for them under the direction of the president of the institution. You can also help these officials come to a balanced view of education and the challenges facing it. Educational institutions have much to do, and they need legislators to recognize the importance not only of scholarships but also, for example, of the special requirements of students and staff members with disabilities. Legislators should know that funding for capital projects is as important as programs for gifted students. Legislative directives must be fair and consistent and recognize the many facets of education.

You can help, too, in dealing with the federal government. Governing board members should press the government for reasonably stable, long-term policies of financial aid that ensure opportunity to students and ease the financial constraints on the institution.

The media can be friends of the institution and should be encouraged to provide a balanced view of issues in higher education. Always on the lookout for the outrageous and bizarre, the media should be offered other views of what is going on in education. Help them see the total picture.

The general public benefits, and so does your institution, when you encourage the institution to bring leaders in business, industry, labor, the professions, and government to campus. Interactions between these leaders and the campus community develop a better understanding between the institution and the community and state.

Effective fund raising begins with you, the governing board member, and with the commitment of your institution to listening to its constituencies in making long-range plans. Your responsibilities are not only group tasks—making policies, establishing procedures, evaluating progress—but also personal ones. Your own understanding of and participation in the fund-raising process, and all that underlies the usefulness of that process, is essential to the success of fund raising for your institution.

In many ways, fund raising is one of the most important activities you can engage in. Like education, philanthropy is, as William Boyd (1989, p. 1) says, "one of the most powerful influences shaping the future of our society." In enabling voluntary giving, in helping others to express their hopes and dreams for your institution and for education, you are contributing to a mighty and powerful force for good.

CHAPTER 11

Strengthening Relationships with Government Agencies and Political Leaders

Aims C. McGuinness, Jr.

Trustees of public colleges and universities and public higher education systems will face a more challenging external environment in the 1990s than in any period of this century. To some degree, these challenges have always been present, but they will intensify in the years ahead, making the board's role in external relationships more important.

Public boards face a basic contradiction. Political leaders, reflecting public opinion, clearly perceive colleges and universities as keys to the future—keys to fulfilling individuals' aspirations as well as contributing to communities, the states, and the nation. Yet higher education is the target of growing frustration stemming from perceptions that it is not sufficiently responsive to major societal concerns, for example, the quality of public elementary and secondary schools, teacher education, or the need for accessible graduate and professional programs. Critiques of educational quality, initially focused on the public schools, are increasingly aimed at undergraduate teaching and learning. Highly publicized controversies involving intercollegiate athletics and indirect overhead cost rates for sponsored research only serve to further undermine public confidence.

The public board's relationships with the external environment are further exacerbated by an increasingly uncertain economic climate. With almost no exception, states now face more severe economic constraints than at any time in more than two decades. Public boards face the wrenching decisions that are required when demands far exceed available resources. These decisions are made more difficult by the tensions among competing priorities and interests.

Few states are immune from intense regional competition. Growing urban centers, for example, demand greater accessibility to graduate and professional programs, These demands threaten the positions of traditional university centers struggling to sustain high-cost programs in the face of declining federal research funding and stabilizing enrollments. Community colleges seek adequate funding to serve expanding enrollments, while other sectors struggle to improve quality with stable or declining resources.

Funding formulas and decision-making processes adequate for times of growth are ineffective in handling the difficult choices in periods of decline. The political balance necessary for consensus building in state legislatures is lost as there are far more losers than winners and one region of the state is pitted against another. These inequities in the overall state political and economic scene are amplified in states' higher education systems, making the task of the public board even more difficult.

The high turnover of state political leaders, accelerated by the drive for term limitations for state legislators, complicates funding problems. The traditions guiding relations between higher education and a state and the origins of state coordinating and governing structures can be quickly lost as senior legislators are replaced by newcomers. High turnover of elected officials may reinforce the role of legislative and executive branch civil servants in ensuring continuity over political cycles.

Given these conditions, it is not surprising that concerns about the quality of public board members are intensifying. Effective board behavior is one of the most important prerequisites for effective external relationships. Not only is it difficult to get people who have the requisite commitment to higher education and civic leadership and experience in governing complex organizations to serve on boards, but the quality of board appointments and of candidates for board election is likely to reflect unstable political leadership (see Kerr and Gade, 1989). Educational issues, intensified by economic and political conditions, can breed concerns about governance structures. Since the mid 1980s, thirty states have either completed or seriously debated major redesigns of their educational systems.

In this environment, public boards of trustees must perform at least three seemingly contradictory external roles. They must be

- Advocates and interpreters to the general public of the values, aspirations, and needs of the institutions they govern, even when these may clash with external priorities.
- Buffers between the external political and economic pressures and the academy, striving to foster an environment of continuity and stability that is essential for creativity, open debate, and sustained attention to academic pursuits—even when the external environment may be in turmoil.
- Connecting points between the concerns of the broader society, including the state, and the academy. Public colleges and universities must be seen as responsive to the needs and concerns of the states in which they are located. If they are not, the danger of inappropriate political intrusion increases.

The skill of public boards in balancing—if not juggling—these roles will determine their success in the hostile external environment of the 1990s.

Patterns of Public Board Structures and External Relationships

Much of the literature on boards of trustees is written from the perspective of the board of a single institution and, in many cases, a private nonprofit institution or corporation. However, the single board is the exception in U.S. public higher education. Kerr and Gade (1989, pp. 116–117) identify three forms of governance by public boards:

- *Consolidated governance systems.* One board covers all two-year and four-year public campuses ("fully consolidated") or one board covers all four-year public campuses, including research universities and other four-year institutions ("partially consolidated"), with separate arrangements for two-year institutions.
- *Segmental systems.* Separate boards cover separate types of campuses, such as research universities, comprehensive colleges and universities, and community colleges.
- *Campus-level boards.* These boards (five hundred of them) are "autonomous" where they have full authority over a single campus and are not covered by a system board. They exercise "delegated authority" where they exist within a system but can make some decisions on their own. They are "advisory" where they exist within a system but can only give advice, not make binding decisions. Most systems have no campus-level boards.

In all but three states—Delaware, Michigan, and Vermont—a statutory state coordinating or governing board oversees the relationship between the public institutions and the governor and state legislature. The authority of these state coordinating boards varies from limited statewide planning to extensive budgetary and regulatory roles. To complicate the picture even more, in twenty-three states, the statewide board plays a dual role of being both the consolidated governing board for most of the state's public institutions as well as the board responsible for statewide coordination. As discussed later in this chapter, this dual role places special burdens on boards to balance internal governance with statewide coordinating and policy leadership. The complexity of these variations in relationships between public boards and state governments is illustrated in Table 11.1.

Beyond the relationships with state higher education boards, most public governing boards must maintain extensive relationships with many other state agencies and offices: executive branch fiscal agencies, state attorneys general, facilities commissions and public works departments, state personnel departments, economic development commissions, legislative committees and research staffs, and so on.

Relationships with state governments are also heavily influ-

Table 11.1. Patterns of Campus Governance.

Consolidated Governing Boards		Coordinating Boards						Planning Agencies (i)		
		Regulatory Coordinating Boards (f) Patterns of Campus Governance			Advisory Coordinating Boards (g) Patterns of Campus Governance			Patterns of Campus Governance		
Board for All Public Institutions	Separate Board for All Senior Institutions. Separate Agency for Community Colleges	Multi-campus or Segmental Systems	Mixed Single Institutional Boards and Multi-campus or Segmental System	Primarily Single Institutional Boards	Multi-campus or Segmental Systems	Mixed Single Institutional Boards and Multi-campus or Segmental System	Primarily Single Institutional Boards	Multi-campus or Segmental Systems	Mixed Single Institutional Boards and Multi-campus or Segmental System	Primarily Single Institutional Boards
Alaska (b) Georgia Hawaii Idaho (a) Maine Mass. (D) Montana (a) Nevada	Arizona Florida (a, b) Iowa Kansas Mississippi New Hampshire (b)	Connecticut Florida (a) Illinois	Alabama Arkansas Colorado (d) Maryland New Jersey Oklahoma S. Carolina Texas	Ohio (I)	Alaska (b) California Connecticut Louisiana Minnesota Nebraska New York (h, A) Oregon	Indiana Mass. Missouri New Mexico Pennsylvania	Kentucky (I) Virginia (I) Washington (I)	District of Columbia	Delaware Vermont	Michigan

North Dakota	North Carolina (D)
Rhode Island	Oregon (b)
South Dakota	West Virginia (j)
Utah (D)	Wisconsin
Puerto Rico	(e)
	Wyoming

(b, e)
Tennessee

Notes: (a) States with agency responsible for all education levels.

(b) Alaska, Florida, Oregon and New Hampshire have coordinating agencies in addition to a consolidated governing board.

(c) Maine Maritime Academy and vocational-technical institutions are under separate boards.

(d) Colorado Commission recommends to legislature the relative proportions to be appropriated to each institution.

(e) Office of Educational Policy & Planning is in governor's office and is not a separate board.

(f) Regulatory boards produce a consolidated budget for all institutions or an aggregated budget.

(g) Advisory boards review and make recommendations to the governor and legislature on separate institutional budgets.

(h) New York Board of Regents does not have budget authority.

(i) Planning agencies have neither program nor budget authority.

(j) West Virginia has two multi-campus boards, the University of West Virginia System and the State College System, that together coordinate the public system.

Institutional Boards: (I) Each public institution has an independent, autonomous board.

(A) Each institution under the jurisdiction of the multi-campus system has a board with limited advisory authority.

(D) Each institution under the jurisdiction of the multi-campus system has a board with authority delegated by the system board.

Source: Reprinted from McGuinness and Paulson, 1991, p. 9. Used by permission.

enced by legal provisions defining the degree to which public colleges and universities are autonomous or exempt from state laws applicable to general state agencies. In many cases, differences in autonomy or exemption reflect different institutional origins. State universities that evolved from normal schools, for example, are often closely tied to state personnel and budgetary systems. Examples include the California State University System, the New Jersey State Colleges, and the State University System of Pennsylvania. Many older state universities were formed as publicly chartered private corporations, with a degree of autonomy from state procedural controls. Examples include Pennsylvania State University, Rutgers University, and the University of Maine System. Constitutional autonomy, most clearly illustrated by the legal status of Michigan's public four-year colleges and universities, provides for an even stronger insulation of public governing boards from the actions of executive and legislative branches of the state government.

Beyond formal legal constitutional or statutory provisions, the relationships between public institutions and state governments are most often shaped by subtle cultures and traditions developed over many years. In some states, acrimonious relationships are the tradition, while in others, the relationships are characterized over many years (including difficult economic times) by mutual respect (Newman, 1987).

The public board's external relations are most often on behalf of several institutions, if not a system. Several state agencies are usually involved besides the governor and state legislature. And the board often plays a dual role as the governing board for several institutions and as the coordinating body for a system of public institutions or the state's higher education enterprise as a whole. A key challenge facing a public board, then, is that it must serve the interests and priorities of both the state and the academy.

Principles of Effective Board Relationships

Common sense, conscientious board performance, and open communication are the key ingredients of a successful relationship with government agencies and political leaders. Three principles should guide boards, despite great variations among them:

Both Institutional and Governmental Priorities and Perspectives Are Important and Legitimate

Some people argue that institutional autonomy is intrinsically good and state involvement intrinsically bad. A more constructive conception is that, depending on the issue, both perspectives are important and legitimate. Strong colleges and universities should have a high degree of autonomy in certain matters and should, ideally, operate in a highly decentralized system of governance. At the same time, the state, and the board and agencies that represent the state, has an obligation to ensure that certain societal and system needs are addressed that transcend the needs and perspectives of the single campus. Campus leaders often do not recognize that the state or system provides positive external leverage for internal campus priorities by checking mission drift through the program approval process and by providing budgetary and other incentives for innovation and resource reallocation.

Newman (1987, p. xiii) notes that "the real need is not simply for more autonomy but for a relationship between the university and the state that is constructive for both, built up over a long period of time by careful attention on the part of all parties." In other words, just as the state should value institutional autonomy so also should higher education boards be concerned with the needs and perspectives of state government—the system needs.

One of the best ways a public board can guard institutional autonomy is by giving conscious, ongoing attention to accountability. The board should provide clear information to the public about the institution's performance in relation to its mission, its use of public resources, and its contributions to important public priorities. The board should also work at building trusting relationships and sustaining a climate of openness and respect for different perspectives. In these ways, a governing board can lay the foundation for the resolution of serious conflicts between state and institutional priorities that will inevitably arise from time to time.

Advocacy for Higher Education Should Be
Tempered by Sensitivity to the State's
Other Priorities and Economic Condition

Some people argue that the primary responsibility of the public board is to advocate the interests and needs of the institution or institutions it governs, placing secondary priority on the needs, concerns, and economic conditions of the broader society and state government. Most public boards, especially those of consolidated and multicampus systems, play a dual role of being both institutional governing boards and system (and in some cases, statewide) coordinating boards. The board's governing responsibilities include defending essential values of the academy (especially in the face of inappropriate ideological, political, or bureaucratic intrusion); advocating for educational values, needs, and priorities; and seeking the public resources necessary to carry out the institutional missions. At the same time, public boards have a special responsibility, far more pronounced than that of their private counterparts, to be sensitive to and, at times, to defend and advocate for viewpoints of the broader society and the state government. Balancing these roles is a difficult challenge.

Many higher education systems were created by state governments to address essentially political and economic concerns, that is, to achieve greater coordination, eliminate duplication, and ensure a more rational distribution of resources among competing higher education interests—especially between regions. Governors and state legislators expect system boards to carry out basic functions of coordination: systemwide policy leadership and planning, budget recommendations consolidating the needs of all campuses within a systemwide framework, program review and approval, and regulatory and accountability functions carried out on behalf of state government.

One of the most important roles of a public governing board is to articulate a vision that connects the interests of the academy with the broader public interest. The board has a special obligation to coordinate the demands of society with the perspectives of the academy. As described by Robert Berdahl (1971, p. 15), the public board must serve as a "suitably sensitive mechanism" for transmitting the state's wishes to higher education and higher education's needs to the state.

Of course, positive ties between the state and higher education are far easier to sustain in good than in difficult economic times. When the state government must make severe cuts in higher education funding, the board must balance a sensitivity to the state's economic conditions with its obligation to articulate higher education needs and the potential long-term educational consequences to the state if these needs are not met. It is not uncommon for a public board to face these questions: Should the board stand on principle and defend to the end the needs of the higher education system, even if doing so is unrealistic because of state economic conditions? Or should the board capitulate to political and economic pressures and accept budget cuts that may be devastating for higher education? If a governing board builds open, trusting relationships, these relationships will serve it well in times of stress. Also, a deliberate effort to project the future economic position of the state and to see public higher education as integral to that future can assist a board in attuning its internal aspirations and priorities to external realities. In all but the most extreme situations, confrontations should be avoided.

Board Performance and Leadership Are Keys to Effective Relations Between Public Higher Education and State Government

It is a serious misconception that board performance, both of individual members and of the board as a whole, is a private, internal matter unrelated to the board's external relations. In fact, a board may do more to lead both internal and external constituencies through the values exhibited by individual and group behavior than by its formal policy actions.

Inappropriate political intrusion into a board's affairs can almost always be traced to actual or perceived poor performance by the board, such as inept handling of a presidential search; insensitivity to, or even violation of, open meeting laws; failure to ensure proper accountability for expenditure of public funds; public perceptions of arrogance and insensitivity to state economic conditions; and blatant use of the board for partisan political purposes or to advance a member's political aspirations. Intervention by governors and state legislators in such matters may be inappropriate, but it can be openly invited and encouraged by the governing board's own actions. A public governing board must keep foremost in mind that, in a very visible way, it is modeling the values and interpersonal behavior that it believes should characterize actions on the campus and interactions between higher education and the broader society.

Board Actions for Effective Relationships

The following questions are relevant to external relationships of a public board. A public governing board should address these questions in periodic reviews of its own performance.

Does the Board Have a Concise Mission Statement for the Institution It Governs or for the System and Each of the Campuses?

Mission statements can make clear to both internal and external constituencies that an enterprise is focused, understands its aspirations and limits, and is sensitive to both higher education and public priorities. To be useful in external relationships, a mission statement should have several characteristics. It should be concise— perhaps no more than a brief paragraph. It should be crafted to have meaning for the general public and the academic community. Although it should be subject to extensive review and comment prior to being adopted, it should be the board's statement and not necessarily the consensus of all the constituencies who are consulted. The mission statement should convey both what will be done as well as what will not be done. Statements that imply no sense of limitations or give the impression that the institution intends to be "everything to everybody" have little credibility.

System boards often concentrate on institutional mission statements but fail to give attention to the system's mission. This focus can lead to too much emphasis on matters of internal institutional governance and neglect of system policy leadership, coordination, and relations with external constituencies. The general public and even state legislators grasp far more quickly what an institution should be doing than what a system should be doing.

A good system mission statement, in addition to the points mentioned above, should reflect two distinct but complementary roles. First, the statement should make clear the system's role in developing and sustaining each of the institutions according to its unique mission. Mission statements that blur distinctions among constituent units and between institutions and the system can undermine the system's diversity and make delegation ambiguous. Systems can also focus excessively on perceived system imperatives (coordination, eliminating unnecessary duplication, achieving the benefits of economies of scale) while failing to give appropriate attention to how the system can stimulate and support the creativity, innovation, and productivity of each campus.

Second, a good system mission statement should articulate the unique roles of the system. How does the system contribute to the whole being more than the sum of its parts? By expanding student opportunities to move throughout the system? By promoting coordination and sharing of resources? By making services available more effectively and efficiently than would be possible if each institution were separately governed? Above all, how will the system carry out the critical yet potentially contradictory roles of advocating for the needs of colleges and universities, serving as buffer for the system and its constituent units against inappropriate external intrusion, and building constructive relationships between higher education and the broader society?

Does the Board Have a Clearly Stated Vision of How the Institution or the System Contributes in Concrete, Measurable Ways to Major Public Priorities?

Some public priorities for higher education include raising the educational attainment of the population, increasing minority participation and achievement, and contributing to job creation and economic development. There is certainly no single way for an institution or system to contribute to these goals. Boards may use planning documents, a statement of goals and objectives, or other vehicles to state how the institution or system will contribute. Or they may urge their administrators and faculty members to respond creatively to specific social and other problems of concern to the general public and elected political leaders. Mobilizing the talents and energies of the university to address carefully selected public policy issues can go a long way toward building public confidence in the institution or system.

The statement or action, and the process by which it is developed and renewed, should be highly visible to both internal and external constituencies. The aim is to create both the reality and perception of focus, action, responsiveness, and progress, expressed in ways that are understandable to the general public and political leaders. Extensive planning documents worded in obscure academic jargon and reams of data, all produced in the name of accountability, will do little to build public confidence in the institution or system. They will do even less to give a sense of direction, excitement, and progress to the institution or the system.

Does the Board Consciously Seek to Support and Build Constructive Relations with the State Higher Education Board?

As explained earlier, most states have some form of statewide coordinating agency. In some cases, this body and the public governing board are one and the same. In half the states, however, public governing boards relate to a state board that has planning, budgetary, and regulatory responsibilities but no authority to govern institutions.

A degree of tension between governing boards and coordinating boards is common. To an extent, this is a natural consequence of differences in perspective between institutional and state priorities, as suggested earlier. What governing boards occasionally fail to recognize is that they share responsibility for statewide coordination and for building constructive relationships between institutions and the coordinating structure. In fact, one of the strongest forces leading to increased centralized authority for coordinating boards is the reaction of state political leaders to the perceived infighting and parochial behavior of institutional governing boards, presidents, and higher education lobbyists. The following are some of the questions that governing boards should ask about relations with coordinating bodies:

- When reports or recommendations are forwarded to the coordinating board, has the governing board fully exercised its own authority and responsibility? Or is it just passing the difficult choices on to the next level, thereby relinquishing its governing authority? For example, if a multicampus system board fails to exercise its responsibility to scrutinize a proposal for a new high-cost graduate program that will clearly duplicate a program on one of its other campuses, it will force the coordinating board to assume that responsibility.

- Does the governing board make conscious use of data and reports submitted by the institutions to the coordinating board? For example, many states now require institutions to report information on student achievement and retention or on periodic review of academic programs to the state coordinating agency. The governing board may be failing to assume its own responsibility to evaluate the effectiveness of the institutions under its jurisdiction if it gives these reports only perfunctory attention.

- Does the governing board consciously support efforts of the coordinating board to resolve differences among institutions and sectors within the higher education community? Or does the board allow or encourage political "end runs" to the governor and legislature whenever an institution or the system perceives that its self-interest is not being served by a coordinated process? While end runs may result in short-term gains, especially in good economic times, they invariably lead to long-lasting antagonisms, lost confidence in higher education, and stronger coordinating mechanisms.

Does the Governing Board Inform Political Leaders About Institutional and System Developments That Affect Their Constituents or That Will Receive Media Attention?

The board should inform political leaders about actual or potential problems or crises and good news. Consistent efforts to brief key leaders so that they are fully prepared to respond to inquiries from the media and constituents can build support and trust. However, there is an important distinction between efforts to keep political leaders informed and efforts to draw them into the decision-making process that is uniquely the board's prerogative. The aim is to avoid the surprise, if not the anger or embarrassment, that can motivate political leaders to intervene directly in an effort to solve the problems themselves.

Does the Board Exhibit Values That Characterize Exemplary Public Bodies in All Its Actions?

As suggested earlier, good external relations are inextricably tied to good board performance (and the performance of individual board members). A board will earn respect and influence among state political leaders to the extent that it shows respect for diversity and exhibits openness, fairness, and objectivity in its deliberations. Above all, an effective governing board must function as a group, not merely a collection of individual members each pursuing his or her separate interest. These points should all be addressed in the board's periodic evaluation process.

Ambiguities about who speaks for the board and how board positions are developed and expressed to state government can be sources of serious problems. Does the board have clear policies and procedures on communications with state government? How are positions developed? Who speaks for the board? Are the roles of the board chair and the system or institutional chief executive clear? What are the board's expectations about how individual board members are to communicate with key political leaders? Is there a clear understanding of board ethics, especially in terms of members' use of the board for their own political interests?

The issues discussed in this chapter are only some of those that will arise as public boards address the challenges of the 1990s. Policy leadership that draws together the priorities of the academy and those of the broader society in a constructive relationship will continue to be one of the most important functions of a public board.

CHAPTER 12

Maintaining
Sound Relations
with System Campuses

Robert L. Carothers

Service as a governing board member for any one of the nation's 120 multicampus systems is among the most challenging assignments any of us can accept. Today, more than half of all students enrolled in higher education institutions in the United States attend a college or university that is part of one of these public systems. Some of the systems, such as the California State University System or the State University of New York, enroll over 350,000 students each year. The ratio of students to trustees in these systems is immense, on the average about 10,000 to 1. Obviously, trustee responsibility in such a system must be understood differently from service on the board of a liberal arts college enrolling 1,500 students. But service on these system boards differs substantially even from service on the board of a single large land-grant university. This chapter examines some of these differences and discusses how members of system governing boards can best serve their many constituents.

The multicampus systems in the United States and their governing and executive structures vary significantly. They range in size from 365,000 students at the sixty-two campuses of the SUNY system in 1988 to several systems with two or three campuses and enrollment of less than 30,000. They vary in mission from segmental, like the Minnesota Community College System, to comprehensive, like the University of Wisconsin System, which includes nearly all public institutions of higher education in the state.

Each system has a chief executive officer, whose title may be chancellor (most common for multi-institutional systems), president (most common for multicampus, single-institution systems), commissioner (usually a governor's appointee), or executive director (more common for coordinating boards than for governing boards). For the purposes of this chapter, however, I shall refer to the system chief executive as the chancellor and the campus chief executive as the president. The authority of the system CEO varies greatly, depending on whether the board—and the culture of the system—sees the CEO as the chief line officer of the system or as the chief of staff to the board itself. The role of the system CEO in relationship to the campus CEOs also varies a great deal, ranging from that of convener of the system's campus CEOs to that of supervisor, with authority to appoint and evaluate campus chief executives.

The appointment and tenure of system board members follow different procedures in different systems. Most system board members are appointed by the governor of the state, although in several states, the members are elected either directly by the voters or by the state legislature. Board members may include the governor and other constitutional officers, the superintendent of public instruction, key members of the legislature, or alumni of one or more institutions, each designated by either the state constitution or statute. Other members may represent geographical regions or be appointed at-large. Terms vary from two to eight years, and reappointment may or may not be permitted. The chair may be elected from among the board members or specifically appointed by the governor. The system board may be the only board that relates to the campuses, or there may also be campus-level boards, with varying responsibilities.

But despite all these differences (and more), the higher education systems have a great deal in common, and their boards face many similar problems and opportunities. Members of these boards have many constituents—ranging from the governor who appointed them to the state legislature that funds their system, from faculty members to students, from parents to alumni. And constituent groups may be segmented by college or university within the system. Therefore, the most basic challenge of these boards is to develop and oversee policy that is clear and fair. In multicampus or multiuniversity systems, boards must convey a sense of balance, equity, and fairness, consistent with well-defined system and institutional missions, goals, and objectives. Maintaining that sense of balance, equity, and fairness is essential to building a positive and productive relationship between the system board and its constituent universities or campuses.

Knowing the Facts and the Players

In multicampus systems, a major problem for the governing board is acquiring sufficient, relevant knowledge of the many programs and people in the system in order to be equipped to make informed and intelligent decisions. Since individual campuses are continually evolving, staying knowledgeable will be a great challenge for board members. Thus the orientation and development of board members is extremely important. Beyond a clear understanding of their role as policymakers and trustees of the common good, new board members must quickly grasp the organization of the system and its member institutions, particularly the complex relationships among the board, the system office and its officers, and campus executives and their vice presidents and deans.

The number of people seeking the board member's attention, all with their own agendas, may be immense. Local constituent groups from each institution within the system—faculty members, student government, unions, alumni, and foundations—will want to assure themselves that the board member understands and appreciates their role in the life of the campus or university. Special-interest groups, ranging from athletic booster clubs to gay and lesbian caucuses to chambers of commerce, will want to see where each board member stands on sundry matters near and dear to their hearts. How these various groups are received and heard the first few months after a board member's appointment may well determine effectiveness throughout that board member's tenure.

It is in everyone's best interest to begin an orientation of board members quickly, and board members themselves should demand to see the "syllabus" for the orientation program. The orientation should respect the trustees' time constraints and be available at their convenience. But an investment of time early in a trustee's term of office may help avoid long and painful sessions later. Elsewhere in this book, orientation of board members is discussed in detail. I will focus here on matters most relevant to service on system boards.

Board members should approach the orientation process with three fundamental questions in mind:

1. What is the mission of the system as a whole, and what is the mission of each institution within the system?
2. Who is responsible for fulfilling those missions, and what are their basic strategies (sometimes—but not always—found in long-range or strategic plans) for achieving success?
3. What are the principles under which resources are allocated within the system and on the campus, and to what extent are the allocations consistent with the respective missions?

The orientation process should attempt to address these questions, although it is unlikely that clear answers will immediately emerge. Particularly in a system, board members are most likely to discover that opinion varies with regard to these questions, depending upon the perspective of those questioned. But rather than seeing ambiguity as a problem, new board members should see variance of opinion as fundamental to the challenge that lies before them. Indeed, working toward answers to these questions and creating within that effort a sense of balance, equity, and fairness are what service on a system board is all about. It is important, then, that board members listen carefully and respectfully to constituents to begin the process of seeking balance.

The chancellor should have basic responsibility for the orientation of new trustees. But the chair of the board may be the logical person with whom to begin discussions, first, to gain some sense of history and, second, to understand "hot" issues, which, when encountered without warning, might distort the larger picture. The chancellor should provide articulate responses to the three basic questions—such matters of policy are his or her chief concern. But those answers should be considered in the context of the chancellor's role and sphere of interest. System academic and finance officers should be able to refine those answers even further. Board members will want to require from the officers a more detailed explanation of processes, particularly with regard to program approval and the allocation of funds to campuses—matters likely to come up as the orientation proceeds.

The next step in the orientation is meeting the university or college presidents and learning how the world looks from their perspective. Since it is unlikely that any one board member will have the time to learn about every campus during the first few months of service, it is probably best for a new board member to pick one institution for a relatively close look, seeking to identify the generic issues from the prevailing point of view on that campus. If the member lives in a region served by a particular institution and is associated in some way with that school, it may be wise for the member to spend time on a campus elsewhere in the state. The board chair and the chancellor can help guide the member in selecting a campus, and the chancellor should make the practical arrangements for a first campus visit and for introducing the board member to the campus president. It is often helpful to have a knowledgeable staff member from the system office accompany the board member on this first visit, although once on campus the staff member should fade into the background.

The board member should also seek answers from the campus presidents and the various campus constituents to the same fundamental questions presented earlier. Presidents, deans, and faculty members are proud of their institutions and of their students, and it is only natural that they will want to show the board member their accomplishments. But although it is important to honor this pride of achievement, campus visits must be more than show-and-tell exercises. The board member must have the opportunity to question the campus leaders about issues important to the future of the institution and the system. Some private time with the campus president is important, not just for the education of the board member but also for the president to listen to the board member's perceptions and priorities. Board members are very significant in the life of college and university presidents, and it is important that presidents and board members come to know and understand each other as well as possible.

As time permits, the board should visit each campus in the system. Despite similarities, each campus is unique, each president and faculty member different, and each curriculum special. Every community also has different assets and problems. Visiting each campus may be difficult in large systems such as SUNY or the California State University System or where campuses are spread over very great distances such as in the University of Alaska System or the University of Missouri System. But with balance, equity, and fairness as the goals, board members should make every effort to learn about each institution and its people.

Several simple, relatively efficient strategies can help board members build their knowledge base about campuses. First, they can ask the chancellor and the campus president to prepare a summary description of the campus (no more than three pages) that identifies the five greatest assets that the institution can build upon for the future, as well as the five greatest challenges it will face. Second, they can ask for summaries of the most recent regional accreditation report. In these reports, the recommendations of the visiting team are particularly important. Third, board members can seek and accept invitations to systemwide meetings and conferences, especially those which bring together faculty members or students from the various campuses around some common concern or interest (for example, meetings of student government officers, minority faculty and staff members, financial aid officers, or alumni). Fourth, whenever possible, meetings of the board and its committees should be scheduled on the different campuses, allowing the board members to get orientations to the campuses as well as allowing the constituents on those campuses the opportunity to meet board members and see how their work is accomplished. At each step in this orientation process, the board members should seek further clarification of the fundamental issues—mission, strategy, and resources—to begin to develop the kind of leadership that will allow them to serve the system and the public and earn the respect of the campus communities.

Governing the Far-Flung Empire

The role of any higher education governing board is to set policy for an organization that is both complex and contentious. In a multicampus system, the board's responsibility to set policy is complicated by the diversity of history, character, and aspirations among the member universities or campuses. To meet the needs of all these institutions, the board must achieve a working balance between institutional autonomy and system coordination.

This balance is the single most important factor in improving relationships among the board, the system officers, and the various campus constituents. Most of the criticism of systems of higher education results from a lack of such balance, and much of the frustration system board members experience comes from not understanding the dynamics that make this balance so critical. A brief look at the roots of the problem may make the problem clearer.

Systems of universities or colleges are relatively new, especially in the context of the traditions and history of the university. Systems are political creatures, designed to assist governors and legislatures in implementing public policy at public institutions. System boards set operating policy and seek to ensure that this policy is implemented in a way that uses public resources—tax dollars—effectively and efficiently at the various institutions. The assumption behind these actions is that the universities that make up the system exist as instruments of public purpose, which will be revised by the state from time to time.

Universities, on the other hand, seek to set their own agendas, consistent with abstract principles involving the search for truth and "the good"—whether that truth be philosophical or scientific, and whether that good be aesthetic, social, or political. Over the centuries, universities have been moderately successful in preventing narrow social or political causes from overwhelming this fundamental mission, and the term *academic freedom* has come to stand for a frame of mind that resists intrusion from the outside. Even within the university, faculty members tend to have loyalty first to their disciplines—methodologies for seeking the truth—and to their departments and only then to the college or university itself. Given this hierarchy of commitment, board members should not expect faculty members, students, or alumni to be ready to sacrifice their immediate interests for the system.

The system board plays a central role in reconciling the tensions between public purpose and academic freedom. It is, of course, the board that translates the demands of government into policies that honor the traditions of the academy and respect the rights of faculty members and students. And it is the board that translates for government the values and purposes of the universities, enabling the public to see current controversies in the context of the larger commitment to free inquiry and free speech—without which an academic institution has no meaning or validity. But the universities are apt to see the board itself as government—the philistine force at the temple gates. Therefore, the board must walk a narrow line if it is to accomplish public purposes in such a way as to honor and preserve the nearly sacred principles of academic freedom and institutional autonomy.

This tension is at play everywhere, but nowhere more clearly than in the relationship between the system chancellor and the campus president. The board, of course, wants each to be a strong leader, respected on the campus and around the state for his or her vision and management skills. However, since the chancellor and campus president are likely to have well-developed egos (otherwise, they could not be in the positions), the potential for conflict is significant—as many former presidents and chancellors around the country can attest.

The board can do several things to help make this difficult relationship work. First, as much as possible, the board, particularly the board chair, should develop broad working definitions of the respective roles of the chancellor and the presidents. For example, it is helpful simply to affirm, often and in public, that neither the board nor the chancellor intends to manage the individual colleges or universities from the central office. The board members should say that they respect the principles of institutional autonomy. And the board should act in ways that reflect that respect, allowing the presidents as much room as possible to set their own agendas within the broad policy goals established by the board. On the other hand, board members should expect the chancellor to lead in developing and articulating these broad policy goals. And they should make it clear to the presidents and to various external constituents that it is the chancellor who speaks for the system.

Second, the board should view the chancellor and the presidents as a team; all of them are officers of the system with responsibility for the good of the system as a whole. The board needs to encourage a collaborative style, making clear that in most matters it expects the chancellor and the presidents to achieve consensus.

Academic institutions in general have a strong tradition of collegiality. People on the campuses have far greater expectations regarding consultation than do board members who work in the business world. Campus presidents, pressed on every side for decisions, may complain about all the "process" on their campuses, particularly where collective bargaining agreements have codified much of the process. Nonetheless, as products of the academic culture, they are zealous about assuring appropriate consultation on matters to be resolved at the system level. The board should expect that matters that the chancellor brings before the board have been fully discussed with the presidents.

At the same time, the chancellor, while recognizing that the presidents must represent their institutions in the development of system policy, also has a right to expect that each president will act in ways that are respectful of other institutions in the system and that promote the general good. The board can reinforce that perspective.

The board should also establish procedures for resolving disagreements between the chancellor and the presidents. An effective chair can usually act as the mediator in these disagreements. It is inevitable that in matters such as resource allocation, for example, a given president and the chancellor will sometimes be at odds. But the board should make clear that it expects disagreements to be brought to the board in an open and candid way. The chancellor will not be effective if end runs by presidents to individual board members or, worse, local legislators are permitted.

A balancing of local and system agendas is required in many circumstances. For example, the system leaders, subject to pressure from the governor or the legislature, may see completion of mandated studies and reports as very high priorities. Campus leaders, wrestling with the operational problems of the day, may regard the studies as bureaucratic impositions that divert time and energy from the fundamental work of the university. Where faculty members are organized for collective bargaining on a system level (increasingly the case), the system's need for consistency in contract implementation will often be at odds with the university's desire to solve its disputes in the way local circumstances seem to dictate. A campus dean may feel that he or she cannot be creative in solving personnel problems because of policy concerns in the central office that seem abstract or unimportant. Similarly, administrative vice presidents, who are under daily pressure to fix leaking roofs or create additional parking, may resent system budget priorities based on such broad public policy goals as increasing the number of women in science and mathematics programs.

The board needs to hear and recognize the perspectives of people in the system and in the individual universities. It should think carefully about what work it wants its officers to do and how it wants them to spend their time. Although there is a very legitimate need for analysis and review of the programs and expenditures of both the system and its institutions, universities do not exist for institutional research and self-study. Complying with collective bargaining agreements is important, but contracts should be negotiated that provide for good local management and creative solutions to problems. The board and the chancellor have a responsibility to plan for the future and to design strategies to meet complex social challenges. But these strategies are not likely to be effective if the basic infrastructure of the institutions is neglected. Again, balance is critical.

One final note of caution. If the board is to play this very important role of balancing the needs of the system and the campuses, its integrity, impartiality, and credibility must be maintained. Board members should resist the temptation to become advocates for individual colleges or universities at the expense of others, particularly if they happen to live in one of the communities where a university is located. Similarly, they should avoid private dealings with presidents, unions, or special-interest groups. And they must be certain that they have no conflicts of interest, whether real or perceived, in matters before them. The chair of the board should vigorously protect the board and the system against breaches of such a standard. If the challenge before system boards is the creation of a sense of balance, fairness, and equity, that challenge can only be met if the board itself has the respect of the entire system.

Acting as Champion and Advocate

Although multi-institutional governing boards were created to manage and coordinate rapidly increasing state and federal expenditures for education, system governing boards also retain the board's traditional role as champion and advocate for the member institutions of the system. Indeed, it can be argued that the ability to make the case on behalf of higher education from a statewide perspective and the power boards have to insulate institutions from direct political control are strengths of the system board.

Playing the roles of champion and advocate well enables the board to develop credibility on the campuses. This credibility becomes immensely important when the board must make difficult decisions. In an economic climate where governors and legislators are struggling to balance budgets and yet meet the needs of many supplicants, it should not be surprising that higher education, a major budget item in nearly every state in the union, is subject to political maneuvering of all kinds. It is important to the board and to the campuses that board members navigate the political seas with skill and style. They must listen carefully to the ideas and concerns of state officials, while at the same time safeguarding their own authority to make the decisions that govern the universities. If the institutions in the system come to believe that the board is unable to defend their legitimate interests or if they see the board only as a surrogate for more powerful political interests in the state, system relationships will deteriorate rapidly.

Political realities make the establishment of clear missions, goals, and objectives by systems and institutions all the more important. System boards should make their mission statements memorable, avoiding the kind of vague and general jargon under which nearly anyone can do anything. The boundaries of appropriate activities should be drawn as explicitly as possible. And the mission statements should be displayed and repeated frequently. Proposals for new ventures, as well as the maintenance of existing activities, should be tested against mission statements that are well known and accepted by all parties. In this way, the board can be prepared to react to a variety of pressures and criticisms, whether from regional legislators seeking a new medical school or the governor who faces revenue shortfalls and wants to close a campus. The system mission statement is also a necessary part of explaining to a given university why some grand venture it envisions for itself cannot be supported or why it must reorder its priorities to accomplish some statewide initiative.

The relationship between system boards and legislatures is complex. Typically, the legislature appropriates half or more of the resources a public system relies on and expects the system and its institutions to be accountable to it for the kind and level of services provided to students and the public. Because they control the funds, legislators may feel that they can set policy for the system. In a practical sense, of course, resources can drive policy, and the board must work with the legislature and yet stand apart, protecting its role as the policy-setting body for the system.

In most instances, cooperation and collaboration between the board and the legislators are better strategies than confrontation. The chancellor and the board chair have a particular responsibility to interact with the leadership of the legislature. They must articulate the system's mission and needs and listen carefully to the aspirations and concerns of the legislature. To the greatest extent possible, the board should seek to build a consensus with the legislature on the agenda established by the board. To do so will give the board credibility with the legislature when it is called upon to explain and defend policies ranging from tuition to course credit transfer and from allocations to athletics.

In several states, higher education coordinating boards have a significant influence on higher education policy. Like the legislature, these boards may have agendas that can be at odds with those established by the system governing board. The state may also have other system or institutional boards. Minnesota, for example, has four distinct system boards—the University of Minnesota Board of Regents, the Minnesota State University System Board of Directors, the Minnesota Community College Board of Directors, and the Minnesota Technical College Board of Directors—as well as a higher education coordinating board. The Minnesota Private College Council, which represents the state's private colleges before the legislature, plays an equivalent role to the system boards' in the development of public policy. Interacting and negotiating with other boards and their leaders can be immensely time consuming and frustrating, but protecting the prerogatives of the system board and the interests of the member institutions will lead to success in dealing with its constituent campuses.

The board can serve its member institutions well by establishing broad alliances with key actors at the state level. Coalitions of business organizations; statewide labor councils; large foundations; professional associations of teachers, school administrators, or school boards; associations that serve ethnic or racial minorities; and other groups may prefer to work with a state association of universities and colleges toward common goals. Joint efforts to raise funds for scholarships for minority students, to effect changes in pension law that benefit faculty members, or to highlight such broad concerns as the level of achievement in foreign languages can be very successful and will allow the institutions in the system to see the board working actively in the interests of its institutions.

Recognizing Excellence

Although the system board is rarely involved in the day-to-day operation of its constituent institutions, it can play an important role in recognizing the achievement of stated goals and objectives. Appropriate strategies to identify and reward success can make concrete what may often seem to the universities and their constituent groups to be the distant and abstract vision of the board.

The board must recruit and retain the very best people for executive management positions. Selecting chancellors and presidents may be the most important work that a governing board does. Equally important, however, is encouraging and reinforcing these leaders when they are successful in achieving goals the board has set.

Often, this encouragement simply involves saying, both in

private and in public, that the president is doing well. Attention to the achievements of a particular institution and its president may seem too basic to mention here, but system boards, focused on the big picture, may neglect to notice success in an individual institution. Positive comments will be taken to heart by the president and by the entire university community as signs of what is really valued by the board. Board members' acknowledgments are very important to presidents. Presidents should not have to guess what the board feels about their work or rely on formal evaluations to find out.

Recognizing excellence also means working to secure adequate compensation for all members of the university community. Among the most sensitive matters that confront the board are the salary and benefits it grants to presidents. Although most presidents are still compensated at levels far below individuals with similar responsibilities in the private sector, there is great public scrutiny of presidents' compensation packages. Some presidents have lost their credibility, if not their jobs, over expenditures made for the president's residence, deferred compensation agreements, or similar matters. The board must make clear to presidents the exact terms of their compensation, but it must also step forward and defend the terms of any compensation package to which it has agreed, especially when that agreement is criticized by the public.

A number of boards around the country have developed programs that recognize the scholarly achievement of faculty members, usually through awards or the establishment of special chairs. But boards can also recognize the accomplishment of the faculty and staff members of the system institutions by working for competitive compensation packages. This task has become more difficult as collective bargaining has gained ground in higher education systems and as both boards and executive officers have assumed responsibility for bargaining collectively with their employees.

Some board members may fear that statements made in support of better compensation may return to haunt them across the bargaining table. But the limits of salary and benefits settlements are largely established by the revenue available to the system, some 75 to 80 percent of which will usually go for compensation to employees. In an age when both labor and management have access to the same data, both parties know what can be agreed to. Little is lost and much is gained by the board's advocacy of appropriate compensation.

Above all, system boards need to find ways to recognize and highlight the achievement of students. It is a painful reality that members of system boards will come to know only a tiny percentage of the students enrolled at the institutions they govern, most often those who take on leadership roles in student government. Yet if system boards want to signal to the campuses that students are the top priority of the system, they need to develop strategies to find examples of student achievement and to recognize and reward them.

One way to recognize the achievements of students is to schedule student presentations before the board, presentations that highlight student artists, for example, or students working on public service initiatives. On campus visits, board members should ask to meet with students, not just to listen to their concerns but also to allow students and their faculty mentors to show off their best efforts. System publications should also feature student work, and board presentations before the legislature or congress should include students (who, in any event, are often the best lobbyists). The board should watch carefully to determine that student input is a part of any recommendation brought before the board by the chancellor or others. This action signals that it expects everyone to listen to the views of the primary object of higher education: the students.

Once again, the key to the board's relationships with all its constituents is its commitment to balance, equity, and fairness, consistent with well-defined and frequently articulated missions, goals, and objectives. If it can lead in this way, the board can create a system that as a whole is greater than the sum of its parts—a good definition of a happy and productive family.

CHAPTER 13

Responding to Political, Social, and Ethical Issues

Paul N. Ylvisaker

It has become a truism to start each decade with a declaration of impending change. But even if a truism, the statement still has to be repeated: each decade of this century has seen the pace of change speeding up. And trustees of colleges and universities will find in the 1990s another dizzying rearrangement of the social and institutional landscape, already nearly unrecognizable.

The most problematic aspects of this change are the causes and consequences of increasing diversity, the onrush of pluralism in every aspect of life and quadrant of the globe. Spirits and voices so long held quiescent by traditional constraints have shaken loose and been given expression and power by today's electronic and photonic magnifications of the printing press. Both globally and locally, the haunting question is whether the center can hold, whether any known or putative form of governance can contain, let alone harness, the centrifugal genie that modernization has freed from the bottle.

One can therefore expect leadership and decision making to become ever more precarious and diffuse. The law of negotiated consent within a constantly differentiating constituency fastens itself with titanic force to all social institutions, especially to the academy, where it has so long held sway. A second and possibly

226

countervailing force will also gain strength during the coming decade: the dwindling of resources and the cost-price squeeze. Higher education has become a big and expensive enterprise, with essential outlays needed for physical plant, staff salaries, complicated student needs, and regulatory requirements. Fiscal constraints could invite more decisive leadership; but leadership could also shatter against the call for pluralism and negotiated consent.

Both these contending forces will be intensified in the 1990s. Pluralism will intensify through the swirling mix of cultures, religions, and divergent interests, now global in their reach. It will intensify through demographic shifts within our own and the world's population that will steadily diversify applicant pools, faculties, and student bodies, and through the erosion by advancing technology of the insulating barriers that have traditionally kept academic and social communities as stable enclaves. Fiscal constraints will intensify as societies pay the accumulated costs of environmental damage, poverty, health deficits, and social insecurity as the agenda of the cold war shifts to regional and internal conflicts that are accentuated by struggles over diminishing resources. It is not beyond imagination to see a human race—and the academy— surviving and even flourishing in that contentious environment. But the learning curve and the art of social invention will have to move sharply upward for the continuation of progress and even for survival.

Communications technology and global migration have made all sorts of boundaries permeable and in many ways obsolescent. The boundaries of the campus are no exception. No longer a walled city, the academy is more liquid than fixed. Administrators, faculty members, and students flow outward, and electronic messages, competing values, and social violence gush inward. No longer is the academy a protected and exclusive terrain; and it becomes less so with each passing year.

So far, implosion is more evident than explosion. External forces have had more of an effect on the campus than the campus has had on the culture outside. There are exceptions: scientific and technological discoveries, such as the discovery of DNA, that have radically altered the thinking and agenda of the global community; the ingenuity of "Sesame Street"; and the pedagogical artistry of peripatetic scholars on television. But these are individual sorties rather than collective assertiveness on the part of the academy.

Governance in such a fluid environment, even establishing an identity, becomes all the more a mercurial endeavor. But that is the challenge of the 1990s and beyond. The challenge begins and ends precisely at the point of establishing an identity: a distinguishable and distinctive mission, a forceful statement of what colleges and universities are all about. Trustees bear the ultimate responsibility for ensuring that such a statement is made. The mission statement must be a declaration of the values that the institution stands for, values that must be conspicuously practiced amidst the swirling pluralism of the life surrounding the institution.

The irony of pluralism is that it simultaneously demands and resists efforts to reach consensus on values. It sheds light on our diversity yet resists the imposition of any one code. Anarchy reigns at one end of the continuum, authoritarianism at the other.

But trustees do not have to adopt either extreme. Pluralism admits of its own resolution. The resolution lies in nurturing diversity while professing and practicing one's own creed. And this is precisely what trustees and their institutions will be called upon to do in the years immediately ahead. The squeeze on resources will not allow institutions and individuals to be all things to all people; but the grounds for making choices—of general mission and particular stands—will have to be explicit and clear. This task will not be easy but it will be essential, especially as the din of conflicting voices becomes ever louder and the issues to be settled grow even murkier.

The primary thrust will have to be on campus: campus leaders, including trustees, will need to define and model the behaviors they believe are critical. But no such candle can or should be hidden under a campus barrel. Those values need also to be extended into the world beyond.

Guiding Principles

In responding to political, social, and ethical issues, trustees have three essential responsibilities. First, they must discern critical influences in the external environment. Given their growing intrusion, external factors, such as demographic shifts, economic trends, social forces, and cultural tensions, need constantly to be identified and assessed by trustees. All of these factors occupy center stage and require far more attention from trustees than the casual reading of relevant newspaper articles. Trustees need to examine these factors at periodic retreats that feature, at least in part, the scanning of the future and involve faculty members and experts skilled in such assessments.

Second, trustees need to translate an understanding of the significance of external developments into campus policy and practices. Being aware is half the battle; the rest is a matter of making certain the college or university is prepared to deal with what lies ahead. Presidents, administrators, and faculty members need to be regularly questioned as to whether they have anticipated and laid the groundwork for handling selected issues as they emerge.

Third, trustees should monitor the social, political, and ethical performance of the institution through recurrent questioning and discussion. It is one thing to profess the virtues of good citizenship, quite another to live up to those ideals. Trustees bear the ultimate responsibility for institutional performance; their own example sets the tone and the standard. Simply by raising concerns regularly and insistently, trustees can effectively discharge that responsibility.

Values to Uphold

Governing boards, together with campus leaders, should periodically take inventory of their values. What do we and the institutions we serve stand for and strive to advance? There are many possible answers, of course, but here are five to help start a conversation with other board members.

Academic Freedom

The signal contribution of any institution of learning is to ensure society access to "the independent voice," that is, to be a forum for persons given freedom and sanctuary to address problems and issues—sometimes with detachment, sometimes with passion, but always unfettered by chains of enforced conventionality. That free-dom is not simply the function of tenure, which seems often to be more the ultimate fringe benefit than the guarantee of an indepen-dent voice. It is, or should be, the value pervading the entire insti-tution and the essential contribution of that institution to society.

In the coming decades, society will badly need the indepen-dent voice: for its creativity, criticism, advocacy, and challenge. Dur-ing times of turmoil, as clearly the 1990s will be, society tends to close in on such freedom, just at the time such freedom becomes more essential. So, unfortunately, does higher education. Witness the constricting response to McCarthyism in the 1950s and the cur-rent wave of "political correctness" now insinuating itself on so many U.S. campuses. Commandment number one for trustees will be to preserve academic freedom, often against the odds and at heavy cost.

Excellence and Equity

In the years ahead, with rapid demographic shifts producing rising proportions of minority members in the actual or potential appli-cant pool for higher education, the two academic values of excel-lence and equity will have to be considered in tandem. There is evidence of success and ingenuity in dealing realistically with these values. The Algebra Project in Cambridge, Massachusetts, has dem-onstrated the capacity of minority students to achieve high levels of competence in mathematics, and the relatively new notion of mul-tiple intelligences has challenged the myopic insistence on IQ as the single indicator of human potential. But colleges and universities will have to stretch their imagination and energies to create new approaches to the resolution of tensions between the twin values of excellence and equity. In the process, they must make a greater commitment to K-12 educational reform and to improving their own recruitment, counseling, and curriculum.

Tolerance and Caring

The decade of diversity will put a premium on the virtue of toler-ance. Tolerance has always been considered the cornerstone and product of higher learning. It is the essential capacity to understand not only the human condition that gives rise to diversity but also to appreciate the extraordinary human benefits of diversity. Whether colleges and universities can maintain this tradition of tolerance in the face of expanding differences, challenging so much of the status quo, is a central question. Crimes of hate are rising across the country, and tension and violence already abound on U.S. campuses. More than tolerance will be required. An atmosphere of caring is needed, to assure those who are different that they and their education are treasured by everyone associated with the institution.

Academic Accountability

Academic freedom carries with it the reciprocal obligation of being accountable to the constituencies of higher education and to the general public that has ensured the freedom the academy enjoys. The boundaries of accountability are constantly and progressively being expanded through laws and regulations; an enlarging conception of the social and ethical role and responsibility of higher education; more explicit definitions and expectations of institutional performance, output, and value added; and ever more sophisticated consumer demand. Trustees will often find this complex environment of expectations perplexing. But failing to study it assiduously will place them and their institutions in peril.

Institutional Neutrality: A Value Open to Exception

It has been persuasively argued that institutions of higher education ought generally to remain neutral on controversial issues. This argument posits that colleges and universities should encourage individuals within their orbit to express themselves freely and vigorously but refrain from taking institutional stands that could inhibit the freedom of individual expression and mire the institution in prolonged, acrimonious, and divisive debate. Colleges and universities, it is contended, are not public legislatures; they should not become partisan but should seek to enlighten public debate by providing access to the independent voices of individual members of the academic community.

So far, so good. But as a rigid orthodoxy applied to every political, social, and ethical issue, this rule would morally cripple higher education. Too many institutions have hidden behind the rule, dodging the responsibility of wrestling with the knottier and more troubling issues that confront them and of giving force to the ideals they profess. Colleges and universities with religious affiliations and more codified sets of values usually find it easier to take positions on difficult issues. But even they find the going rough, when, for example, campus dialogue centers on such issues as abortion. More and more, they, like their secular counterparts, will find themselves pressed to declare institutionally where they stand on issues such as investments in South Africa, U.S. participation in regional and global conflicts, the implications of genetic engineering and biotechnology, race relations, and the allocation of social energy and resources.

There is no general formula for resolving the question of whether to remain institutionally neutral or to take a stand. But there is the imperative of regularly confronting the question and determining openly whether this is the place, this is the time, to say as Martin Luther once did, "Here I stand; I cannot do otherwise."

The Art of Defining Whether an Issue
Is Political, Social, or Ethical

If one could clearly distinguish between political, social, and ethical issues, it might be easier to sort out which issues should find their way onto trustees' agendas and how trustees should respond to those issues. For example, issues judged to be purely political in nature might appropriately fall under the rule of institutional neutrality and be left to the tug and pull of individual opinion and partisan interplay. But most issues are not so unambiguous. What may begin as one development, for example, the widening of social disparities, quickly takes on the coloration of politics and the suspicion of ethical impropriety.

Weighing the response to such issues is exceedingly difficult. When and how should the debate continue as essentially a matter for individual expression, and when and how should the institution intervene? How a response is arrived at is often as critical as the response itself. Should it be proactive or reactive? Determined in open debate or behind closed doors? Made by the entire academic community or only a ruling segment? Arbitrary, or in some way honoring the academy's credo of converting each provocation into a learning experience?

Trustees are likely to face ambiguous political, social, and ethical issues frequently during the next decade. Trustees would do well to anticipate and lay the groundwork for their responses. Their rule should be: no surprises.

Critical Issues and Likely Provocations

Several issues are likely to seriously affect college and university campuses in the next decade. These include globalization, equity and social justice, integrity, due process, and ethics.

Globalization

Driven by technology, especially communications, the world is rapidly converting, as Marshall McLuhan said it would, into a global village. Already we have an instantaneous global market, a global political forum, a globalizing consciousness and response to a deteriorating environment, and a nascent world order evolving through a reaffirmed United Nations. That all this might be undone by a proliferation of isolated tongues, the collapse of another Tower of Babel, is entirely possible. But either alternative will be played out on a global stage. And higher education cannot avoid the consequences nor stand aside as an uninvolved observer.

The consequences of globalization will be both positive and negative. Just as with *Sputnik,* a powerful set of stimuli will be applied to all of U.S. society, and the responses will be varied: to reach out, to be part of, to compete, to learn, to grow. On the other hand, conflict will be universalized. Disputes outside the campus— whether in adjacent or distant communities—will be replicated within the campus, particularly as campus populations increasingly represent diversities of class, race, and national origin. Curiosity about people from other cultures and backgrounds will grow and produce healthy innovations in curriculum, research, and outreach. Fear of others will also grow, hopefully not apace. This fear will result in tensions and even violence flaring both on and off campus.

Those contrasting trends are already visible. Stanford University and Connecticut College are expanding their curricula sympathetically and constructively to be more global in content and perspective. The campuses of the universities of Michigan, with heavy Arabic concentrations, reflect the tensions of the Persian Gulf War. Brown University and scores of other institutions are scarred by hostility and campus violence inflicted upon them both from within and without. In the swirl of these developments, colleges and universities will be hard pressed to mediate conflicts of culture, politics, and values; to accept differences without surrendering their own distinctive values and rules of conduct; to prepare the campus and surrounding community so that the ground rules for handling disputes and resolving differences are understood and agreed upon; and to make of each controversy an opportunity for learning.

In the 1990s, conflict will be especially likely over military operations and service. Another debate may arise over the social role of both higher education and government. What should the response of higher education and government be to poverty, both local and worldwide, environmental degradation, the ethics of competition, and other accumulating dilemmas of moral choice?

Each of these issues will provoke trustees to consider whether to adopt an institutional position or follow the rule of neutrality. If there is any general principle that may help resolve the question (and ultimately there may be none, only personal and collective judgments), it is that institutional stands should be taken when basic values are challenged and the very survival of the institution and what it stands for are in question.

Equity and Social Justice

Higher education will find the century-long tension between elitism and equality exacerbated in the years immediately ahead, for a number of reasons. Demographic shifts are producing a population that is increasingly minority, poor, and less prepared for higher education than students of the last several decades. Harold Hodgkinson, the Paul Revere of educational demographers, has been sounding the warning (1990, p. 1): "At the moment, over 30 percent of our youth are at risk of school failure when they show up at kindergarten on the first day." A 1989 report of the U.S. House of Representatives Select Commmittee on Children, Youth, and Families cites the following statistics (p. 2): "Athough the number of children has fallen since the 1970s, the size of the overall population has continued to increase. Thus, children now make up a smaller fraction of the total population—26 percent—than they did in the past—36 percent in 1960. By 2010, children will represent only 23 percent of the population. Minority group members will continue to grow as a proportion of all children, comprising one in three children by 2010."

The more exclusive U.S. universities and colleges might be able to conduct their business as usual, comforted by the fact that their applicant pools, even when shifting toward greater proportions of minorities, will always yield enough students to sustain both their present numbers and standards. "There will always be," as one institutional officer remarked to me nonchalantly, "the number we need of our kind of students." But most colleges and universities will not have the luxury of standing aloof, and even those who presume to do so will not be immune to confrontations erupting over the social, political, and ethical issues arising from demographic shifts.

An even more fundamental reason for heightened tension is higher education's inherent identification with the current and emerging elite. Not only are colleges and universities dependent financially and otherwise on the more favored and affluent members of society, but it is also their declared purpose to produce those who will exercise leadership. And now that knowledge has become sine qua non for success in this age of information, higher education will become ever more the gatekeeper for entry into and progress in lucrative professions, particularly the professions that are the aristocracy of the service economy. Access to higher education is critical. But access will not be easily ensured for the growing pool of disadvantaged and less prepared members of the population, not with rising costs and declining student aid and the pressure and need to raise standards to meet the requirements of economic competitiveness and the general sophistication of modern life.

There are some ameliorating influences. The need of many institutions simply to fill classrooms to survive will make entry into college easier. But what implications does this easing of standards have for quality and financial aid? As a result of the Persian Gulf War, another influx of veterans with another GI bill can also be expected, and with greater numbers of minority applicants. One can find encouraging signs of institutional sensitivity, given the determination of leading colleges and universities to be more aggressive in recruiting less privileged students and making the necessary accommodations in financial aid, instruction, and counseling.

Trustees will need to attend to the issue of equity and social justice, anticipating the effects of the issue not only on institutional practice but also on the larger society. The cause of social justice will be a constant provocation during the 1990s because of imbalances of opportunity within the United States and globally, the reverberating disparities between populations in the Northern and Southern hemispheres, and the haunting predicaments of foreign populations seeking refuge and a better life in the United States. It would be surprising if trustees were not called upon to engage themselves personally as well as institutionally in these issues.

Integrity

The first victim of increased competition among colleges and universities is likely to be truth. Institutions will be tempted to advertise falsely, misrepresent what they can actually provide, cut corners and engage in cutthroat competition, allow inequities in faculty and staff compensation, tilt financial aid packages toward favored clientele, bury deferred maintenance under accounting covers, profess one set of ideals and ignore them in practice, and withhold from recruited presidents and faculty members the harsh realities they will discover when appointed. These practices are, sadly, already in evidence. And if truth becomes the victim, what is left of the soul of higher education?

Above all else, trustees have to be the guardians of truth. They do so, first of all, by insisting on and practicing integrity in their own relationships and deliberations. Second, they need to assure the campus community that truthfulness will be honored rather than penalized. Third, they will have to monitor the institution's performance in every aspect of its work and processes, asking hard questions and being willing to face equally hard answers. Fourth, they need to examine their institution's external relations and communications, to make as certain as they can that the general public's rightful expectation of academic integrity is being satisfied.

Now that the age of big higher education has arrived, the most predictable and most damning scandals will involve the loss of integrity. What has happened in collegiate athletics, scientific research, the advertising of academic wares, financial aid, and all too many other areas of higher education are all indications of what may follow and recur. Trustees should see these events as warning signs and move aggressively to prevent them from recurring.

Due Process

In recent decades, the public has increasingly insisted on fairness in every facet of institutional life and on governmental response to unfairness through increased regulation of vital academic processes that were long carried out without public scrutiny. For example, the public has become concerned about affirmative action, research on human subjects, facilities for the handicapped, genetic research and engineering, environmental impact, sexual harassment, and financial aid and repayment. The lengthening list shows no signs of shrinking, despite recent moves toward deregulation in the general economy and spreading resistance to regulations within the academic community.

Fairness is a powerful concept. Whether it is realized through governmental action or the voluntary response of colleges and universities, it will continue to be high on the agenda for higher education. Much of the agenda will be defensive, that is, simultaneously resisting the further intrusion of regulation while fighting counterattacks by those who would do away with innovations that on balance have advanced the cause of fairness. Affirmative action will continue to engender debate. So will judicial entry into tenure-granting processes, interinstitutional communication of policies of financial aid, secrecy in standardized testing, and confidentiality in a wide variety of traditional academic practices.

Knottier than any of these issues may well be the growing concern over freedom of expression on campus. Will equal opportunity and equal protection be given to views, either from the right or from the left, contrary to those prevalent (the current term is *politically correct*) on campus? What provisions or constraints should govern the appearance of outside speakers on campus? What latitude should be allowed for the unpopular, the unconventional, even the obscene?

Although these concerns involve the substantive aspects of due process, they also directly raise the question of fairness: equity among the various claimants and fairness in the procedures by which policies are adopted and carried out. Trustees will obviously have to familiarize themselves with the law and make certain they have sound legal advice. But they will also have to make certain that their institutions take the initiative in ensuring fairness and anticipating and containing the disputes that are bound to arise.

Ethics

Everything that has been discussed thus far has an ethical dimension. Still, there are other domains in which trustees will increasingly face ethical dilemmas that will demand a constant consideration and restatement of moral standards and values.

Science and technology, particularly biotechnology, will be the focus of many ethical concerns. The possibilities of altering reproductive and emotive behavior, of expanding the whole range of human choice in which divine or statistical law once prevailed, are bringing on a new age of ethical debate. Equally provocative are the exploration of space and consequent issues of priorities; revolutionary developments in communication, raising privacy questions; and environmental research that will force a rethinking of cultural norms and possibly the entire premise of economic development and the social order.

Higher education should be a major forum for such debate, divisive though it will surely be. The fact that the top two campus life issues of concern to college and university presidents are substance abuse and student apathy suggests that the academic forum is far from realizing its potential and responsibility (Carnegie Foundation for the Advancement of Teaching, 1989).

Being a trustee is no longer a passive exercise in civic distinction. It is a demanding role that requires focused attention on emerging issues of global scale and consequence. The campus cannot be isolated from the contentious questions that will be placed on society's agenda. It will in all likelihood be center stage, where most of these dramas will be played out. And trustees will bear the ultimate responsibility for making certain that the debate will be conducted openly, fairly, and with enlightenment and reason.

What will be expected of trustees is due diligence, the honoring of higher education's fundamental values and traditions, and a very healthy dose of self-education. One wonders whether there is in Oklahoma's recent legislation requiring governing board members to enroll in continued education an augury of what is to come.

CHAPTER 14

The Board's Role in Collective Bargaining

Kenneth P. Mortimer

In 1963, Milwaukee Technical Institute became the first postsecondary institution to sign a collective bargaining contract for faculty members. The first strike ever called at a higher education institution was at Henry Ford Community College in Michigan in 1966. In that same year the faculty of the Merchant Marine Academy became the first at a four-year institution to organize. Faculty unionization in 1968–69 at the City University of New York and Central Michigan University, the first at major four-year institutions, attracted substantial public attention.

Two major points can be made about the status of collective bargaining with faculty in higher education. First, faculty collective bargaining is mainly a phenomenon of public higher education. Eighty-five percent of all higher education institutions with faculty unions are public institutions and more than 66 percent of the bargaining units are in two-year institutions (Andersen, 1991, p. 1).

Second, the growth of faculty collective bargaining has closely paralleled the enactment of state collective bargaining laws. Between 1965 and 1972, faculty collective bargaining occurred mostly in a few heavily populated and relatively industrialized states in the East and Midwest that had adopted enabling legislation before 1970. Collective bargaining activity accelerated in the late

1970s and the early 1980s, when enabling laws were passed in Maine, Connecticut, Florida, California, and other states. In 1989, nearly 470 collective bargaining agents represented about 217,000 faculty and professional staff members, or about 30 percent of the total number (Andersen, 1991, p. 1).

This chapter is an overview of the status of collective bargaining with faculty in U.S. higher education. It begins by discussing why faculty members have chosen to unionize and describes the assumptions undergirding the industrial experience with collective bargaining and the five stages of the process. Throughout this discussion, policy issues that trustees should be aware of are highlighted. The chapter concludes with seven suggestions designed to help trustees of institutions with faculty unions understand the collective bargaining process.

Why Faculty Members Choose Collective Bargaining

Although it is difficult to pinpoint the precise reasons why faculty members choose to join unions in specific situations, the literature and scholars of the topic agree on the importance of five major factors. The first factor is the increased size and changing nature of the professoriate, which appears to have encouraged the rise of collective bargaining—especially in the 1960s. At the start of the 1960s, there were approximately 275,000 instructional staff members. But by 1975, the professoriate had added another 352,000 faculty members, an increase of 127 percent (Jacobs, 1990, p. 44).

As a result of this growth, the U.S. professoriate in the 1960s and 1970s was made up of young people who were especially likely to support collective bargaining. Several surveys of faculty members in the 1970s showed that young faculty members were consistently more supportive of unionization throughout U.S. higher education than older faculty members were (Mortimer and McConnell, 1978).

The second major reason for the growth of unionization was the changing national and state legal environment. In the absence of specific legislation, applicable law concerning the right to organize, join unions, and engage in collective bargaining is derived from three sources: common law, as expounded in judicial decisions; municipal law and legislation defining the power of local governments; and constitutional law. In 1970, the National Labor Relations Board reversed an earlier ruling and extended the provisions of the National Labor Relations Act to private colleges and universities. This change in the national law had an impact on enabling legislation in the states. By 1990, twenty-six states had legislation granting faculties of public institutions the right to unionize and requiring public employers to bargain with duly constituted bargaining agents. Three other states have no such state legislation, but the governing boards of more than one institution in these states have taken the position that they will bargain with faculty on their own authority.

A third factor contributing to the popularity of collective bargaining in the public sector is the rise of the community college. Community colleges now account for about one-third of all postsecondary institutions and for one-sixth of the faculty members. But they account for about two-thirds of the bargaining agents in the public sector. Community colleges often have closer ties to the traditions and culture of the public schools than to those of universities and find unionization more palatable than universities do.

A fourth factor is that some faculty members see collective bargaining as an effective response to the financial pinch of the last two decades. Public financial support for postsecondary education has fallen from the levels characteristic during the rapid growth of the 1960s. Jack Schuster (1990, p. 34) explains in stark detail how the decrease in support has affected faculty members: "The real income of faculty declined sharply. From the historic high reached in 1972–1973 real income plummeted over the next eight years. Then, over the following eight-year period (from 1981–1982 through 1988–89), faculty salaries rebounded as increases averaged 1.7% per year above the Consumer Price Index. . . . This rebound amounts to a partial recovery, but the cumulative loss of real earnings for faculties since the early 1970's appears to be greater than that for any other major non-agricultural occupation."

A fifth factor in the rise of collective bargaining is the perceived impotence of many traditional faculty governance mechanisms in the face of demands for increased efficiency, control, productivity, and accountability from outside agents. Faculty members at many institutions have become increasingly frustrated with what they regard as legislative, judicial, and executive interference in internal academic affairs. Many faculty members regard collective bargaining as a countervailing force to this external intervention.

Characteristics of Collective Bargaining in Higher Education

Trustees must understand the characteristics of collective bargaining that have evolved in industry over fifty years, because the same characteristics apply to collective bargaining in higher education. Five characteristics tend to govern the conditions under which collective bargaining operates in academe:

1. Assumption of a fundamental conflict of interest between the employer and employee
2. Principle of exclusivity
3. Formal negotiation of a contract that is legally binding on both parties
4. Use of formal grievance procedures ending in binding arbitration
5. Legitimacy of sanctions as devices to settle disputes

The assumption that there is a fundamental conflict of interest between an institution's administration and faculty members contradicts the traditional ideal of the university as a community of scholars. In that ideal concept, the faculty dominates educational policy and has major influence on issues of organizational structure related to academics, such as the creation of new departments. Members of the academic community are seen as bound in an inescapably interdependent relationship in which some of the basic functions of management, such as quality control, are in the hands of the faculty.

Advocates of collective bargaining almost unanimously condemn the extent to which the ideal of the community of scholars actually prevails in colleges and universities. Some people argue that collective bargaining is a countervailing force to increased administrative power and a way to restore the ideal of the academic community. Others claim that a faculty member is an employee in every classic, measurable sense of that term and should have the same rights as any other employee. This view has caused difficulty in several cases involving a faculty member's rights as an employee as opposed to rights as a professional and is a subject to which I will return.

The posture that usually accompanies the assumption of conflict of interest is the familiar adversarial tone that most people expect to characterize negotiations. Faculty unions typically prepare "laundry lists" of demands, many of which they know they have no hope of achieving, and management counters with equally unrealistic proposals.

Trustees should consider whether collective bargaining necessitates an adversarial relationship. Many scholars of the topic have argued that the process encourages it but that relationships can be cordial, even while adversarial. The key is to try to keep the adversarial nature of the process limited to collective bargaining issues and to prevent it from affecting other aspects of employee relations.

The *principle of exclusivity* is that management can deal with one, and only one, bargaining agent and that it is illegal to deal with any other agent regarding terms and conditions of employment. This principle generally arises in the debate over the relative roles of the union and the faculty senate. The union may argue that a faculty senate is, in fact, an employee organization as defined by the relevant labor legislation. Therefore, it could be regarded as a competitor to a union. Certainly, the relationship between a senate and a union will be a major topic of discussion between the administration and the union and perhaps a subject of negotiation at the collective bargaining table.

The industrial approach to collective bargaining involves the negotiation of a legally binding document. This document, or contract, is part of academic negotiations as well, and it will be discussed later in this chapter. In public institutions, the financial aspects of the contract often are determined by the governor or the legislature. The contract may need to specify the particular roles of campus officials in matters of governance and academic policy as they interact with others at the systemwide or state level.

Academic collective bargaining also involves the use of third-party binding arbitration as a dispute mechanism. Trustees must understand that under the formal appeal system set up in most collective bargaining agreements, the social context for handling grievances changes. Instead of answering the question Have we been right and fair in our dealings with employees? management must be prepared instead to answer the question, Do we as managers think this is a decision so fair and right that we can prove it to an experienced neutral party? The use of third-party binding arbitration also calls into question the status of other governance documents in force at the institution, including the faculty handbook and other employment contracts.

The strike is a possible dispute and settlement mechanism in academic collective bargaining. There are, of course, intermediate steps short of a strike, including mediation, fact-finding, and binding arbitration of disputes. Some state statutes do not give public employees the right to strike.

In general, the academic experience with collective bargaining reflects precedents set by the origins of the process in industrial labor relations. Over the last fifteen or twenty years, however, a body of case law has developed in which academe has begun to be recognized as a "special industry," particularly in restrictions placed on the bargainability of such governance items as selection of deans. Further, it is possible that institutions can develop an approach to collective bargaining that will lessen the influence of industrial precedents.

Process of Collective Bargaining

Collective bargaining is a process with at least five stages (1) collective bargaining statutes, (2) unit determination, (3) the collective bargaining election, (4) negotiation of a contract, and (5) administration of a contract. Each of the stages is discrete and should reflect the unique setting of the academic environment and the particular institution involved.

Legal Framework

The legal framework that initiates collective bargaining introduces stringent policy considerations (Figuli, 1984). It is crucial that trustees understand these considerations.

Most statutes dealing with collective bargaining set up a legal requirement that, after elections occur, a union is designated as the exclusive bargaining agent and management must bargain in good faith and eventually sign a legally binding document. The statute may set up rules and procedures under which the collective bargaining process will occur. Normally, the law creates a public employee labor relations board (PERB) that will issue a series of rules and regulations under which the collective bargaining process can take place. Elections will be monitored and mandatory subjects of bargaining will be defined according to the provisions of the statute and the rulings of the labor relations board. The statute may also specify appropriate mechanisms for resolving disputes and grant some public employees the right to strike as a settlement mechanism. The PERB usually is the agency designated to monitor elections, define terms, and settle disputes.

Trustees should be aware that state collective bargaining statutes rarely recognize college and university faculty members as a distinct category of public employees. The Supreme Court has acknowledged that faculty members in "mature" private universities have managerial authority over many issues and therefore ought not to have the right to unionize (*National Labor Relations Board* v. *Yeshiva University*, 1980). This ruling has yet to be sustained in the public sector, however. For the most part, then, case law and precedent from nonacademic settings will set the framework for academic settings.

Unit Determination

Before an election is held or a bargaining agent certified, there must be an agreement concerning the appropriate bargaining unit; that is, it must be determined which groups will be eligible to vote in the election and will be covered by any subsequent agreement. Decisions on a bargaining unit may be reached in three principal ways. In the first method, the administration and the union can agree on an appropriate bargaining unit and sit down to bargain. This happens in fewer than 20 percent of the cases.

A second and more common method of determining the bargaining unit is for the administration and the union jointly to petition the state labor relations board to conduct an election. In the petition, the two parties can agree about the appropriate bargaining unit and move ahead to the election phase of the process.

The third method is probably the most common way to determine a bargaining unit and is used when the administration and union disagree on the definition of the unit. In this case, a petition is normally made to the appropriate PERB. In many cases, the board appoints an examiner to hear both sides' arguments on what is an appropriate unit. The examiner then makes recommendations to the board, which in turn decides what constitutes an appropriate community of interest. Several variables are important in defining the appropriate community of interest and will have a major impact on the board's eventual decision.

The makeup of the bargaining unit can be hotly contested and ambiguous. It is useful to answer the following four questions in the process of determining what the bargaining unit will be: What campuses, colleges, and schools should be included in a bargaining unit? What is the status of certain professional schools such as law and medicine? How is the definition of faculty/teaching staff to be formulated? What are the distinctions between management and labor?

In a multicampus institution, the question arises as to whether all campuses should be included in one overall bargaining unit or whether separate campuses can bargain individually. The answer varies around the country. Typically, the large public systems like the State University of New York, the California State University System, the City University of New York, the Florida State University System, and the University of Hawaii are merged into one bargaining unit. In several states, including Michigan, Ohio, and Oregon, the pattern of single-campus elections prevails. In these states, the system-level governance mechanisms are relatively weak compared to those of the multicampus systems mentioned above.

A second important question is whether certain professional schools—notably, schools of law, medicine, and dentistry—should be included in the bargaining unit. In many cases, professional schools have argued successfully that their special salary structures, close affiliation with practicing professionals, differences in the academic calendar, and accreditation standards are so peculiar to the schools that they ought to be allowed to determine their own position on unionization.

A third major question is how to define a faculty member. Do those who are not regular teaching faculty members—such as librarians, student personnel staff, other nonteaching professionals, and part-timers—share a community of interest with full-time faculty members?

The status of part-time faculty members is ambiguous in higher education. In many instances, the benefits of university employment, such as insurance programs or office space, are not extended to part-time faculty members. Often, part-time positions are used to support candidates for graduate degrees and are regarded as part of graduate education. Unit determination forces the administration to consider the extent to which part-time faculty members should be counted among the regular faculty members.

In some cases, librarians, laboratory assistants, technicians, counselors, and student personnel staff are included in the bargaining unit with faculty. A major concern, of course, is that if these nonteaching professionals are not in a faculty bargaining unit, they certainly have a right to organize separately from that unit. Some people have pointed out that the inclusion of these classes of employees in the faculty bargaining units inevitably leads to demands to extend faculty perquisites to them.

A fourth important question is how to define management and labor. The process of unit determination requires a legally binding definition of who is management and who is labor. Academic deans are quite clearly management and are excluded from the bargaining unit, although assistant and associate deans may belong to some units. However, whether department chairs should be considered managers or faculty members is unclear. Trustees should be aware that the inclusion of department chairs in units with the faculty may affect the extent to which these positions can be relied upon for administrative purposes. Almost certainly, if department chairs are in the bargaining unit, there will have to be discussion about how the position of chair is defined and filled.

Elections

When there is an agreement about the definition of a bargaining unit and a determination that at least 30 percent of the faculty members show interest in that unit, the labor relations board usually will order an election. The ballot will include the associations that have petitioned or intervened in the petition as well as an opportunity for faculty to vote not to unionize. The labor laws of most states require that an option must eventually receive the majority of the votes cast to be certified. If neither a single agent nor the no-union option receives the majority vote on the first ballot, a runoff ballot will be ordered between the top two vote getters on the first ballot.

The trustees and administrators have the right to try to persuade faculty members not to unionize, but they must be careful not to engage in behavior that could be interpreted as threatening, intimidating, or coercive. Opposition to unionization is legal and has been effective at many public universities, including the University of California, Berkeley and Los Angeles; Pennsylvania State University; and the University of Minnesota.

The way the issue is phrased in an election campaign may have an extremely important influence on the results of the election. In some elections, the issue clearly is whether or not to unionize, not which union to choose. The choice is between one agent or no agent at all. In some elections at public institutions, however, the issue seems to be which agent to choose. In the early stages of collective bargaining in higher education, faculty members at many institutions assumed, or were led to believe, that unionization was inevitable. Once this assumption is established, the question of whether to unionize is disregarded.

In institutions with significant organized opposition to unionization, there appears to be a greater chance that unionization will be defeated than in institutions without organized opposition. Opposition may take the form of organized groups within the faculty or statements by the administration about the disadvantages of unionization. If opposition to unionization is not organized or has not achieved much stability, faculty members are likely to regard the issue as a choice between unions rather than as a choice of whether or not to unionize.

Most experienced observers would argue that the election campaign should be treated as a political contest rather than an organized debate about academic principles. Although the actual tenor of the debate will depend on campus relationships, an election is a political contest and political norms usually prevail.

If the no-representative option wins, the matter is resolved for at least a year, often longer. The labor board will not entertain a petition for a new election until a year has elapsed. If an agent is chosen, the fourth stage of the collective bargaining process, negotiations, comes next.

Negotiations

The negotiation process requires careful preparation by the administration. Trustees should make clear the parameters under which the administration will be allowed to negotiate. For example, if the governing board has the authority to set faculty salaries, it should have a basic understanding with the administration about the parameters of any economic settlement before the bargaining process begins or offers are made.

Trustees may want to be involved in discussing the composition of the bargaining team. In some community colleges, for example, trustees themselves may be part of the bargaining team. Trustees are more likely to be part of the team if the community college governing district is closely associated with local school boards.

Generally, however, the negotiation of the contract is a matter best left to a competent administration. The trustees' role in the negotation process is to question, prod, and assure that basic policy questions are answered.

Figuli (1984), an experienced collective bargaining professional, argues that the composition of the bargaining team is of critical concern to trustees. The team must consist of people with complementary skills, compatible personalities, and strong physical and mental resources. A properly constituted negotiation team must have among its members people who communicate well, assimilate large amounts of information quickly, know the institution's working conditions, and can be seen as trustworthy by both sides.

Trustees should learn which issues are negotiable in a collective bargaining arrangement. They can obtain this information from applicable statutes and court decisions on the subject of bargaining. Or they can determine which issues are discussed at the bargaining table and which are codified and therefore put into a contract. In practice, however, what is negotiable will depend on local circumstances, past practice at the institution, and the demands and strategies of the parties at the table.

In general, a collective bargaining statute establishes the obligation of both parties to engage in good-faith bargaining over wages, hours, and terms and conditions of employment. Some legislation is permissive, or laissez-faire, about what is negotiable. Other statutes specify certain issues as mandatory subjects of negotiation and prohibit agreements on other issues. An example of a permissive statute would be one that defines the scope of negotiations as wages, hours, and "other conditions of employment." The intent of such language is probably to let the negotiation process itself place any limits the parties wish on the scope of bargaining. Other statutes may have a management-rights clause that says the employer is not required to bargain over matters of inherent managerial policy. The clause ensures that employers cannot be forced to bargain on these issues, but they may do so if they choose.

A more realistic approach to determining what is negotiable would be to examine what appears in a variety of collective bargaining contracts. The most common topics fall into five categories: salaries and fringe benefits, grievance procedures, union rights and security, work load and personnel policies, and reduction-in-force procedures. Other items in a contract would include management-rights clauses, governance items, and other matters of institutional policy. Grievance procedures are included in most contracts, and approximately 70 to 80 percent of them in effect in four-year institutions specify binding arbitration as a final step in the grievance process.

Most collective bargaining agreements have provisions covering compensation of faculty members. Although the most heated disagreement in negotiations often involves faculty compensation, there is little disagreement about its negotiability. In collective bargaining negotiations in public higher education, the most common problem is whether or not the administration can negotiate financial settlements that have not been approved by the legislature or the executive branch of state government. The authority of administrations will vary, depending on the statutory authority of the institution in question.

The debate over the financial and organizational status of the union may focus on such issues as the choice between a *union shop* and an *agency shop*. Under a union shop, faculty members must become dues-paying members of the union within thirty days of being hired and remain members in good standing for the duration of their employment. Under an agency shop, employees must pay the agent a fee, approximately equal to union dues for the duration of their employment. Some contracts include office space for the union; release time for union officials; and the use of telephones, bulletin boards, and campus mail.

Practical personnel policies in collective bargaining contracts may include the procedures and criteria for promotion and tenure decisions; work-load provisions relating to such matters as office hours, length of the work week or year, teaching overload, class size, the number of course preparations, calendar, and advising loads; and so forth. Governance issues in contracts can take many forms. Some contacts have provisions for the formation of joint faculty-administration committees to handle or study a variety of issues. These kinds of arrangements may provide for faculty involvement in such matters as the selection of department chairs, deans, and even presidents.

The institution must develop a philosophical position on its approach to negotiations. This position should outline what is to be negotiated and a general set of assumptions about how collective bargaining fits into the total governance pattern of the institution. Figuli (1984) urges the board and the president to seize the initiative by beginning to develop policy parameters as early as the stage of unit determination. He recommends making an inventory of all policy statements relating to the subject of bargaining and carefully assessing the acceptable and optimal limits of possible proposals for each potential subject of bargaining. The key determinant should be, according to Figuli, how to obtain a contract consistent with sound principles of education and management..

One bargaining philosophy is that of comprehensive negotiations. In this approach, management agrees to use the faculty contract as a surrogate for the faculty handbook. The administration then agrees that the union will be its chief vehicle for communicating with the faculty, and the negotiation process takes the form of extensive discussions about a full range of issues to be included in the contract.

Another approach to negotiations is to limit the actual contract to such employment issues as wages, fringe benefits, and other working conditions and to exclude issues of governance and educational policy. Bucklew (1974) argues that collective bargaining has brought into focus the dual roles—employees and professionals—played by faculty members in the university. As employees, faculty members have an understandable concern for their personal welfare and financial interests. As professionals, they are centrally involved in the development and execution of the instructional, research, and service missions of their institution.

To avoid the adversarial posture inherent in collective bargaining, academic decisions, which by their nature require open and deliberative processes, should not be included in contracts. This limited approach to bargaining recognizes that academic decision making should be a multilateral, rather than simply bilateral, process and that matters of professional judgment are difficult to incorporate into a collective contract.

Trustees and the administration may find it difficult to impose a limited approach to the scope of negotiations. A consistent and well-articulated set of conceptual limits will help in setting the tone for discussions.

Contract Administration

Contract administration requires an adequate number of staff members and great care since it is the process through which the contract is interpreted. The administration will need to prepare careful inventories of the actions required of both parties after the contract is negotiated. The board and the president may consider the establishment of some formal structure to oversee the administration of the contract and provide consulting services to assist with the process.

Ambiguity in the contract language or its intent can modify what the parties may have thought they agreed to at the bargaining table. In such cases, both parties may find themselves in disagreement about a matter and will have to either negotiate it again during the next round of negotiations or develop a procedure to settle such disputes. Grievance and arbitration settlements can be costly and can involve serious questions of principle if the contract language and administration is not monitored carefully.

Advice for Trustees

To be effectively involved in, or prepared to monitor administrative involvement in, collective bargaining, trustees must be fully informed about the process of bargaining and the circumstances at their own campuses. Specifically:

- Trustees should become familiar with existing contracts, policies, and the social context of labor relations issues at their institution.
- Trustees must require administrators to provide regular briefings on the bargaining strategies and tactics to be adopted.
- Trustees should ensure that the administration articulates a consistent conceptual approach to bargaining.
- Trustees should set clear expectations for the parameters of any potential settlement or changes in policy. This is particularly true for the financial details of the contract.
- Trustees must be aware that collective bargaining may be accompanied by public statements, political posturing, and even strikes. The board must be united in its public posture and remain steadfast in the pursuit of its objectives.
- Where important issues such as salaries, management rights, or arbitration are involved, trustees must review or approve, where necessary, the final details of the contract before it is signed. Distinctions between policy and matters of administration should continue to be a subject of debate by trustees.

• Trustees must monitor these important issues through contract administration and receive periodic reports on arbitration and grievances.

Academic institutions with collective bargaining contracts keep life interesting for administrators and governing boards. Governing boards whose members understand the origins, complexities, and nuances of the process can be enormously helpful to the administrators who are charged with negotiating the institution through the minefields. The first step is for the board and its members to understand their own roles and responsibilities and to be mindful of the fact that, because most trustees and regents come to their volunteer responsibilities without understanding these complex matters, continuing education should be made available to them, beginning when they are first elected or appointed, as part of their orientation to the institution and to their trusteeship.

Court Cases Cited

National Labor Relations Board v. *Yeshiva University.* 444 U.S. 672 (1980).

CHAPTER 15

Setting Tenure and Personnel Policies

Richard P. Chait

This chapter highlights some key issues and policy options that should concern governing boards.

Why Are Academic Personnel Policies So Important?

Faculty members are the heart and soul of academic institutions. Their motivation, working environments, morale, and productivity depend on effective and enlightened policies that are properly administered and monitored.

The Heart of the Enterprise

Colleges and universities offer students academic programs staffed by faculty members. The academic programs largely define the institution's mission, and the faculty largely determines how well that mission is fulfilled. When we list the great universities or the strongest departments of universities, our judgments are inevitably assessments of the caliber of the faculty. Thus, although administrators, architects, athletic directors, and even trustees sometimes like to think otherwise, the quality of the faculty and the quality of the university are very nearly synonymous. Because professors are so crucial to an institution's success, trustees must understand the policies and practices that govern the employment and influence the performance of faculty members.

The Bulk of the Budget

The faculty's direct relationship to an institution's reputation might be reason enough to carefully consider policies and practices affecting academic personnel. However, an equally powerful economic argument can be made. Compensation for faculty members and related instructional expenses consume the lion's share of an institution's budget.

In any year, instructional expenditures may represent between 30 and 35 percent of an institution's operating budget (Taylor, Meyerson, Morrell, and Park, 1991, p. 59). Over the long term, the salary and benefits for a faculty member who is tenured at age thirty-five could easily exceed $1.25 million by the time the professor elects to retire. Thus, compensation of faculty members is expensive, and tenure decisions are costly. A decision to tenure five faculty members, for example, could represent a $6.25 million obligation. Colleges and universities need to be as attentive to tenure decisions as to construction decisions entailing a comparable capital outlay.

Proliferation of Procedures

In the late 1960s, a spate of externally imposed rules and regulations started to direct the behavior of higher education institutions. Examples of these rules and regulations are plentiful: legislation for the handicapped, the Family Educational Rights and Privacy Act (Buckley Amendment), and even decisions by the Environmental Protection Agency.

Although many kinds of regulations have had an impact on colleges and universities, the most dramatic effects can be observed in the area of personnel administration. In 1968, President Johnson signed Executive Order 11246, which together with Titles VI and VII of the 1964 Civil Rights Act and Title IX of the 1972 Education Amendments Act, provides the basis for affirmative action. Other prominent examples of regulations affecting personnel decisions include the Equal Pay/Equal Work Act and the Occupational Safety and Health Act. These statutes and orders govern the recruitment, appointment, promotion, and compensation of faculty, as well as the entry and advancement phases of their employment. In addition, many states adopted legislation that enabled the faculties of public colleges to unionize. Salaries, work loads, evaluations, retrenchment, and leaves have all become contractual matters.

Other rulings and regulations affect the exit process for faculty members. In 1972, the *Roth* and *Sinderman* decisions by the Supreme Court set standards for procedural due process at public colleges as a protection against dismissal (*Board of Regents* v. *Roth,* 1972; *Perry* v. *Sinderman,* 1972). And the Age Discrimination in Employment Act was amended to prohibit mandatory retirement by colleges and universities, effective January 1, 1994. Taken together, all these rules, laws, goals, timetables, underutilization analyses, regulations, orders, policies, and procedures have affected the lifeblood of the university—namely, the flow of faculty into, up, through, and out of the institution.

Increase in Litigation

Not unexpectedly, the proliferation of procedures and statutes has spawned a noticeable increase in litigation. A casual observer may wonder whether academics spend more time in the courtroom than the classroom. Between 1970 and 1984, 160 cases of academic employment discrimination on matters such as appointment, promotion, pensions, and retirement were decided in court. Of these 160 cases, nearly 70 percent involved public institutions. In the same period, there were 156 decisions on procedural and jurisdictional issues in public and private colleges and universities (LaNoue and Lee, 1987, p. 25).

Perhaps of some solace to boards of trustees is the fact that plaintiffs have enjoyed only modest success in these cases. As La-Noue and Lee reported (1987, p. 30): "Of the 156 procedural/jurisdictional decisions, 58 have been in favor of the plaintiff and 77 for the defendant, and 21 have been split decisions in which both parties have won and lost on different issues. On the other hand, plaintiffs have won only 34 of 160 decisions that reached the merits (6 were split)."

Even though colleges and universities prevailed in nearly four of every five substantive cases, few organizations relish the prospects of a court appearance. And, in any case, the costs in time, money, morale, and goodwill are often substantial. Therefore, boards of trustees should ensure that their institutions have clearly defined, broadly disseminated, and faithfully followed policies, procedures, and performance criteria for personnel actions.

Scarcity of Resources

As the overall economy falters, states derive less revenue from corporate, individual, sales, and property taxes. Consequently, state governors and legislatures, especially in the Northeast and West, have had to dramatically reduce appropriations to higher education. In some cases, there were sizable midyear rescisions and furloughs as well as absolute and permanent budget reductions.

In an era of equilibrium or retrenchment, personnel decisions will be more critical and mistakes more costly than during a time of plenty. The academy can no longer cover over mistakes with more people and more money. Colleges and universities have far less maneuverability to change people and hence programs exactly at a time when the ability to respond to changes in student demography and interests may be a top priority.

The link between people and programs in higher education cannot be overstated. In higher education, product changes almost always require personnel changes. Unlike autoworkers on an assembly line, who can turn with relative ease from the production of one model to the production of another, few classicists could shift from a course on Plato to a course on pollution. In other words, since there will probably be limited opportunities in the near future to change people or expand programs, each personnel decision will assume added significance and each mistake will be magnified. Now, perhaps more than ever before, the human resources of colleges and universities must be managed effectively.

Scarcity of Faculty Members

Although estimates about the supply of and demand for faculty members over the next twenty years vary, the disagreements focus on the magnitude of the shortage of qualified faculty members, not on whether there will be a shortage. Bowen and Schuster (1986) forecast a 4 to 6 percent yearly attrition rate of full-time faculty members between 1990 and 2010. "At the annual rate of 4 percent, over ten years about 32 percent of all faculty positions would become vacant through attrition, and over twenty-five years 70 percent would become vacant" (p. 186). Recent annual turnover rates at public colleges fall close to the predicted range: 6.1 percent for four-year colleges and 4.3 percent for two-year colleges. In 1990, administrators at colleges and universities anticipated that over the next two years searches would have to be conducted to fill about 9 percent of all currently occupied full-time faculty positions (El-Khawas, 1990, pp. 21–22).

With limited financial resources and an expected shortage of faculty members, the competition for academic personnel will be keen. Already, 63 percent of the institutions surveyed by the American Council on Education reported "difficulty in getting top applicants to accept positions" (El-Khawas, 1990, p. vi). This concern was most pronounced at public four-year institutions, where 74 percent of the respondents expressed concern about the predicted shortage of faculty members (p. 5).

Colleges and universities will need, therefore, some comparative advantages to recruit and retain the best teachers and researchers. The competition for faculty members will only heighten the need for personnel policies and practices that are workable, attractive to faculty members, and conducive to productive careers. Yet, ironically, many boards of trustees of public colleges and universities lack the authority or autonomy to determine crucial personnel policies, which are often set by a state agency or through collective bargaining. To compound the problem, public college boards frequently have limited control over the volume and flow of financial resources.

Even under these circumstances, however, boards of trustees must be well versed in the terms and conditions of faculty employment and well informed about the effectiveness of key policies. If the policies are inadequate, perhaps the board can adopt changes "at the margin" that will have an ameliorative effect. And where policies are ineffectual despite everyone's best efforts, the administration should document the policy's deficiencies and the board should try to influence the appropriate authorities to make changes.

Managing Human Resources

Most colleges and universities recognize the need to manage their physical and fiscal resources. Capital and operating budgets are routinely developed, and fiscal projections of three to five years are common. Although the management of human resources also requires planning and monitoring over the short and long terms, many institutions fail to carry out these tasks.

Nearly all boards receive a balance sheet and a statement of changes in fund balances annually. The balance sheet presents a financial picture at a particular moment, and the statement of changes helps a board to compare current circumstances with conditions twelve months ago. But how many boards receive similar information about personnel generally and faculty in particular? Planning for the management of human resources might begin with an inventory of current staff members. For example, the data for faculty members might be arrayed by department or school, age, sex, race, salary, work load, tenure status, highest degree attained, and retirement date.

Computer programs are available to store and display these data (Nevison, 1980). The programs permit simulation exercises based upon various policy assumptions made by the institution. One can manipulate policy variables that affect the flow of faculty members through the institution, such as rates of promotion and tenure, length of probationary periods, retrenchment plans, and voluntary attrition. Through the application of these models, a college and its board can routinely examine historical patterns and trends, up-to-date profiles of faculty members, and forecasts of the likely effects of contemplated policy or environmental changes.

A particular college or university can also be compared to other institutions without much difficulty. The American Associ-

ation of University Professors (AAUP) publishes an annual com-
pendium of salary levels and tenure ratios. Other valuable annual
statistical summaries include *The Condition of Education* (National Center for Education Statistics) and *Campus Trends* (American Council on Education). If appropriate comparative data are
not available, an institution can initiate an information exchange
with a group of similar institutions. In any case, trustees should
ensure that the institution has an appropriate faculty data base,
periodically makes projections and conducts simulations, and mon-
itors the college's condition and performance against comparative
data from similar institutions. For a superb guide to the scope and
use of comparative data, trustees should consult *Strategic Analysis*
(Taylor, Meyerson, Morrell, and Park, 1991), which has special sections on faculty members and instruction and three case studies on
public two- and four-year institutions.

With respect to the faculty and the curriculum, trustees worry
most—and occasionally too much—about institutional flexibility.
Despite all the expressed concerns, very few colleges or universities
attempt to measure or gauge flexibility, except to monitor the ratio
of tenured to untenured faculty members. This ratio may communicate something about flexibility if the bases for the calculation are
sound. Trustees should understand whether, for example, the denominator of the ratio includes research and teaching assistants,
librarians, and part-time faculty members.

Some other useful measures of flexibility can be charted. Colleges can calculate the percentage of instructional salary dollars
committed to tenured and untenured faculty members respectively.
This measure would give some sense of the institution's financial
flexibility, which is necessary to achieve curricular flexibility. Faculty turnover rates should also be monitored. What are the average
employment periods for tenured and untenured faculty members?
How have these rates changed over the past five years? How do they
compare with rates at similar institutions? Since more program
changes and innovations may have to be generated from within
colleges and universities in the near future, boards might ask how
often courses are substantially revised, replaced, or discontinued.

Considering Changes in Personnel Policy

Before considering changes in personnel policy, the board should ask a crucial question: Does the problem derive from an inadequate policy or from the ineffective administration of a sound policy? Obviously, an institution should not mistakenly change policies when it should actually change people or, conversely, change people when it should change policy. Sometimes both policies and people may need to be changed. A simple example may illustrate the point. In an eastern state, College A and College B, both public four-year colleges, opened in 1971. Both schools are subject to the same state statutes on tenure and are governed by the same collective bargaining agreement. By 1989–90, 79 percent of faculty members at College A were tenured, while only 58 percent were tenured at College B. There may well be defensible reasons for the higher tenure ratio at College A. But if the board at College A suddenly became disturbed by the school's tenure density, should tenure policy be the focal point of criticism? Obviously, institutional practice and not tenure policy accounts for the difference.

Many schools have tenure levels below 60 percent. The average tenure ratio in 1987–88 was 64.9 percent for all colleges, 65.9 percent for public four-year colleges, and 74.2 percent for public community colleges (National Center for Education Statistics, 1990, p. 227). The variations are attributable not so much to dissimilar tenure policies as to differences in implementation of policies.

If a policy change seems advisable, the president and the board need as much hard data as possible to supplement opinions, impressions, and intuitions. Moreover, the board should ask the administration to articulate the problem to be resolved or the objective to be achieved by a change in policy. The board (or the appropriate board committee) should be actively engaged in discussions about policy objectives through questions (Chait, Mortimer, Taylor, and Wood, 1985) such as: What are the main purposes the policy is intended to serve? Is the proposal aimed at a new objective, or is it a new approach to an established goal? Are there any conflicts among various policy objectives? Does the weakness lie with the policy or with its implementation? How will we know whether our purposes have been realized? How will we monitor and evaluate the impact of the policy?

The administration should then explore with the faculty policy alternatives that are congruent with policy objectives and periodically update the board as a preferred course of action emerges. Eventually, the administration should present a draft policy for discussion by the board or the designated trustee committee. The board should not draft, edit, or revise personnel policy statements. The board should express any reservations it has about the policy and if necessary, direct the administration to rewrite the policy to satisfy the board's concerns.

If policy changes will affect faculty members directly, faculty members should be consulted, for three reasons. First, faculty members may have some valuable ideas to contribute to the discussion. Second, consultation suggests that the board and the administration respect the legitimate role of the faculty in the process of shared governance, a central tenet of most colleges and universities. Incidentally, "meaningful participation of faculty in the governance process" has a very positive effect on faculty morale, stronger even than "institutional financial support and faculty salaries" (Anderson, 1983, p. 6). Third, consultation improves the likelihood that the change will be effective, especially in those instances such as promotion and tenure reviews or curricular changes where the faculty will actually be called upon to implement the new policy. At a minimum, the board should understand, preferably firsthand, the dominant sentiment of the faculty on the issue under consideration. Many institutions adopt procedures such as multiconstituency task forces, faculty representatives on trustee committees, and regular reports from the leadership of the faculty senate—all coordinated by the president—to gain input from faculty members.

When the moment arrives to write the final version of a new policy, the college or university should always select language appropriate to the institution. The board of trustees should seek assurances that the proposed policies have not been borrowed wholesale from other colleges or from professional associations without very careful analysis of each and every provision. Furniss (1976, 1978), for example, questions the status of policies on tenure and retrenchment recommended by the AAUP and cautions institutions not to adopt the association's policies word for word.

Although policies are enormously important, personnel actions speak louder than personnel policies. Tenure decisions communicate far more about institutional standards than does tenure policy. Likewise, promotions, merit pay, or awards of sabbatical leave communicate far more about institutional values than do policy pronouncements. Personnel decisions are clear signals that are widely broadcast. The board's actions should closely fit the intended message.

Understanding Academic Tenure

Few faculty personnel policies are more perplexing to trustees than those surrounding the institution of academic tenure. The first step in reducing the confusion is for trustees to understand the origins and purposes of tenure.

Definitions

Among personnel policies and actions, none looms larger than academic tenure. As noted earlier, tenure decisions involve substantial economic and contractual commitments to individuals and to programs. Despite the central importance of tenure, many trustees (and some academics) are uncertain about the provisions and purposes of tenure policy. This confusion adds to the larger controversy over the value and wisdom of a tenure system.

Some definitions may help to minimize the confusion. Traditionally, the academic community has regarded the Statement on Academic Freedom and Tenure presented by the AAUP in 1940 as the definitive exposition on tenure. In part, that statement declares: "Tenure is a means to certain ends—specifically, (1) freedom of teaching and research and of extramural activities and (2) a sufficient degree of economic security to make the profession attractive to men and women of ability. Freedom and economic security— hence, tenure—are indispensable to the success of an institution in fulfilling its obligations to its students and to society" (American Association of University Professors, 1984, p. 3).

As much a characterization as a definition, the AAUP statement might be compared to a more operational definition offered by the Commission on Academic Tenure, cosponsored by the AAUP and the Association of American Colleges. The commission defined tenure as "an arrangement under which faculty appointments in an institution of higher education are continued until retirement for age or physical disability, subject to dismissal for adequate cause or unavoidable termination on account of financial exigency or change of institutional program" (American Association of University Professors and Association of American Colleges, 1973, p. 256).

Taken together, these statements provide a useful definition of academic tenure. However, trustees should remember that general definitions by associations and commissions do not supersede the specific policy provisions adopted by a board of trustees, enacted by a legislature, or negotiated by a faculty union. Academic tenure will be neither more nor less than what official institutional policy stipulates, although absent any specific institutional statement, national norms may be brought to bear (*Krotkoff* v. *Goucher College*, 1978). With these caveats in mind, I can speak broadly of the primary purposes of academic tenure.

Purposes

As the AAUP statement suggests, tenure aims to safeguard academic freedom and ensure a measure of economic security. Like the term *academic tenure,* the term *academic freedom* has no common definition. To critics of academic freedom, the term suggests a license to speak irresponsibly on any issue. To defenders, academic freedom represents a hallowed doctrine and a prerequisite to teaching at a college or university.

Academic freedom has three essential components: (1) the freedom to conduct and publish research, (2) the freedom to teach and discuss issues pertinent to the course or subjects without introducing into the classroom irrelevant matters, and (3) the freedom to speak or write as a citizen without expressly speaking or writing on behalf of the institution unless authorized to do so. In short, academic freedom is meant to provide an atmosphere conducive to the open and unfettered pursuit and exchange of knowledge. Tenure safeguards academic freedom, it is argued, because the award of tenure formally and explicitly confers the three privileges mentioned above. Tenured personnel are thereby assured that their research and teaching can be guided by their best professional judgments and not by outside pressures, institutional orthodoxy, or concerns for continued employment.

Unlike academic freedom, economic security is a well-established and easily understood concept. By carefully specifying the grounds and procedures whereby tenured personnel may be dismissed, tenure protects against arbitrary and capricious personnel actions, thus providing significant job security for faculty members.

As originally conceived, tenure was to benefit the institution as well as the individual, and many proponents of tenure argue that the benefits are indeed mutual. Traditionally, tenure is seen as creating an environment that encourages faculty members to undertake long-term and high-risk projects. Tenure is said to help develop a coterie of professionals loyal to the college yet sufficiently secure to act as constructive critics. And perhaps most important, the very nature of a tenure decision presumably forces the institution to assess each candidate carefully and thus to exercise quality control. It is important for board members to understand the espoused goals and objectives of tenure policies. Only then can trustees fruitfully examine actual tenure practices.

Prevalence

Formal academic tenure in the United States is a product of the twentieth century. Although various forerunners of tenure were available to some faculty members in the 1800s, academic tenure as a systematic policy was not well established until the early 1900s, when universities such as Harvard and Johns Hopkins adopted the policy. Tenure was not generally accepted as a fundamental precept of the profession until the Declaration of Principles in 1915 by the newly formed AAUP.

Today, however, academic tenure operates on almost all college campuses. About 85 percent of all colleges and universities have a tenure system, and these institutions with a tenure system employ about 90 percent of all full-time faculty members. All universities, nearly all four-year colleges, and about 67 percent of all two-year colleges have a tenure system (National Center for Education Statistics, 1991, p. 10).

Although nearly all institutions have tenure systems, obviously not all faculty members have tenure. Only 64.9 percent of faculty members had tenure in 1987–88, virtually the same percentage reported in 1980–81. Seventy percent of all male faculty members and fifty percent of all female faculty members were tenured in 1987–88 (National Center for Education Statistics, 1990, p. 227). In all, a good many faculty members hold tenure; a reasonable estimate might be about 317,000 of the 489,000 full-time faculty members.

Slightly more than half (54 percent) of all faculty members responding to a survey in 1989 considered tenure more difficult to achieve than in 1975. But that number represents a steep decline from 1975, when 73 percent of the respondents believed the chances for tenure were dimmer than five years earlier (Carnegie Foundation for the Advancement of Teaching, 1989, pp. 110, 124).

Procedures

The criteria, standards, and procedures for the award of tenure differ from institution to institution (and often from school to school within a university). But there are enough commonalities to construct a generalized description of the bases and processes that govern tenure decisions.

How do tenure decisions arise? Normally, a faculty member automatically stands for tenure at a fixed time, generally one year before the expiration of the probationary period. In exceptional cases, a candidate may be considered a year or two earlier. In rare instances, a college or university may offer an extremely well-established scholar at another university an appointment with "instant tenure." Denial of tenure at the end of the probationary period almost always means that the unsuccessful candidate must leave the institution at the end of the contract. Such provisions are referred to as the up-or-out rule.

Tenure decisions typically reflect assessments of performance and judgments about potential. Minimum eligibility requirements usually include:

1. *Service in a probationary period.* A probationary period of about three to seven years offers a faculty member an opportunity to develop and refine the skills necessary for the position and offers the institution a chance to observe and evaluate the faculty member's performance. Service elsewhere may be counted toward fulfillment of the probationary period, although credit for prior service usually does not exceed half the total probationary period. Satisfactory completion of the probationary period represents one measure of professional experience.

2. *Attainment of appropriate academic credentials.* To receive tenure, a faculty member usually must attain the highest degree, such as a doctorate, normally awarded in his or her discipline. In the current marketplace, four-year colleges and universities usually tenure only faculty members who already possess a terminal degree.

3. *Appointment to an appropriate academic rank.* Usually, a faculty member must hold or be qualified to hold the rank of assistant or associate professor before receiving tenure. It is commonplace, but by no means required, to link the tenure decision to promotion in rank.

4. *Successful past performance.* Past performance is normally assessed in three broad areas: teaching, scholarship (or research), and service to the college and the profession. Depending upon the institution or the department, these criteria are weighted differently. Some institutions require excellence in all three areas, but most institutions usually require excellence in one or two areas with solid performance in the others.

5. *Growth potential.* An individual's capacity and ability to continue to develop as a teacher and scholar are also considered in tenure decisions. Most often, forecasts of potential growth are based upon past performance and the value attached by students and colleagues to work done thus far by the faculty member.

Although tenure decisions are ultimately subjective in nature, a body of evidence is usually assembled to inform the deliberations. A typical dossier includes letters of recommendation from students and campus colleagues, letters from outside references (usually in the same or an allied field) that address the quality of the candidate's scholarship, the candidate's publications and scholarly reviews of these works, student evaluations of the candidate's teaching, course syllabi and examinations, and a self-evaluation or personal statement that includes the candidate's goals and objectives for the future. Not all institutions collect all these materials, and each institution obviously assesses the evidence differently.

The review process usually entails a sequence of deliberations and recommendations, often beginning at the departmental or program level. In many universities and some liberal arts colleges, the recommendations of the department and department chair carry great weight. Beyond the department, the process moves to the dean, a schoolwide or collegewide committee, the academic vice president, and the president. In nearly all cases, the president eventually places a recommendation for action before the board of trustees.

Since the board bears ultimate as well as legal responsibility for the adequacy and equity of the tenure-granting process, it should determine that the procedures are fair, reasonable, manageable, comprehensive, and appropriate to the mission and structure of the institution. From time to time, the academic affairs committee of the board or its equivalent should ask the dean or provost to "walk" the committee through the process. During the review, trustees might ask questions such as: What documents do faculty members receive that explain the process? Does the process allow an evaluative record to be constructed from the start of the probationary period? How do the procedures guarantee faculty members due process? Are the procedures acceptable to a large majority of the faculty members? Are there any significant differences in procedures across academic units and, if so, why? The committee's role is not to write procedures but to ensure that there are procedures in place that are widely understood and appropriate to the task.

Establishing Tenure Policy

Although boards should be generally acquainted with the procedures that govern tenure reviews, the more important aspects of the process are establishing tenure policy and making tenure decisions. Before examining tenure policies, a board should first recognize that these policies exist within a larger institutional context. Therefore, the board must have a working knowledge of the following documents and how they interrelate: (1) existing bylaws, rules, regulations, and relevant state statutes; (2) contracts and negotiated agreements, especially those that directly affect staffing patterns; (3) the affirmative action plan; (4) the operating budget; (5) strategic priorities and the mission statement; and (6) a profile of the institution's faculty, as described earlier.

Tenure policies and practices are unusually sensitive issues for faculty members. Therefore, the need to be clear on policy objectives and to consult widely with faculty is especially acute. Moreover, certain aspects of tenure policy involve contractual obligations between the institution as employer and the professor as employee. Changes in policy may require that some faculty members who have been at the institution for a long time be exempted from any change.

What tenure-related policies should a governing board establish? With appropriate and substantial participation by the college community, a board, unless restricted by union contracts or state law, ought to set policies governing the probationary period, credential or degree requirements, and rank requirements for tenure. On the advice and recommendation of the faculty and academic staff, the board should also set general guidelines on the relative importance of teaching, scholarship, and service. Criteria affecting judgments of past performance and future contributions are best determined by faculty peers and academic administrators, although the board should insist that such criteria be plainly stated and clearly supportive of the institution's mission.

In considering tenure policy, a board might raise the following questions:

- Does the probationary period provide adequate time to evaluate a faculty member's performance?
- Are assignments sufficiently varied during the probationary period to test a faculty member's abilities in all areas of his or her responsibility?

- Are the degree requirements appropriate to the institution's mission and the conditions of the marketplace?
- Is the relative importance assigned to teaching, research, and service consistent with the institution's mission? Is there sufficient latitude to accommodate faculty members with different interests and strengths?
- What policy statements do faculty members receive? How are standards and expectations communicated to the faculty? Have standards and expectations changed over the past five years?
- Are institutional needs, strategic priorities, and affirmative action recognized as appropriate criteria for promotion and tenure decisions? If not, why not?

Making Tenure Decisions

A tenure decision requires considerable familiarity with an individual's qualifications. The decision requires a sophisticated assessment of the candidate's professional expertise—an assessment best rendered by other experts. Yet a tenure decision also requires familiarity with institutional needs and priorities. Trustees are more likely to be acquainted with the institution's needs than with the individual's strengths. A governing board should consider the "fit" between individual merit, as judged by academic professionals, and institutional needs, as judged by the board in consultation with the academic administration. Such a role implies that the board will ask a somewhat different set of questions than the faculty and administration and will require a somewhat different set of materials to make an informed decision.

With its focus on institutional needs, a board may ask questions such as:

- Do we have the financial resources to support these tenured appointments?
- Are these permanent appointments consistent with the school's strategic priorities, curricular needs, and affirmative action plans?
- Will these decisions unwisely constrain institutional flexibility or unduly bind a particular department?

- Do enrollment and placement patterns warrant a permanent appointment?
- Will these decisions prevent even more attractive appointments to tenure within the foreseeable future?
- If tenure were denied, would the dollars "saved" be allocated to the same position, another program, or a different department?

These questions suggest the kind of data that a board needs to participate effectively in tenure decisions and in the review of tenure policies. All too often, administrators furnish boards with the very same information provided to faculty members and deans, even though trustees have (or should have) a markedly different set of concerns. If trustees receive only information about the individual merit of a candidate, how can the board help but dwell on that aspect of the decision? If the board receives information on enrollments, placements, finances, flow of faculty members through the institution, tenure levels, and affirmative action, however, a very different discussion might ensue.

The division between individual merit and institutional need can be too sharply drawn. Surely, faculty deliberations on merit should be made within the context of institutional needs, and, conversely, trustees should be acquainted with the qualifications of tenure candidates. In general, however, the board should concentrate on the extent to which individuals with strong credentials for tenure meet institutional needs.

As a rule, if the board feels assured that the prescribed process has been followed and the appropriate criteria have been applied, it should rarely have cause to review tenure recommendations for individual merit. A fair question might be whether a president or a board *can* determine the academic quality of highly specialized experts working in so many diverse fields.

The board may receive assurances of a candidate's merit formally or informally from the president or from its normal review of faculty portfolios. On occasion, the board or one of its committees may elect to review a tenure recommendation more meticulously than usual solely to ensure that the prescribed process has been followed, the proper documentation collected, and the appropriate criteria applied. If carefully limited to questions of procedure and discreetly conducted, such a spot check would probably not be seen either as an intrusion on faculty prerogative or as lack of support for the president. Some circumstances may warrant an in-depth review by the board, such as widely disparate evaluations of the same candidate or a conspicuously disproportionate number of either positive or negative recommendations overall by race or sex.

Although a board may be tempted to investigate the merits of tenure recommendations from the president that generate an up-roar on campus, care should be exercised to review only cases where the board has considerable reason to believe that established policy has been violated. In other words, unless state policy or a labor contract requires otherwise, a board should not serve as a court of last resort for faculty members considered talented by some but found wanting by others when established policies and procedures have been equitably applied.

The risks associated with a review on merit by the board are substantial. Very likely, the board's action will be perceived by fac-ulty members as an intrusion on their autonomy. Morale may sink as tension heightens. The president, too, may regard the review as an inappropriate interference or as a vote of no confidence. Thus, such reviews should be conducted only rarely and then with great care.

In certain cases, institutional bylaws, state policy, or a labor contract may require that upon petition the board review a tenure decision or hear a grievance. Boards should have guidelines that anticipate and address these circumstances. These guidelines should include:

- A statement of the board's authority to render a final decision
- Establishment of a review procedure that ensures due process and respects confidentiality
- Assignment of the responsibility for review to an appropriate board unit, such as the education or faculty affairs committee
- Prescription of the range of sanctions and remedies that can be applied
- Description of the general circumstances, such as a charge of unlawful discrimination, under which the board might consider questions of individual merit

Prior to undertaking any review, the board and the president should consider the need for legal counsel to assist them in such matters as due process, need for transcripts, sources and uses of evidence, and personal liability. However, as in all personnel policies or individual personnel actions, the board should first ask itself Is it fair? and *then* ask the university counsel Is it legal? What is legal is not always fair, but what is fair is almost always legal. Institutions that are consistently equitable and fair-minded are less likely to encounter lawsuits and more likely to win the few cases that do arise than are other institutions.

Revoking Tenure

As difficult and unpleasant as a decision to deny tenure may be, any attempt to revoke tenure will prove doubly so. Because tenure policies are designed to guard against capricious and arbitrary dismissals, such proceedings are typically cumbersome and weighted to favor the tenured faculty member. In general, tenured faculty members can be dismissed for three reasons: adequate cause, financial exigency, and program discontinuation. In all three cases, the burden of proof rests with the institution, and due process must be provided.

Dismissal for adequate cause traditionally encompasses professional incompetence, acts of moral turpitude, neglect of duty, insubordination, and dishonesty in teaching or research. Dismissals for cause are rare, not so much because colleges and universities have no incompetent faculty members, but because the political costs of such proceedings are steep and because few administrations systematically document inadequate performance over time. Usually, the problem is not with the policy per se—most schools have reasonable statements about adequate cause—but with the execution of the policy. With the end to mandatory retirement, the need for methodical longitudinal data on faculty performance will become even more critical, lest some unfit professors continue to serve.

Until the 1970s and the onset of a no-growth era, policy statements about dismissal due to financial exigency were little more than boilerplate buried deep within the faculty handbook. More and more, however, colleges and universities have been compelled by financial stringency to exhume and apply the policy. As a rule, tenure policy permits the dismissal of permanent faculty when fiscal conditions are so severe that institutional survival requires the release of these persons. Institutions may, however, set a different standard, for example, one that permits layoffs due to chronic financial stress across the campus or solely within a particular department (*Scheur* v. *Creighton University*, 1977; Furniss, 1976). In most instances, the dismissal of untenured faculty members within a program or department precedes the release of tenured personnel, although boards enjoy wide latitude to determine the criteria that govern layoffs (*Johnson* v. *Board of Regents of the University of Wisconsin System*, 1974).

Several court cases address the issue of retrenchment generally and the dismissal of tenured faculty members in particular (Kaplin, 1978, 1980). On the whole, these cases suggest that the administration and board of trustees enjoy considerable authority to determine whether or not true financial exigency exists and considerable latitude to determine the most prudent means of reducing expenses. In the absence of violations of institutional policy, a negotiated agreement, or evidence of subterfuge, the courts have afforded universities broad discretion to determine the programs and personnel to be terminated. In *Johnson* v. *Board of Regents of University of Wisconsin System* (1974), the court required state institutions to ensure due process by providing: (1) a written statement of the basis for the decision to lay off employees; (2) a reasonable description of the manner in which that decision was reached; (3) reasonable disclosure of the data the decision makers used; (4) an opportunity for terminated faculty members to argue that the decision was arbitrary, capricious, or unlawful; and (5) adequate notice and appropriate compensation to terminated employees.

Tenured faculty members may also be dismissed when an institution elects to discontinue or curtail a particular program or department. Very often, dismissals due to program discontinuation relate closely to financial considerations. However, the decision may be motivated solely by a department's quality or its centrality to the institution's mission.

From all the court cases on retrenchment and layoff one extraordinarily important principle emerges, a principle that simply cannot be overemphasized: "Each case is subject to its own contractual provisions" (*Lumpert* v. *University of Dubuque,* 1977, p. 10). What an institution can or cannot do, within the broad confines of the law, depends chiefly on the stipulations of relevant institutional policies.

Whatever the substance of an institution's retrenchment policies, the policies ought to be adopted in advance of the need to use them. The moment of crisis is not an opportune time to formulate policy, least of all retrenchment policy. Moreover, as a matter of sound practice, academic personnel and programs should be evaluated periodically. Such evaluations will help identify problems early, establish a history and habit of review, and provide valuable data to inform retrenchment decisions should cutbacks some day be deemed necessary.

Considering Modifications and Alternatives to Tenure

Although a well-established concept and a widespread practice, academic tenure has always been subject to criticism, especially in the last decade or so. Briefly stated, these criticisms are

Tenure reduces accountability. Critics argue that tenure is a one-sided contract, binding the institution to the teacher but not the teacher to the institution. With a "lifetime contract," a tenured faculty member is effectively removed from accountability and the incentive for good performance implicit in periodically having to seek contract renewal.

Tenure constrains an institution's flexibility. Each time an institution confers tenure, it makes a long-term financial commitment to an individual and a commitment to a program. Since these commitments are not easily withdrawn, the institution becomes more rigid and less capable of making commitments to other individuals and programs.

Tenure impedes affirmative action. Tenure removes positions from the job market for extended periods of time. The larger the percentage of positions filled with tenured personnel, the fewer the vacancies. Consequently, the institution must wait for retrenchment, death, or dismissal for cause before it can diversify the faculty.

Tenure establishes a class system. Tenure policies limit academic freedom and other privileges to the tenured faculty. If academic freedom is essential to professors and tenure is essential to academic freedom, how can untenured faculty members successfully practice their profession?

Tenure duplicates other protection. Critics of tenure maintain that state and federal law and numerous court decisions afford faculty all the freedom needed to teach, conduct research, and speak out. Furthermore, in the opinion of some observers, collective bargaining agreements render tenure superfluous, since these contracts provide due process, employment security, and academic freedom.

Whenever demographic and economic trends are unfavorable for higher education, criticisms of tenure seem to intensify. Thus colleges with many tenured faculty members are searching for a way to reduce the number of tenured positions, and colleges not yet tenured to capacity are looking for strategies and policies that will enable them to stay that way. From these efforts, some alternatives have emerged that either introduce modifications into a tenure system or replace tenure with a contract system. The variations arise more often at private colleges, which typically have greater flexibility to experiment (see Chait and Ford, 1982). However, some of the less radical deviations from convention are widely practiced in the public sector as well.

The simplest, although not always most desirable, modification is a tenure quota, that is, the establishment of a ceiling on the percentage of faculty members who may hold tenure at any given time. The only options are to waive the quota or wave farewell. Tenure quotas or guidelines do ensure some flexibility and the introduction of new blood. They also force hard choices, since the fixed number of tenure slots available allows only so many among eligible individuals to be accommodated. However, because only untenured faculty members are adversely affected in a direct manner by tenure quotas, the burden of resolving an institutional problem falls unevenly on one constituency. Moreover, junior faculty members, faced with bleak prospects for tenure, start to think more of enhancing their mobility than of serving the campus community.

More and more institutions have elected to extend the probationary period, normally three to seven years, that a faculty member must serve to qualify for tenure. Extended probation affords a longer time to observe and evaluate untenured faculty. Of course, the longer an untenured faculty member remains at an institution, the more likely that his or her anxiety will increase and the more difficult the decision to terminate the faculty member will become. Although the AAUP sets seven years as a standard probationary period, numerous institutions, particularly research universities, have longer probationary periods.

A modification related to extended probationary periods is a waiver of the up-or-out rule. Several independent colleges no longer require faculty either to earn tenure or to leave the institution at the conclusion of the probationary period. Instead, faculty members may be retained without tenure on renewable multiyear appointments. The so-called tenurable faculty may be considered for tenure at some future date should a tenure slot open.

Although they retain the essence of traditional tenure policy, the modifications discussed thus far do alter the notion of tenure as originally conceived. The periodic evaluation of tenured faculty, however, is not inconsistent with conventional policy. More and more institutions now evaluate tenured faculty members intermittently, perhaps every four or five years (absent an evaluation for some other purpose, such as promotion or sabbatical leave). Although few institutions have used these assessments as a means to terminate the employment of weak faculty members, the process, at its best, may lead to improved performance (Licata, 1986).

For colleges and universities that wish to abandon rather than modify conventional tenure policies, term contracts represent the only alternative. Although relatively few campuses use contract systems, most notably two-year colleges, each system has a different name and at least one different wrinkle. There are, for example, growth or learning contracts, rolling contracts, and variable-length contracts. Despite the different catchwords, all these systems share a common element: an appointment for a specific and limited time period with no assurance (or proscription) of continued employment beyond the expiration date of the contract.

In most cases, initial contracts are for a relatively brief period, such as one to three years. As a contract term draws to an end, the institution evaluates the candidate's performance to date, and the candidate presents a prospectus or statement of goals for the next contract period. Under the rolling contract system, the faculty member's multiyear contract extends, or rolls, at the end of each year as long as favorable evaluations continue. Should there be a negative evaluation, the faculty member has a fixed period of time to remedy the deficiencies noted.

In theory, contracts offer opportunities to exercise discretion, cut losses, minimize long-term commitments, maximize institutional flexibility, and make personnel changes. But not many institutions exercise these opportunities. Almost all institutions renew nearly all their contracts (Chait and Ford, 1982).

Thus far I have presented some modifications of tenure and some alternatives to tenure. Another option would be a combination of modifications and alternatives. In some ways, the "peaceful coexistence" of tenure and nontenure systems hardly represents an innovation. Nearly all institutions have had part-time and adjunct faculty in nontenured positions working side by side with tenured and tenure-track faculty. Now, however, there are more appointments of full-time faculty members to positions expressly designated as outside the tenure track, where service does not apply toward fulfillment of a probationary period. Limited-term, nontenured positions do ensure some turnover of faculty members, although the same turnover could be achieved by not reappointing probationary faculty members. However, the nontenure positions do not raise false hopes of tenure and do not leave any ambiguity about long-term prospects.

Each modification and alternative to tenure entails some tradeoffs that need to be assessed within a specific institutional context. In all cases, changes in tenure policy should be approached carefully and investigated thoroughly because these changes can touch many nerves and spawn much controversy.

Administering Promotion and Tenure Policies Effectively

Among all the alternatives to tenure, the most obvious option is often easily overlooked: to administer current policy more effectively. As noted earlier, many colleges and universities are able to make discriminating and discerning judgments and thereby hold tenure ratios to a reasonable level, perhaps between one-half and two-thirds of the full-time faculty. Although one cannot generalize too broadly, colleges and universities that do exercise selectivity share certain common policies and practices.

First, these institutions approach faculty excellence as a matter to be judged, not measured. Although some aspects of a faculty member's performance can be quantified, most cannot. Therefore, parties to the tenure process collect and review evidence appropriate to the decision at hand. Something of a judicial model applies. A jury of peers, usually at the departmental or institutional level, examines the evidence and offers a judgment, sometimes unanimous and sometimes divided. These recommendations are often appealed, reviewed, and even reversed at higher levels. Ultimately, though, informed professional educators reach a final decision.

Second, the judgments are based on clear criteria that are spelled out to the faculty member at the time of appointment. Again, clear criteria are not necessarily mathematically measurable criteria, although there may be some quantitative data to support criteria such as "effective class presentation," or "scholarly productivity." Whatever the particular criteria, they normally do not change between the time of appointment and the tenure decision. Standards of performance may change—the institution may expect more from a full professor than from an assistant professor—but the bases of judgment remain relatively constant.

Third, the criteria are not limited to individual merit. Institutional priorities are also considered. As suggested earlier, college presidents and boards of trustees must make tenure decisions against a backdrop of institutional priorities such as financial equilibrium, affirmative action, and enrollment patterns.

Fourth, the institution usually uses interim evaluations, especially at the earlier stages of a candidate's progress. Many colleges and universities employ, either formally or informally, a threshold or break-point evaluation at or near the halfway point to tenure and usually one year before the candidate's current appointment expires. (Probationary faculty members normally have one- to three-year contracts, renewable at the institution's option.) These comprehensive interim evaluations are clearly understood by all to be a significant hurdle en route to tenure. At the conclusion of the assessments, the appropriate academic officer informs the weakest fac-

ulty members that their probationary appointments will not be renewed. This process is referred to as "weeding out."

Fifth, nearly all institutions with well-managed tenure practices require multilevel reviews at the time of the tenure decision.
Each level introduces a somewhat different perspective. To maintain institutional quality, a department must be made answerable
to a larger constituency, for example, colleagues at the same institution but in allied fields, peers in the same field but at other institutions, or perhaps both. Divisional or collegewide committees
can actually serve to protect strong departments against weak departments with lesser standards.

Sixth, these institutions employ someone at or near the top
able to say no on close votes if institutional priorities so dictate. To
retain the confidence and goodwill of faculty members party to the
decision and to ensure the integrity of the process, however, the
president or provost shares his or her thinking with the collegewide
committee, the dean, and the department head.

These policies and practices are by no means surefire solutions to the tenure problem. Much depends on the institutional
context, local tradition, and individual leadership. But any steps
taken to administer tenure policies more effectively are likely to
have a more immediate, positive, and pragmatic effect than are
rhetorical assaults against the concept of tenure.

Auditing Promotion and Tenure Policies

To audit promotion and tenure policies, a board of trustees or its
academic affairs committee should ask a series of questions of the
administration approximately every year. Some of the questions
concern the evaluation process that underlies promotion and tenure
decisions; others concern the outcomes of the review process.

With respect to the evaluation of faculty members, the board
might ask:

- What are the primary purposes of faculty evaluation?
- What areas of responsibility are evaluated and what criteria are
  applied?
- Are the standards based on performance relative to others on

campus, national norms, or the achievement of certain objectives?

- What evidence does the college gather and from whom? How are student evaluations incorporated into the process?
- Who participates in the evaluation? What role, if any, do students, peers, administrators, and outside experts play in the decision-making process?
- How often do evaluations occur? Are all faculty members, tenured and untenured, evaluated regularly?
- Who manages the evaluation process?
- How are faculty members informed of the results of the process?

The board should be satisfied that the faculty and the administration together have articulated reasonable purposes for and areas of evaluation and suitable criteria, standards, and sources of evidence.

From time to time, professors and administrators may suggest that the work of an academic, especially a teacher, simply cannot be evaluated. Trustees should be skeptical of such assertions. Numerous books describe in detail workable, sensible faculty evaluation programs as well as tools and techniques that can be instituted to collect valid data from students, colleagues, and administrators to gauge faculty performance in teaching, research, and service (see, for example, Seldin, 1984; Centra, 1979.) The failure to adopt a well-designed, comprehensive system for evaluating faculty members may reflect, therefore, a lack of political will and desire more than the absence of sound evaluation technology.

To understand the results of the promotion and tenure process, the board should request certain outcome data on a regular basis, probably once a year. Although these data should not be construed as indicators of quality, they will familiarize the board with the results of promotion and tenure decisions and should provoke a discussion with faculty and staff about the effectiveness of the tenure system and whether the institution's objectives are being met. The data presented to the board should answer the following questions:

- What percentage of a faculty cohort (people appointed in the same year) reached the point of the tenure decision? What per-

centage resigned and why? (Absolute numbers may be more informative for small colleges.)
- Of those people considered for promotion or tenure, what percentage were successful?
- How many promotion or tenure decisions led to a grievance on substance? On procedure?
- Are there any marked differences in success rates among various academic units?
- What is the tenure ratio and how is it calculated? What percentage of the instructional payroll is committed to tenured faculty?
- What is the projected tenure level five and ten years from now?
- Are there any marked differences in the success rates of women and members of minorities in achieving promotion and tenure compared with other faculty members?

Although an institution's ability to recruit and retain a talented and diverse faculty is not immediately germane to the promotion and tenure process, trustees may be concerned with the issue. To gain information about the issue, trustees might ask: How many appointments offered by the college were declined and why? How many faculty members whom the college would have preferred to retain resigned and why? Were women and minorities disproportionately represented among these categories? What steps can the institution take to reduce the number of rejected offers and unwanted resignations?

Promotion and tenure success rates and the institution's ability or inability to attract and retain faculty should be critical concerns of trustees, particularly in regard to female and minority faculty members. Despite some twenty years of formal affirmative action programs on almost every campus, the numbers reveal little progress. African Americans constitute little more than 1 percent of all full-time faculty members at public colleges and universities, exclusive of historically black colleges—a proportion virtually unchanged over the past decade. The percentage of black faculty members nationwide (4.1 percent) has actually dropped somewhat since 1977. Hispanics make up about 1.6 percent of the full-time professoriate. Although the proportion of female faculty members has increased slightly over the past 30 years to about 27 percent, women represent only 11 percent of full professors and 23 percent of associate professors. Furthermore, women at all ranks earn less than men, and the overall salary gap between men and women has actually widened (National Center for Education Statistics, 1990, pp. 219, 223).

Policy recommendations to advance affirmative action are not in short supply (Washington and Harvey, 1989; Blackwell, 1988; Brown, 1988) and have not changed dramatically over the past fifteen years (Carnegie Council on Policy Studies in Higher Education, 1975). Boards of trustees should be especially mindful that successful affirmative action programs require a very visible commitment by the institution's leadership, which surely includes the board. Evidence of that commitment includes heartfelt rhetoric as well as concrete actions, such as the recruitment and advancement of a multicultural faculty (Hyer, 1985; Washington and Harvey, 1989). Boards and institutions committed to affirmative action should vigilantly audit the effects and results of promotion and tenure policies on efforts to diversify the faculty.

Personnel policies extend well beyond promotion, tenure, and affirmative action. There are, for example, the questions of salaries, work loads, benefits, and professional development. Not all of these issues can be addressed in a single chapter, perhaps not even in a single volume. Yet policy formulations on all these issues can be approached in a similar manner. Above all else, there should be a clear understanding on the board's part of the purposes to be served and the goals to be attained by a particular policy or practice. Against that backdrop, the administration should draft policies in concert with the faculty and then seek the board's counsel and reactions. Once adopted, the effectiveness of a policy—the degree to which it attains the stated objectives—should be monitored by the administration and reported periodically to the board, with changes recommended as necessary.

Sound personnel policies and procedures are neither a panacea nor a substitute for talented faculty and adequate resources. However, poor policies or ineffective implementation of policies can reduce motivation, provoke dissatisfaction, and waste human and fiscal resources. By contrast, well-reasoned and well-administered policies can help to create an overall environment that is conducive to bringing out the best in people. And is that not another way of stating the principal goal of education?

Court Cases Cited

Board of Regents v. *Roth*, 408 U.S. 564 (1972).

Johnson v. *Board of Regents of the University of Wisconsin System*, 377 F. Supp. 230 (1974).

Krotkoff v. *Goucher College*, 585 F. 2d 675 (1978).

Lumpert v. *University of Dubuque*, 255 N.W.2d 168 (1977).

National Labor Relations Board v. *Yeshiva University*. 444 U.S. 672 (1980).

Perry v. *Sinderman*, 408 U.S. 593 (1972).

Scheur v. *Creighton University*, 260 N.W. 2d 595 (1977).

CHAPTER 16

Defining, Assessing, and Nurturing Quality

E. Grady Bogue

Conventional assumptions about collegiate quality often appear in the conversations of academic leaders, board members, and civic leaders. These assumptions include, for example, the notions that only a few colleges can be of high quality and that high-quality schools are expensive to attend, large and comprehensive, highly selective, or nationally recognized or have impressive resources.

This cluster of assumptions evokes a pyramidal image of quality. Old and large research universities cluster at the apex of the pyramid. Former teachers colleges (now universities) reside in the middle. Community colleges dominate the base. Liberal arts colleges may be sprinkled throughout this pyramidal structure, depending upon their perceived attributes. Is this pyramidal image a narrowly conceived model of collegiate quality that fosters an unnecessary and unhelpful arrogance? As noted in *Trustees and Troubled Times in Higher Education* (Association of Governing Boards of Universities and Colleges, 1992c, p. 22), it is a model "driven by the prestige of research" and designed "to stoke academic egos instead of students' dreams." Let us consider a contrasting image.

Peter Senge, author of *The Fifth Discipline* (1990), offers this conviction: "I do not believe great organizations have ever been

287

built by trying to emulate another, any more than individual greatness is achieved by trying to copy another 'great person'" (p. 11). Under this assumption, high quality results not from imitating another institution or individual but in reaching for and discovering one's own promise and distinction, whether personal or organizational. Our assumptions, our "mental maps," may be both confining and facilitating as we attempt to impart meaning to the world about us.

Questions of Quality

What do we hope to achieve and how good a job are we doing? Questions of this type about purpose and performance are premier leadership questions for any organized enterprise, corporate or collegiate. These questions of quality are surely critical to board members and others who hold institutions in trust. In this chapter, I hope to expand the understanding of how collegiate organizations define, assess, and nurture quality. A second purpose is to identify a cluster of "governing ideas" that will enable the board member to evaluate both the intent and the impact of campus quality-assurance programs and policies.

    To recite here the evidence of our national concern with quality in both business and government is unnecessary. This concern is apparent in U.S. colleges and universities, as a review of newspapers, magazines, contemporary books, and electronic news media coverage will attest. The board member interested in specific citations of such evidence will find them in Resource D.

    The current national debate on quality has raised a range of questions and issues for the public and the academic community to consider, including:

- Is quality in limited supply? Can only a few institutions be of high quality?
- Is quality to be expressed in a single performance indicator, or does it take more data than that from a single indicator to illuminate organizational performance?
- How can a definition and assessment of collegiate quality rec-

ognize the diversity of institutional missions and simultaneously respect meaningful performance standards?

- To what extent should information on quality be subject to public disclosure?
- Are quality and funding always linked in positive and direct correlation? What variables, other than money, directly affect the quality of programs and services?
- What is to be the primary purpose for the assessment of quality—improvement or accountability?

With the last question in mind, the question of purpose, I will begin with a story that highlights the issue of accountability and reveals the most fundamental purpose of our quest for quality.

The First Accountability

Years ago, I remember agonizing over the performance of a graduate student, which I described in *The Evidence for Quality* (Bogue and Saunders, 1992, pp. 5-6), as follows: "A thirty-year old woman enrolled in a graduate course has submitted a major paper. This paper is not just grammatically incorrect; it is incoherent! Her performance in the course has been marginal on every dimension, culminating in this disappointing and heartbreaking final paper. Any reasonable standard of acceptable performance would not encourage a passing grade for this paper, much less for the course. It might be argued that each person contributing to the meaning of this student's bachelor's degree has committed an act of malpractice, cheating this woman of her potential and dignity."

How could this have happened? This woman is a graduate of an institution that is regionally accredited and of a program that is professionally accredited. Think of the simple attitudes and actions it would have taken to discover whether this student could write a grammatically correct sentence, a coherent paragraph, a sensible essay. Think of the corrective action that could and should have been taken early in her collegiate career. "This example illustrates a mind left wasted, a mind left dispirited and disengaged. To know that this student has been exposed to a lower quality climate requires no great philosophical agony in defining quality nor any technological feat in measuring it" (pp. 5-6).

Is not the first accountability of an institution to its students? Board members can and should ascertain whether every campus within the circle of their care is meeting this first accountability. Conversations built on hazy and narrow notions of quality should yield to more thoughtful and substantive exchanges. Having in hand a definition of quality is an essential first step.

Definition of Quality

Few themes have occupied the attention of such a diverse array of minds over such a long period of time as the theme of quality. Poets and philosophers, executives and employees, scholars and statesmen, those who teach and those who are taught recognize that the search for quality is never ending.

Although defining quality is a challenge of the highest order for higher education, it is not a challenge unique to colleges and universities. A widely recognized writer on the corporate sector, Philip Crosby, defines quality simply as "conformance to requirements" (1984, p. 60). A book published by the American Management Association—*I Know It When I See It: A Modern Fable About Quality*—touts customer satisfaction as the principal indicator of quality: "Customers aren't interested in our specs. They're interested in the answer to one simple question: did the product do what I expected it to do?" (Guaspari, 1985, p. 68). In his book *Managing Quality* (1988), David Garvin describes the multiple dimensions of quality as follows:

- Performance—the "fitness for use" test: Does the product do what the consumer wants?
- Features—the "bells and whistles" that supplement the basic functions and add competitive edge.
- Reliability—how long till the first failure or need for repair?
- Conformance—the extent to which the product meets established specification and manufacturer standards.
- Durability—the length of product life.
- Serviceability—speed, cost, and ease of repair.

- Esthetics—a highly subjective but measurable aspect of product appeal.
- Perceived quality—is a Honda built in the United States perceived as a Japanese car? Is it perceived to be of higher quality than a car with an American brand name?

The spirit of those people who put heart and meaning into our organizations, whether corporate or collegiate, and the importance of the perception of quality that they create is nicely presented by Jan Carlzon, president of Scandinavian Airlines, in *Moments of Truth* (1987, p. 2): "But if you ask our customers about SAS, they won't tell you about our planes or our offices or the way we finance our capital investment. Instead, they talk about their experiences with the people of SAS." Think about the thousand collegiate "moments of truth" created in any week through the interaction of students with faculty and staff. Here is an important governing idea of collegiate quality: it is the people, the faculty and staff members, who give operational meaning to the word *quality*.

The man who gave impetus to the rapid enhancement of quality in Japanese industry and perhaps the most renowned and oft-quoted American authority on the issue of quality, W. Edwards Deming, furnishes still another aspect of the definition of quality. The first item in Deming's list of fourteen points for management is to "create constancy of purpose for improvement of product and service" (1986, p. 24). The essence of quality, from Deming's perspective, is the commitment to constant improvement—a second governing idea and theme to which I will return.

Are academic definitions of quality different from those cited for the corporate sector? There are similarities and serious points of departure. Among the leading researchers and writers in U.S. higher education is Alexander Astin, who gives this definition of quality (1985, p. 61): "The most excellent institutions are, in this view, those that have the greatest impact—add the most value, as economists would say—on the student's knowledge and personal development and on the faculty member's scholarly and pedagogical ability and productivity." This definition moves away from an emphasis on size and selectivity and accents results rather than reputation.

Another statesman of U.S. higher education is Lewis Mayhew. He and his coauthors offer a slightly different definition of quality in *Quest for Quality:* "Quality undergraduate education consists of preparing learners though the use of words, numbers, and abstract concepts to understand, cope with, and positively influence the environment in which they find themselves" (Mayhew, Ford, and Hubbard, 1990, p. 29). This definition, while useful, fails to acknowledge the idea that education at every level in our society is a moral enterprise. Whether it acknowledges the role of passion, appropriately celebrated in such books as Peters and Austin's 1985 work, *A Passion for Excellence,* is another question. The role of passion in the nurturing of quality will be discussed later.

In *The Evidence for Quality,* Robert Saunders and I ventured this definition of quality: "Quality is conformance to mission specification and goal achievement—within publicly accepted standards of accountability and integrity" (Bogue and Saunders, 1992, p. 20). What we hoped to achieve in this definition was to recognize, respect, and reinforce the concept that there are varieties of excellence in U.S. higher education, from Stanford University in the West to Samford University in the South, from Centenary College to Central Piedmont Community College, from the Air Force Academy to Antioch University. Anyone who takes in the grand sweep of U.S. higher education will immediately and intuitively sense the folly of the pyramidal image described earlier, an image that so often fashions our notions of quality. Respect for diversity, for varieties of excellence, is another governing idea that is essential to an effective quality-assurance program.

Saunders and I also wanted to ensure that our definition of quality embraced an ethical test. Contemporary news coverage, reports and critiques on higher education, and conference themes on public trust in higher education highlight current concerns with integrity in higher education. A pattern of unfortunate administrative and faculty behavior is leading to what some commentators describe as a loss of sanctuary for higher education. In the eyes of some, higher education is no longer a place where "Mr. Chips" lives. Although any one ethical abuse may be seen as an exception to a more general rule of integrity, we cannot claim to be nurturing quality while stealing from our institutions, governments, and clients.

A definition of collegiate quality cannot rest on the assumption that quality is in limited supply. It must be based on the idea that quality is attainable and essential to each and every campus for which a board member is responsible. And it must include the idea that quality will always be related to mission and that the mission of any campus, no matter how comprehensive, will always be limited. A campus or system of campuses with units or programs differing in mission is understandable. A campus or system of campuses with second-class units or programs is more difficult to defend.

A preference for closure and a discomfort with ambiguity might urge the selection of a "best" definition of quality from among those presented here. There are, however, informative and helpful elements in each of these definitions. Astin's definition (1985), for example, suggests that a school making no developmental contribution, no value-added contribution, to its students would hardly be considered a quality institution. The definition of Mayhew, Ford, and Hubbard (1990) affirms that a school not equipping its graduates to cope with and positively influence the environment could not be considered a high-quality institution. Saunders and I urge (1992) that collegiate quality must be related to mission and goals, to the educational and ethical performance of the institution. The complex nature of quality requires a multifaceted approach to the assessment of quality, a matter to which I now turn.

Assessment of Quality

Can we trust the assertion, cited earlier, that customer satisfaction is the primary indicator of quality (Guaspari, 1985)? Perhaps under some conditions. But academic leaders and governing boards can do better than that. Board members can assemble concrete and specific evidence on quality. They can, and should, know as much about their students on exit as they do on entry—about changes in their knowledge, skill, and attitudes. There are several questions that can inform and focus discussions on assessing quality.

1. How can we improve decision making? In the corporate

world, we make design, production, and marketing decisions. In the collegiate world, we make decisions to implement, revise, and terminate programs and to admit, place, advance, suspend, and graduate students. Such decisions should be informed by assessment. A simple decision-making model suggests that most decisions about quality in collegiate work turn on the need to establish accountability for programs and services and to support action leading to the improvement of programs and services.

2. What indicators will we accept as evidence of quality? Earlier, I noted David Garvin's citation of factors such as fitness for use, reliability, conformance to specification, and durability for use in assessing the quality of industrial products. Higher education has fashioned a wide array of factors that give evidence of quality, including:

• Accreditation—the test of achievement of mission and goals
• Rankings and ratings—the test of reputation
• Outcomes—the test of value added
• Licensure—the test of professional standards
• Program reviews—the test of peer review
• Follow-up studies—the test of client satisfaction

Each of these factors has strengths and liabilities. Perhaps the oldest and best-known seal of collegiate quality, accreditation, is built on the premise and promise of mission integrity and performance improvement. But the accreditation process has been criticized and has been called, for example, a periodic exercise in professional back scratching. Ranking and rating studies, including the well-known annual ranking of schools in *U.S. News and World Report* and media ratings of "America's best colleges," keep discussions about quality alive but offer little help in efforts to improve quality and are often referred to as quantified gossip. Student satisfaction is legitimate and essential evidence of quality. However, student satisfaction may be inversely related to quality in educational settings. A more detailed evaluation of these different types of evidence can be found in *The Evidence for Quality* (Bogue and Saunders, 1992).

Earlier I discussed the importance of relating quality to mission. To that idea, I add another governing idea—the importance of assembling multiple sources of evidence on quality. The nature of both personal and institutional performance is too complex and diverse to be captured in a single point of data. Consider the leadership and educational posture of the accounting department chair who knows that his or her students have the highest pass rate on the certified public accountant examination of any institution in the state, who has a trend line of high satisfaction from graduates over recent years, whose files are filled with complimentary letters from employers of her graduates, whose students regularly perform better than students in other departments on campuswide assessments of communication and critical thinking skills, and whose department was praised by a recent program review panel of accounting faculty from other institutions. This chair has a cluster of evidence about performance that is useful in making both decisions and improvements. Just as physicians do not have a "health meter" in their offices but assess our health by examining a cluster of medical evidence, so do academics need a cluster of performance evidence to make quality judgments about students, programs, and institutions.

3. What standard of performance will be acceptable? Identifying performance evidence raises the question of standards. There are three types of standards:

- Criterion standards—comparing performance to a predetermined criterion level
- Comparative standards—judging performance against a "normed" population of students or programs
- Connoisseurship standards—evaluating performance through the opinions and values of a panel of judges

Accreditation and program reviews are built heavily on the connoisseurship standard, in which the evidence of quality is evaluated according to the knowledge, values, and experience of the visiting team. Whether a program or an institution gets a pass or fail, an excellent or unsatisfactory rating, depends on the judgment of the team. And this leads to the final question.

4. Who will make the judgments of quality? In its early

rankings of schools by reputation, *U.S. News and World Report* asked college presidents to rank institutions. An argument could be made that the president of Vanguard University may know little about Coastal College, beyond his or her friendship with the president or limited anecdotal evidence. From such tangential knowledge can come reputational rankings circulated over the land. To the credit of *U.S. News and World Report,* later rankings revealed increased sophistication of criteria and judges. A single rater using a global criterion was replaced with multiple raters using multiple criteria. Both campus officers and board members need to know whether those people judging the quality of programs and services have sufficient knowledge and experience to warrant their confidence.

The principal reason for an aggressive quality-assurance program on any campus should be to inform the decisions made about students, policies, and programs—the call of first accountability. Unfortunately, too many campuses still require assessment exercises having no utility in decision making or no application whatsoever. For example, a two-year college and a university required their graduates to take a test of general education. But neither institution used the results in its decisions about programs or student performance. It would not be difficult for a board member to discover whether a campus was using information about quality in its policy and program decisions. Quality-assurance ventures should be ventures in learning and discovery.

The search for truth certainly involves the theoretical but can involve elements of empiricism and accident as well. Reflection and action are complements in the search for truth.

Nurturing Quality

What questions can board members use to evaluate quality-assurance policies and programs on the campus or campuses for which they are responsible? Here are themes and questions to help examine campus commitment to quality assurance—a summary look at the governing ideas I have been advancing.

Distinctive Mission Statement

Does the campus have a distinctive mission statement? Questions of ends encourage questions of beginnings. Inquiries about performance will eventually lead to inquiries about purpose. The architecture of the campus mission furnishes an essential foundation for an effective quality-assurance effort. Does the campus have a concise statement of mission and values, a statement that clearly and forcefully reveals what the campus stands for? If the name of the campus were masked in the mission statement and the content were so vague and undistinctive that it could describe a hundred other campuses, the institution could have a quality problem.

Evidence of Improvement

Can the campus offer evidence of improvements that have been made to programs and policies as a result of assessment and inquiries about quality? This question should be posed and answered for every organized unit on a campus. A campus or program unit that cannot offer a reasonably prompt and substantive answer to the question What did you do with what you found out? deserves skepticism about the strength and substance of its quality assurance efforts.

Links to Teaching and Learning

How have quality-assurance activities been used to improve teaching and learning, to enhance student, faculty, and staff growth and development? Are quality-assurance and assessment activities "faculty friendly?" Board members will not have to search their memories very deeply to remember who the primary architects of quality are. They are the faculty members who elevate our vision, lift us from the poverty of the commonplace, and push us to the far edge of our potential. Assessment and quality-assurance exercises unconnected to improving teaching and learning are empty exercises.

Multiple Indicators

An effective quality-assurance program will involve multiple sources of evidence on both student and program performance. Does the campus have a variety of quality evidence from conventional tests, program reviews, accreditation, licensure results, client satisfaction and follow-up ratings, and perhaps more innovative sources that facilitate assessment?

External Standards

In the early history of U.S. higher education, one of the principal roles of board members was to "examine" the proposed graduates. Thus, to the judgments and standards of the faculty was added the "external standard" of the board. The use of external standards continues to be found in externally referenced assessment exercises and the use of external teams in accreditation and program review.

There is a philosophical tension inherent in this governing idea. Some contemporary philosophies of quality, total quality management (TQM), for example, justifiably insist that those people responsible for the product are responsible for quality. Is it a misplacement of trust to insert a third party or external standard into the quality-assurance process? I think not. An essential feature of the academy is testing ideas against the larger community of scholars. The results of our work must come into the public forum at some time.

Strategic Perspective

Does the campus have a strategic and unifying vision of quality? This vision will be built on the idea that there is no policy, no behavior, no practice that does not influence quality. Moreover, there will be a coherent and logical system of interactions among the various institutional approaches to quality assurance. The philosophy and components of the quality-assurance system will be characterized by awareness and allegiance, that is, the system will be known and owned by faculty and staff.

A campus whose quality-assurance efforts consider these governing ideas will experience the power of renewal inherent in these ideas. Such a campus will rediscover its purpose and priority, promote the development of its faculty and staff members through continued learning, and strengthen its community. There can be no quality in an educational enterprise without caring, and there can be no caring without community. With this note on community and quality in mind, let us examine a concept currently in vogue, that of total quality management, and ask what potential it offers for collegiate quality assurance.

Total Quality Management

The term *total quality management,* or *strategic quality management,* has emerged from the work of a cluster of writers that includes W. Edwards Deming, Walter A. Shewart, Philip Crosby, Joseph Juran, and David Garvin. An informative and integrating work that discusses the application of TQM to higher education is Daniel Seymour's *On Q: Causing Quality in Higher Education* (1992). Seymour is "convinced that accrediting agencies, program reviews, standing committees, control-minded governing boards, and the occasional well-intentioned task force" will not be the instruments for causing quality in higher education (p. x). He offers TQM as an answer to his question, Is there a better way to manage higher education?

Seymour identifies these principles as the operational embodiment of strategic quality management:

> Quality is meeting or exceeding customer needs.
> Quality is everyone's job.
> Quality is continuous improvement.
> Quality is leadership.
> Quality is human resource development.
> Quality is in the system.
> Quality is fear reduction.
> Quality is recognition and reward.
> Quality is teamwork.
> Quality is measurement.
> Quality is systematic problem solving.

Most of these principles are not inimical to the governing ideas I have offered in this chapter. Although Seymour's commentary on TQM is compatible with what I have built thus far, his advocacy of TQM warrants thoughtful review. Seymour suggests that current and conventional quality instruments, such as program reviews and accreditation, make little significant contribution to collegiate quality. He sees these instruments as occasional devices that convey the appearance of quality and that establish a "good enough" mindset. Those people who have been on both the giving and receiving end of program and accreditation reviews will know the liabilities of these and other measures of quality previously cited in this chapter. Both these instruments are built, however, on the premise and promise of improvement, an idea central to TQM and one of the governing ideas of quality emphasized in this chapter.

Is it necessary to deprecate the contributions of the quality-assurance instruments already in place in order to appreciate what TQM has to offer? I think not. Space constraints do not permit scrutiny of all the principles of TQM. Having accented the principle of continuous improvement, I elect to examine two additional ideas from TQM: client satisfaction and systematic problem solving.

The driving principle of TQM is the principle of client satisfaction. Few would argue that faculty and staff listen enough to students and other clients. There are, however, critical differences between corporate and collegiate settings in the application of this principle. Any faculty member who has found his or her caring for students in tension with caring for standards knows the limitation of this test of quality for colleges and universities. Students do indeed, as Seymour (1992) suggests, vote with their feet. It is sad when they occasionally vote for shoddy and shallow options. But when they do, the ideal of quality should not be exchanged for the notion of satisfaction.

Seymour offers a chapter in his book titled "Choosing to be Distinctive." It is a clarion call that opens with this painful but accurate note: "The reason so few people have a clear understanding of their institution's vision is because there is really nothing in it worth remembering" (1992, p. 62). As Seymour notes, the more "filler" and generalities one can find in a mission or vision statement, the less likely that a campus can translate that vision into a high-quality reality. Linking quality to mission requires a thoughtfully constructed mission statement, as I affirmed in an earlier governing idea.

Many campuses are trying TQM as a problem-solving tool. For most, it has offered an exciting and renewing agenda. Although some faculty members and administrative officers see TQM as appropriate for improvements in the admissions office, business office, facilities maintenance office, campus security office, or other administrative settings, others note, as does Seymour, that these are not the only settings where "we degrade, we hassle, and we ignore" (1992, p. 115). Will we be as quick to see opportunities for listening to our clients, for continuous improvement, for problem solving in the academic heart of colleges and universities—where students can be put in harm's way by low and empty expectations, by assessment exercises having little or no utility in decision making, by a vision of quality depending more on faculty publication counts than teaching and caring for students? This is a question that board members can legitimately explore.

Whether the initial euphoria and the subsequent quiet passage of some previously heralded management concepts will, in retrospect, also describe the fate of TQM in colleges and universities remains a test of time. An argument can be made that many of the philosophical principles of TQM have been at work in academia for some time. The quest for quality is a continuous process, and there is no reason to neglect any conceptual tool that will aid us in that quest. As with any tool, the effectiveness of its application turns on the artistry of the user in ensuring that it fits the time, task, and place.

Heart First: A Vision of Quality

Boards can ascertain whether campuses under their care can offer a range of evidence of collegiate quality; whether these campuses can furnish evidence on policy, program, and personnel improvements that have been made as a result of inquiries about quality; and whether educational and management decisions are being informed by information about quality. These are conceptual or "head first" concerns, and they are among the most important governing ideas of quality cited in this chapter.

But the principal guarantor of quality is not "head first" but "heart first" actions of caring and daring. Academic leaders and trustees should care enough for truth, service, and human growth and dignity to ensure that their vision of quality pervades the campus. The vision should call students and colleagues from the poverty of the commonplace, through higher standards, consistent encouragement, active compassion, respect for diversity, and renewed dedication to the highest ethical standards. Such a promise can be realized if we conceive of academic quality as synonymous with the campus as a community of caring (Bogue and Saunders, 1992).

In *Sand and Foam*, Kahlil Gibran wrote: "Your heart and my mind will never agree until your mind ceases to live in numbers and my heart in the mist" (1973, p. 30). Not all that is real, not all that is meaningful, not all that is beautiful in colleges and universities, or any other learning organization, will yield to numbers. There are, however, governing ideas that encourage colleges and universities to effectively address questions of performance—questions as legitimate and essential to collegiate organizations as to others. In fact, these questions are more legitimate and essential in colleges and universities than in other organizations. A mind and heart cheated of promise and potential—is this not a more painful mistake than a faulty computer or stereo? In recommending the governing ideas of quality to trustees, I seek not so much consensus or closure as to promote a more open curiosity about the nature and nurture of quality, to encourage a vision of collegiate quality assurance as a venture of both decision and discovery, and to promote an agenda of caring and daring.

PART THREE

Developing
the Public Board

Governing boards are only as effective as their individual members: how they conduct themselves in meetings, how they educate themselves and are educated by their leaders, how well they are led, and how well they are served by their chief executives and staffs. None of these matters should be left to chance or to ad hoc attention.

The five chapters in Part Three are devoted to the process of developing effective trustees, of ensuring that good boards are on the path to becoming better boards. Offering suggestions on subjects ranging from the orientation of new board members and in-service education programs to the responsibility of boards to study their own performance periodically, these chapters provide practical guidelines for trustee and staff leaders.

Two individuals bear most of the responsibility for developing the board: the board chair and the president or chancellor. The position of board or university secretary continues to evolve as an important influence in helping the board chair and chief executive fulfill their own and their board's responsibilities. Two chapters address these leadership positions and their relationships with the governing board.

In sum, Part Three suggests a variety of options available to governing boards and their leaders to strengthen their abilities to meet the high expectations held for them by so many people. Effective trustees and governing boards are the result of good planning, teamwork, and focused attention on their education and development.

CHAPTER 17

Orienting Trustees and Developing the Board

Robert L. Gale
Frances Freeman

The boards of independent colleges and universities have the advantage of being able to select their own members, but members of public boards are appointed or elected by others. In states where the governor appoints trustees, incumbent board members can seek appropriate ways to inform the governor of the skills that are needed. Some governors may welcome lists of nominees. In that case, the creation of an external body to recruit, screen, and recommend nominees is an excellent means of injecting more objectivity into the process. In states where boards are elected, incumbent trustees might make known the qualities and areas of expertise that are needed in potential candidates. In the hands of appropriate people, guidelines, checklists, and matrices that deal with the key needs of the board and the desired qualifications of candidates can have significant impact on how decisions are made.

Candidates for public boards should be considered on two separate dimensions. The first is diversity, that is, personal characteristics such as age, sex, ethnicity, and so forth. The second is professional position and expertise, as well as the individual talents that enable a board to do its job effectively. Some of the desirable characteristics sought in trustees are financial acumen; legal expertise; lobbying or political skills; knowledge of higher education;

305

and knowledge of areas such as marketing, government relations, athletics, medicine, hospital management, investments, real estate, or physical plant management.

Today's board members are expected to be strongly committed to the integrity and development of their institution and willing to devote time to that commitment beyond the hours spent in board or committee meetings. They are expected to consciously seek opportunities to spend time on campus, attend ceremonies and special events, and be continually aware of their responsibility to ensure that the fundamental mission of the institution is fulfilled to the greatest degree possible. These expectations border on the unrealistic, as few trustees come to their volunteer duties fully understanding the time and energy required of them.

Need for Trustee Orientation

A well-conducted orientation process is an essential requirement for effective trusteeship. In many cases, trustees of public institutions have not had previous experience with the institution or as a trustee, nor have their appointments been based on a particular expertise or background relevant to the board's responsibilities. Once new board members have been made aware of how the responsibilities of the board and the individual trustee differ and complement one another, they must be shown how to discharge the responsibilities.

In a public institution or system, the orientation of new trustees can be the province of an orientation committee or a small ad hoc committee of thoughtful, respected board leaders or elected board officers. The committee need not conduct the orientation program but should provide leadership and oversee the program. A small committee of the board can help to ensure that the program is comprehensive and credible. It is especially important for the board's elected leaders to assume a visible role in the orientation process.

The chief executive should have the primary responsibility for guiding the committee in the planning and implementation of the orientation program. He or she should be recognized as the person most responsible for the new trustee's understanding of the institution or system. The administrator should keep a low profile in carrying out this duty to encourage the involvement of respected members of the board.

All trustees share the same basic responsibilities, but the unique aspects of system and multicampus governance require special attention during the orientation of new trustees. The trustee on a multicampus board holds in trust not just one campus or university but possibly up to twenty or more. Moreover, the trustee on a system board is entrusted with a legal and political abstraction, more than an institution or set of institutions or campuses.

In addition to imparting practical information on trusteeship, orientation programs need to engender identification with institutional and corporate entities and missions and make multicampus and system trustees sensitive to the need to be evenhanded in dealing with the needs and aspirations of all their campuses. The challenge of the trustees, along with that of the chief executive, will be to ensure equity among campuses, effective and intelligent coordination of educational objectives, and recognition of diversity and individual institutional pride while fostering creativity and initiative at each campus.

Guidelines for Orientation Programs

The first step in preparing an effective orientation program is to acknowledge that such a program is needed. Boards should adopt a statement of trustee responsibilities that emphasizes the importance of an orientation program, the goals of the program, and the desired results of the program. The involvement of appropriate members of the administration in the orientation program is also essential.

Boards should also consider adopting a brief statement of individual trustees' responsibilities to clarify what board members expect of one another. An institutional code of conduct for individual members helps new board members understand the obligations and commitments they assume in accepting a trusteeship. The prospective code demands careful consideration by the trustees in consultation with the chief executive. A code might include the following requirements for trustees:

- Devote time to learning the major responsibilities of governing boards and how the particular institution functions.
- Prepare for, regularly attend, and actively participate in board meetings and committee assignments.
- Accept and abide by the legal and fiscal responsibilities of the board as specified by the institutional charter, bylaws, and statutes and regulations.
- Vote according to one's individual conviction, challenge the judgment of others when necessary, and yet be willing to support the majority decision and work in a spirit of cooperation with fellow board members.
- Maintain the confidential nature of board deliberations and avoid acting as a spokesperson for the entire board unless so designated.
- Avoid participation in administrative functions and learn and use appropriate institutional channels when conducting board business.
- Know and comply with board policy on conditions that constitute conflict of interest, vehicles for disclosure, and procedures to be followed when a conflict of interest is perceived to exist.
- Support the institution's fund-raising efforts through personal giving according to one's means and share in the solicitation of others.
- Refrain from actions and involvements that might prove embarrassing to the institution and resign if such actions or involvements develop.
- Make judgments on the basis of the best interests of the institution and avoid serving special interests.

Trustees should be asked as soon as possible after their appointment or election to participate in an orientation program scheduled sometime within their first few months in office. They should plan for a minimum of one day on campus, although two days are preferable. Arrangements should be made for trustees to be housed on campus and to meet faculty and students in relaxed, comfortable settings.

Each new trustee should be assigned to a "trustee sponsor," that is, an experienced board member who can help the new person learn the ropes. Restraint should be exercised in the amount of written material given to new board members in preparation for their orientation: avoid overloading them with too much too soon.

The three basic objectives of the orientation program are to acquaint the new trustee with the institution (or institutions, in the case of a multicampus board), the responsibilities of the board as a whole, and the responsibilities of the trustee as an individual. The trustee should spend time on campus, taking a walking tour and visiting a class or two—with advance permission from the instructors, of course. Scheduling orientation around some major campus event, such as a cultural activity or lecture, provides further opportunity for the trustee to experience campus life. The trustee should also have free time for relaxation and wandering. If the board is responsible for more than one campus, the new board member might be invited to visit a campus that he or she would otherwise rarely visit. Happily, most multicampus boards do rotate their meetings from campus to campus.

The new trustee should be briefed, with an opportunity for questions, on administrative and academic organization, programs, and priorities; budget, finance, and fund-raising programs; physical plant priorities, maintenance, and energy; and highlights of institutional objectives. Concise summaries should be provided of institutional data on enrollment, faculty size and characteristics, budget and endowment, legislative information, state laws, and schools and programs. Other material might include a description of the institution's history and development; a one-paragraph biographical sketch of each trustee (along with committee assignments and offices); and a list of key administrators, faculty members, and student leaders. To avoid inundating trustees with more than they want or need to read, a board may provide new trustees with a two- or three-page summary of key institutional data, particularly if more than one campus is involved.

The orientation to the responsibilities of the board as a corporate entity should include information on board bylaws, minutes, and meeting schedules; fund-raising activities; and foundation information (if relevant). Board responsibilities should be clearly elucidated. A good framework to use is the list in Chapter Six of this volume.

Bringing in a trustee from another institution or an outside consultant to discuss trustee and board responsibilities and policy and administrative functions with new trustees is a useful way to broaden the orientation program. New board members also should be given an opportunity to meet with the institution's chief executive and the board chair to ask additional questions or make comments. An evaluation of the entire orientation program should be requested from participants before their departure from campus.

The Association of Governing Boards of Universities and Colleges has compiled an orientation package for boards of public institutions, called *Fundamentals of Trusteeship* (1991), that includes a videotape outlining board responsibilities, an audiotape for each new board member that addresses his or her individual responsibilities, and a user's guide.

In-Service Education and Board Development

Orientation programs should be only the first step in a process of continuing education for trustees. Periodic board workshops and retreats offer an important and necessary opportunity for members to step back, review and assess past performance, and take an in-depth look at the mission and future of the institution.

The effectiveness of such educational programs depends on several factors. Timing is important. The program should be scheduled at a time that will not be occupied with routine board business or conflict with holidays. A date that is chosen several months in advance and based on the preference of the majority of the board members should ensure maximum attendance. The setting is also significant. A meeting place away from the institution is preferable, ideally one that is comfortable, invites reflection, and provides new stimulation.

The objectives of retreats and workshops should be clearly defined and can include issues such as:

- Improving board organization, staffing, and performance
- Reviewing institutional mission
- Discussing strategic planning objectives
- Improving relations between the board and the chief executive

- Reviewing relationships with state administration, the legislature, and statewide educational policy agencies
- Discussing existing and proposed educational programs
- Reviewing the board's role and effectiveness in fund raising

An outside facilitator can bring objectivity, insight, and additional information to the proceedings. Frequently, outsiders also can generate more candor on the part of participants. Two highly respected individuals acting as cofacilitators can provide variety in style and help to maintain momentum. A facilitator may be an experienced trustee from another institution, such as the trustees available through the Board Mentor Program of the AGB, a former college president, or an expert in higher education. Trustees should be sent a short survey of questions or issues that will be the subject matter of the retreat. The questions can be a joint effort of the facilitator, the chief executive, and the board chair. If the answers are sent in advance of the retreat, the results can be tabulated and distributed at the retreat for discussion.

A board should be mindful of open meeting laws but should not use them as an excuse to avoid workshops or retreats. It is better to have workshops and retreats with members of the press present than not to have such sessions at all. Although New Jersey apparently requires training sessions and workshops for public college and university boards to be open to the public, most other states do not. However, the board should consult the state attorney general or local legal counsel before scheduling such an event. A final agenda for an event that demonstrates that no institutional policies or procedures will be decided may help to obtain a favorable decision from the appropriate authority. The best agendas are issue oriented and include a few key questions, with a brief background statement for each one.

Some states have unreasonably strict sunshine laws—laws that hinder a board's effectiveness. One public university board, in a state with sunshine legislation that permits flexibility, found that it could conduct a workshop only under the auspices of an outside consultant. Legal counsel reasoned that such a workshop did not constitute a board meeting because the agenda was developed by the consultant and the board was not convened to transact business binding on the institution. The trustees attended on the same basis that they would attend any other conference.

A workshop or retreat should include an evaluation to help plan future programs. Answers to a few pertinent questions should be sufficient to determine the usefulness of the format and content. Chapter Twenty-One offers many other useful ideas for planning and conducting in-service programs for trustees.

Board Development in Board Meetings

Frequently, board members can be encouraged to work more closely together and to be more involved simply by having more exciting agendas for regularly scheduled board meetings. Far too often, agendas are filled with relatively dull reports and provide little opportunity for discussion of policy issues involving the future of the institution.

Regular board meetings should be occasions not only for conducting business but also for provocative discussion and stimulating exchange. Some approaches to varying meeting agendas include: inviting a trustee from another institution to share experiences with common concerns, asking trustees other than the chair or committee chairs to lead discussions on certain issues, encouraging board members who may have attended educational meetings or conferences to share information and insights, and making site visits that are appropriate to items scheduled for discussion.

To involve all trustees in meetings, a variety of issues should be brought up at each meeting that will elicit participation from different trustees. Trustees usually have a great deal of experience in many areas, and their ideas should be useful to the institution. Agendas should concentrate on policy issues that board members can make useful contributions to, however, and not on administrative detail.

Some variation in meeting sites can be helpful, particularly at a university. Sessions could be held at the various schools, with the dean of each school having an extensive role in that particular meeting. An interesting recent article might also be sent to members in advance of a meeting to form the basis for a discussion. A panel of students or faculty members discussing a subject of current importance during a board meeting can strengthen trustee involvement. There are many ways to lend variety to meetings, but the important thing is to use every means possible to see that meetings are consistently interesting and productive.

Programs for trustee orientation and board development are essential if voluntary trusteeship is to be effective. Good programs require large investments of time and effort; great ones build on the successes of earlier programs and on candid evaluations by participants. Casual attention to these matters simply does not work.

The responsible exercise of academic trusteeship must be learned. Notwithstanding the fact that trustees bring considerable life experience to their volunteer responsibilities, including the credentials of service on the boards of other enterprises, there is no experience comparable to serving on the board of a college or university. Ambiguities in decision making are much more prevalent there than elsewhere, many individuals and groups claim ownership of the academic institution, and the issues addressed in the boardroom are extremely complex. There is no substitute for orientation and opportunities for reflection away from preoccupation with routine business.

CHAPTER 18

Making Board
Meetings Work

George David Kieffer

Complaints about board meetings are legion. And yet some boards routinely participate in meetings that their members consider informative, interesting, fun, and productive. Invariably, these boards are associated with institutions viewed as successful by students, faculty, and the public. The chief executive or the board members or both understand that board meetings are not only a policy-setting arena but also a window on the institution and powerful tool for leadership. The relationship between good board meetings and good institutions has not been diminished by requirements of open meeting laws. On the contrary, open meeting laws have simply enlarged the window while requiring a broader range of meeting skills from trustees.

This chapter will suggest ways to improve board meetings in the age of open meetings. But public board members must recognize that their most important tasks in this era are not only to improve board decisions but also to motivate, empathize, support, discipline, inspire, reaffirm, disaffirm—in short, but in the broadest sense—to *lead* through the conduct of meetings.

Problems and Opportunities

Every meeting is different. However, if one understands the basic problems and opportunities inherent in board meetings, under-

314

standing, applying, and modifying practical suggestions found here or elsewhere will be easier.

The Meeting Is Often the Message

A meeting is a medium of communication, and as Marshall McLuhan preached, the medium is the message. In other words, the way we acquire information may affect us more than the information itself. A meeting, like McLuhan's medium of communication, bumps people around. Thus, the tenor of a particular meeting (or series of meetings) can affect those who get "bumped around," including the board, the institution, and the community—in fact, anyone who sees, hears, or reads about the meeting—more than the subject matter discussed. Furthermore, the medium and the subject matter act upon each other so that substantive decisions, including the basic institutional agenda, are fundamentally influenced over time by the manner of conduct of the board.

Every board meeting sends a message, and every board meeting teaches. Most board members judge a meeting as good or bad in terms of their enjoyment of the discussion. But this judgment requires an assessment of what the meeting "said," not only in terms of decisions reached but also with respect to how its tenor influenced the board members, the staff members, the students, the faculty members, and the broader community.

Poorly conducted board meetings are like a slowly crippling disease that can, over time, cause dire consequences for the institution. What once may have appeared to the college community as foolish behavior by the board in time becomes acceptable and then normal behavior and then, pity the institution, admirable behavior. At this point, the institution is in trouble. On the other hand, the board that understands the impact of its meetings upon the institution can over time help turn around a troubled institution by changing the tenor of the board meetings. Or, to put it another way, one manages the institution by first managing the board meetings. To miss this point or dismiss its importance borders on negligence.

The first step to improving board meetings is to understand the huge impact, intended and unintended, that they have on the educational community and the institution. The second step is to recognize what stands in the way of a good meeting and why meetings fail.

Board Behavior and the Phenomenon of Collective Incompetence

It is generally recognized that while individuals may behave reasonably, when they assemble in large groups they may institute mob rule. I call this idea as it relates to board meetings the *phenomenon of collective incompetence*, whereby very wise individuals can coalesce into very foolish groups.

All assemblages of people are different from the individuals who comprise them, and all boards are different from the individual board members. In one sense, a board is like the human centipede sometimes seen at parades; the group cannot go faster than its slowest member, even when all members are heading in the same direction. And, of course, individual board members do not always want to go in the same direction. There are certain maneuvers human centipedes cannot do. And the nature of boards (as opposed to individuals) means that there are certain things boards do not do well.

The Group Mind

Nobel laureate Herbert Simon, in studying the human mind in relation to computers, has shown that the most that human beings can hold in short-term memory without forgetting something is six or seven pieces of data. Therefore, some miscommunication and misunderstanding are inevitable in any meeting. But in addition, when a group of people meet, more is going on than a series of voices or votes that reflect how the individuals think and what they remember. The individuals interact and influence each other. Out of the exchanges by individuals, the group generates information, goals, solutions, and decisions. Particular thoughts may be expressed by individuals, but these thoughts are as much the product of the group and its chain of thinking as the creation of any one person.

In this sense, the whole board has far greater capacity than the sum of the parts, particularly when the whole governs the institution and therefore can enforce its will. Along with other goals, board members seek collective wisdom and institutional force in board meetings. There is value in not only the collective knowledge of the participants but also the additional knowledge, wisdom, or creativity—added value—born of the dynamic mix of a group that is intended to reflect the community.

A "group memory," a common language and a common set of assumptions, is crucial to the functioning of a group. Individual expertise cannot be shared and the whole cannot "think" without certain common foundations. Every group brings to a meeting the separate, distinct perspectives of all individuals within the group, which contribute to the "group mind," but there must be a common memory composed of information and experience shared as a group for the group to process new information and reach decisions.

In the absence of the common memory that must underlie every board action, group thought—and therefore effective group action—are severely disabled. We see this most commonly when we recognize that a discussion has gotten off the subject. Clearly someone, perhaps everyone, perceived the discussion as on the subject, at least for a moment. At all times around the meeting table, minds are skidding off the subject, whether or not the individual reveals it or the group recognizes it. Therefore, one person's perspective on what is happening is almost never exactly the same as the group's perspective.

Following is a brief discussion of the types of disorder inherent in all meetings. Knowing that they exist and must be dealt with is key to recognizing the problems and opportunities of all board and committee meetings.

The Natural Disorder of Meetings

Cognitive dissonance is the mental conflict that occurs when beliefs or assumptions are contradicted by new information. The unease or tension that the conflict arouses in a person is relieved by rejecting, explaining away, or avoiding the new information. Board members may convince themselves that no conflict really exists and thus reconcile differences that are irreconcilable. When information challenges group beliefs, reactions are fast and furious as the group races to protect established beliefs.

Because group thinking can be so difficult, individuals tend to dissociate from the task before them. This is done in a number of ways. For example, some board members may believe that the rest of the group is more informed about an issue and choose to drop out of the discussion even when they disagree with the opinions being voiced. Others may daydream and miss some important information. Or, commonly, a mechanical task will replace the substantive issue before the group. For example, a substantive proposal is presented with charts and graphs. The group criticizes the charts and graphs instead of the proposal, dissociating from the real task.

Individuals come to a meeting with different abilities, experience, intelligence, and communication styles. Each sentence is heard or spoken within a particular history or context of the speaker and listener. Furthermore, people communicate with more than the spoken word. Body language, clothing, and personality all say things to meeting partners. Some miscommunication is inevitable, and there is a continual need for clarification. Board members must assume that miscommunication is occurring continually and that frequent summaries and clarifications are required to keep the group focused.

A meeting is often the focal point for decisions made elsewhere. Thus, debate within the meeting may affect the outcome of the meeting far less than pressures brought to bear on participants from outside. These pressures cloud the apparent discussion and alter the meaning of everything said. Some participants will respond only to literal statements and presumed intentions, while others may also understand the pressures behind the statements.

The most powerful forces in any meeting, far more powerful than the institution itself, are the basic human needs of the participants. These include economic well-being, a sense of belonging, and the need for recognition and control. These needs are expressed at nearly every point in a meeting, whether or not a participant gives voice to them directly. The wise board member recognizes that fulfillment of these needs presents both a problem and opportunity for leadership.

A meeting provides a forum for assessing and expressing

status within the group, and this competition will affect the behavior of group members. Board members compete on a number of levels: to win a debate, to appear tough or intelligent, to attract attention. What is said at a meeting may be unrelated to the stated subject matter, although some board members may respond as if it were related. Competition can bring confusion to any discussion.

Every meeting will have distractions, including late arrivals, early departures, uncomfortable surroundings, telephone interruptions, poor technical facilities, and so on. Even when there are few outside distractions, all participants tend to wander from time to time.

Distractions short-circuit the group process. Board members must assume that someone will be distracted at any point in a meeting and must reduce the distractions that are within their control.

There is a saying that the time spent on any item of an agenda will be in inverse proportion to the amount of money involved. Furthermore, I believe the time spent will be in inverse proportion to the complexity or difficulty of the issue: this is the *law of avoidance.*

Complex matters, irrespective of money, tend to be ignored, and simple matters tend to be belabored. People are simply more comfortable discussing what they know than what they do not know. And most people would rather demonstrate what they know than struggle with what they do not know. Therefore, the group will avoid tough questions and concentrate on easy, phony, comfortable ones, dragging the meeting toward contented failure.

The personalities of board members can also cause problems in meetings. Some personalities simply do not mix well together. Some relationships carry limitations. Personal and professional feelings can distort communication. Regardless of personalities, individuals naturally take on certain roles in a group: the facilitator, the disrupter, the complainer, and so on. Nearly everyone adopts a role of some kind during a meeting, in view of the other participants. Nearly everyone harbors feelings about the other participants, feelings that sometimes cripple communication.

A single participant can derail a meeting. He or she may force others to respond to peripheral issues and encourage dissociation from the task. Fear of hurt feelings and blind reverence for democracy may allow that member to take the meeting's steering wheel and drive where he or she wants to go. The group tends to defer, dropping the discussion to the lowest common denominator, or falls into prolonged argument. If one of these types of people is on a critical, controversial committee the risk of failure is substantially increased.

Control Is Not a Dirty Word

These underlying disorders and the phenomenon of collective incompetence tell us that running a good board meeting is hard work. Like democracy, the board meeting requires more discipline, more direction, and more control than do its individual members. From cognitive dissonance to insecurities to normal distractions—there is so much that cannot be controlled that it is critical to reduce the other risks and disorders that can be controlled. That is why boards name a chair to lead meetings, create committees, and meet in person rather than by telephone. That is the whole purpose of *Robert's Rules of Order* (Robert, 1971): to provide order to board decision making.

In the end, the control necessary for board meetings is really a matter of carrying out a democratic process, a process that permits the group—this human centipede—to decide its direction and move in that direction together as fairly and effectively as a group can possibly move. Not only does this control permit the fairest, best decisions, but it also generates a clear message to the institution and community through the powerful medium of the board meeting. The recommendations for improving board meetings in the following sections are nearly all directed at honing this focus to permit the best decisions and the cleanest messages to the educational community.

A Perspective on Open Meeting Laws

Open meeting laws have enlarged the skills required of chief executives and board members, reinforcing the role of the board meeting as a message as well as a leadership and management tool. I will not review in detail the kinds or applications of open meeting laws;

this task has been done by others. The point to be made here is that to the extent a board or committee meeting is a medium and a management tool, its leverage—for good or ill—is made greater by open meeting laws. Since an open meeting says more to the broader university community, open meetings must be clearer in process and message than closed meetings.

Often called sunshine laws, open meeting laws vary from state to state. Many of these laws were first adopted in looser form in the mid 1950s. After Watergate, more comprehensive open meeting laws were passed.

In essence, open meeting laws require that all or a substantial portion of a public board's work be done in public. For a review of the costs, benefits, and application of such laws, I suggest Harlan Cleveland's study (1985). Cleveland calls the application of open meeting laws a "trilemma," whose elements are the public's right to know, the individual's right to privacy, and the public institution's mandate to serve the public interest. These elements must be weighed carefully in the context of particular issues.

The generally stated benefits of open meeting laws are that openness can be a necessary check and balance; facilitates public scrutiny and deters misappropriation, conflicts of interest, and all forms of official misbehavior; enhances public confidence and encourages fact-finding; helps to inform those affected by the governmental process; creates more accurate press accounts; and helps in identifying and correcting public officials' incorrect assumptions. The generally stated costs of open meeting laws are that openness may harm individual reputations and infringe on privacy, constrains the nature of discourse, changes the decision-making process, encourages participants to make speeches for the benefit of the audience and waste too much time in the process, and results in "lowest common denominator" decisions.

Cleveland (1985, p. 31) suggests that there is a "wide consensus that an appropriate balance of the three elements of the public interests would allow—indeed, encourage—the following kinds of exemptions:"

- Personnel matters, when a specific individual is being discussed
- Collective bargaining strategy and the negotiations themselves

- The attorney-client relationship in discussions concerning actual or potential litigation
- Real estate matters
- Security issues
- Evaluation procedures, whether of an individual, a group, a program, or the institution as a whole
- Self-education sessions of governing bodies
- The presidential selection process

Much can be said for open meeting laws, and legitimate concerns have been raised against them. In any event, they are here to stay. Often, too much time is spent in applying open meeting laws in the context of a particular issue of intense public interest, and too little time is spent clarifying the applicability of the laws and board policy in general.

The best approach to protecting the board's integrity and message is to set aside specific time on the agenda every year or two to achieve an understanding of state law and its applicability to the board. Boards should demand an opinion of counsel; too much time is spent debating personal views in open meetings (including the above stated pros and cons) without regard to the particular law. The counsel should be directed to prepare a policy statement summarizing the applicability of the law to given situations. That policy statement should be discussed, modified if necessary, and approved by the board. It should then be a part of board orientation and development programs.

Kieffer's Laws of Meetings

In the succeeding sections, I discuss fundamental decisions affecting the conduct of meetings and problems and opportunities inherent in meetings. However, it may be useful for board members and the chair to keep in mind the following "laws."

Meetings Tend to Fail in Direct Proportion to the Number and Variety of Tasks Being Undertaken

The narrower the defined task, the better the group does and the better individual board members will do. The more issues and tasks undertaken in the same meeting, the more difficulty the group has in thinking successfully. Getting the group to think is difficult. Reduce the issues and tasks to the smallest number possible and make clear exactly what the task is.

Meetings Tend to Fail in Direct Proportion to the Number of People Actively Participating

Each additional person brings basic needs, competitiveness, aspirations, an agenda, personality, and feelings (as well as talent and abilities) to the meeting. Moreover, with each person added to the meeting, the number of relationships between members increases geometrically. When three people meet, the dynamics are A versus B, A versus C, and B versus C, or three sets of relationships between individuals. But four people meeting creates seven sets of relationships between the individual participants. (Not to mention those situations where two of the parties may gang up on a third.) A ten-person meeting potentially creates forty-five different relationships.

As a meeting grows in size, productivity decreases dramatically. Each additional person potentially increases the risk of failure, so each person's participation in the meeting must be fully justified. The board has a given size, but in committees, as a general rule, seek to reduce the size of all meetings.

Meetings Tend to Fail in Inverse Proportion to Preparation Time and in Direct Proportion to Meeting Time

The most important work for any meeting is done before the meeting. Once the meeting begins, options for leadership are severely constrained. A good share of time should be spent in preparation and consultation. In addition, the attention span of the average person in a meeting falls substantially after about one or two hours. A meeting should be as short as possible. Ironically, meetings are shortened if board members prepare more for them.

Most people spend too little time in preparation and too much time in meetings. Time is often wasted doing things that should have been handled before the meeting, or great energy is spent in a meeting averting a disaster that could have been avoided with a little forethought.

The process of preparing for a meeting is something like the process suggested by Timothy Gallwey (1974) in his popular book, *The Inner Game of Tennis.* Gallwey says that picturing each shot in your mind before and as you hit it will substantially reduce the number of misses. Preparing for a meeting is much the same. Visualize the meeting in advance. Picture the perfect attitude of the group, the perfect location, the perfect proposal, the perfect discussion, the perfect argument. Visualize the perfect response to the difficult participant. Visualize the perfect meeting and then make the necessary preparations to make that vision a reality.

Meetings Tend to Fail When the Environment
Is Inconsistent with the Purpose

Everything possible should be done so that the environment for the meeting by its nature encourages attention to the particular task. This means matching the desired task with the proper location, seating, and timing as well as the appropriate participants. This match is discussed further in connection with the "theater" of the meeting.

Fundamental Decisions Affecting Conduct of the Meeting

The ability of the chair to preside at meetings, anticipate the flow of business, manage people, exercise wisdom, and maintain flexibility is key to a successful meeting. Equally important are shaping the agenda and supplementing it with advance information.

Selection of the Chair

Not everyone has the ability or skills to be an effective chair. Still, many boards choose to pass the chairmanship around as if the post were the equivalent of blackboard monitor in the third grade. The selection of a chair is the most important decision influencing the effectiveness of board meetings. If that choice is made on any basis other than considering who would be best for the job, the board will compromise everything else it does in the meetings. Once the wrong choice is made, it cannot be corrected by manipulating the chairperson during the meeting. Correcting or challenging the chair will only undermine the meeting further. The key is in the selection.

The board chair should have the ability to imagine the meeting before it ever takes place and the ability to align the meeting with the fundamental goals of the group, cause, or organization. Just as important as this vision is the ability to share it with meeting partners.

Managing a meeting is managing people. Board members with poor "people skills" seldom make successful chairs. A successful meeting manager has developed the skills to motivate and lead in a positive way; listen and hear what meeting partners are saying; sense when there is confusion or harmony, discord or agreement; and bring people and ideas together in a constructive way.

Closely allied with people skills is what Warren Bennis and Burt Nanus in their book *Leaders: Strategies for Taking Charge* (1985) have called "emotional wisdom." Emotional wisdom includes the following skills:

- The ability to accept people as they are, not as you would like them to be
- The capacity to approach people, relationships, and problems in terms of the present rather than the past
- The ability to treat those you are close to with the same courteous attention you extend to strangers and casual acquaintances
- The ability to trust others even if the risk is great
- The ability to do without constant approval and recognition from others

A chair also needs to be flexible. Adhering to the spine of the meeting does not involve a militaristic devotion to the agenda or the time schedule if it appears that a deviation can focus the contributions of meeting members toward the desired goal.

Some boards permit the chair to appoint committee chairs; others elect committee chairs directly. In either case, the selection of the committee chairs is a critical choice because so much board work is handled in committee. The committee chair should have the same qualities discussed for the board chair. Volunteering should not be the sole criterion; the board will get weak chairs.

Establishment of the Agenda

A brief agenda should not be confused with a brief meeting. Most agendas simply list the topics to be discussed without further elaboration, telling the participants almost nothing. This is the laundry-list approach. But the agenda is an important road map. Each item should tell the participants enough to allow them to prepare and to understand the goal of considering the item and should bring people back to the map whenever they lose their place.

An agenda usually involves different types of tasks. It is useful to tell participants whether a particular item is for information, discussion, action, or all three. Meetings fail because participants are not clear about what is on the table at a particular moment and what is ultimately expected. Let them know so that they can direct their preparations and contributions accordingly.

Here is an example of a typical board meeting agenda distributed in advance:

1. Minutes
2. President's remarks
3. 1995 budget (to be distributed)
4. Conference report
5. Committee reports
   a. Finance
   b. Long-range planning
6. New business
7. Adjournment

Here's how the agenda might be improved:

1. *Minutes:* ACTION ITEM. Approval of minutes of meeting of January 15, 1993. Minutes attached.
2. *President's remarks:* DISCUSSION ONLY. Report attached.
3. *Budget for 1994-95:* ACTION ITEM. BUDGET INCLUDED IN MATERIALS. The 1994-95 budget was approved by the

finance committee at the December meeting. Action by the full group was deferred at the December meeting, pending receipt of a staff report regarding the MacArthur Program, appearing on page 8. The staff report, preceded by an executive summary, is enclosed for your review. Staff recommends approval.

4. *Report on conferences:* DISCUSSION ONLY. At the October meeting, we requested a report by staff enumerating the various conferences to which we are invited to send a representative and an analysis of the strengths and weaknesses of particular conferences. The report is attached. It is the intention of the president to recommend action at the next meeting.

5. *Committee reports:*

   a. Finance committee: ACTION ITEM. The report of the committee is attached. Recommended actions appear on page 1 of the report.

   b. Long-range planning: A draft report is attached for discussion. The final report is expected to be approved by committee at its meeting in two months.

6. *New business.*

7. *Adjournment.*

Once prepared, the agenda should be circulated enough in advance to allow review by board members; they may want to do a little homework. But it should not be distributed so far in advance that it will be laid aside, unless another copy will be sent later. In any event, the meeting leader should always have extra copies of the agenda at the meeting. It is the board's agenda and to the members' advantage to have it in front of all meeting partners.

Indicate the time when the meeting will begin and end. As much as possible, stick to those time limits. Work will expand to fill the time available. The schedule can always be relaxed, but there must be something to relax. Also, try to estimate the time to be spent on each item of the agenda. Note it on the agenda whenever practicable.

An executive summary is not necessary, of course, for all meetings. But whenever the material is more than three pages in length, an executive summary can focus on particular items, summarize reports, and clarify what is expected of members. The chief executive and board chair should always consider, therefore, whether an executive summary of the item would be useful.

Some people make the error of assuming that an executive summary is an insult to intelligence. Actually, the more sophisticated the meeting partners and the more effort they devote to policy formation, the more they will be used to and expect executive summaries. They expect summaries because they know and accept the limits of their role and their time. The executive summary should be distributed before the meeting.

Time and again, someone will pass out a report at a meeting with the obvious expectation that it will be seriously considered. It will not be. In fact, it will distract from discussion and derail group thought. And unless there is a strong incentive to do so, any paper delivered at the meeting will not be read after the meeting. Papers distributed at the meeting are of little use unless very brief—no more than one-half page.

Board Meetings as Theater

All board meetings are part theater. You cannot eliminate the theatrical aspects of a meeting any more than you can eliminate location, costume, or seating. There is always some location, some mode of dress, some seating—some theater—all of which conveys a message. Theater can make meetings proceed well or poorly. And it is important that the theater that accompanies a board meeting be consistent with the message the institution wants delivered.

People listen and contribute more effectively when they are engaged, but holding the attention of meeting partners is difficult. It is not just what you put on the table that is important; more important is what the meeting participants can digest. Facts alone do not taste good. Some degree of entertainment is required to hold people's attention, particularly as the meeting goes on. Holding the attention of the participants is no less the responsibility of the board chair than the success of the meeting itself. Although an interesting meeting is not necessarily a successful one, a boring meeting is almost never a good meeting, because the group was less than fully engaged.

If you are not interested in the meeting, why should anyone

else be? Show your own interest in the matters under discussion at a meeting. Your interest will be infectious. Your attitude should be enthusiastic, even if the task at hand is rather routine and mundane. Enthusiasm is infectious, too.

Meetings are affected by the spirit of the meeting place. For example, the lighting in nightclubs is soft and dark. Schoolrooms are well lit, with upright desks. Corporate boardrooms reflect power and authority. The meeting location subconsciously tells board members who they are and what the institution is about. The public view of the board will be shaped in part by the spirit of place. The location should reflect how the board wants to be seen. Keep in mind that discussions will tend to be more orderly in an orderly room and that participants' behavior will be influenced by location. The board can raise expectations and performance by selecting a location that seems to require more of participants.

Practical Suggestions for the Chair

How does the chair maintain discipline in a group of peers so that he or she can keep the meeting on track? Among peers, authority and discipline come from the chair's perceived commitment to the group and the group's objective as well as from the chair's skill in assisting the group in meeting the objective. If the chair is perceived to have his or her own agenda or to favor some group members over others, the chair's authority will be limited to that which he or she can muster on a particular vote. If, however, the chair can embody a commitment to every member of the group and a common objective, his or her strength and authority go deeper. In maintaining order and discipline, the chair will be seen as imposing not his or her will upon the individual who may be endangering the process but rather the group's will. Thus, the chair's voice will represent many others, and his or her authority will be greater.

The chair, more than anyone else at the meeting, should keep in mind the statement less is more. The chair's comments and goals should be limited. The less the chair says about particular issues, the greater the chair's strength. The chair's primary concerns should be the welfare of the group, the integrity of the meeting process, the achievement of the group objective, and the aim and objectives of the institution as a whole. The less the chair imposes his or her views on particular matters, the more able the chair is to serve these higher goals.

If you are the chair, review the meeting agenda with the chief executive before the meeting. Envision what might happen at the meeting. Discuss special problems with particular board members. Be prepared and encourage others to be prepared. At the meeting, time is wasted if the chair walks the group page by page through materials about routine items that were distributed well before the meeting. This practice also sends a message to every member that preparation is unnecessary. It removes responsibility from others. Whenever you can, you want to encourage responsibility from others. Because there are enough things that can go wrong during the meeting no matter how well you prepare, do not add poor preparation to the list.

There is more to starting a meeting on time than simply getting through earlier. Starting on time is the first test of a chair's control. It sets a subconscious expectation with respect to your ability to perform throughout the meeting. If you can not do the first thing you said you were going to do, why should your leadership be taken seriously? Starting on time also establishes a presumption that the meeting as a whole will be a success. It establishes the ground rules for others who are presenting, reporting, or discussing issues.

The beginning of the meeting sets the stage for the remainder of the meeting. There should be no doubt that the meeting has begun, no weak start. Bang the gavel or speak louder than you have to; do whatever you can theatrically to make it clear that you have begun. Your opening statement sets out the tasks, problems, and opportunities at hand and focuses the group for the entire meeting.

Do not draw attention to latecomers by restating what has preceded or admonishing them for their tardiness. In either case, you are only adding a further distraction. Presume there is unspoken confusion or drift (remember the phenomenon of collective incompetence) and periodically remind the group why they are there and what is being sought at a given moment.

The eyes of meeting partners tend to fix on the chair. Therefore, what the chair says and how he or she looks or sits become the mirror for the group in assessing itself. Be careful at all times to reflect what you believe the group (and the institution) should think of itself. Ninety percent of what you say should be reflective of the group or the process rather than of you as an individual.

If you argue about your positions with peers in a meeting, you will have difficulty paying attention to the process and you will risk losing your authority. Your attention must be directed almost entirely to the process of the meeting, not to its substance. Therefore, your time for substantive involvement during the meeting is limited, and you must make up for that by focusing more on the substance before the meeting. Form preliminary judgments with the chief executive but refrain from expressing them in meetings, except where the issue is of highest priority and where your position will make a difference.

Do not force anyone to speak during a meeting, but make sure that the more reticent board members have the opportunity to speak. Ask them, from time to time, whether they have something to add on a particular point. Actively look for disagreement so that it can be dealt with. Find what is positive about a contribution from any member of the group rather than what is negative. Look for opportunities to make members feel good about themselves and their contributions. Record their contributions; it is a sign of respect. Be generous with compliments.

Make sure that minority views are expressed. Look out for the stampede that generally follows the presentation of an idea. Many people want to jump on the bandwagon by either criticizing the idea or praising it; the group (like a mob) wants action. Ask those in favor of an idea to consider potential problems, and ask those opposed to consider possible good points of the suggestion.

Do not permit long pauses. Attempt to feel when the issue is ripe for conclusion and offer your summary. It is up to you to summarize the *group's* thoughts back to the group. Attempt to give the meeting a sense of momentum and continuing success.

In ending the meeting, summarize what has been accomplished and relate the conclusions to the original intent of the meeting as stated in your agenda and opening remarks. Review the next steps. End in a positive, upbeat fashion. Make the members feel the meeting was worth their time and effort. The end of the meeting should be as clear as the beginning. Try to end on time.

Practical Suggestions for Board Members

Just because you are not chairing the meeting does not mean it is not your meeting. Every player has a stake in every meeting. Your role may vary and your control may be circumscribed. The quarterback may call the plays, but it is every bit as much the halfback's football game.

There is almost no excuse for not doing the necessary homework required for a meeting. Yet many people do not do it. Not only does this lack of preparation slow the meeting terribly, but it sends a message to all attendees that the person who fails to do homework for this meeting probably fails to do homework in other endeavors, too. It is a sign of disrespect for yourself and for others.

All board members should be familiar with the basic concepts of *Robert's Rules of Order Revised* (Robert, 1971). Nothing can destroy a meeting so much as incompetent use of *Robert's Rules* and nothing reflects so obviously on your preparation and meeting skills as how you use these rules. The participant who is both comfortable and familiar with these parliamentary rules will run circles around the unknowledgeable participant in both formal and semiformal meetings.

Buy a copy of *Robert's Rules of Order* and read it. At a minimum, be aware of the following points:

1. A motion should be made and seconded *before* discussion of *any* issue starts. This ensures that a subject merits discussion.
2. The chair should restate the motion after it has been made and seconded so it is clear that it has been ruled in order. This also provides some control for the chair.
3. Reports of committees do not always have to be "approved" or "accepted." They can simply be "received" if no immediate action is desired. Approving or accepting means that all items within the report have been approved by the group. Usually, the treasurer's report should be received rather than approved, since it is unaudited and sometimes incomplete.

4. It is customary for the chair of the committee to move that the report be received or approved. This places responsibility on committee chairs for running good committee meetings. It also permits the committee chair to explain committee actions and gives the committee chair some credit.

5. Only one main motion can be considered at a time. A main motion is the one that brings an action before the group. For example a committee chair might say, "I move adoption of the report" or "I move approval of the minutes." Considering two main motions at the same time is a mortal sin.

6. A subsidiary motion is one to change or dispose of a main motion. For example, "I move the report be amended to delete paragraph three," or "I move that the minutes be amended to reflect my vote." The subsidiary motion must be discussed and voted on before the main motion can be discussed and voted on, although it cannot be made unless the main motion is already on the table.

7. A privileged motion, for example, "I move that we recess," is one that calls for immediate action of the *whole group*. It must be considered before *any other motion* and is not debatable. (Courtesy has a very high place in parliamentary procedure.)

8. A motion to reconsider a previous vote must be made by someone on the previous winning side.

9. When someone "calls for the previous question," he or she is only making a suggestion to end the discussion and vote. If a single person objects, the discussion keeps going. If someone "moves the previous question" and there is a second, the group must vote on whether or not to end the debate. If the motion fails, the discussion continues.

10. As a general rule, do not attempt to draft substantive language longer than a single sentence in a formal meeting. Refer it to a committee or back to staff.

Many disagreements in meetings have to do not with what has been said but rather with what someone thinks has been said. Presumptions enshroud the message. Poor presentations make the message more confusing still. To limit miscommunication, offer to repeat back to the meeting partner with whom you think you disagree what was said. Before you attack a point, restate it in its most positive sense. Then ask your meeting partner to restate your point of view.

You may never agree with your meeting partner on a particular issue, but if you fail to understand his or her position, you will undermine the opportunities for agreement and understanding on related issues. Watch out for your own "combative listening"—the tendency to take issue with what is said because you strongly disagree. Try to diffuse this combative listening in your meeting participants. Find what is positive in what has been said rather than only what is wrong. Just because you are willing to listen to an idea does not mean you have to agree with it.

By the time you have arrived at any meeting, you have had every opportunity to avoid it or to change it. By the time you have arrived for the meeting, you have had every opportunity to determine what you want to accomplish in general and with each participant in particular. You have prepared as much as you could prepare or were willing to prepare. The issues are before you. Your role in relation to your meeting partners is established. Whether they are absolutely necessary or not, the participants are there; it is too late to eliminate or include anyone.

The meeting is on. So now is the time for *being there.* No excuses—you will only weaken your position. No complaints— complaining will only undermine the meeting. You cannot be anywhere else. This meeting is the only place you can be. You are here, and others are relying on you, so give everything you have to make the meeting work.

CHAPTER 19

Understanding Chief Executive and Board Chair Responsibilities

Richard T. Ingram

The relationship between the chief executive of an institution and the governing board's chosen leader is vital to how well the governing board will perform. The synergy between these two individuals can make possible what neither individual could accomplish alone. The gap between the board's leadership potential and actual performance, whether narrow or wide, inevitably reflects how these individuals work together.

The purpose of this chapter is to explore the special relationship between the chief executive and the board chair within the context of helping the board to do its job well. Although the president is responsible for managing the institution, the chair is responsible for managing the board, and they are jointly responsible for leading the board. At times, the president takes the lead, and at other times, the board chair does so. Certain prerogatives are reserved for the board chair, while others are reserved for the president. Understanding the differences between the two roles marks an effective relationship, but no less than knowing when the president and the chair must act jointly.

An Appropriate Relationship

The prerequisites of an ideal relationship between the chief executive and the chair include a board chair who is the clear choice of

335

the large majority of trustees, does not serve for too little time nor for too long, has earned the respect of trustees and administrators alike, understands fully the commitment required of the position, and has proven ability in the presiding role at meetings. There are others prerequisites, of course, but I begin with these.

The chief executive should appreciate the chair's responsibility to serve the institution and public trust first and the president's needs second, manage the board's affairs, speak for the board in certain situations, and see to it that the board does its job. The president or chancellor and the chair must trust one another and realize that one can be only as effective as the other.

A leader's personal style complements substance and competence. The multitude of personal qualities and interpersonal skills that make or break would-be leaders are a crucial determinant of the relationship between the chair and the chief executive. The styles of these two leaders do not have to be alike, but they should not conflict with one another. Mutual respect, adjustment to one another's style, clear understanding that there can be only one chief executive and only one board chair, keeping one another informed and aware of travel schedules—all make for an ideal relationship.

Just as not everyone should have a turn at being president of an academic institution or system, neither should every trustee have a turn at being chair. Too much is at stake for such a policy. Few decisions a board makes carry more importance to more people than that of who should be the next chair. And, unfortunately, few decisions can be more political. It is never easy to select a chair, but a nominating process within the board, perhaps led by past chairs who may be continuing service on the board, is crucial to a civilized process. In the end, however, tenure on the board should never be more than one of several considerations, and it should be a less important one than many other considerations.

When the chair–chief executive team is what it should be, new opportunities present themselves:

- Trustees and staff members are motivated to higher expectations and, therefore, better performance.
- The board is much more likely to function as a team rather than as a collection of individuals with their own agendas.

- A deliberate strategy for strengthening the board's performance is more likely to develop.
- Ambiguities between board and management roles are reduced.
- Institutional priorities are more clearly identified and more quickly addressed.
- The confidence of external and internal stakeholders in the board and institution or system is enhanced.
- The morale of trustees and staff members is bolstered as trusteeship becomes more fun than drudgery.
- The president is made to feel comfortable in seeking advice from the chair on any matter, personal or institutional.

There Can Be Only One Chair

Among the important personal qualities to be sought in the board's elected leader are listening and communication skills, objectivity, sensitivity, decisiveness, influence over others, foresight, and presiding skills. These qualities will be discussed in this section.

An effective leader should consistently demonstrate not only the ability to listen, but also the ability to *hear* the views of others. The chair understands that his or her personal views on issues must often be modulated and sometimes sacrificed to those of others. It is nearly always better for the chair to express personal positions after all others have had their say.

Trustees appreciate hearing from their chair directly from time to time. Along with the occasional memo or fax, the personal phone call goes a long way toward establishing and maintaining rapport and the flow of information. Personal communication takes time, but it is always a good investment. Board members want to hear from their president and chancellor, too, of course, and thus coordination of communication is important. And the chair should remember that good communication with the president is a two-way proposition; there is room for initiative here as well: it is as appropriate for the board chair to initiate a telephone call to the president or chancellor as it is for the president to do so with the chair. Keeping in touch is a joint responsibility.

Ideology, arrogance, or insensitivity, especially on the part of the chair, have no place in the boardroom. The chair should be seen as having a sense of fairness and openness on all issues and information coming before the board. This stance is especially important in maintaining good rapport with the chief executive and staff members. How the chair responds to bad news or rumors, for example, has much to do with building trust. Indeed, a chair who overreacts to an unexpected and unpleasant happening on campus or to a surprise adverse newspaper article about the institution is not helpful to the board, the chief executive, or the institution. Everyone expects the chair to be sophisticated and temperate, to collect all the facts in consultation with the president or chancellor, before expressing a point of view. Trust is built on nothing less.

When it is time to make difficult decisions among competing options and when these decisions are within the chair's prerogatives, the chair must take the lead. The chair can do so without sacrificing sensitivity to others' opinions, most especially the chief executive's views. Trust is built on the chair's ability to explain his or her position clearly, decisively, and consistently once discussion is concluded.

The chair should be well connected with those outside the institution or system who can do it some good. Thus, the influence of a potential chair must be considered carefully during the selection process. But the chair must also be willing to use such influence when it best serves the institution's interests.

Foresight is another important quality in a chair. Fortunate are the chief executive, board, and institution when they have a chair who possesses the ability to predict likely consequences of proposed actions (or a decision not to act). An ability to read the likely reactions of the trustees, for example, can be immensely helpful to the president.

The chair accepts the responsibility for helping the board to accomplish its aims. Such leadership is exercised in particular through the chair's ability to conduct good meetings. Chapter Eighteen provides some useful advice for conducting meetings.

There are several other qualities to be sought in the chair. The chief executive normally has only one place to look for dependable and consistent support in his or her difficult role, and that is to the board. The board's elected leader bears much of the responsibility on this score. Ideally, the chair is capable of being a trusted adviser and even friend to the chief executive. He or she must be accessible to the president and alert to the president's professional and personal needs, morale, health, and welfare. The board chair should also be concerned about recognizing any and all special contributions of the president's spouse.

Keeping confidences and willingly taking some of the criticism directed at the presidency are also among the chair's responsibilities. And the chair should take the lead in acknowledging the board's appreciation for a job well done. One experienced former university president who has since joined the ranks of trustees, Harold Envarson, president emeritus of Ohio State University, has observed that trustees should be "loving critics." But there is also much room for praise. Chapter Eight elaborates how a board can support its chief executive, especially through its chair.

The Chair's Responsibilities

Most of the chair's responsibilities fall into four broad categories: to be knowledgeable about the institution or system in all of its complexity, to develop ways to strengthen the board's effectiveness, to speak for the board when appropriate, and to serve as the board's conscience and disciplinarian. In sum, the chair's job is to motivate trustees and lead the board in partnership with the chief executive.

Be Knowledgeable

A common lament of chief executives is that their boards are more comfortable with immediate, short-term matters than with helping to shape a vision for the long term. The chair should be the most knowledgeable of all trustees about the institution in order to help the board to focus on the future. This is a difficult but essential responsibility.

Being knowledgeable means having a command of the information—the statistics, the strengths and weaknesses of major programs and services, the campuses, the senior officers, the condition of the physical plant, and so on. But it also means keeping abreast of demographic trends, emerging issues and trends in the field of higher education, the changing political landscape, economic developments, and so on. The chair must be a voracious reader.

The chair should perennially ask these two questions: Are we addressing the real issues that set, affect, and maintain the institution's course? Are we making the best use of our time and energy? The chair should help the board and president to see themselves as others see them.

The university or system of universities is an exceedingly complex web of traditions, values, decision makers, constituencies, and individual faculty entrepreneurs. And it has enormous resistance to change. The university has been likened to a giant supertanker that requires considerable time and space to change course— the secret of the academy's strength for centuries and, some would argue, its weakness. It is the chair's ability to explain (to faculty, media, legislators, alumni, donors, and parents) and defend the uniqueness and complexity of the institution that enables him or her to help the president navigate the institution through troubled water.

Strengthen the Board's Effectiveness

The chair and president should periodically discuss how the board is doing in meeting its responsibilities. All boards can be and do better. A thorough and candid diagnosis may lead to discussion along these lines: On what specific dimensions is the board especially strong and weak? Are the committees functioning well? Which are and are not and why? Are board agendas and supporting materials on target? Do the trustees likely share our assessment or do we need to test our conclusions with them? The next order of business is for the chair and president to develop a strategy to fix what seems to be broken by setting specific goals and objectives within a realistic time frame.

Chapter Twenty-One addresses the need for all boards to periodically conduct self-assessments, but the assessment process begins with private and candid deliberation between the board chair and chief executive. The fact that only about 33 percent of all types of public boards of higher education responding to an AGB survey reported conducting a self-study of their performance between 1986 and 1991 is discouraging indeed (see Resource B).

The chair has a key role in the orientation of new trustees as well: first, by insisting that a solid and interesting orientation program be designed and second, by actively participating in it. Surprisingly, the 1991 survey by the AGB reveals that about 25 percent of all public boards still do not provide such programs (see Resource B). Chapter Seventeen also offers useful ideas and resources for orientation programs.

Speak for the Board

The chair will be called upon to explain, defend, or advocate for a variety of board deliberations, decisions, or institutional actions. Reporters love ambush interviews and may seek out the chair in person or by telephone. Faculty leaders, students, and political leaders want and need to hear from a board spokesperson from time to time, as do alumni and athletic boosters. This responsibility should be understood and accepted by board chairs.

Who should take the lead, the chair or the chief executive, depends on the situation, the issue, and the anticipated reactions of those most directly affected by what is said and who says it. Good judgment by the chair and president are needed in this area. The best guidelines are these: remember that the integrity of the institution and the presidency must be first priorities, avoid speaking to a matter that is clearly within the president's portfolio except in the most compelling or unusual circumstance, and fully disclose what is in the public domain.

One mark of an effective board is the tradition or practice accepted by all trustees whereby inquiries or requests for comment are referred to their board chair or president. Some trustees may like to see their names in newspapers, but their speaking for the board is an unhealthy and dangerous practice.

Be the Board's Conscience and Disciplinarian

Another characteristic of a good board is its ability to keep its house in order—no small task if some trustees believe, mistakenly, that they have legal rights or responsibilities as individual board members. They do not.

It occasionally falls to the chair to admonish, cajole, or speak privately and candidly with the misguided or inexperienced trustee. Such actions will not be needed frequently, but the chair should not be reluctant to meet this responsibility. How he or she handles delicate situations determines the measure of respect earned from the trustees and president.

There is no place for factionalism among trustees, party politics in the boardroom, or grandstanding by the occasional trustee who seeks political gain by using the trusteeship as a platform. These serve only to harm irreparably the reputation of the board and the institution. Not only must the chair be certain that he or she is not part of any such problem, and step down should that be the case, but he or she must also work to enable the board to function as a team rather than a collection of individuals.

Furthermore, there is justifiable concern about the decline in ethical standards in academe, conflicts of interest in the boardroom, and violations of individual rights to privacy. In serving the public trust, the board and president look to the chair to help them balance what has been labeled a "trilemma": the institution's and board's mandate to do their job, the public's right to know, and the individual's right to privacy (Cleveland, 1985). The chair more than any other trustee or institutional officer serves as gatekeeper in matters of organizational conscience. He or she sets the moral, ethical, and legal tone for the entire board through personal example and by being its conscience.

There Can Be Only One Chief Executive

According to Kerr (1984), the academic presidency is increasingly beleaguered. The ever-increasing expectations from group and individual stakeholders have taken their toll on the president's ability to provide academic leadership. And one of the sources of pressure on this office is the board itself.

Trustees understandably expect a great deal from their president or chancellor. After all, their own effectiveness is determined in large measure by the chief executive's competence. Successful chief executives spend a large measure of their time with trustees, and for trustees. Chief executives accept the fact that their own and their institution's or system's effectiveness will be little better than that of the board. Thus, trustee education and board development are a presidential responsibility along with everything else.

On a few basic matters, there should be no ambiguity between the board and the chief executive. There can only be one chief executive; neither the chair nor the board members are capable of substituting their judgments on matters properly reserved for the president or chancellor. Although the chair must manage the board, he or she must have sustained and committed help from the chief executive. And although the chair and the president share responsibility for leading the board, there are some particular expectations of the president in this regard.

The Chief Executive's Responsibilities

The chief executive should accept responsibility for educating the board, communicating effectively with the board, preparing the board and its committees for their work, and implementing the board's policy decisions promptly. A new profession has emerged to help presidents with these responsibilities. The professional staff position of board secretary continues to develop within the field of administration (see Chapter Twenty).

Educate the Board

Whether the board gives a clear mandate for the president to be the board's chief educator or not, he or she should assume the role. Virtually every board meeting should have an educational component in one of three categories: in-service trustee development, academic programs of the institution or system, or trends and issues in higher education that are especially relevant to the institution's future.

The role of educator calls for some reserved meeting time and creativity on the president's part. A timely article sent in advance for discussion, a faculty member who has just returned from participating in an exchange program, a guest speaker on the responsibilities of trusteeship or higher education finance or fund raising, a student newspaper editor who has can share student perspectives on issues confronting the institution—all are obvious sources that can inform and engage the board.

Other ideas to educate the board include distributing an informative set of multiple-choice questions (and answers) that cover basic institutional facts and characteristics to enable the individual trustee to assess his or her personal knowledge, asking a trustee who attended a regional or national meeting to report highlights to the board, and inviting a trustee to engage the board in a discussion of a subject related to his or her other volunteer or career experience that may have relevance. Board members will have other ideas.

Of special note is an apparent trend for boards to designate one meeting each year as a retreat or special workshop to address long-range issues affecting the institution or system. Such a meeting provides the opportunity to help trustees review their performance and renew their commitment.

Communicate Effectively

The doctrine of "no surprises" prevails in communication between the chief executive and board. Bad news and good news must be provided to trustees as soon as practical, before it is delivered by someone else. The need for confidentiality sometimes presents problems, but it should not be used to rationalize waiting for an executive session to deliver information. The fax machine offers new opportunities, but the telephone works best in spite of the time it requires. Trustees like to hear their president's voice.

Prepare Trustees for Their Meetings

Trustees expect their chief executive and staff members to prepare good agendas with solid supporting material in advance of meetings. The president should solicit ideas from the trustees for future agendas and otherwise help them to set priorities for the use of their time. Although trustees do not mind occasional written materials distributed at committee and board meetings, these materials should be the exception rather than the rule. Except in very unusual circumstances, financial data should *always* be sent in advance, particularly if action on them is required or expected.

Trustees often complain that they get too much paper and information or too little. But they universally admire good presentations, occasional use of slides or other visual aids, tightly written executive summaries, information and analysis rather than raw numbers, and evidence of good proofreading.

Implement Board Policies Promptly

Implementing the board's policies is an obvious responsibility of the chief executive, but it sometimes becomes a source of needless tension. The key to this responsibility is threefold: promptly and accurately capturing the board's action, decision, or policy in meeting minutes; giving good feedback as soon as possible, with information about how the implementation process seems to be going; and offering subsequent assessment about the impact of the board action.

Shared Responsibilities

The board chair and president share the responsibility of leading the board. Trustees, like any group in any enterprise, will rise only to the level of expectation held for them by their leaders. Together, the chair and the chief executive should clarify what is needed and expected; design a plan to strengthen the board's effectiveness; continuously discuss how the talents, experiences, and influence of individual trustees can be used to the institution's or system's advantage; and work to motivate their colleagues to higher levels of performance. When trusteeship is rewarding it is usually because the chair and president make it so.

CHAPTER 20

The Role of the
Board Staff Secretary

Bonnie M. Smotony

The increasing complexity of the trustee's role and growing demands on both trustees and presidents of academic institutions make it essential that appropriate staff support is available to facilitate the business of the governing board. The character and structure of staff support are generally shaped by decisions made by the president and the board—decisions concerning the needs of the board and the resources available to meet those needs. In *The Role of the Board Secretary*, Daniel Perlman (1989, p. 2) said that "administrative support for the governing board assumes several characteristics, depending on the size, complexity, and organizational structure of the institution; its historical development; its mission; and often on the style of its executive officer."

Staffing Patterns

The way in which staff support is provided and by whom varies. In many institutions, staff support is provided by a board secretary or by someone who fills that role but perhaps has a different title. Sometimes the title is indicative of the level of support provided to the board, but more often one must look at the functions performed by the board secretary to gain some sense of that person's place within the institution.

346

Several surveys conducted in collaboration with the Association of Governing Boards of Universities and Colleges (Smotony and Summers, 1979; Smotony, 1986, 1992) reveal that administrative staff support generally falls into one of four types. In the first type, a *secretary to the president and secretary to the board* provides support that is often *executive secretarial* in nature. One person typically fills a dual role, serving as secretary to the board and administrative or executive secretary to the chief executive officer of the institution. Duties generally encompass management of the clerical component of the president's office, distribution of materials, and preparation of board minutes and other documents.

In the second type, the position of *secretary to the board and assistant to the president* is also a dual role, but with the board secretarial function paired with the title and responsibility of a special assistant or executive assistant to the chief executive officer. This is generally a *staff* position.

In the third type, a *secretary of the board/administrative officer* combines the secretarial function with such varied assignments as secretary of the university, development officer, legal counsel, vice president in a functional area with line responsibilities, or legislative advocate for the institution. Responsibilities in both roles are principally *administrative* in nature.

The fourth type of support, the type most generally required at large public multicampus institutions, is that typically provided by an *officer of the board/corporate secretary*. In addition to fulfilling the board secretarial function, this person would exercise broadly delegated authority as an officer of the corporation, including the execution of legal documents, either acting alone or in concert with the chair of the board. In some institutions, this officer is appointed by and reports solely to the board. In others, he or she may report to the president or be a member of the executive administrative team. The duties and responsibilities of an officer of the corporation are typically prescribed in the board's bylaws, with other duties generally assigned by the president. This position is *executive* in nature.

There are various combinations of the above types, and some board members volunteer support services, with minimal clerical assistance from the institution. Substantial staff support is also provided to the board by the president and his or her administrative team through, for example, the numerous studies and reports, position papers, and policy statements prepared by the administration that are vital to the board's capacity to govern the institution.

In an unpublished survey of board secretaries that I conducted in 1991 (Smotony, 1992), respondents were asked to determine which of the four types of support most closely matched their own positions. Figure 20.1 shows these patterns within the 188 public institutions responding.

In considering the level of staff support needed by the governing board, the method of delivery, and by whom that support is to be provided, the answers to the following questions can be helpful:

- What is the minimal level of support that is acceptable and the optimal level possible? Certainly, a board would expect a different level of support from a corporate officer than from the president's secretary functioning in a dual role. What is needed and expected?
- Should the board secretary report to the board or to the president? Is a joint reporting relationship preferable or possible?
- Where the board secretary holds an additional position, is that an appropriate pairing of assignments? Are there institutional positions that are inherently in conflict with the position of board secretary?
- What is the appropriate placement of the board secretary's position within the institution? Is it important to provide visibility? Does placement in the hierarchy determine acceptance as a key player?

The staff support person must first meet the needs of the trustees. He or she should ensure efficient functioning of the board so that it may fulfill its principal mission—the governance of the institution. The support person should assist the president in fulfilling his or her substantial responsibilities for leading and managing the institution. And the support person must foster the vital communication and the personal relationship necessary between the trustees and the president.

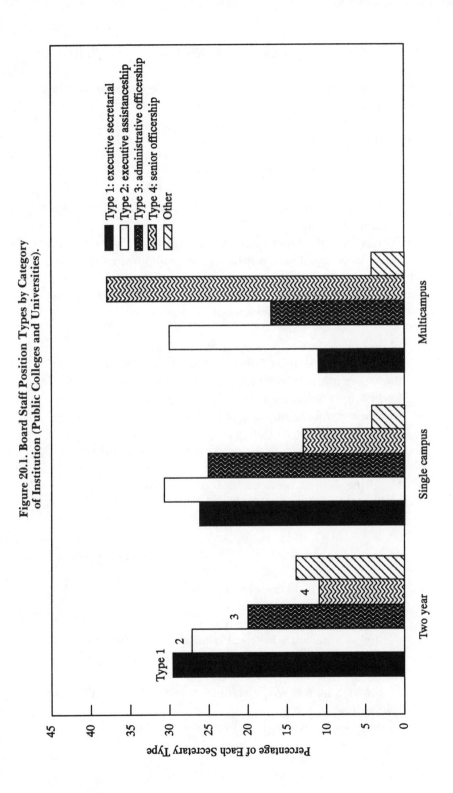

Figure 20.1. Board Staff Position Types by Category of Institution (Public Colleges and Universities).

Many long-tenured board secretaries observe that they often feel they are most effective when their activities are largely invisible. Their function is one of coordinating and facilitating, much of it done behind the scenes.

Responsibilities

Other than the duties and responsibilities reflected in the board's bylaws and standing orders, there is rarely a job description that clearly sets forth the expectations of the board and the president for the board secretary. There is little literature about the role, and the variations that exist make the development of a model job description almost impossible. Some common functions, however, typically fall within the secretary's scope of responsibilities:

- Planning meetings, preparing agendas, giving official notice, and staffing meetings of the board and its committees
- Preparing minutes, resolutions, and certifications
- Codifying and disseminating board policy statements
- Reviewing and maintaining bylaws and standing orders
- Drafting or reviewing policy proposals
- Serving as custodian of the corporate seal and of official corporate records
- Handling the arrangements for board meetings, including travel and hotel accommodations, security, meals, ground transportation, and so forth

Less common, but still frequent, are such functions as:

- Advising on jurisdictional matters
- Orienting new board members
- Assisting in presidential recruitment
- Acting as a liaison with legal counsel concerning trustee obligations and board actions
- Acting as a liaison with former trustees
- Acting as a liaison with media representatives or with campus information officers
- Drafting speeches and remarks for the board chair

- Drafting communications and correspondence to and on behalf of board members
- Coordinating board retreats
- Assisting with logistics and questions of protocol for academic convocations, graduations, or visits to the campus by special guests or other dignitaries

Planning Board Meetings

The board secretary plays a major role in the planning and coordination necessary for meetings of the board. Although the secretary's level of involvement may vary according to the reporting relationship, the board secretary generally takes the lead in overseeing the myriad details such meetings entail.

Planning for board meetings often begins with the development and adoption of a meeting calendar that sets forth the dates of the meetings and, for boards of multicampus institutions, the locations of those meetings. As indicated in Resource B, public boards hold approximately ten meetings each year. A calendar that calls for meetings at the same time each month (for example, the second Friday of each month except for August and December) encourages good attendance. Advance scheduling also makes possible the timely presentation of major policy and planning issues that require a significant amount of staff work. In developing the meeting calendar, the secretary must address these considerations. If changes in the date or location of a meeting become necessary, the secretary should immediately notify each member of the board, as well as the public.

Physical arrangements for board meetings, again a responsibility of the secretary, should provide the kind of environment most conducive to accomplishing the board's business. A meeting room, in pleasant surroundings and preferably on a campus, should have adequate accommodations not only for the board but also for attendance by appropriate officers and staff members and the public and the press. It is also helpful to assist with travel arrangements and hotel accommodations for those board members who must travel from their home city to attend a meeting.

The environment of a board meeting is often affected in subtle but unmistakable ways by the content of the agenda. For example, an item of high public interest may create external pressure from special-interest groups, which, in turn, may attract greater attention from the media. This external pressure can range from the demand for public attendance that exceeds the capacity of the facility to a full-scale demonstration aimed at disrupting the meeting. Preparation for increased public attendance and the accompanying media attention often requires security measures for public safety. In making the necessary physical arrangements in such circumstances, the secretary must balance the legitimate concerns of the public with the requirement for an atmosphere that will allow the board to conduct its business.

Developing the Agenda

Agendas for meetings of the board and its committees are typically driven by the board's bylaws and standing orders. Action items on the agenda generally propose adoption of a policy to be implemented by the president, request approval of a policy of action in an area where the board has reserved authority for itself, request an exception to a policy previously approved, or direct or authorize the president to take specific action beyond that which the board has previously delegated. Items for information or discussion will inform the board of actions taken by the president under delegated authority, where such reporting is required by the delegation; serve as a forum for discussion of matters of significance under study by the administration and that may become action items on a future agenda; and inform the board of activities by faculty, staff, and students and of major events planned by the institution.

The secretary can be particularly helpful in the development of the agenda by paying close attention to the items proposed for inclusion. Is the proposed action by the board clearly and definitively stated in writing? Is it accompanied by sufficient information to inform the board of the necessity for the action or of any implications of failure to act? Have the alternatives been sufficiently explored, and are those arguments submitted clearly and concisely? Can the action proposed be accommodated within authority already delegated to the president? Will approval of the action being requested have an explicit or implicit effect on current policy? Is the action an exception to current policy, or will it supersede a previously approved policy?

The secretary can also help coordinate the internal review of agenda items as they are proposed to ensure that all institutional concerns are addressed before the items are carried forward to the board. Where there are standing committees of the board, the secretary should be sensitive in determining the committee of jurisdiction to which the matter will first be referred. Direct consultation with the committee or board chair, may be appropriate, but the board secretary should always be mindful of the possible need to first consult with the president or other senior executives.

Ensuring Compliance with Sunshine Laws

Since 1977, all fifty states have had some form of open meeting legislation. These laws, when applied to a public university, dictate the conditions under which a board may meet in private and the matters that may be discussed in a closed session. Often, there are penalties for violation of the open meeting regulations. The secretary must know the provisions of the state's sunshine laws and must ensure that the form and time of the notice of the meeting and the content of the agenda are in compliance with the laws.

Preparing the Minutes

The board secretary is responsible for creating a record of the proceedings of the board and its committees. Recording the proceedings can be accomplished in a variety of ways, depending on personal preferences and available resources. The meetings can be recorded on tape, either by a simple tape recorder placed on the meeting table or a very elaborate sound system that provides amplification as it records the meeting and is operated by a technician from a remote location. Or the services of a court reporter might be used. These two methods of recording the meeting produce a verbatim transcript of the proceedings, from which an edited version can be prepared to serve as the record. The record could also be taken by someone skilled in shorthand or speed-writing. It could be produced from summary notes taken by a clerk, secretary, or other staff member, who would then produce written minutes from those notes, a good memory, and an understanding of the background material presented to the board.

Minutes can take different forms. For example, action minutes serve some boards very well; only the actions taken by the board are recorded and all discussion and background material are omitted from the record. For some boards, a verbatim record is preferred, with only a minimum of editing. Other minutes are narrative, where the writer records the relevant discussion, makes passing reference to the not so relevant, and ignores the irrelevant.

In preparing the minutes, the secretary must understand the importance of these records to the institution—to its history, governance, administration and management, and various constituencies. Minutes must serve the purposes of the corporate body. They should provide a record sufficient to guide the current administration in implementing the board's actions and should serve succeeding administrators in carrying out the board's direction. I prefer narrative minutes that reflect the relevant points of discussion so as to clearly reveal the intent of the board in taking the action. The minutes should contain enough information so that they can under most circumstances stand alone, that is, afford the reader who was not at the meeting and does not have background material full comprehension of what was under consideration and the rationale that determined the action taken.

Since the board derives its authority from its charter or other enabling legislation, its policy statements often have the force of law. The minutes are an important means by which the board is able to document its authority and jurisdiction. This record may have to stand the test of a legal challenge.

The minutes must be accurate, complete, fair, impeccably honest, and a record on which the trustees, the administration, and all constituencies of the institution can rely. They must serve both the immediate and long-term interests of the institution. It is the board secretary who must deliver that record.

The secretary can create an index of board minutes to permit the prompt retrieval of information. Without such a retrieval system, the minutes lose a great deal of their value. Depending on the needs of the institution and the resources available, this index may be a simple subject-matter card file or a fairly sophisticated computer-based index. Here again, the size and complexity of the institution, as well as the period of time covered by the records, would determine what is needed.

Advising on Bylaws and Standing Orders

The bylaws and standing orders provide the framework within which the governing body operates and are often the vehicle by which authorities delegated by the board to the president or other administrative officers and to the faculty members are codified. The secretary should be thoroughly familiar with the bylaws and should be able to provide advice both to the board and to the administration concerning their provisions. To be most useful, the bylaws should be kept current. The secretary can help identify the need for revisions or additions to the bylaws and oversee their reprinting and redistribution as necessary.

Keeping the Seal

The form and design of the corporate seal is often prescribed in the bylaws and standing orders, and the secretary is charged with the custody and use of the seal. The seal is normally used only in connection with the transaction of business of the board. For example, the seal may be affixed by the secretary to documents signed on behalf of the corporation. Often, the seal is used as a symbol of the institution for official purposes (for example, on diplomas) or in connection with alumni, student, or public projects.

Acting as a Certifying Officer

On behalf of the corporation, the secretary is often called upon to provide confirming documentation to funding organizations, government agencies, and other legal entities. In this capacity, the secretary certifies the action of the board; the identity, appointment, and authority of the officers of the institution; the provisions of the bylaws and standing orders; and excerpts from the minutes of the board.

Developing a Policy Manual

If the board does not have a policy manual that codifies board policy statements, it would be appropriate for the board secretary to develop one. The manual should contain those institutional statements on faculty governance, tenure and academic freedom, faculty and student codes of conduct, and other major policies adopted by the board and requiring board action to revise. The manual might be divided into categories reflecting the organization of the university, for example, administration, business and financial, educational policy, buildings and grounds, legal matters, personnel, student affairs, and so forth. Revisions to the policy statements included in the manual should be submitted to the board for action in a format designed to clearly indicate the language being added or deleted.

Having a policy manual ensures that trustees know what their policies are. The administration may also find the manual to be a very useful tool in ensuring that administrative procedures are in compliance with board policy and in proposing changes from time to time.

Orienting New Trustees

Orientation of new board members is often a collaborative effort by the board chair, the president, and the secretary. The board chair or a fellow trustee is best equipped to help the new trustee understand the role of governance. The president is most qualified to explore with the new trustee the mission of the institution, its organization, and the issues confronting the institution that the board faces in the years ahead. The secretary can most effectively introduce the new trustee to board procedures. For example, promptly upon the announcement of his or her appointment, the trustee should receive information about the members of the board, including mailing addresses, telephone numbers, biographical data, and photographs, where available. A copy of the board's bylaws and other policy documents and a calendar of board meeting dates and locations should also be provided.

Often the secretary serves as the initial contact for the new trustee who has general questions about the board's activities or specific questions about the institution. The secretary plays "traffic director," responding to those requests directly or channeling them to the president or other members of the administration.

Reporting Relationships

To whom does the secretary report? A recent survey (Smotony, 1992) indicates that 52 percent of board secretaries in public institutions report to the chief executive, 23 percent report to the board, and 18 percent report to both. Clearly, the board secretary who reports solely to the board seeks direction from the board. When an individual is appointed by and reports directly to the president, it is the president who provides the direction. However, when an individual has a dual reporting relationship, to the board as its secretary and to the president in some other capacity, perhaps as an executive assistant, that person is as much an agent of the board as of the president and must often balance competing or sometimes conflicting interests and objectives. Regardless of reporting lines, the secretary is expected to facilitate the relationship between the chair and the president. At all times, the secretary must have the confidence of both the board and the president.

Cooperative and supportive relationships between the board secretary and key members of the administration are crucial. The secretary often serves as an important communication link with other university personnel, legal counsel, members of the media, and other constituent groups. This liaison role also extends to assisting the president in keeping former trustees sufficiently informed about institutional matters so that they remain part of the university family.

As previously noted, the secretary's role is often one without a well-defined job description. When one considers the vastly different demands made upon the board secretary as a consequence of his or her varied assignments, it is easy to understand why the role differs so greatly among institutions and why the perception of the role differs among presidents, trustees, and other members of an institutional community—even among board secretaries. The expectations for the performance of the board secretary differ according to who is doing the expecting.

The perceptions of the appropriate role of the secretary held by the secretary, the president, and the trustees must be fairly similar. If there are significant differences in the expectations for the secretary's performance, friction is likely in one or more of the relationships.

The secretary's role becomes an even more sensitive one should there be conflict or tension between the president and the board. The board secretary must demonstrate an allegiance to the president and an unquestioned loyalty to the board, remaining neutral during periods of conflict. For a president or a trustee to require that the secretary take sides in such a situation is more than unfortunate. And the secretary cannot offer personal loyalty to the president at the risk of compromising his or her obligation to the board. Actions that undermine the position of the president at a time when the incumbent may be at odds with the board are equally wrong.

Whatever decisions are made by the trustees and the president with respect to the nature and structure of the board secretary's role, there are certain responsibilities delegated to the secretary. In carrying out these responsibilities and in exercising authority delegated in the bylaws of the board, the secretary must not encroach or seem to encroach on the president's or any other officer's authority and responsibility. Whether the secretary is a member of the president's staff or an independent employee of the board, congenial and cooperative relations must be maintained with the president and members of the administration. As Kerr and Gade (1989, p. 99) found, "The best board secretaries are models of discretion, diplomacy, and devotion to duty."

Profile of the Board Secretary

Much has been learned about the board secretary in recent surveys, although it is very difficult to find a model for the position. A 1985 survey revealed that "the board secretary is well educated . . . [and] women outnumber men but not by a great margin . . . with 80 percent at age 40 or more" (Smotony, 1986, p. 34). Results of my 1991 survey (Smotony, 1992) do not change that picture. Board secretaries continue to serve for an average of eight years, but many exceed fifteen years of service. When vacancies do occur, the method of recruitment varies. Twenty-two percent of secretaries are selected from within the institution. Anecdotal evidence, however, suggests that vacancies are filled more frequently now through regional or national recruiting than was true a decade ago.

There is little literature concerning the board secretary, there is no model job description, and there is no academic program leading to certification for the position. Despite this, the role of board secretary is continuing to emerge as a more visible and better defined role in higher education. Perhaps institutions are placing a higher value on the functions typically performed by the board secretary, or boards are now recognizing the need for an increased level of staff support. It may also be that those people who perform the functions associated with the board secretary are beginning to evolve a clearer sense of themselves as professionals and as contributing and effective members of the institution's management team.

Supporting this latter premise is the work of a task force, composed of board secretaries from six public institutions, formed in 1990 and charged with examining the feasibility of a formal course of academic work focusing on the role of the board secretary. This task force concluded (in an internal memorandum) that although a formal course of study did not appear feasible at that time, the board secretary should possess a certain body of knowledge. The task force's recommendations in the memorandum led to the development of a comprehensive list of topics and subtopics on which the effective secretary must be informed. For example, the secretary should have knowledge of the institution's history and mission, as well as the history and development of higher education. He or she must understand the concepts of academic freedom and shared governance. The secretary must be informed about legal and ethical issues of concern to trustees—constitutional and statutory provisions affecting the institution as well as federal and state regulations such as the Freedom of Information Act and conflict of interest laws. The task force also recommended that the board secretary be skilled in the organization and management of the work environment in order to effectively manage the board administrative support process. Of particular importance to the continued effectiveness of the board secretary is an understanding of the unique role he or she must play within the institution and an interest in developing and enhancing the role. The secretary should also be informed about current issues, both internal and external, facing the institution.

At the task force's urging, a series of seminars and workshops have been developed in collaboration with the Association of Governing Boards of Universities and Colleges. These workshops are offered annually in conjunction with the National Conference on Trusteeship of the AGB, held each spring. Trustees and presidents should encourage the board secretary, especially the secretary who is new to the position, to attend.

The position of board secretary continues to evolve in academic institutions as an increasingly important part of good management and governance. Although the scope and function of the position vary widely, presidents and chancellors depend increasingly on the position to ensure that the board and the institution are well served. Board secretaries are enormously helpful to the chief executive when the presidency is beleaguered with pressures and demands from everywhere. And board secretaries can help trustees function more effectively as expectations about their performance and demands on their time continue to multiply.

CHAPTER 21

Assessing
Board Performance

Barbara E. Taylor

Colleges and universities depend on their governing boards for skilled leadership, and yet few boards operate as effectively as they might. Reflecting on this problem, researchers and practitioners have cited regular assessment as an essential tool for improving board performance.

Alderfer (1986, p. 50) remarked that "a key factor" of successful boards is the presence of "an active mechanism for the board to review its own structure and performance." Studies of employees and groups have shown a connection between regular appraisal and improved performance (Lawler, 1973; Zander, 1982). And recent empirical research has demonstrated that one feature of effective college boards is their practice of engaging in self-reflection and seeking feedback on their performance (Chait, Holland, and Taylor, 1991). Houle (1989, p. 157) emphasized this point by asserting that "the capacity for self-criticism is the surest impetus for improving the quality of the board and the work it does."

There is little mystery to the connection between assessment and better performance. Skillful assessment produces systematic feedback on performance that boards otherwise would not receive. According to Zander (1982, p. 113), "When members get no feedback on their group's performance . . . they tend to believe that the out-

361

put of their group has been good, that they can be satisfied the unit has succeeded. Members who get little feedback also expect their group will do well in days to come and do not fear failure. No news is good news." Few trustees have contact with a variety of boards, and so most lack broad experience on which to base comparative judgments about their accomplishments. What board members experience on a particular board is usually assumed to be acceptable performance.

Moreover, a common view is that it is unfair to expect boards to be self-critical and concerned about improving their performance because, after all, their members are uncompensated volunteers with time-consuming professional and personal commitments that usually take precedence over board responsibilities. But board assessment need not be extremely time consuming, and the improvements that may result from the assessment process are likely to make board service far more satisfying. (See Chait and Taylor, 1989, for a discussion of some of the frustrations that members of underperforming and dysfunctional boards feel.)

Boards must also take self-assessment seriously for other reasons. Boards are usually involved in appraising the performance of the chief executive, and many also require that faculty, staff, and campus heads, if any, be evaluated regularly. It may strike constituents as unfair when a board that imposes assessment requirements on others is unwilling to evaluate its own performance.

Although most governing boards are formally accountable to themselves alone (assuming that they act in accordance with law and public regulations), they depend on the public for financial and other forms of support. If they are seen as ineffective and intransigent, they risk losing the support of governors, legislators, donors, parents, prospective students, and other key stakeholders.

A board is a corporate entity, usually composed of individual achievers. One of the most difficult lessons for any trustee to learn is that the activities of an individual board member, regardless of how valuable, are no substitute for group strength and success. The need to develop group strength is particularly acute in the public sector, where board members rarely know one another well prior to joining the board and where there may be deep divisions within the board about its proper role and performance. Regular board assessment helps create a sense of collective responsibility and collective achievement, and the candor that honest self-reflection entails can help bind board members together in pursuit of common goals.

By definition, systematic assessment requires open and honest discussion among all board members, yet it can be extremely difficult to be candid about a board's performance and aspirations in a public setting. Fortunately, some states allow public boards to meet in executive session and conduct retreats and other group development activities in private, so there should be few legal barriers to pursuing the suggestions that follow.

However, retreats and development efforts can be valuable experiences even in states that require them to be open to the public. Open meetings laws should not be used as a rationalization to avoid the assessment process. Assessment is too important to the quality and cohesiveness of a board to be neglected, for whatever reason. If a board assesses its performance regularly, both in retreats and as part of its normal business, the press and public will eventually grow accustomed to the effort and, one would hope, grow to respect the board's commitment to improving its effectiveness.

Assessment and Board Development

Assessment is just one facet of a continuing effort at board development that all boards and their leadership, including the board chair and the chief executive, should plan and undertake. Board development has both formal and informal aspects; that is, it includes specific activities aimed at enhancing board performance, and it also emanates naturally from a board operating style that encourages openness to innovation, tolerance for diverse opinions, and an emphasis on learning by board members. Some aspects of this broad concept of board development include:

- Orientation programs that inform new board members about the institution's or system's history, mission, and characteristics and about the board's role and responsibilities
- Continuing education in the form of workshops and conferences, common readings, issue-oriented discussions during

board meetings, or board retreats that teach trustees about the institution or the board's responsibilities

- Periodic determination of goals and priorities by the board in support of its own responsibilities or the larger goals of the institution or system
- An environment of openness within the board and among the board and institutional leaders that encourages careful analysis of problems, brainstorming, receptivity to questions by trustees or regents, and willingness to take constituent views into account
- Regular opportunities for social interaction that help board members know one another as individuals and contribute to solidifying the internal relationships that bind trustees together as a corporate unit
- Opportunities for social and substantive interaction among the board and important constituents, such as faculty members, students, legislators, alumni, and the community, in order to reinforce the board's responsibility to others and to keep trustees apprised of the needs and aspirations of other institutional stakeholders

Conducting Board Assessments

The process of assessing board performance has been advanced significantly in recent years. Higher education boards probably have more experience with it than those of other enterprises. Many helpful lessons have been learned, and new tools are available.

Goals and Standards for Achievement

A prerequisite for useful board assessment is the articulation of standards and goals against which to measure performance. Consider, for example, a few of the possible indicators of success that individual members of a board might think are meaningful: 100 percent attendance at board meetings, good relations with the legislature, lack of controversy within the board, lots of free exchange within the board, success at attracting appropriations, good relations with the chief executive, and frequent, candid feedback offered to the chief executive.

These indicators are diverse, and some are contradictory. Yet one or more might reasonably be held as valid by any given member of a board. Therefore, even if each trustee were willing and able to assess the board's performance accurately, board members might well come to very different conclusions about the board's strengths and weaknesses.

Setting standards and goals for board performance should be part of a long-term program of board development. Such a program requires free and open exchange within the board and between the board and the chief executive concerning institutional or system priorities and the board's role in advancing those priorities. For example, the board's role may include direct involvement in attaining certain goals, such as in helping secure a needed appropriation. And the board may also participate in developmental activities that strengthen the board's ability to function effectively on the institution's behalf, such as efforts to interact more effectively with constituents or to enhance communication within the board.

Three views of what constitutes exemplary board performance are found in the literature, and embedded in each are assumptions about a board's fundamental goals. The first and by far the most prevalent of these views centers on the responsibilities of boards, such as those outlined in Chapter Six. The assumption here is that a board that performs these responsibilities well is effective (Paltridge, 1980). The second view concentrates on satisfaction with internal board operations, including meetings, participation, board leadership, bylaws, committee structures, attendance, and quality of meetings (Ingram, 1980). The third view considers board success almost entirely from the perspective of group process, that is, the *means* by which goals are achieved. Thus, process becomes as important as substance, and performance is judged not only according to whether or not, for example, the money was raised or the new program launched but also by the breadth of involvement by constituents and the satisfaction of stakeholders with the results (Chait, Holland, and Taylor, 1991).

Aspects of all three of these approaches can be combined to reflect a particular board's understanding of what constitutes exemplary performance. It is wise to think broadly about what success is and to consider seriously the proposition that satisfactory performance includes tackling the right issues, using the right processes, and organizing the board in ways that support both good substance and good process. Before embarking on any board development or assessment effort, it is important for board members, with their chief executive, to discuss their assumptions about what constitutes effective board activity, what their board's short- and long-term goals are, and what indicators would signify success.

Self-Assessment Instruments

Various self-assessment instruments can assist boards in gauging their performance. As valuable as such instruments can be as springboards for discussion, most cannot claim to present an accurate picture of a board's performance. Ashford (1989) found that self-assessments of performance are rarely accurate because the environment provides few unambiguous clues about what successful performance is; opinions vary so much about what valid indicators of success are; and to maintain a positive self-image, most people tend to reject or reinterpret negative information about performance.

   In research focused specifically on college and university boards, Chait and Taylor (1987) examined the results of self-assessments by sixty-one boards of public and independent institutions that had completed a frequently used evaluation instrument. They found extremely small variations in responses across institutions and among individual board members. Although experience and intuition suggest that board performance varies considerably among institutions, most board members in this study reported that their boards were performing at an above-average level across the range of their responsibilities. In other words, there is serious doubt that these self-assessments provided an accurate picture of actual board performance.

   However, it is important to note that a board does not need a perfect self-assessment instrument to benefit from using one. The key to the value of most instruments is found in the interpretation of what might seem to be rather fine differences in responses by individuals, the skill of a facilitator who can assist the board in understanding what the instrument might be reflecting (and not reflecting), and, most of all, the willingness of board members to reflect candidly on their performance and what can be done to improve it.

Perhaps the most frequently used board self-assessment instrument is the Self-Study Criteria of the Association of Governing Boards of Universities and Colleges (see Resource C for one illustration of survey forms available from the AGB for various types of institutions or systems). This instrument is intended to be used primarily in conjunction with the board mentor workshop of the AGB, which is a self-study retreat facilitated by a specially trained peer trustee. The Self-Study Criteria asks board members to rate their board's performance across a variety of substantive areas, such as institutional planning, academic oversight, and fund raising, as well as with respect to the state of relations between the board and significant constituents, such as the chief executive, students, and faculty. Individual responses to the criteria are aggregated and used as a springboard for discussion at the workshop, where the facilitator encourages the board to reflect on reasons for variations in ratings of particular criteria.

Other board assessment instruments include:

- The simple Rating Scale for Boards, developed by Houle (1989), that asks board members to rate their board in twelve areas dealing with board structure, constituent relations, and goal setting.
- The Board Self-Rating Schedule, developed by Savage (1982), that asks trustees to rate their board's structure, knowledge, practices, performance, relationships, and other qualities.
- A questionnaire created by Chait, Holland, and Taylor (1991) in connection with an empirical study of board effectiveness. The questionnaire is used to assess board performance in six competency areas, most of which concern board process.

The questionnaire developed by Chait, Holland, and Taylor (1991) has been subjected to extensive field testing and revision and to date shows modest evidence of validity and reliability. However, the authors' less than spectacular success in this effort highlights again the difficulty of creating a self-assessment instrument capable of reflecting actual board performance.

Use of Outside Consultants and Facilitators

A board can profit greatly from the use of outside consultants and facilitators in its self-assessment. A skilled facilitator can listen objectively and reflect back to the board what is being said, noting apparent areas of dissension and disagreement. If selected properly, the facilitator will not be seen as having a particular ax to grind, as might be the case if a board member or the chief executive were to act as facilitator.

An experienced facilitator should be knowledgeable about board performance and able to help a board understand how it might go about enhancing its efforts. The facilitator can often read between the lines of a self-assessment instrument and help a board understand its own view of its performance, as well as help structure group discussions and exercises that encourage creative thinking and consensus building.

Consultants and facilitators are usually used to help plan and facilitate board retreats and other extended sessions aimed at goal setting, assessment, and board development. They may be used to lead short board development and assessment sessions during or in conjunction with regular board meetings, at which board responsibilities, goals, and performance are discussed. Where relationships within the board or between the board and one of its constituent groups have broken down, a consultant can interview all parties and provide feedback to the board about the problem and potential solutions.

A consultant may be used to conduct an assessment of board performance by observing the board, reviewing documents such as board and committee minutes, and conducting confidential interviews with board members and constituents. This type of assessment by a consultant is quite rare, and it is not a substitute for honest self-appraisal by the board. However, as one part of a larger effort to understand as thoroughly as possible the board's performance, an honest assessment by a knowledgeable outsider is likely to benefit a board.

Role of Board Leadership

A board's leaders, particularly the chair and the chief executive, play a crucial role in board development and assessment activities. The ability of board leaders to create a climate in which candor and open discussion about the board's responsibilities and performance can flourish is essential to the success of any form of board assessment. Board leaders create this climate by encouraging members to participate and maintaining an environment in which there are few forbidden topics. Such practices encourage good decision making and a high level of commitment by the board members, and they are particularly useful in preparing a board to assess its performance honestly. In other words, the habit of candor, developed in other contexts, carries over into the self-assessment process.

Board leaders are especially central to encouraging ongoing and less formal approaches to board assessment. Assessment is usually equated with the periodic board retreat or appointment of a consultant to undertake a major study of the board's operations. However, assessment should be a normal part of the board's regular operations.

Assessment as an Ongoing Process

Self-assessment can be included in a board's ongoing work in several ways. For example, the chair can ask board members to complete a short questionnaire about desirable board goals, attitudes toward their trusteeship, and ways to improve the board's performance. Or the chair, perhaps with the chief executive, can interview individual board members for responses to such questions.

At the end of a regular board meeting, perhaps in executive session, the chair can go around the table and invite members to comment orally or in writing on the meeting. Was it interesting and well conducted? Did the board consider issues of real consequence for the institution? Did board members have the information needed to make good decisions on a timely basis? What could be done to make the board's next meeting even more profitable?

With the chief executive's assistance, a chair might prepare an occasional "pop quiz" to be distributed to board members at a meeting. The quiz might include simple multiple-choice or fill-in-the-blank questions about the university's budget, enrollments, or programs or about the board's obligations and stated priorities. Board members should complete and score the quiz individually, and their responses should not be collected. The exercise reinforces in an enjoyable way the obligation trustees assume to be informed about the institution or system and the board.

All boards make mistakes, but too few reflect on their errors and the lessons they learned. A chair can encourage the board to step back after a significant mistake and discuss what happened, why, and what lessons the board should draw from the incident. In this way, boards learn to avoid similar errors in the future and, perhaps equally important, learn the habit of candor within the board group.

It was argued earlier that a board must set goals for itself. Board leaders can reinforce the importance of these goals and the board's commitment to them by leading trustees in an annual review of the board's successes and failures in achieving its priorities.

With assistance from the chief executive, the chair can also lead the board in collecting periodic feedback on its performance from senior administrators, campus officials, faculty leaders, and students. Although valuable, this exercise can be tricky for two reasons. First, it can be difficult for some constituents, especially those in administrative positions, to be completely candid. One solution is to ask a consultant or other neutral third party to interview individuals privately and report their comments anonymously. Second, relatively few faculty members and students know the board's work intimately enough to comment knowledgeably on it. Therefore, the logical people to talk to are constituent representatives to the board or its committees or student and faculty leaders who have regular commerce with the board, though in such cases the board should be careful not to assume that the opinions expressed are necessarily representative.

Board leaders should encourage the creation of a board committee on trusteeship or a board affairs committee that is charged with evaluating the performance of individual board members and monitoring the achievements of the board as a whole. The committee can help plan orientation programs, retreats, and other board development activities and can advise the chair and chief executive about areas of weakness within the board and suggest remedies.

Conducting Board Retreats

Periodic retreats can be powerful board development tools. Many boards recount as a watershed the experience of going away together as a group and spending a day or two discussing nothing but the board's goals, aspirations, and performance.

For too many boards, a retreat is the only setting in which open discussion is encouraged (or even possible), large issues are tackled, attention is given to the board as a corporate whole, and time is set aside for social interaction. Although most boards could improve their normal operations by adopting some of the features associated with retreats, the periodic retreat still provides an important opportunity for board members to step back from the press of normal business and focus exclusively on the board's performance. Capably handled, retreats can pay major dividends.

The discussion of retreats that follows draws on Savage (1982), which is the most thorough treatment available of the steps involved in planning and carrying out a board retreat. Primary leadership for proposing and developing a retreat rests with the chair and the chief executive. In the absence of their individual and mutual support for the effort, it is unlikely to succeed.

There is a lesson for chief executives, in particular, in this emphasis on joint responsibility. Many chief executives, thinking assessment is good for boards, plan and offer a retreat with token or no involvement by board members. In the absence of real support for the effort by all or the vast majority of trustees, the retreat will not succeed. If board support cannot be secured, it would be better for the chief executive and chair to embark on a less intensive (and perhaps less threatening) series of board development and assessment activities, such as those mentioned earlier in this chapter, and accustom the board gradually to the idea of more thorough assessment in a retreat setting.

The steps involved in developing and conducting a successful retreat can sound time consuming and onerous, but Savage emphasizes that "every step the board takes in this process is a model of how the board should normally operate" (1982, p. 13). What may look like an overly complex approach to securing board input into, support for, and involvement in the process actually reinforces the authority, accountability, and commitment of the board. A successful retreat involves seven stages: (1) agreement on shared assumptions, (2) profile of the board, (3) formal action by the board, (4) appointment of an agenda committee, (5) information gathering and agenda development, (6) the retreat, and (7) postretreat action.

1. *Agreement on shared assumptions.* At the outset, the chair and chief executive should reach agreement concerning their assumptions about the board's role and goals, its relationships with important constituents, public expectations of the board, the function of board development and assessment activities, the qualities the institution or system values in its board members, the relationship between board and institutional priorities, problems the institution is facing, and any other matters that seem pertinent to setting the board's priorities and analyzing its performance. Individuals hold such assumptions but rarely articulate them. When the implicit assumptions board leaders hold are in conflict, a successful board development program is difficult or impossible to achieve. If necessary, other board members or an outside consultant can be brought in to facilitate agreement between the chair and chief executive on issues deemed crucial to the success of board development.

After the chair and the chief executive reach general agreement about common assumptions, priorities for board development, and the specific idea of a retreat, the chair should indicate to the board that a retreat is under consideration. The chair should also explain its possible purposes, describe steps to be taken subsequently, and invite the input of other board members.

2. *Profile of the board.* At this stage, alone or with a consultant, the board should conduct a preliminary review of its own goals, structure, and practices—both to test the group's readiness to undertake a more thorough analysis of its performance and to highlight issues needing further consideration in a retreat. The board chair, members of the board affairs committee, or a consultant, with advice from the chief executive, might interview individual board members to inquire about their experiences as board members; their perceptions of the board's strengths, weaknesses, and priorities;

their impressions of the problems facing the institution; and their general interest in the idea of a retreat.

3. *Formal action by the board.* Once assumptions are clarified and a preliminary assessment of the board has been undertaken, the chair should ask the board for a formal resolution agreeing to proceed with plans for a retreat. If an outside facilitator is to be used, the resolution should identify the person, and, if possible, he or she should be present at the meeting and introduced to the board. The resolution should specify the purposes of the retreat, the time and commitment involved, and the obligation of board members to be present and to participate.

Although this step may seem overly formal, it is important to ensuring that no board member is surprised by the retreat or its purposes and that all trustees assume a sense of responsibility for the retreat's success. Even if a handful of board members remain unconvinced of the value of the retreat, it is important that they not feel they were misled or hoodwinked into supporting it.

4. *Appointment of an agenda committee.* At this stage, the chair appoints an agenda committee to prepare for the retreat. If the board decides not to use an outside facilitator, this committee also prepares to conduct the retreat. The agenda committee may be comprised of members of the board affairs committee or it may be an ad hoc group. In either case, the board chair and the chief executive should be committee members, and the facilitator, if any, should work closely with the committee to develop plans for the retreat. The agenda committee's major responsibilities are to determine the specific purposes of the retreat, set its location and dates, develop the agenda, and issue invitations.

The site of the retreat should be quiet, comfortable, and away from campus. It should offer overnight accommodations and dining facilities and be accessible to as many board members as possible. The dates of the retreat should be selected to encourage maximum participation, and the retreat should extend at minimum over a period of twenty-four hours to allow sufficient time for meeting and socializing.

The agenda for the retreat must be carefully planned, as detailed below, and the assistance of a skilled facilitator is strongly encouraged, especially for boards not accustomed to regular retreats.

However, the agenda committee should resist the temptation to turn all further responsibility for the retreat over to the facilitator. If the board is to gain maximum benefit from the experience, its members must retain ownership of the planning effort.

Attendance at the retreat should be limited to board members and the chief executive, if open meeting laws allow. The presence of spouses and administrators other than the chief executive—much less the press—can be distracting and can undermine candor. (Other retreats, such as those intended for strategic planning or board education, may profitably include spouses, administrators, faculty members, students, and others.)

5. *Information gathering and agenda development.* Boards and facilitators preparing for a retreat usually find it useful to gather detailed information about members' perceptions of the board's responsibilities, priorities, and performance. Assessment questionnaires were described earlier in this chapter; however, the agenda committee and facilitator may wish to modify whatever standard instrument is selected to reflect the goals and priorities of a particular board.

Questionnaires should be completed privately and anonymously and returned to the facilitator or to the institution so that responses can be aggregated. The facilitator and the agenda committee can then prepare a specific agenda, based in part on responses to the survey.

If possible, the proposed agenda should be shared with the full board for comments and modifications. If time prohibits this, the committee should circulate the agenda as widely as possible. Again, the idea is to enhance as much as possible the commitment of all board members to the retreat process.

6. *The retreat.* The facilitator or other individual chairing the retreat assumes responsibility for keeping the meeting on schedule, encouraging each board member to feel a sense of ownership of the process and of the board's performance, and ensuring that the retreat concludes with specific suggestions for postretreat action.

The retreat and its agenda should be based on the following:

- A clear statement of retreat purposes that are reasonable and achievable in the time allotted and at the board's current level of commitment and sophistication.

- Thorough discussion by the board of the results of the self-study instrument, if any. To facilitate this process, each board member should be sent a copy of the survey results at least a week before the retreat.
- Small-group sessions that encourage participation by involving everyone in devising strategies for enhancing board performance.
- Plenary sessions to enable small groups to report their findings and for the board as a whole to come to consensus about next steps.
- Leadership opportunities for as many board members as possible. The facilitator, chief executive, and chair should not dominate the proceedings.
- Sufficient flexibility to accommodate unpredictable shifts in board members' energy levels or interest in pursuing particular issues.
- Social time to enable board members to relax and build their relationships with one another.

The retreat should end with a reasonable consensus among board members about board goals, issues the board faces, priorities for improving group performance, and steps to be taken after the retreat concludes. Board members can be invited to complete an evaluation of the experience. The chair, chief executive, and agenda committee can use these evaluations in planning future development activities for the board.

7. *Postretreat action.* On the basis of the discussions and recommendations from the retreat, the facilitator should write a report summarizing the highlights of each session, the agreements reached, and recommendations for further action. The agenda committee should review the report for accuracy and completeness and prepare to commend it to the full board for adoption. The chair or a member of the agenda committee should contact members who were unable to attend the retreat and brief them about it so that the entire board can be brought into the spirit of the retreat.

Once the report is reviewed and adopted by the entire board, the chair should assign responsibility for specific tasks and priorities to the board, particular committees, or the chief executive. The board should be involved in monitoring progress toward achieving the goals adopted at the retreat or subsequent to it. Those responsible for follow-up should report periodically on progress achieved and seek advice on modifications. It is essential that the chair and chief executive demonstrate ongoing and visible leadership in carrying out the improvement strategies devised at the retreat. It would probably be better not to hold a retreat at all than to fail to follow up after the event is concluded.

Some boards wisely commit themselves to board development retreats, both to monitor progress in achieving goals set previously and to outline future priorities. This practice reinforces the idea that board development is not a one-time effort but an ongoing responsibility.

Sample Statements of Board Members' Responsibilities and Desirable Qualifications for Trustees and Regents

In 1988, the Minnesota legislature established the Regents Candidate Advisory Council. The council's purposes are to develop criteria for the selection of regents of the University of Minnesota, prepare a description of the responsibilities and duties of regents, identify and recruit qualified candidates, and recommend at least two and not more than four candidates for each position to be filled by the legislature. This panel of twenty-four distinguished Minnesotans publishes a report of its work by March 15 of each odd numbered year. (The council's address is 85 State Office Building, St. Paul, Minnesota 55155.)

In its 1991 report to the legislature, the council included several exhibits: a fact sheet on the council and its policies and procedures, a statement on candidate conflict of interest, a statement on diversity in candidate selection, the results of a survey of legislators concerning the council's work to date, a statement on the responsibilities of individual regents, and a statement of criteria for university regents. The latter two statements are included here.

Responsibilities of Individual Regents

1. To seek to be fully informed about the university and its role in the state and in higher education and to be responsive to the changing environments which affect it

2. To support the mission of the university
3. To speak one's mind at regents' meetings but to support policies and programs once established
4. To understand that the regents' role is policy making and not involvement in administration or the management process
5. To strengthen and sustain the president while being an active, energetic, and probing board member exercising critical judgment on policy matters
6. To communicate promptly to the president any significant concern or complaint and then let the president deal with it
7. To defend the autonomy and the independence of the university
8. To maintain an overriding loyalty to the entire university rather than to any part of it or constituency within it
9. To represent all the people of Minnesota and no particular interest, community, or constituency
10. To help enhance the public image of the university and the board of regents
11. To recognize that authority resides only with the board as a whole and not in its individual members
12. To recognize that the president is the primary spokesperson for the university and the chairman of the board is the only other person authorized to speak for the board
13. To foster openness and trust among the board of regents, the administration, the faculty, the students, state government, and the public
14. To maintain a decent respect for the opinions of one's colleagues and a proper restraint in criticism of colleagues and officers
15. To recognize that no board member shall make any request or demand for actions that violate the written policies, rules, and regulations of the board or of the university
16. To maintain the highest ethical standards and never to allow any personal conflict of interest to exist

Qualifications Sought in University Regents

A. *Personal*
   1. Integrity, with a code of personal honor and ethics above reproach.
   2. Wisdom and breadth of vision.

    3. Independence.

    4. An inquiring mind and an ability to speak it articulately and succinctly.

    5. Ability to challenge, support, and motivate university administration.

    6. An orientation to the future with an appreciation of the university's heritage.

    7. The capability and willingness to function as a member of a diverse group in an atmosphere of collegiality and selflessness.

    8. An appreciation of the public nature of the position and the institution, including the open process of election and service.

B. *Professional/experiential*

    1. Valid knowledge and experience that can bear on university problems, opportunities, and deliberations.

    2. A record of accomplishment in one's own life.

    3. An understanding of the board's role of governance and a proven record of contribution with the governing body of one or more appropriate organizations.

C. *Commitment*

    1. Commitment to education.

    2. Enthusiastic understanding and acceptance of the university's mission.

    3. An understanding of the land-grant nature of the university and the higher education system in the state.

    4. A willingness to commit the time and energy necessary to fulfill the responsibilities of a university regent.

    5. Willingness to forego any partisan political activity while a regent that could be disruptive or harmful to the university.

    6. The capability to foresee six to twelve years of constructive and productive service.

    7. Overriding loyalty to the university and to the public interest rather than to any region or constituency.

D. *Student Regent*

    1. A student regent candidate will be judged by the same criteria as other regent candidates and preferably be a current student.

RESOURCE B

Survey of Public Governing Board Characteristics, Policies, and Practices

In 1991, the Association of Governing Boards of Universities and Colleges, with support from Teachers Insurance Annuity Association/College Retirement Equities Fund (TIAA-CREF), conducted a survey of its member boards. Responses were received from 214 governing boards of public two-year and four-year colleges and universities and multicampus systems—an 81 percent response rate.

This survey included a section on board composition that allows for comparison with data from other surveys dating back to 1917. However, survey methodologies and sample sizes vary from study to study.

The highlights of the 1991 AGB survey given here include tables comparing data for different types of institutions and some data in the text that were not provided in the tables because of space limitations. Although based on a sample of public college and university governing boards, the data are believed to give a reliable and valid representation of the public sector of higher education. (Percentages in the data may not always total 100 percent as a consequence of rounding.)

380

Board Size and Composition

The public college or university governing board has an average of eleven members, but ranges from five to more than thirty members, depending on the type and location of the institution. The boards of 40 percent of four-year single-campus institutions and 41 percent of multicampus systems include students as voting members, compared to 15 percent of the boards of two-year institutions. The number of voting faculty trustees from within the institution range from none (two-year institutions) to 9 percent (four-year institutions and multi-campus systems). Boards of two-year institutions have members from designated constituencies, including alumni and ex officio members from state government, less frequently than do boards of four-year institutions and multicampus systems (see Table B.2).

Diversity of Board Members

Early in this century, males made up 96 percent of the membership of governing boards of public colleges and universities (Nearing, 1917). About fifty years later, males constituted 88 percent of all trustees in these boards (Hartnett, 1969). Change has accelerated since then, however, and public college and university governing boards more closely reflect the demographics of U.S. society.

Female membership on public boards grew from 4 percent in 1917 (Nearing, 1917) to 12 percent in 1969 (Hartnett, 1969) to 25 percent in 1991 (see Table B.3). Among public sector institutions, the percentage of female board members is the highest (31 percent) on boards of two-year colleges.

Hartnett reported in 1969 that 3 percent of all public board members were from minority groups. That number increased to 17 percent in 1991. African Americans currently account for 13 percent of board members of public institutions overall, more than double the proportion in 1977. In 1991, 3 percent of board members were reported to be of Hispanic origin, 1 percent of Asian origin, and less than 1 percent of Native American origin (Table B.3).

Trustee Term Limitations

About 37 percent of board members of four-year single-campus institutions and 29 percent of board members of multicampus systems are limited to an average of two consecutive (typically six-year) terms. About 11 percent of the boards of two-year institutions have consecutive term limits (see Table B.4). Most trustees with term limits will be eligible for reappointment to the board after a two-year waiting period, with the exception of two-year institutions, which on average have a five-year waiting period. Board chairs serve as chair for an average of three years, but nearly 33 percent are limited to an average of two years as chair.

Board Meetings

Public boards meet an average of ten times per year for three hours per meeting. On average, a board member devotes fifty-four hours to board and committee meetings annually. Board members of multicampus institutions commit an average of seventy-two hours per year to meetings. Those at two-year institutions devote an average of fifty-seven hours to meetings, and board members at four-year single-campus institutions devote about thirty-seven hours. (These figures do not include preparation time for meetings or time spent in other duties between meetings.)

Standing Committees

The standing committees used most frequently by governing boards of all public institutions or systems are, in descending order, finance (61 percent), executive (43 percent), academic affairs (38 percent), and buildings and grounds (25 percent). Table B.5 shows the use of standing committees by type of institution or system.

A typical public board committee has five members, and a minority of committees include faculty members and students as voting members. Of the faculty members who are voting members on committees, 20 percent are on academic affairs committees, 12 percent are on finance committees, and 12 percent are on student affairs committees. When students are voting members, they are most frequently on the following committees: student affairs (44 percent), academic affairs (27 percent), buildings and grounds (19 percent), and development (14 percent).

Board Staff

Virtually all public boards have a designated person to assist them with their responsibilities. But except in multicampus boards, these support people usually have part-time responsibilities for the board combined with other institutional duties (see Table B.9).

Board Policies

More than 67 percent of the boards of two-year institutions, more than 50 percent of the boards of multicampus institutions, and approximately 33 percent of the boards of four-year single-campus institutions have adopted statements defining conflicts of interest for board members. This is an increase from the 42 percent of all public boards reported to have such statements in the AGB's 1988 survey (Association of Governing Boards of Universities and Colleges, 1989).

The percentage of boards whose members are required to file disclosure statements on their assets and business affiliations increased from about 50 percent in 1988 to about 60 percent of boards in 1991. A formal orientation program for new trustees is now offered by 75 percent of public boards, an increase from 58 percent in 1988.

Chief Executive

Boards of multicampus systems are significantly more likely to have established procedures or written policies to guide the presidential search process than are boards of four-year single-campus institutions and two-year institutions. About 64 percent of the boards of two-year institutions and four-year single-campus institutions and 48 percent of multicampus systems have adopted formal policies to guide the review of the chief executive's performance (see Table B.10).

The incumbent presidents of public colleges and universities had served an average of six years in 1991. Their predecessors had served an average of eight years. Table B.12 shows variances in length of service by type of institution or system.

Few chief executives are voting members of their institution's governing board (5 percent), and virtually none serve as voting members of community college boards. The percentage of presidents and chancellors with academic rank, tenure, or both is 76 percent in four-year single-campus institutions, 57 percent in multicampus systems, and 26 percent in two-year institutions (see Table B.13).

Table B.1. Methods of Selecting Trustees in Public Institutions of Higher Education.

	Type of Institution		
	Four-year single-campus (%)	*Two-year single-campus (%)*	*Two-year and four-year multicampus (%)*
Gubernatorial appointment with legislative approval	69	32	73
Appointment by the legislature	8	6	3
Popular election	1	43	12
Other (varying approaches)	22	19	12

**Table B.2. Public Institutions of Higher Education
with Students, Faculty Members, Alumni, and
Ex Officio Representatives as Voting Board Members.**

	Type of Institution		
	Four-year single-campus (%)	Two-year single-campus (%)	Two-year and four-year multicampus (%)
Students	40	15	41
Faculty members (within the institution)	9	0	9
Faculty members (other institutions)	2	2	1
Alumni elected or appointed by alumni or association	13	4	11
All other alumni	34	6	28
Ex officio state government members as required by state law	16	4	31

Table B.3. Gender and Racial/Ethnic Background of Trustees
in Public Institutions of Higher Education.

	All (%)	Four-year single-campus (%)	Two-year single-campus (%)	Two-year and four-year multicampus (%)
Type of Institution				
Male				
1917	96	*	*	*
1969	88	*	*	*
1977	82	*	*	84
1985	77	76	75	80
1991	73	74	69	77
Female				
1917	4	*	*	*
1969	12	*	*	*
1977	18	*	*	16
1985	23	24	25	20
1991	27	26	31	23
White				
1969	97	*	*	*
1977	93	*	*	89
1985	85	*	*	86
1991	83	81	81	85
Black				
1969	3	*	*	*
1977	6	*	*	8
1985	11	*	*	10
1991	13	16	12	10
Hispanic				
1985	3	*	*	3
1991	3	2	7	3
Other minorities				
1969	>1	*	*	*
1977	1	*	*	3
1985	>1	*	*	1
1991				
Asian	1	1	1	2
Native American	>1	>1	>1	1
Other	>1	1	0	>1

Note: * = data not available.
Source: Data from Nearing, 1917; Hartnett, 1969; Atelsek and Gomberg, 1977; Association of Governing Boards of Universities and Colleges, 1985, 1991.

**Table B.4. Term Limitations of Trustees in
Public Institutions of Higher Education.**

	Type of Institution		
	Four-year single-campus (%)	Two-year single-campus (%)	Two-year and four-year multicampus (%)
Boards limiting the number of consecutive trustee terms	37	11	29
Boards permitting trustee reelection or reappointment	56	60	59
Boards having a mandatory retirement age for trustees	0	0	3

**Table B.5. Types of Board Committees in
Public Institutions of Higher Education.**

	Type of Institution		
	Four-year single-campus (%)	Two-year single-campus (%)	Two-year and four-year multicampus (%)
Executive	49	17	55
Academic affairs	39	19	51
Student affairs	31	9	25
Planning	9	11	24
Development	21	4	11
Finance	59	40	80
Buildings and grounds	20	28	32

Table B.6. Use of Executive Committees and Executive Sessions by Boards in Public Institutions of Higher Education.

	Type of Institution		
	Four-year single-campus (%)	Two-year single-campus (%)	Two-year and four-year multicampus (%)
Boards whose members not on the executive committee regularly attend executive committee meetings	19	0	31
Boards whose formal minutes of executive committee meetings are shared with the full board			
Yes	54	29	63
No; minutes are taken, but are shared only with executive committee members	12	14	11
No formal minutes are taken	35	57	26
Boards that routinely use executive sessions (a portion of the meeting restricted only to the board members and often the chief executive)	61	52	70

**Table B.7. Open Meeting Policies of Boards
in Public Institutions of Higher Education.**

	Type of Institution		
	Four-year single-campus (%)	Two-year single-campus (%)	Two-year and four-year multicampus (%)
Boards whose meetings are open to the public/media			
Yes, as required by state law	93	100	97
Yes, as a voluntary board decision	5	0	1
Boards whose committee meetings are open to the public/media			
Yes, as required by state law	64	81	85
Yes, as a voluntary board decision	7	0	8

**Table B.8. Board Self-Assessment Patterns in
Public Institutions of Higher Education.**

	Type of Institution		
	Four-year single-campus (%)	Two-year single-campus (%)	Two-year and four-year multicampus (%)
Boards that have undertaken a formal self-evaluation within the past five years	29	34	36
Boards with self-evaluation policies			
Board policy requires periodic formal board self-evaluation	14	19	11
By tradition, the board evaluates its performance on a regular basis	23	63	11
Formal board self-evaluation occurs on an irregular basis	68	38	82
Boards that have undertaken formal self-evaluation using an outside facilitator	62	53	67

Table B.9. Board Staffing Patterns in
Public Institutions of Higher Education.

	Type of Institution		
	Four-year single-campus (%)	Two-year single-campus (%)	Two-year and four-year multicampus (%)
Boards employing support staff with the following titles:			
Secretary to the board/university	24	18	38
Assistant to the president	32	11	14
Administrative assistant to the president	6	11	7
University counsel/general counsel	4	0	3
Other titles	34	60	39
Boards with a designated staff person to assist them			
Full-time	12	13	54
Part-time	88	87	46
Boards with a staff person who directly reports to the			
Chief executive	87	80	52
Board chair	6	14	20
Other	7	5	28

Table B.10. Presidential Search and Assessment Policies in
Public Institutions of Higher Education.

	Type of Institution		
	Four-year single-campus (%)	Two-year single-campus (%)	Two-year and four-year multicampus (%)
Boards with a written board policy or an established procedure to guide the search process for the chief executive	44	33	61
Boards using an executive search firm or other outside consultant to assist with the process of selecting the current chief executive	34	33	48
Boards with a written board policy to guide the comprehensive review of the chief executive's performance	63	64	48

**Table B.11. Use of Presidential Contracts in
Public Institutions of Higher Education.**

	Type of Institution		
	Four-year single-campus (%)	Two-year single-campus (%)	Two-year and four-year multicampus (%)
Boards whose incumbent chief executive currently serves under the terms of a written contract	69	96	62
Boards whose chief executive received a written contract at the time of appointment	70	89	61

**Table B.12. Length of Chief Executives' Service in
Public Institutions of Higher Education (in Years).**

	Type of Institution		
	Four-year single-campus (%)	Two-year single-campus (%)	Two-year and four-year multicampus (%)
Average term of current chief executive	7	7	5
Average term of previous chief executive	9	9	7

Table B.13. Chief Executives' Academic Rank and Tenure Status in Public Institutions of Higher Education.

	Type of Institution		
	Four-year single-campus (%)	Two-year single-campus (%)	Two-year and four-year multicampus (%)
Boards whose chief executive holds academic rank or tenure			
Both academic rank and tenure	62	15	49
Academic rank only	13	2	7
Tenure only	1	9	1

**Table B.14. Prior Position of Chief Executives in
Public Institutions of Higher Education.**

	Type of Institution		
	Four-year single-campus (%)	*Two-year single-campus (%)*	*Two-year and four-year multicampus (%)*
Boards whose chief executive held the following positions immediately prior to their current one:			
Chief executive of another higher education institution	26	30	33
Administrator in this or another higher education institution	69	64	41
Professor in this or another higher education institution	0	0	4
Other position within higher education	5	6	12
Other position outside higher education	1	0	10

RESOURCE C

Self-Study Criteria
for Public Multicampus
and System Boards

Recognizing the importance of periodic self-assessment by boards of trustees and regents, the Association of Governing Boards of Universities and Colleges has developed and published four separate surveys of self-study criteria: one for public four-year (single-campus) institutions, one for public community colleges, one for statewide coordinating boards and commissions, and one for public multicampus boards, as reprinted here. Individual board members and the chief executive complete the surveys anonymously. Their responses can then be easily aggregated to provide a useful profile of how a board perceives its relative strengths and needs.

The survey form for public multicampus and system boards presented here includes a criteria section that covers basic matters of board responsibility, organization, and performance and helps elicit matters of concern to individual board members. The separate trustee audit enables individual board members to take stock of their knowledge and commitment. Experience suggests that involving a third-party facilitator who is skilled in group process will provide the best discussion and outcomes. A separate user's guide is also available from the AGB on request.

Criterion 1: System and Institutional Missions

No university or college can be all things to all people. Each should have a clearly defined mission, a statement of purpose, if it is to have rational direction. The board that governs a system of institutions must be cognizant of the educational needs of the people of the state and the special abilities of each institution within the system to fulfill its part of those needs.

The board should ensure that educational programs are carefully planned on a systemwide basis to avoid unnecessary duplication of programs of high unit cost and programs of high necessity but low enrollment potential. The system has an obligation to define its mission clearly so that the campuses understand their relationship to the system. The board should make certain that the specific and unique goals of each institution are clearly enunciated to each academic community so that these goals can serve as guides to the faculty members, prospective students, state policymakers and the general public.

		Yes	*No*	*Don't Know / Can't Judge*
1.	Is there a statement of mission and related goals applicable to the system as a whole?	____	____	____
2.	Is it important to have a published mission statement for the system as a whole?	____	____	____
3.	Does each institution within the system have its own statement of institutional mission?	____	____	____

4. Are board members familiar (in general terms) with each mission statement? ___ ___   ___

5. Have these institutional mission statements been developed in relation to one another and to the system's statement? ___ ___   ___

6. Are these statements sufficiently clear and specific so that they can serve as guides to academic planning, decision making, and budgeting? ___ ___   ___

7. Does the board periodically review the statements of mission for
   a. The system as a whole? ___ ___   ___
   b. Each institution within the system? ___ ___   ___

8. Are these statements of mission periodically reviewed by
   a. Campus executive officer? ___ ___   ___
   b. System chief executive officer? ___ ___   ___
   c. Faculty senates? ___ ___   ___
   d. Administration? ___ ___   ___

9. Have the statements of mission been related to the statewide plans and the plans of other sectors (such as private higher education)? ___ ___   ___

Summary: In relation to this criterion, I believe the board's performance has been

Very Good ___ Good ___ Adequate ___ Poor ___ Don't Know/Can't Judge ___

Further comments or suggestions related to this criterion:

Criterion 2: Academic Planning and Policy

The board should be certain that each institution in the system has a documented academic plan to fulfill its declared educational mission. In addition, the board should ensure that the faculty and administration have formulated the necessary educational and personnel policies to achieve approved educational goals.

	Yes	*No*	*Don't Know/ Can't Judge*
1. Does the board demonstrate a good understanding of trends in higher education and of the changing needs of society and today's students?	—	—	—
2. Are the institutions and the system living up to their stated missions through the educational programs they deliver?	—	—	—
3. Do the institutions have documented long-range academic plans that are integrated with an overall system plan?	—	—	—
4. If so, has the board reviewed these plans within the last three years?	—	—	—
5. If not, is a planning process for academic programs soon anticipated?	—	—	—
6. Does the board routinely receive copies or summaries of reports from visiting accreditation teams?	—	—	—
7. Does the board receive timely reports from the system executive officer on the progress of implementation of educational policies?	—	—	—

8. If so, are these reports useful in assessing the quality of educational programs and their appropriateness?   ___ ___   ___

9. Are academic personnel policies reviewed periodically (tenure, promotion, sabbaticals, retirement, and so on)?   ___ ___   ___

10. Is systemwide, regional, or national information on policy implementation shared with the board for comparative purposes?   ___ ___   ___

11. Does the board take an active role in long-range planning for academic programs and planning?   ___ ___   ___

Summary: In relation to this criterion, I believe the board's performance has been

Very Good ___ Good ___ Adequate ___ Poor ___ Don't Know/Can't Judge ___

Further comments or suggestions related to this criterion:

Criterion 3: Financial Management and Planning

Requesting public funds from the governor, the legislature, and state financial departments is an important function and, perhaps, one of the most difficult for the governing board. Louis H. Heilbron (1973, p. 178), veteran trustee in public higher education, has said: "The condition of success is credibility. The trustees must have a record of fiscal responsibility in operations. They also should have a reputation for making supportable budgetary requests, for asking for what is needed, taking into consideration a realistic approach to the state finances. . . . This posture—affirmative to obtain appropriations to meet demonstrated needs, yet restrained to show credibility—is difficult to establish and maintain."

	Yes	*No*	*Don't Know / Can't Judge*
1. Are the fiscal plans and budgets consistently related to institutional and system master-plan goals?	——	——	——
2. Has the board established credibility in its funding requests?	——	——	——
3. Is the board's review of budget requests carried out with sufficient care, so that the resulting submission to state officials is truly the board's decision?	——	——	——
4. Has the board had to defend proposed budgets before state officials or agencies in recent years?	——	——	——
5. Has the board demonstrated its ability to be effective with state agencies in supporting system-wide and institutional needs?	——	——	——
6. Is the board provided with meaningful and useful "yardstick information" to judge expenditures, such as trend information, ratio data, data on economic inflation factors, and comparisons with institutional costs in other states?	——	——	——

7. Has the board approved and implemented a financial plan, with a widely understood distribution methodology, that allocates funds fairly and equitably among the institutions, consis-

tent with their respective
missions?   ___   ___   ___
8.   Is the financial plan discussed
     and reviewed with the campuses
     prior to its implementation?   ___   ___   ___

Summary: In relation to this criterion, I believe the board's performance has been

Very Good ___ Good ___ Adequate ___ Poor ___ Don't Know/Can't Judge ___

Further comments or suggestions related to this criterion:

Criterion 4: Physical Plant

It is the board's responsibility to create and maintain a physical environment conducive to scholarship and learning and consistent with reasonable expectations of future funding. Decisions that involve campus master plans and capital funding requests are the major concerns. Prudence demands that maximum use be made of existing physical plants before construction or remodeling is considered. Efficiency of the board's time and effort require that the board be concerned only with those matters that cannot be properly delegated to the administration.

	Yes	*No*	*Don't Know/ Can't Judge*

1.   Is the board informed about and
     does it periodically review the
     status of
     a.   Deferred maintenance?   ___   ___   ___
     b.   Energy conservation
          methods?   ___   ___   ___
     c.   Renovation as an alternative
          to new construction?   ___   ___   ___

  d. Accessibility of facilities to
   the handicapped?   —— ——   ——
2. Has the board approved master
  plans for the institutions that reflect present and future needs?   —— ——   ——
3. Have these plans been reviewed
  within the last three years?   —— ——   ——
4. Do the physical plans support
  the long-range educational master plan?   —— ——   ——
5. Before it approves proposals for
  enhanced or new construction,
  does the board assure itself that
  present space and instructional
  areas are effectively scheduled
  and utilized at maximum levels?   —— ——   ——
6. Has the board established credibility in its capital funding requests by equating the necessity
  of proposed projects with the
  ability of the state to support
  them?   —— ——   ——
7. Does the board, or do individual
  trustees, become involved in decisions on details related to the
  physical plant that are within
  the delegated responsibility of
  the executive officers and their
  staffs?   —— ——   ——
8. In relation to new buildings or
  major enhancements, does the
  board ensure the appropriate involvement of
  a. Faculty members?   —— ——   ——
  b. Students?   —— ——   ——
  c. Alumni?   —— ——   ——
  d. Other constituencies?   —— ——   ——

Summary: In relation to this criterion, I believe the board's performance has been

Very Good __ Good __ Adequate __ Poor __ Don't Know/Can't Judge __

Further comments or suggestions related to this criterion:

Criterion 5: Board Membership

The concept of a "balanced board," with sufficiently diverse backgrounds, points of view, interests, and skills, has been given increased attention recently, particularly as it applies to lay governing boards of public institutions. Boards need responsible and dedicated members with an array of specialized knowledge and skills if they are to govern effectively. The opportunity for a system board to select its own members is limited, but a board should be aware of its membership needs and make these known through whatever means are appropriate.

	Yes	*No*	*Don't Know/ Can't Judge*
1. Is the board's composition sufficiently diverse to reflect the backgrounds, interests, and perspectives of the citizens of the state?	__	__	__
2. Does the board make its membership needs known to the governor's office, legislature, or other appointing or confirming authority?	__	__	__
3. Do board members have sufficient knowledge of the history and role of the system and its individual institutions to make			

confident decisions on issues and
recommendations before them? ___ ___ ___
4. Does the board have an established orientation program for
new trustees? ___ ___ ___
5. If so, is the program comprehensive and thorough in its orientation to the system as well as to
the board's responsibilities? ___ ___ ___
6. Does the board understand and
accept the distinction between
policy and procedure, and does it
avoid involvement in operational matters that fall within
the responsibility of its principal
executives? ___ ___ ___
7. Do board members take advantage of in-service education or
other regional or national meetings to keep abreast of issues and
trends in public higher
education? ___ ___ ___

Summary: In relation to this criterion, I believe the board's performance has been

Very Good ___ Good ___ Adequate ___ Poor ___ Don't Know/Can't Judge ___

Further comments or suggestions related to this criterion:

Criterion 6: Board Organization

The effectiveness of a board depends on its decision-making process
and the conduct of its meetings. An effective board should periodically take time to review and assign priorities, review organizational structure, consider rules of procedure, and update its bylaws

and policy or operational manual, as needed. It should review its procedures for preparing agendas and conducting meetings and ensure that key policy decisions are carefully considered and that time is not wasted on trivia or administrative detail.

	Yes	*No*	*Don't Know/ Can't Judge*

1. Within the last three years, has the board reviewed its structure and the way it conducts its business? ___ ___ ___

2. Do you receive the board's agenda and supporting information for meetings in enough time to prepare yourself confidently? ___ ___ ___

3. Is the information you receive in advance of board meetings typically
   a. About right in quality and amount? ___ ___ ___
   b. Too extensive? ___ ___ ___
   c. Too little or generally lacking in quality? ___ ___ ___

4. Does the board meet annually
   a. About the right number of times? ___ ___ ___
   b. Too often? ___ ___ ___
   c. Too infrequently? ___ ___ ___

5. Does the present committee structure of the board provide for timely and effective communication of the status and direction of issues to the entire board? ___ ___ ___

6. Does the committee structure give the whole board the opportunity to consider all matters of key importance to the institu-

tions and the system?   ___ ___   ___
7. Does the board make certain, in
    the way it is organized and con-
    ducts itself, that the interests of
    all institutions within the system
    are considered equitably with re-
    spect to their respective
    missions?   ___ ___   ___
8. Does the board ensure that it has
    access to reports or the view-
    points of
    a. Faculty leaders/union
        representatives?   ___ ___   ___
    b. Student leaders?   ___ ___   ___
    c. "Classified" employees (not
        exempt from overtime pay)?   ___ ___   ___
    d. The general public?   ___ ___   ___
9. Does the board provide for rea-
    sonable rotation of its committee
    leaders and board officers?   ___ ___   ___

Summary: In relation to this criterion, I believe the board's performance has been

Very Good ___ Good ___ Adequate ___ Poor ___ Don't Know/Can't Judge ___

Further comments or suggestions related to this criterion:

Criterion 7: Selection and Assessment of Executive Officers

The selection of executive officers for the system and institutions is
a major responsibility of the governing board. Each selection
should be preceded by a thorough review of the institution's or
system's mission and priorities and a clear definition of the qualifications sought in candidates. Selection committees should solicit

viewpoints and nominees from all segments of the academic community.

It is important that the board and each executive officer agree in writing on goals and objectives to be used in assessing the officer's performance. These goals and objectives should be supported with appropriate timetables and procedures for assessment. The entire process should be perceived as beneficial to the incumbent chief executive and the system.

		Yes	*No*	*Don't Know/ Can't Judge*
1.	Do written board procedures exist to guide the process of search and selection of principal executive officers?	—	—	—
2.	Is it clear where the responsibilities lie for the distinct activities of searching, screening, and selecting executive officers at the system and institutional level?	—	—	—
3.	Have search procedures been reviewed for effectiveness within the last two or three years?	—	—	—
4.	Has the board considered an outside executive search firm to assist with the search process?	—	—	—
5.	Does board policy or practice provide that the system executive officer will select executive officers for the institutions, subject to board ratification?	—	—	—
6.	If so, does the institution's board provide procedural guidance for the system executive and convey to him or her its expectations with respect to selection criteria?	—	—	—

7. Do the search policies and procedures ensure participation by important constituent groups (students, faculty members, alumni, and the community)? ___ ___ ___

8. When incumbent executive officers were selected in recent years, were the following in place:
   a. Written statements of duties and responsibilities of the office? ___ ___ ___
   b. A written set of priorities and performance expectations? ___ ___ ___
   c. A set of conditions of employment, including perquisites (home, car, retirement plan, and so on)? ___ ___ ___

9. Did the executives participate in the development of written performance expectations for their office? ___ ___ ___

10. Do a procedure and schedule exist for a formal assessment of performance for principal executive officers? ___ ___ ___

11. Is the need for a formal assessment process understood and agreed to by the board and the executives of the system and institution? ___ ___ ___

12. Have the incumbent executives participated in the formulation of assessment policies and procedures? ___ ___ ___

Summary: In relation to this criterion, I believe the board's performance has been

Very Good ___ Good ___ Adequate ___ Poor ___ Don't Know/Can't Judge ___

Further comments or suggestions related to this criterion:

Criterion 8: Board Relations with
Executives of the System and Institutions

The quality of the relationship between a board and the executives of the system and institutions is critical to the effectiveness of the entire system. Although the board must take responsibility for basic policies and their consequences, it also must give the executives the authority they need to act decisively. The board must promote and support effective and appropriate communication between the executives of the system and the institutions.

	Yes	*No*	*Don't Know/ Can't Judge*
1. Is there a climate of mutual trust and confidence in the board's relationships with its system executive?	___	___	___
2. Does the system executive demonstrate his or her understanding of the board's responsibilities by			
a. Sharing information in a timely fashion?	___	___	___
b. Ensuring that the board decides major policy issues?	___	___	___
c. Finding creative ways to keep the board aware of the strengths and needs of each			

institution in the system? ___ ___ ___
3. Does the board demonstrate its
   responsibility for supporting the
   system chief executive by
   a. Demonstrating interest in
      his or her health and
      morale, need for perfor-
      mance feedback, need for va-
      cations or professional
      leave, family circumstances,
      compensation, and so on? ___ ___ ___
   b. Advising informally on the
      system executive's relation-
      ships with individuals or
      groups within and outside
      the system? ___ ___ ___
   c. Willingly "taking the heat"
      when necessary on difficult
      policy decisions? ___ ___ ___
   d. Maintaining a spirit of
      openness and candor with
      the system executive? ___ ___ ___
4. Are the professional and personal relationships between the
   system chief executive and board
   chair what they should be? ___ ___ ___
5. Do the executives of the institutions see the board as generally
   supportive of them? ___ ___ ___
6. Do these executives generally see
   the system executive as being
   supportive of them? ___ ___ ___
7. Has the board clearly stipulated
   each executive officer's authority
   to act decisively and negotiate
   firm settlements in crisis
   situations? ___ ___ ___
8. Does the board have an under-

standing with the administration
with regard to affirmative action
goals and objectives?   ___ ___   ___

Summary: In relation to this criterion, I believe the board's performance has been

Very Good ___ Good ___ Adequate ___ Poor ___ Don't Know/Can't Judge ___

Further comments or suggestions related to this criterion:

Criterion 9: Board-Faculty Relations

An important part of a board's success is the nature of its relationship with the faculty. Most board members lack the professional expertise to legislate in the area of academic affairs, yet they share the burden of responsibility with administrators and faculty members for the quality of instruction and for achieving the institution's academic missions. The board should rely upon professionals for advice in formulating governing policy and delegate to them authority to carry out operational policies and procedures. These responsibilities are particularly difficult to meet in a public system of higher education, where boards are so removed in time and distance from the institutions they govern.

The liaisons for the board-faculty relationship should be the executives of the system and institutions because they work with the faculty members on a day-to-day basis. The line between governing policy and operating policies and procedures should be established with reasonable clarity. The institutions needs to be given academic direction, but the faculty members need the freedom to perform their professional services.

The presence of a faculty union may influence board-faculty relationships. In fact, state laws sanctioning faculty bargaining or collective negotiation or "meet and confer" laws have often been cited as major deterrents to traditional governance procedures. Trustees must understand their policy-making roles and establish guideline policies that enhance the flexibility needed in the bargaining process while retaining the authority necessary to protect the welfare of students and the quality of institutional programs.

	Yes	*No*	*Don't Know/ Can't Judge*
1. Is there an effective and appropriate communication channel for gathering information, opinions, and advice from faculty leaders?	___	___	___
2. Is this communication channel between the board and faculty supported by the executives and administrators of the system and institutions?	___	___	___
3. Have the respective roles of the board, the administration, and the faculty been effectively delineated in the formulation of academic policy?	___	___	___
4. Does the board exercise authority over			
a. More aspects of educational affairs than it needs to?	___	___	___
b. Fewer aspects of educational affairs than it needs to?	___	___	___
c. Neither. (Its participation in educational affairs is appropriate.)	___	___	___
5. Has the administration proposed and the board approved up-to-date policies concerning			
a. Selection of new faculty members?	___	___	___

b. Standards of performance
    and peer-review
    procedures?   — —   —
c. Faculty promotion and
    tenure?   — —   —
d. Faculty retrenchment,
    whenever or wherever it
    may be necessary?   — —   —
e. Acceptance of "outside"
    work or consultancies by
    faculty members?   — —   —
f. Conflict of interest?   — —   —
g. Faculty sabbaticals or pro-
    fessional leave?   — —   —
h. Faculty grievances?   — —   —
i. Faculty benefit programs,
    including fee-waiver
    policies?   — —   —

6. Were faculty leaders involved in
    the formulation of these
    policies?   — —   —
7. Are the faculty members in
    general agreement with these
    policies, and do they view them
    favorably?   — —   —

(Optional for Collective Bargaining Environments)

8. Has the board effectively differ-
    entiated collective bargaining
    issues from administrative/gov-
    ernance issues?   — —   —
9. Does the board play an appro-
    priate role in the collective bar-
    gaining process?   — —   —
10. Has the board reviewed and dis-
    cussed the following related to
    the collective bargaining
    process:

a.   The development of a
     clear-cut set of goals and
     objectives relevant to its
     bargaining philosophy?   ____ ____   ____

b.   The selection and role of
     the management bargain-
     ing representative?   ____ ____   ____

c.   The appropriate communi-
     cation channels between
     the board and the manage-
     ment and faculty bargain-
     ing representatives?   ____ ____   ____

d.   The appropriate roles for
     individual board members
     and the chief executive
     officer in the bargaining
     process?   ____ ____   ____

Summary: In relation to this criterion, I believe the board's performance has been

Very Good ____ Good ____ Adequate ____ Poor ____ Don't Know/Can't Judge ____

Further comments or suggestions related to this criterion:

Criterion 10: Board-Student Relations

The board has a clear obligation to protect the welfare of the students and their expectation of an educational experience conducive
to scholarship and intellectual and personal development. Student
safety, health, and comfort are essential to learning. The students'
freedom to learn independently is a basic tenet of academic freedom
and, like other freedoms, it must be exercised with respect to protecting the welfare of the community as a whole. The board must
be sure that it has established lines of communication with students
through appropriate channels.

	Yes	*No*	*Don't Know/*
			Can't Judge

1. Does the board have an effective and appropriate organizational channel to solicit information, opinions, and advice from students? ___ ___ ___

2. Has the board approved policies that provide for the students' noncurricular (cultural and recreational) activities? ___ ___ ___

3. Has the board reviewed campus safety policies and procedures within the last two years? ___ ___ ___

4. Does the board, or a committee of the board, periodically review student satisfaction with
    a. The content and quality of academic programs? ___ ___ ___
    b. Faculty performance? ___ ___ ___
    c. Student services? ___ ___ ___
    d. Extracurricular programs? ___ ___ ___
    e. System and institutional response to high visibility social issues (such as apartheid/divestiture, affirmative action, campus crime, AIDS, and substance abuse)? ___ ___ ___
    f. Administration of financial aid policies and programs? ___ ___ ___

5. Is the board satisfied with the adequacy of student due process and grievance policies and procedures? ___ ___ ___

6. Does the board understand the structure of student government

within the system, and is it satisfied that the program of student
government addresses the needs
and interests of students?   ___ ___   ___

Summary: In relation to this criterion, I believe the board's performance has been

Very Good ___ Good ___ Adequate ___ Poor ___ Don't Know/Can't Judge ___

Further comments or suggestions related to this criterion:

Criterion 11: External Relationships of
the System and Its Institutions

The system and its institutions need to reassure their constituencies
that they are effectively carrying out their stated missions. Available
channels of communication should be used to convince these constituencies to support the needs of the system and the institutions.
The board also needs to evaluate the quality of program initiatives,
including appropriate board and trustee involvement in advocating
for the system and its individual institutions.

	Yes	*No*	*Don't Know/ Can't Judge*
1. Does the board ensure that the institutions have programs in place to inform the public and other interested parties about educational and scholarly accomplishments?	___	___	___
2. Have the board and the system executives established good working relationships with state officials, the legislature, and			

state agencies dealing with postsecondary education?   ___ ___   ___

3. Are most board members sufficiently knowledgeable of system
and institutional strengths and
weaknesses to be effective
spokespersons?   ___ ___   ___

4. Has the board experienced events
or situations that caused concern
regarding its responsibility to
safeguard the system's autonomy
and freedom from unreasonable
political intrusion?   ___ ___   ___

5. If so, has the board been willing
to take a public stand against
unwarranted intrusion by public
officials or agencies?   ___ ___   ___

Summary: In relation to this criterion, I believe the board's performance has been

Very Good ___ Good ___ Adequate ___ Poor ___ Don't Know/Can't Judge ___

Further comments or suggestions related to this criterion:

Trustee Audit

The responsibilities of individual trustees are different from the
responsibilities of the board as a corporate body. The following
checklist has been designed to help you assess the extent to which
you have absorbed the breadth and depth of your role. There is no
perfect score.

    Your candid response can be helpful in the design or en-
hancement of orientation programs for new and experienced trustees or in the planning of workshops or retreats. Questions in the
audit are adaptable to the unique characteristics of your system and

institutions or campuses. Responses will constitute a useful supplement to a board self-study process. The questions are the result of the scrutiny of a number of trustees and chief executives.

	Yes	No	Somewhat or Sometimes

Background

1. Do you have the required information and opportunity to understand your obligations and responsibilities as a trustee? ___ ___ ___

2. Are you familiar with the stated missions, plans, and current policies of the institutions within your system? ___ ___ ___

3. Do you stay abreast of higher education trends, legislation, and other public policy by reading the *Chronicle of Higher Education*, AGB's *Trusteeship* magazine, or other material? ___ ___ ___

4. Have you taken advantage of opportunities to meet with trustees and educators from other institutions? ___ ___ ___

5. Through scheduled board programs and activities or through your own initiative, have you had the opportunity to get to know your fellow trustees? ___ ___ ___

6. Do you find any conflict between your responsibility for the welfare and advancement of the various institutions in your system and your responsibility

to the citizens of your region,
state, or nation?   ___   ___   ___

7. Please indicate with an *x* your
   three strongest areas of expertise based on your background
   and experience.

Budget/finance	___	Student affairs	___
Investments	___	Faculty affairs	___
Management	___	Fund raising	___
Planning	___	Public relations	___
Legal affairs	___	Marketing	___
Plant		Government	
management	___	relations	___
Real estate	___	Other:___	
Education	___	___	

8. Now go back and place a check
   mark beside three areas of interest to you outside of your background and expertise.

Knowledge of the System

9. Are you well informed about
   the type and quality of your
   system's educational programs?   ___   ___   ___

10. Have you visited one or more
    institutions within the system
    in the last year?   ___   ___   ___

11. Can you accurately assess the
    leadership effectiveness of
    a. Your system's chief
       executive?   ___   ___   ___
    b. The key administrators in
       your system's office?   ___   ___   ___
    c. The chief executives of the
       individual institutions?   ___   ___   ___

12. Are you acquainted with the
major aspects of physical plant
needs at all institutions, including buildings and maintenance
needs, deferred maintenance,
planned new construction or
enhancements, and so on?   ___   ___   ___

Board and Committee Meetings

13. Are you comfortable with your
attendance record at board and
committee meetings?   ___   ___   ___
14. Do you read the minutes of
meetings to determine whether
they faithfully represent the
proceeding's decisions as you
recall them?   ___   ___   ___
15. Do you consistently and tho-
roughly familiarize yourself
with the information prepared
for you in advance of board and
committee meetings?   ___   ___   ___
16. Have you found it necessary to
remind your fellow trustees to
avoid involvement in nonpolicy
matters better left to the execu-
tives and administrators?   ___   ___   ___

Fund Raising and Public Relations

17. Have you recently taken advantage of an opportunity to say a
good word about your system to
a policymaker or organization
at the state level?   ___   ___   ___
18. Do you take advantage of op-
portunities to formally present

information about your system
or higher education in general
to key groups or individuals? ___ ___ ___

Trustee Concerns

19. Have you ever suggested some-
    one who would make an out-
    standing new board member to
    the governor or other appoint-
    ing authority? ___ ___ ___
20. Do you understand the concept
    of fund accounting? ___ ___ ___
21. Do you find your system's fi-
    nancial statements intelligible? ___ ___ ___
22. Are you able to maintain im-
    partiality regarding the con-
    cerns of students and faculty
    members and the needs of the
    system and its institutions? ___ ___ ___
23. Do you make yourself available
    for counsel with your chief ex-
    ecutive in support of his or her
    relationships with individual
    institutions as well as with state
    policy leaders? ___ ___ ___
24. Is it important to keep your
    chief executive informed of any
    personal communication you
    may establish with executive
    and administrative leaders at
    individual institutions? ___ ___ ___
25. If you have such lines of com-
    munication, can you avoid
    prejudiced judgments that
    could result from the
    communication? ___ ___ ___

26. Do you avoid asking special fa-
     vors of the administration?   ___ ___   ___

27. Are you satisfied that you have
     no real or perceived conflicts of
     interest in your service as a
     trustee?   ___ ___   ___

28. If you have not already done so,
     would you be willing to serve
     as a committee chair or board
     officer?   ___ ___   ___

     Why (or why not)?

29. Have you found your trustee-
     ship to be stimulating and re-
     warding thus far?   ___ ___   ___

     Why (or why not)?

30. How would you rate yourself as
     a board member at this time?

     Above Average ____ Average____ Below Average ____

General Assessment

1. What issues have most occupied the board's time and attention
    during the past year?

2. What were one or two successes during the past year for which
    the board takes some satisfaction?

3. What particular shortcomings do you see in the board's organization or performance that need attention?

4. Other comments or suggestions:

RESOURCE D

Recommended Readings

Chapter One: Exercising
Stewardship in Times of Transition

Gardner reminds us in *On Leadership* (1990, p. 42) that leadership is ultimately "the accomplishment of group purpose." Gardner's work is worthwhile reading for anyone who aspires to lead, whether as trustee or chief executive or other institutional officer of an academic institution—where policy decisions are made from the academic department level and up.

    Mason's book, *College and University Government* (1972), is a gem. He was a professor of political science and chairman of the department at Tulane University and chairman of the Committee on College and University Government of the Association of American University Professors at the time he wrote it. Mason's handbook is intended primarily "for those members of academic institutions who are devising a system of government for their colleges and universities" (p. ix). Writing from his unique perspective, Mason makes a strong case for faculty participation in university government. The section called "The Board of Trustees—the Reality of Limited Power vs. the Myth of Unlimited Sovereignty" is especially useful and provocative reading.

Kerr and Gade's research and report card on the state of higher education trusteeship is also required reading, particularly for those who serve the public sector. In *The Guardians: Boards of Trustees of American Colleges and Universities* (1989), Kerr and Gade conclude that most boards can and should function more effectively but that boards are nevertheless essential to U.S. higher education. The authors express particular concern about the trend toward coordination and control in multicampus systems.

Productivity is effectively addressed by eight writers in *Productivity & Higher Education* (Anderson and Meyerson, 1992). This work demonstrates how difficult it is to apply this important business concept to an academic institution but largely convinces the reader that it is possible. This little book is likely to be a precursor to many more articles and books on the same subject over the next several years.

Chapter Two: The New Demography

Two publications by Hodgkinson expand upon many of the points made in this chapter: *All One System* (1988) and "Reform Versus Reality," an article in *Phi Delta Kappan* (1991).

Chapter Three: The Economics and Financing of Public Higher Education

An individual interested in further readings about the economics and financing of public higher education will find a rich and expanding literature available to explore this subject beyond the overview provided in Chapter Three. For people who enjoy data, three annual publications are particularly valuable. The *Digest of Education Statistics*, published annually by the National Center for Education Statistics (NCES) of the U.S. Department of Education provides valuable national comparisons and trends over time, particularly with respect to international, federal, state, and private funding. This digest also includes an analysis of the economic returns to individuals from achieving various levels of education. *State Profiles: Financing Public Higher Education*, published by Research Associates of Washington, provides comprehensive statewide comparisons on funding levels, taxing capacity and effort, and postsecondary participation rates. *State Higher Education Profiles,* also published by the NCES, provides useful trends and comparisons by state, type of institution, and source of funds and expenditures.

For those who wish more information on how changes in price affect students' ability to attend college and decisions about higher education, McPherson and Shapiro's *Keeping College Affordable* (1991) provides an excellent analysis of current research on college costs and attendance. This book also provides a healthy and easily comprehended dose of two economists' perceptions of the financing of higher education.

As described in Chapter Three, two works that provide insight into the factors that have been increasing higher education costs are Arthur Hauptman's article "Why Are College Charges Rising?" (1989) and William Massy's paper "A Strategy for Productivity Improvement in College and University Academic Departments" (1990). For a review of some novel and creative financial responses to the austere fiscal environment of the 1990s, three sources are recommended. The *Tuition Dilemma* (1990), also written by Arthur Hauptman and published by the Brookings Institution, describes the pros and cons of a variety of financing strategies, including prepayment plans, national youth service initiatives, early intervention financial assurance plans, and novel student loan programs. Massy's article "Double Trouble," in the Higher Education Research Program's *Policy Perspectives* (sponsored by the Pew Charitable Trusts) includes a number of suggestions on how to improve productivity in higher education, thus using limited dollars more effectively.

Chapter Four: Coping with a Litigious Environment

A valuable source on the broad range of legal issues facing both public and private higher education institutions is Kaplin's *The Law of Higher Education* (1985) and its update (Kaplin and Lee, 1990). These comprehensive works address constitutional, statutory, and regulatory mandates as well as case law affecting colleges and universities and their constituencies. An excellent annual review of the most important judicial developments relating to higher education, Dutile's "Higher Education and the Courts," is published in the *Journal of College and University Law* each fall, covering the preceding calendar year.

A series of brief, concise reference guides on specific topics and issues of interest to trustees, administrators, faculty members, and legal counsel is available from the National Association of College and University Attorneys in Washington, D.C. Recent titles include *Risky Business: Risk Management, Loss Prevention and Insurance Procurement for Colleges and Universities* (Bennett, 1990), *What to Do When OSHA Comes Calling* (Barber, 1991), and *Crime on Campus: Analyzing and Managing the Increasing Risk of Institutional Liability* (Burling, 1990). A 1985 article by Roderick K. Daane in *The Journal of College and University Law* is the single best analysis of the role of college legal counsel to date.

Chapter Five: Planning for Strategic Decision Making

George Keller's *Academic Strategy: The Management Revolution in American Higher Education* (1983) continues to be one of the best introductions to the subject of planning for colleges and universities. It describes the challenges facing institutions of higher learning in the 1980s (many of which still apply), the role of strategic planning in higher education, and a planning methodology. *Strategic Management in Public and Nonprofit Organizations* (Bryson, 1989) is a more recent text that provides a detailed account of the steps in the planning process as well as examples of successful and unsuccessful planning efforts at several organizations. Firsthand accounts of strategic planning by executives at seven colleges and universities can be found in *Successful Strategic Planning: Case Studies* (Steeples, 1988).

Two popular authors have produced very useful guides on planning and management. Although Michael Porter writes for a business audience, many of the concepts he outlines in *Competitive Advantage* (1985) apply to colleges and universities as well. His thought-provoking books are required reading at many top business schools. They also serve as good reference works for many of the planning concepts successful businesses use. In *Managing the*

Non-Profit Organization (1990), Drucker interviews executives and "thought leaders" in nonprofit organizations on such subjects as managing for performance, building an effective board, and the importance of a mission statement.

Assessing how an institution is performing over time and relative to its peers is an important component of strategic planning. *Strategic Analysis: Using Comparative Data to Understand Your Institution* (Taylor, Meyerson, Morrell, and Park, 1991) examines key strategic indicators in nine areas (students, faculty and administration, instruction, research, plant, tuition and financial aid, student support, giving, and finances) for more than five hundred colleges and universities. This framework can help planning groups assess the performance of their institutions in comparison to national norms.

The *Harvard Business Review* often contains insightful pieces on strategic planning. Although its focus is usually on the business world, analogies can be drawn for colleges and universities. For example, the thesis of Hamel and Prahalad in their article "Strategic Intent" (1989) is that the companies that have risen to global leadership over the past two decades have begun with a goal, or "strategic intent," that exceeds their existing resources. These organizations then rally to close the gap. Henry Mintzberg, in his article "Crafting Strategy" (1987), says that successful strategies emerge over time as organizations innovate and respond to their markets. He thinks that managers need an intuitive feel for the business as well as facts, figures, and forecasts. These ideas may prove useful for strategic planning in higher education as well as in the corporate world.

Change is often an outcome of the strategic planning process. Beer, Eisenstat, and Spector studied organizational change at large corporations. They offer advice on managing change in their article "Why Change Programs Don't Produce Change" (1990).

The literature on the role of board members in strategic planning at colleges and universities is not extensive. However, one authoritative text on strategic leadership by governing boards is *Boards That Make a Difference* (Carver, 1990). This book was written specifically for the governing boards of nonprofit and public organizations.

Chapter Six: Responsibilities of the Governing Board

The Nature of Trusteeship (Nason, 1982) examines thirteen basic responsibilities of college and university governing boards and describes the organizational characteristics that contribute to an effective board. This book is a superb introduction to the nuances and ambiguities of governing boards as well as a valuable reference for the veteran board member.

For a more specific look at the most ambiguous of all board responsibilities, refer to *Trustee Responsibility for Academic Affairs* (Chait, Mortimer, Taylor, and Wood, 1985). This work asks not whether the board should participate in academic affairs but how to do so usefully or more actively than the "benign neglect" exercised by most boards. The work emphasizes shaping basic policies; the effective role of the academic affairs committee; and how to assess academic personnel policies, programs, and budgets.

In *The Guardians* (1989) Kerr and Gade offer answers to three questions: Are boards essential to the functioning of higher education? Do boards work as effectively as they could? Are the roles of boards subject to erosion over time? This report card on the state of governing boards in U.S. higher education reaches a number of interesting conclusions, including that it is easier to serve on a private board than a public board and appointment is a better means of selecting board members than election. Anyone who is interested in trusteeship and governance should read this study commissioned by the AGB.

Part humor, part sociology, part psychology, Mueller's *Behind the Boardroom Door* (1984) looks at the functioning of corporate boards. It confirms that what happens in the boardroom—the ambiguities, subtleties of human behavior, and group dynamics—is the same for boards of for-profit and nonprofit organizations. From his own experiences, Mueller concludes that the practice of trusteeship is more art than science, more similar than dissimilar among types of organizations, and more mystique than a tangible quality. This book is a wonderful source of one-liners and good advice. Mueller reminds us, for example, that there is plenty of room for humility in the boardroom, even though it is rarely found there.

Chapter Seven: Selecting the Chief Executive

The issues discussed in Chapter Seven are treated in greater detail in *Choosing a College President: Opportunities and Constraints* (McLaughlin and Riesman, 1990). This work contains chapter-length case studies of actual searches, as well as many other illustrations drawn from college and university search experiences.

Several excellent manuals can serve as guides to search procedures. Nason and Axelrod's *Presidential Search: A Guide to the Process of Selecting and Appointing College and University Presidents* (1984) is a classic in this area. It was recently revised by Neff and Leondar (1992). *The Search Committee Handbook: A Guide to Recruiting Administrators* (Marchese and Lawrence, 1987) includes useful advice for presidential searches as well as searches at other administrative levels in higher education. Judith Block McLaughlin's chapter on the use of consultants in higher education searches, found in *The Art of Hiring in Higher Education* (Trachtenberg and Stein, 1992), addresses the possible advantages and potential hazards of employing professional assistance in the search. Although now over ten years old, *At the Pleasure of the Board* (Kauffman, 1980) is still one of the best studies of the college and university presidency and has an excellent section on the presidential search. Written for both the profit and nonprofit sectors, *Making a Leadership Change* (Gilmore, 1988) examines the search process in the context of the entire period of leadership transition.

Trustees and search committee members especially interested in issues of confidentiality and disclosure will find *The Costs and Benefits of Openness: Sunshine Laws and Higher Education* (Cleveland, 1985) interesting reading, although continuing litigation in many states makes some of the specifics Cleveland cited somewhat dated. "Plugging Search Committee Leaks" (McLaughlin, 1985) provides a discussion of measures that can be taken to avoid unwanted leaks of confidential information.

Chapter Eight: Supporting the
President and Assessing the Presidency

A number of books and articles have been published on the subject of presidential assessment since the first edition of this was published in 1980. John Nason's guidebook, *Presidential Assessment* (1984) is a comprehensive look at this subject. In addition, several reports in which Clark Kerr was involved have also addressed this subject. The report of the Commission on Strengthening Presidential Leadership, *Presidents Make a Difference* (1984), and the recent Kerr and Gade volume *The Guardians* (1989), both published by the AGB, discuss presidential support and performance reviews.

Several books pertain to the evaluation of administrators, including presidents and chancellors. *Evaluating and Developing Administrative Performance* (Seldin, 1988) is recommended, as is *Developing and Evaluating Administrative Leadership* (Fisher, 1978) and a research report by Robert Nordvall, *Evaluation and Development of Administrators* (1979).

Readers should also be familiar with *At the Pleasure of the Board* (Kauffman, 1980), which contains a chapter on assessment, and the writing of Barry Munitz in the first edition of this book (1980) and in Fisher (1978), referred to above.

A recent publication of the AGB deals with the personal side of the presidency, often overlooked by boards: *Public Roles, Private Lives: The Representational Role of College and University Presidents* (Ostar, 1991). It contains interesting facts and insights, along with excellent recommendations.

Chapter Nine: Ensuring Sound Financial and Plant Management

Fund accounting in higher education can be difficult for trustees to master. Herzlinger and Sherman (1980) explain the advantages of this method of accounting, and Chabotar (1989) and Peat, Marwick, Mitchell & Company (1982) describe the usefulness of ratio analysis. A more comprehensive use of financial data is described in *Strategic Decision Making* (Frances, Huxel, Meyerson, and Park, 1987). Collier and Allen (1980a, 1980b) provide a technical description of fund accounting, while Dickmeyer and Hughes (1980) offer a practical guide to financial self-assessment in higher education.

Chapter Ten: Fund Raising and the Development of University Foundations

William Boyd's description of the synergies created by philanthropy and scholarship is a powerful introduction to the subject of the importance of private support for education. Copies of his unpublished speech are available from the Office of the President, Indiana University Foundation, P.O. Box 500, Bloomington, Indiana, 47402.

Conducting a Successful Capital Campaign (Dove, 1988) is an unusually thorough discussion of the art and science of the major fund-raising campaign. It offers new governing board members a guide and a yardstick for judging their own campaigns. *The Board Member's Guide to Fund Raising: What Every Trustee Needs to Know About Raising Money* (Howe, 1991) is an informative, nuts-and-bolts book that will prepare the governing board member to understand and participate in the fund-raising process.

The Raising of Money (Lord, 1990) delivers thirty-eight important principles of fund raising in a series of short, easy-to-read chapters. The author's understanding of and attitude toward volunteers is one that every governing board member would do well to adopt. *Mega Gifts: Who Gives Them, Who Gets Them* (Panas, 1984) is an anecdotal account of what motivated some thirty wealthy people to make major gifts to colleges and universities. The book offers important insights into the mind of the donor.

Governing board members will certainly want to consult *Fund-Raising Leadership: A Guide for College and University Boards* (Pocock, 1989b). It is a thorough consideration of the role of the governing board member in fund raising, set in the broad context of the mission and long-range plan of the institution and all its external-relations programs. *Raising Money Through an Institutionally Related Foundation* (Reilley, 1985) is a collection of useful articles specifically addressing various aspects of the relationship between separate nonprofit foundations and the institutions they serve.

Chapter Eleven: Strengthening Relationships with Government Agencies and Political Leaders

The best available overview of the relationship between universities and state governments is Newman's *Choosing Quality: Reducing Conflict Between the State and the University* (1987). This work includes numerous examples of both good and bad practices and outlines actions that can be taken by boards and others to improve relationships. Kerr and Gade's *The Guardians* (1989) includes several excellent chapters on the issues facing public boards in their relationships with government, especially the boards of multicampus systems.

Several works, although written ten to fifteen years ago, still provide valuable insights for trustees. These include *Control of the Campus* (Boyer, 1982), *The States and Higher Education: A Proud Past and a Vital Future* (Carnegie Foundation for the Advancement of Teaching, 1976), and *Conflict in Higher Education: State Government Versus Institutional Independence* (Millett, 1984). The Education Commission of the States and the State Higher Education Executive Officers periodically publish issue papers and reference documents on higher education issues. The *State Postsecondary Education Structures Handbook* (Education Commission of the States, 1991) provides an overview of changes in state board responsibilities among the states and profiles the organizational structure of each state.

Chapter Twelve: Maintaining Sound Relations with System Campuses

The literature on academic governance specific to multiuniversity or multicampus systems is rather limited. Lee and Bowen, in their report for the Carnegie Council on Policy Studies in Higher Education called *Managing Multicampus Systems: Effective Administration in an Unsteady State* (1975), offer an overall view of academic affairs, budgeting, student admissions and transfers, and faculty staffing—all within the context of multicampus governance. The authors agree that to survive and remain effective a multicampus system must attain and protect flexibility in all areas.

Especially useful for those board members interested in self-study of their role is the Self-Study Criteria for Governing Boards of Public Multicampus Higher Education Systems of the AGB (see Resource C). Included in the eleven criteria of this self-study are system and institutional missions, academic planning and policy, and financial management and planning. Also presented is a checklist by which board members can assess the extent to which they have learned and assimilated their roles.

Nason, in a postscript to the third chapter of his book *The Nature of Trusteeship: The Role and Responsibilities of College and University Boards* (1982), describes six special, unique obligations of trustees of multicampus systems. Among these special responsibilities are safeguarding institutional interests and needs, maintaining flexibility within the system, and protecting institutions from political control.

The 1987 study *Patterns in Evaluating State Higher Education Systems: Making a Virtue out of Necessity,* by John Folger and Robert Berdahl of the National Center for Postsecondary Governance and Finance at the University of Maryland, is also of interest. This work examines the processes used by statewide systems to assess their colleges and universities.

Of special interest to community college trustees is a research report by Arthur Jensen at San Bernardino Community College District, California, titled *Multicampus Community Colleges: Twenty Years Later* (1984). It provides a historical perspective on the major administrative, communications, and organizational policies and practices of fourteen multicampus districts in five states. It also compares 1984 findings with the findings of a 1963–1964 study of the administrations of multicampus community colleges.

Two works on the composition and structure of different types of institutional governing boards are helpful for trustees in gaining an understanding of the variety of boards that exist in higher education. The first, *Composition of Governing Boards, 1985: A Survey of College and University Governing Boards* (Anderson, 1985), is a special report of the Association of Governing Boards. This work focuses on the characteristics of individual board members and the boards themselves. The second, a report of the Education Commission of the States titled *State Postsecondary Education Structures Handbook* (1991), surveys the legal structures, responsibilities, and memberships of public institution governing boards of all fifty states and the District of Columbia.

Chapter Thirteen: Responding to Political, Social, and Ethical Issues

For a recent discussion of some current ethical issues in higher education, see May's *Ethics in Higher Education* (1991). *The Effec-*

tive Board of Trustees (Chait, Holland, and Taylor, 1991) and *Governing Tomorrow's Campus* (Schuster, Miller, and Associates, 1989) both provide useful guidance for trustees seeking to improve their performance. Gaff explores curricular issues in *New Life for the College Curriculum* (1991), and Richardson and Skinner tackle the difficult issue of equity and excellence in *Achieving Quality and Diversity* (1991). Other useful volumes include *Shaping Higher Education's Future* (Levine and Associates, 1989), *Today's Myths and Tomorrow's Realities* (Millard, 1991), *Culture and Ideology in Higher Education* (Tierney, 1991), *The Racial Crisis in American Higher Education* (Altbach and Lomotey, 1991), *Scholarship Reconsidered* (Boyer, 1990), and *The Prospect for Faculty in the Arts and Sciences* (Bowen and Sosa, 1989).

Chapter Fourteen: The Board's Role in Collective Bargaining

For general resources on collective bargaining with faculty and staff members in higher education, trustees should contact the National Center for the Study of Collective Bargaining in Higher Education and the Professions (Baruch College, City University of New York, 17 Lexington Avenue, Box 322, New York, New York 10010). The center is an impartial nonprofit educational institution that serves as a clearinghouse. It maintains files on contracts, grievances, and arbitration cases.

The Academic Collective Bargaining Information Service (ACBIS) is affiliated with the University of the District of Columbia. It publishes a newsletter and offers seminars and consultation services (ACBIS, 1321 H Street, N.W., Suite M-7, Washington, D.C., 20005).

For a comprehensive overview of collective bargaining, trustees can refer to *Collective Bargaining in Higher Education: The State of the Art* (Julius, 1984). Those concerned with governance issues can turn to Mortimer and McConnell (1978).

Chapter Fifteen: Setting Tenure and Personnel Policies

The Association of Governing Boards of Universities and Colleges has published several useful volumes intended expressly for trustees. *Trustee Responsibility for Academic Affairs* (Chait, Mortimer, Taylor, and Wood, 1985) addresses in detail the roles and responsibilities of the board's academic affairs committee with respect to promotion and tenure as well as academic programs and budgets and faculty evaluation. *Strategic Decision Making* (Frances, Huxel, Meyerson, and Park, 1987) suggests key questions trustees should ask and critical indicators trustees should monitor in the academic area and related realms. A companion volume, *Strategic Analysis* (Taylor, Meyerson, Morrell, and Park, 1991), provides comparative data on faculty tenure, demographics, compensation, support, and development and orients trustees to methods of using such statistics.

The history of academic tenure has been eloquently recounted in *Faculty Tenure* (American Association of University Professors and Association of American Colleges . . . , 1973), a volume that includes nearly fifty recommendations on policy and practice. *Beyond Traditional Tenure* (Chait and Ford, 1982) surveys and evaluates alternatives and modifications to conventional tenure practices and elaborates upon the suggestions outlined in Chapter Fifteen to improve the administration of tenure systems.

Other resources are useful on topics closely related to promotion and tenure. *American Professors* (Bowen and Schuster, 1986) offers a readable and comprehensive overview of the faculty and academic working conditions. *Affirmative Rhetoric, Negative Action: African-American and Hispanic Faculty at Predominantly White Institutions* (Washington and Harvey, 1989) provides an introduction to the issue of affirmative action and offers policy recommendations and conclusions. *Changing Practices in Faculty Evaluation* (Seldin, 1984) and *Determining Faculty Effectiveness* (Centra, 1979) offer practical and clearheaded suggestions to developing faculty evaluation systems. Licata (1986) focuses specifically on the evaluation of tenured faculty members. *Enhancing Faculty Careers* (Schuster, Wheeler, and Associates, 1990) and *Faculty Vital-*

ity and Institutional Productivity (Clark and Lewis, 1985) delineate strategies to foster faculty members' professional development.

Although concerned with the corporate sector, *Managing Human Assets* (Beer and others, 1984) provides excellent and relevant treatments of compensation, incentive structures, and the difficulties inherent in merit pay systems. *Pay for Performance* (National Research Council, 1991) covers the same topics, with a particular focus on government employees. Chronister and Kepple (1987) describe early retirement programs and incentives. To understand the consequences and implications of faculty discrimination litigation, consult Chapter Eight of *Academics in Court* (LaNoue and Lee, 1987).

Chapter Sixteen: Defining, Assessing, and Nurturing Quality

A highly readable source on excellence in American life and education is John Gardner's book *Excellence: Can We Be Equal and Excellent Too?* This work was first published in 1961 and released again in a revised version in 1984. An informative companion volume that describes different models of excellence in collegiate life is Alexander Astin's *Achieving Educational Excellence* (1985).

Three more recent releases are among those cited in Chapter Sixteen. *The Evidence for Quality* (Bogue and Saunders, 1992) furnishes a description and evaluation of current approaches to the definition and demonstration of quality in collegiate life. Lewis Mayhew, Patrick Ford, and Dean Hubbard present a philosophical and historical examination of factors related to quality in colleges and universities in their work *Quest for Quality* (1990). Daniel Seymour's work *On Q: Causing Quality in Higher Education* (1992) is a treatment on how total quality management can and should be applied to higher education.

On a related theme, board members who are curious about how college affects students will find a current volume by Ernest Pascarella and Patrick Terenzini (1991) of interest. It takes an informative and sometimes surprising look at variables related to the impact of colleges on students and also has much to say about collegiate quality. A work by Pascarella and Terenzini that can be mastered in a more modest time frame is found in *Planning for Higher Education* (1992) and is titled "Designing Colleges for Greater Learning."

W. Edwards Deming's book on strategic quality management, *Out of the Crisis* (1986), is a classic. Readers will find a work by Mary Walton, *The Deming Management Method* (1986), an easier introduction to Deming's major ideas. For the board member interested in more specific approaches to the assessment of quality, *Assessing Student Learning and Development* (Erwin, 1991) is recommended as an informative and easy-to-follow resource.

Chapter Seventeen: Orienting Trustees and Developing the Board

The Association of Governing Boards of Universities and Colleges provides a variety of resources for trustees, including *Fundamentals of Trusteeship,* a trustee orientation and development program consisting of a videotape, an audiotape, and a user's guide. The AGB publishes a bimonthly magazine for its members, *Trusteeship,* that contains articles and information directly relevant to trustees. The Trustee Information Center of the AGB is a clearinghouse of information on trusteeship and higher education and is accessible to members by phone, fax, or mail. The Board Mentor Program provides trained peer facilitators who can offer individualized assistance to boards. The AGB also offers a yearly series of seminars and sponsors an annual conference on trusteeship, and it provides an annual list of its publications (free upon request).

Three AGB pamphlets that are especially useful to new trustees are *Trustee Responsibilities* (Nason, 1989), *A Guide for New Trustees* (Axelrod, 1989), and *Trustee Orientation and Development Programs* (Ingram, 1989). All trustees can benefit from a reading of *Effective Trusteeship* (Zwingle, 1984) and John Nason's classic, *The Nature of Trusteeship* (1982). *The Guardians* (Kerr and Gade, 1989) draws upon interviews with presidents, board chairs, and heads of faculty organizations to describe what makes boards effective.

Recommendations for Improving Trustee Selection in Pub-

lic Colleges and Universities (Association of Governing Boards of Universities and Colleges, 1980), a report by a national commission, will be of interest to those concerned about the quality of public higher education governance. Other relevant publications include *The Cheswick Process: Seven Steps to a More Effective Board* (Savage, 1982), a practical and thorough description of the board development process and particularly the steps involved in arranging a successful board retreat, and *The Effective Board of Trustees* (Chait, Holland, and Taylor, 1991). The latter volume describes research involving the development and testing of a model of board effectiveness and contains specific suggestions for improving board performance.

Chapter Eighteen: Making Board Meetings Work

Getting to Yes: Negotiating Agreement Without Giving In, (Fisher and Ury, 1981) is a classic discussion of negotiation that provides a healthy perspective on certain types of meetings. *Robert's Rules of Order* (Robert, 1971) is also a classic. These rules are a statement of present-day parliamentary procedure. *The Strategy of Meetings,* (Kieffer, 1988) takes a more specific look at developing meeting skills in a variety of meeting contexts.

Chapter Nineteen: Understanding Chief Executive and Board Chair Responsibilities

Recommendations on strengthening the board's relationship with the president and the presidency in general are included in *Presidents Make a Difference* (1984), a report of the AGB's Commission on Strengthening Presidential Leadership. Through a three-year study and an extensive series of interviews with presidents and trustees, the commission looked at causes of the growing dissatisfaction of presidents, and ways to correct the problems. The report urges governing boards to give more careful attention to their responsibilities and cautions that unnecessary burdens should not be placed on presidents.

    Fisher's controversial book, *The Board and the President* (1991), offers a disputable view of college and university governance. Among its assertions is that boards have placed too many limits on the president's ability to lead and are the cause for the generally poor condition of the college and university presidency. According to Fisher, the policies and practices of most governing boards are antithetical to effective presidential leadership in that, typically, poorly conducted searches select the wrong kinds of presidents.

For a specific dissection of board chair–president relations, see Pocock's *The Board Chair-President Relationship* (1989a). Pocock notes the basic elements of a successful relationship and makes a number of suggestions. Three situations are examined: (1) when the board chair has the lead—ensuring that the president is kept in tune with the board's policies and that these are supportive of the president's work, (2) when the president has the lead—informing and advising the board and serving as a communication link between institutional constituencies and the board, and (3) joint responsibilities—intermingling responsibilities such as planning, resource allocation, and evaluation.

Chapter Twenty: The Role of the Board Staff Secretary

Most of the material concerning the role of the board secretary is contained in various issues of the bimonthly magazine of the AGB, *Trusteeship*. Fisher (1985) describes the critical role played by the presidential assistant, a position often combined with that of board secretary. Quatroche (1985) also speaks of the pivotal role of the board secretary. Scheid (1989, p. 36) notes that "boards speak through minutes" and stresses the contribution the board secretary makes in ensuring that all appropriate voices are heard.

Relationships between the board and the staff are explored by Houle in *Governing Boards* (1989). For those people wishing more insight into the secretary's role in presidential recruitment, a function in which the board secretary often participates, McLaughlin and Riesman offer helpful advice in *Choosing a College President* (1990). An understanding of the importance of the search for a new president will aid the secretary in contributing effectively to that process.

In *Working Effectively with Trustees,* Taylor (1987) offers great insight into the elements necessary for effective relationships with trustees. Her advice is applicable to all levels of administration.

Chapter Twenty-One: Assessing Board Performance

Since sound board assessment begins with an understanding of a board's goals and responsibilities, John Nason's classic, *The Nature of Trusteeship* (1982), is a fine place to begin exploring the role and authority of governing boards. A useful companion piece to Nason's work is *Governing Boards* (Houle, 1989), which considers board operations, structure, and relationships. Chait, Holland, and Taylor, in *The Effective Board of Trustees* (1991), have developed a model of board effectiveness and specific suggestions for improving board performance that provide guidance in understanding what it means to be a competent board and how boards can enhance their capabilities.

There is little empirical literature relating specifically to college and university boards that describes the usefulness and limitations of assessment processes. The more general, but still very useful, literature on organizational behavior that treats the subject includes Alderfer (1986), Lawler (1973), and Zander (1982). A thorough but technical treatment of self-assessment research and theory is found in Ashford (1989).

Savage's *The Cheswick Process: Seven Steps to a More Effective Board* (1982) is a very practical and thorough description of the board development process and particularly of the steps involved in arranging a successful board retreat. The AGB, whose Board Mentor Program has conducted hundreds of retreats, offers materials describing the retreat process, as well as several versions of its self-study criteria, which are useful for assessing board performance in a wide variety of institutional settings.

References

AGB Notes, 1971, *2*(1), 1.

Alderfer, C. "The Invisible Director on Corporate Boards." *Harvard Business Review,* 1986, *64,* 38–52.

Altbach, P. G., and Lomotey, K. *The Racial Crisis in American Higher Education.* Albany: State University of New York Press, 1991.

American Association of University Professors. *Policy Documents and Reports.* Washington, D.C.: American Association of University Professors, 1984.

American Association of University Professors and Association of American Colleges, Commission on Academic Tenure. *Faculty Tenure: A Report and Recommendations.* San Francisco: Jossey-Bass, 1973.

American Institute of Certified Public Accountants. *Audits of Colleges and Universities.* (2nd ed.) New York: American Institute of Certified Public Accountants, 1975.

Andersen, C. J. "Academics Bargaining Collectively: Some ABC's." *Research Brief,* 1991, *2* (entire issue 2).

Anderson, C. *Composition of Governing Boards, 1985: A Survey of College and University Governing Boards.* Washington, D.C.: Association of Governing Boards of Universities and Colleges, 1985.

Anderson, R. E. *Finance and Effectiveness: A Study of College Environments.* Princeton, N.J.: Educational Testing Service, 1983.

Anderson, R. E., and Meyerson, J. W. (eds.). *Productivity & Higher Education.* Princeton, N.J.: Peterson's, 1992.

Ashford, S. "Self-Assessments in Organizations." *Research in Organizational Behavior,* 1989, *11,* 133–174.

Assembly on University Goals and Governance. *A First Report.* Cambridge, Mass.: American Academy of Arts and Sciences, 1971.

Association of Governing Boards of Universities and Colleges. *Survey of Board Chair Opinion.* Washington, D.C.: Association of Governing Boards of Universities and Colleges, 1973.

Association of Governing Boards of Universities and Colleges. *Recommendations for Improving Trustee Selection in Public Colleges and Universities.* Washington, D.C.: Association of Governing Boards of Universities and Colleges, 1980.

Association of Governing Boards of Universities and Colleges. Commission on Strengthening Presidential Leadership. *Presidents Make a Difference.* Washington, D.C.: Association of Governing Boards of Universities and Colleges, 1984.

Association of Governing Boards of Universities and Colleges. *Composition of Governing Boards, 1985.* Washington, D.C.: Association of Governing Boards of Universities and Colleges, 1986.

Association of Governing Boards of Universities and Colleges. *Financial Responsibilities of Governing Boards.* (2nd ed.) Washington, D.C.: Association of Governing Boards of Universities and Colleges, 1989.

Association of Governing Boards of Universities and Colleges. *Self-Study Criteria for Governing Boards of Multi-Campus Systems.* Washington, D.C.: Association of Governing Boards of Universities and Colleges, 1990.

Association of Governing Boards of Universities and Colleges. *Fundamentals of Trusteeship.* Washington, D.C.: Association of Governing Boards of Universities and Colleges, 1991. Audiovisual package.

Association of Governing Boards of Universities and Colleges. "Fourteen Percent of CEOs Leave Annually; Turnover Is Consistent from Year to Year." *AGB Reports.* 1992a, *34*(6), pp. 2–3.

Association of Governing Boards of Universities and Colleges. *Recommendations for Improving Trustee Selection in Public Colleges and Universities.* Washington, D.C.: Association of Governing Boards of Universities and Colleges, 1992b.

Association of Governing Boards of Universities and Colleges. *Trustees and Troubled Times in Higher Education.* Washington, D.C.: Association of Governing Boards of Universities and Colleges, 1992c.

Astin, A. W. *Achieving Educational Excellence: A Critical Assessment of Priorities and Practices in Higher Education.* San Francisco: Jossey-Bass, 1985.

Atelsek, F., and Gomberg, I. *Composition of College and University Governing Boards.* Higher Education Panel Report, no. 35. Washington, D.C.: American Council on Education, 1977.

Axelrod, N. *A Guide for New Trustees.* Washington, D.C.: Association of Governing Boards of Universities and Colleges, 1989.

Barber, C. A. *What to Do When OSHA Comes Calling.* Washington, D.C.: National Association of College and University Attorneys, 1991.

Beale, J. R. "Delivery of Legal Service to Institutions of Higher Education." *Journal of College and University Law,* 1974, *2*(1), 5–12.

Beer, M., Eisenstat, R. A., and Spector, B. "Why Change Programs Don't Produce Change." *Harvard Business Review,* 1990, *68,* 158–166.

Beer, M., and others. *Managing Human Assets: The Groundbreaking Harvard Business School Program.* New York: Free Press, 1984.

Bennett, B. *Risky Business: Risk Management, Loss Prevention and Insurance Procurement for Colleges and Universities.* Washington, D.C.: National Association of College and University Attorneys, 1990.

Bennis, W., and Nanus, B. *Leaders: Strategies for Taking Charge.* New York: HarperCollins, 1985.

Berdahl, R. D. *Statewide Coordination of Higher Education.* Washington, D.C.: American Council on Education, 1971.

Blackwell, J. "Faculty Issues: The Impact on Minorities." *Review of Higher Education,* 1988, *11*(4), 417–434.

Bloom, A. *The Closing of the American Mind.* New York: Simon & Schuster, 1987.

Bogue, E. G., and Saunders, R. L. *The Evidence for Quality: Strengthening the Tests of Academic and Administrative Effectiveness.* San Francisco: Jossey-Bass, 1992.

Bowen, H., and Schuster, J. *American Professors: A National Resource Imperiled.* New York: Oxford University Press, 1986.

Bowen, W., and Sosa, J. *The Prospect for Faculty in the Arts and Sciences.* Princeton, N.J.: Princeton University Press, 1989.

Boyd, W. B. Address presented at Indiana University, Bloomington, Nov. 1989. (Copies available from the Office of the President, Indiana University Foundation, P.O. Box 500, Bloomington, Indiana, 47402)

Boyer, E. *Control of the Campus.* Princeton, N.J.: Carnegie Foundation for the Advancement of Teaching, 1982.

Boyer, E. *Scholarship Reconsidered.* Princeton, N.J.: Carnegie Foundation for the Advancement of Teaching, 1990.

Brown, S. *Increasing Minority Faculty: An Elusive Goal.* Princeton, N.J.: Educational Testing Service, 1988.

Bryson, M. *Strategic Management in Public and Nonprofit Organizations.* New York: Praeger, 1989.

Bucklew, N. S. "Collective Bargaining and Policy Making." In D. W. Vermilye (ed.), *Lifelong Learners—A New Clientele for Higher Education: Current Issues in Higher Education 1974.* San Francisco: Jossey-Bass, 1974.

Burling, P. *Crime on Campus: Analyzing and Managing the Increasing Risk of Institutional Liability.* Washington, D.C.: National Association of College and University Attorneys, 1990.

Cage, M. C. "How Aggressively Should Colleges Lobby Governors and Legislators for Money in Midst of Recession?" *Chronicle of Higher Education,* Feb. 19, 1992, pp. A1, A12, A23.

Carlzon, J. *Moments of Truth.* New York: HarperCollins, 1987.

Carnegie Council on Policy Studies in Higher Education. *Making Affirmative Action Work in Higher Education: An Analysis of Institutional and Federal Policies with Recommendations.* San Francisco: Jossey-Bass, 1975.

Carnegie Foundation for the Advancement of Teaching. *The States and Higher Education: A Proud Past and a Vital Future*. San Francisco: Jossey-Bass, 1976.

Carnegie Foundation for the Advancement of Teaching. *The Condition of the Professoriate: Attitudes and Trends, 1989*. Princeton, N.J.: Carnegie Foundation for the Advancement of Teaching, 1989.

Carver, J. *Boards That Make a Difference: A New Design for Leadership in Nonprofit and Public Organizations*. San Francisco: Jossey-Bass, 1990.

Centra, J. A. *Determining Faculty Effectiveness: Assessing Teaching, Research, and Service for Personnel Decisions and Improvement*. San Francisco: Jossey-Bass, 1979.

Chabotar, K. J. "Financial Ratio Analysis Comes to Nonprofits." *Journal of Higher Education*, 1989, *60*, 188–208.

Chait, R. P., and Ford, A. *Beyond Traditional Tenure*. San Francisco: Jossey-Bass, 1982.

Chait, R. P., Holland, T. P., and Taylor, B. E. *The Effective Board of Trustees*. New York: American Council on Education/Macmillan, 1991.

Chait, R. P., Mortimer, K. P., Taylor, B. E., and Wood, M. M. *Trustee Responsibility for Academic Affairs*. Washington, D.C.: Association of Governing Boards of Universities and Colleges, 1985.

Chait, R. P., and Taylor, B. E. "Evaluating Boards of Trustees: Theory and Practice." Paper presented at the Association for the Study of Higher Education, Baltimore, Md., 1987.

Chait, R. P., and Taylor, B. E. "Charting the Territory of Nonprofit Boards." *Harvard Business Review*, 1989, *67*(1), 44–54.

Chronicle of Higher Education Almanac, 1992, *39*(1), 4.

Chronister, J., and Kepple, T., Jr. *Incentive Early Retirement Programs for Faculty*. Washington, D.C.: Association for the Study of Higher Education, 1987.

Clark, B. R. "Faculty Authority." *AAUP Bulletin*, Winter 1961.

Clark, S., and Lewis, C. (eds.). *Faculty Vitality and Institutional Productivity*. New York: Teachers College Press, 1985.

Clark, T. D. *Indiana University: Midwestern Pioneer*. Bloomington: Indiana University Press, 1973.

Cleveland, H. *The Costs and Benefits of Openness: Sunshine Laws and Higher Education.* Washington, D.C.: Association of Governing Boards of Universities and Colleges, 1985.

Cohen, M. D., and March, J. G. *Leadership and Ambiguity: The American College President.* New York: McGraw-Hill, 1974.

Collier, D. J., and Allen, R. H. *Higher Education Finance Manual: Data Providers Guide.* Boulder, Colo.: National Center for Higher Education Management Systems, 1980a.

Collier, D. J., and Allen, R. H. *Higher Education Finance Manual: Data Users Guide.* Boulder, Colo.: National Center for Higher Education Management Systems, 1980b.

The Condition of Education, 1990. Vol. 2: *Postsecondary Education.* Washington, D.C.: National Center for Education Statistics, 1990.

Cowley, W. H. *Presidents, Professors, and Trustees: The Evolution of American Academic Government.* San Francisco: Jossey-Bass, 1980.

Crosby, P. *Quality Without Tears.* New York: McGraw-Hill, 1984.

Daane, R. K. "The Role of University Counsel." *Journal of College and University Law,* 1985, *12*(3), 399–414.

Deming, W. E. *Out of the Crisis.* Cambridge, Mass.: MIT Press, 1986.

Dickmeyer, N., and Hughes, K. S. *Financial Self-Assessment: A Workbook for Colleges.* Washington, D.C.: National Association of College and University Business Officers, 1980.

Digest of Education Statistics 1990. Washington, D.C.: National Center for Education Statistics, 1991.

Dove, K. E. *Conducting a Successful Capital Campaign: A Comprehensive Fundraising Guide for Nonprofit Organizations.* San Francisco: Jossey-Bass, 1988.

Drucker, P. F. *Managing the Non-Profit Organization.* New York: HarperCollins, 1990.

Dutile, F. N. "Higher Education and the Courts: 1989 in Review." *Journal of College and University Law,* 1990, *17*(2), 149–242.

Education Commission of the States. *State Postsecondary Education Structures Handbook.* Denver: Education Commission of the States, 1991.

El-Khawas, E. *Campus Trends, 1990.* Washington, D.C.: American Council on Education, 1990.

Erwin, T. D. *Assessing Student Learning and Development: A Guide to the Principles, Goals, and Methods of Determining College Outcomes.* San Francisco: Jossey-Bass, 1991.

"Fact File: 1990-91 Tuition and Fees at More Than 3,000 Colleges and Universities." *Chronicle of Higher Education,* Oct. 3, 1990, pp. A22-A25.

Figuli, D. J. "The Role and Function of Trustees." In D. J. Julius (ed.), *Collective Bargaining in Higher Education: The State of the Art.* Washington, D.C.: College and University Personnel Association, 1984.

Fisher, C. (ed.). New Directions for Higher Education, no. 22. *Developing and Evaluating Administrative Leadership.* San Francisco: Jossey-Bass, 1978.

Fisher, J. L. "Presidential Assistants: An Unsung Resource." *AGB Reports,* 1985, *27*(6), 33-36.

·Fisher, J. L. *The Board and the President.* New York: American Council on Education/Macmillan, 1991.

Fisher, R., and Ury, W. *Getting to Yes: Negotiating Agreement Without Giving In.* Boston: Houghton Mifflin, 1981.

Florida Administrative Code, chapter 6c-4.002(3), Presidential Evaluation, Aug. 11, 1985.

Folger, J., and Berdahl, R. O. *Patterns in Evaluating State Higher Education Systems: Making a Virtue out of Necessity.* Hyattsville, Md.: National Center for Postsecondary Governance and Finance, 1987.

Frances, C., Huxel, G., Meyerson, J., and Park, D. *Strategic Decision Making: Key Questions and Indicators for Trustees.* Washington, D.C.: Association of Governing Boards of Universities and Colleges, 1987.

Furniss, T. "The 1976 AAUP Retrenchment Policy." *Educational Record,* 1976, *57*(3), 133-139.

Furniss, T. "Status of AAUP Policy." *Educational Record,* 1978, *59*(1), 7-29.

Gaff, J. G. *New Life for the College Curriculum: Assessing Achievements and Furthering Progress in the Reform of General Education.* San Francisco: Jossey-Bass, 1991.

Galbraith, J. K. *The New Industrial State.* Boston: Houghton Mifflin, 1967.

Gallwey, T. *The Inner Game of Tennis.* New York: Random House, 1974.

Gardner, J. *Excellence: Can We Be Equal and Excellent Too?* (rev. ed.) New York: W. W. Norton, 1984.

Gardner, J. *On Leadership.* New York: Free Press, 1990.

Garvin, D. *Managing Quality.* New York: Free Press, 1988.

Gibran, K. *Sand and Foam.* New York: Knopf, 1973.

Gilmore, T. N. *Making a Leadership Change: How Organizations and Leaders Can Handle Leadership Transitions Successfully.* San Francisco: Jossey-Bass, 1988.

Guaspari, J. *I Know It When I See It: A Modern Fable About Quality.* New York: American Management Association, 1985.

Hadden, E. M., and Blaire, A. F. *Non-Profit Organization Rights and Liabilities for Members, Directors and Officers.* Wilmette, Ill.: Callaghan, 1987.

Halstead, K. *State Profiles: Financing Public Higher Education 1978 to 1990.* Washington, D.C.: Research Associates of Washington, 1990.

Hamel, G., and Prahalad, C. K. "Strategic Intent." *Harvard Business Review,* 1989, *67,* 63–76.

Hansen, W. L., and Weisbrod, B. A. "The Distribution of Costs and Direct Benefits of Public Higher Education: The Case of California." *Journal of Human Resources,* 1969, *4*(2), 176–191.

Hartnett, R. *College and University Trustees: Their Backgrounds, Roles and Educational Attitudes.* Princeton, N.J.: Educational Testing Service, 1969.

Hauptman, A. M. "Why Are College Charges Rising?" *Higher Education and National Affairs,* 1989, *38,* 5.

Hauptman, A. M. *The Tuition Dilemma.* Washington, D.C.: Brookings Institution, 1990.

Heilbron, L. H. *The College and University Trustee: A View from the Boardroom.* San Francisco: Jossey-Bass, 1973.

Helms, L. B. "Patterns of Litigation in Postsecondary Education: A Case Law Study." *Journal of College and University Law,* 1987, *14*(1), 99–119.

Helms, L. B. "Litigation Patterns: Higher Education and the Courts in 1988." *Education Law Reporter,* 1990, *57,* 1–11.

Herzlinger, R. E., and Sherman, H. D. "Advantages of Fund Accounting in 'Non Profits.'" *Harvard Business Review*, 1980, *58*, 94–105.

Hirsch, E. D. *Cultural Literacy: What Every American Needs to Know*. Boston: Houghton Mifflin, 1987.

Hodgkinson, H. *All One System*. Washington, D.C.: Institute for Educational Leadership, 1988.

Hodgkinson, H. *Demographic Perspectives on Higher Education*. Washington, D.C.: Association of Governing Boards of Universities and Colleges, 1990.

Hodgkinson, H. "Reform Versus Reality." *Phi Delta Kappan*, 1991, *73*(1), 9–16.

Hodgkinson, H. *A Demographic Look at Tomorrow*. Washington, D.C.: Institute for Educational Leadership, 1992a.

Hodgkinson, H. *The Nation and the States*. Washington, D.C.: Institute for Educational Leadership, 1992b.

Houle, C. O. *Governing Boards: Their Nature and Nurture*. San Francisco: Jossey-Bass, 1989.

Howe, F. *The Board Member's Guide to Fund Raising: What Every Trustee Needs to Know About Raising Money*. San Francisco: Jossey-Bass, 1991.

Hyer, P. "Affirmative Action for Women Faculty." *Journal of Higher Education*, 1985, *56*(3), 282–299.

Ingram, R. T. "Organizing the Board." In R. T. Ingram and Associates, *Handbook of College and University Trusteeship: A Practical Guide for Trustees, Chief Executives, and Other Leaders Responsible for Developing Effective Governing Boards*. San Francisco: Jossey-Bass, 1980.

Ingram, R. T. *Trustee Orientation and Development Programs*. Washington, D.C.: Association of Governing Boards of Universities and Colleges, 1989.

Jacobs, F. "Expectations of and by Faculty: An Overview for the 1990s." In L. W. Jones and F. A. Nowotny (eds.), *An Agenda for the New Decade*. New Directions for Higher Education, no. 70. San Francisco: Jossey-Bass, 1990.

Jensen, A. *Multicampus Community Colleges: Twenty Years Later*. San Bernardino, Calif.: San Bernardino Community College Press, 1984.

Julius, D. J. *Collective Bargaining in Higher Education: The State of the Art*. Washington, D.C.: College and University Personnel Association, 1984.

Kaplin, W. A. *The Law of Higher Education: The Legal Implications of Administrative Decision Making*. San Francisco: Jossey-Bass, 1978.

Kaplin, W. A. *The Law of Higher Education, 1980*. San Francisco: Jossey-Bass, 1980.

Kaplin, W. A. *The Law of Higher Education: A Comprehensive Guide to Legal Implications of Administrative Decision Making*. (2nd ed.) San Francisco: Jossey-Bass, 1985.

Kaplin, W. A., and Lee, B. A. *The Law of Higher Education: 1985–1990 Update*. Washington, D.C.: National Association of College and University Attorneys, 1990.

Kauffman, J. F. "Presidential Assessment and Development." In C. F. Fisher (ed.) *Developing and Evaluating Administrative Leadership*. New Directions for Higher Education, no. 22. San Francisco: Jossey-Bass, 1978.

Kauffman, J. F. *At the Pleasure of the Board: The Service of the College and University President*. Washington, D.C.: American Council on Education, 1980.

Keller, G. *Academic Strategy: The Management Revolution in American Higher Education*. Baltimore, Md.: The Johns Hopkins University Press, 1983.

Kerr, C. *Presidents Make a Difference*. A Report of the Commission on Strengthening Presidential Leadership. Washington, D.C.: Association of Governing Boards of Universities and Colleges, 1984.

Kerr, C., and Gade, M. *The Guardians: Boards of Trustees of American Colleges and Universities*. Washington, D.C.: Association of Governing Boards of Universities and Colleges, 1989.

Kieffer, G. *The Strategy of Meetings*. New York: Simon & Schuster, 1988.

Koteen, J. *Strategic Management in Public and Nonprofit Organizations*. New York: Praeger, 1989.

Landry, B. *The New Black Middle Class*. Berkeley: University of California Press, 1987.

LaNoue, G., and Lee, B. *Academics in Court: The Consequences of*

Faculty Discrimination Litigation. Ann Arbor: University of Michigan Press, 1987.

Lawler, E. *Motivation in Work Organizations.* Pacific Grove, Calif.: Brooks/Cole, 1973.

Lee, E., and Bowen, F. *Managing Multicampus Systems: Effective Administration in an Unsteady State.* San Francisco: Jossey-Bass, 1975.

Levine, A., and Associates. *Shaping Higher Education's Future: Demographic Realities and Opportunities, 1990–2000.* San Francisco: Jossey-Bass, 1989.

Levinson, H. "Appraisal of What Performance?" *Harvard Business Review,* 1976, *54,* 30–46.

Licata, C. *Post-Tenure Faculty Evaluation: Threat or Opportunity?* Washington, D.C.: Association for the Study of Higher Education, 1986.

Lord, J. G. *The Raising of Money: Thirty-Five Essentials Every Trustee Should Know.* Cleveland, Ohio: Third Sector Press, 1990.

McGuinness, A. C. *State Postsecondary Education Structures Handbook 1991.* Denver: Education Commission of the States, 1991.

McGuinness, A. C., Jr., and Paulson, C. *State Postsecondary Education Structures Handbook.* Denver: Education Commission of the States, 1991.

McLaughlin, J. B. "Plugging Search Committee Leaks." *AGB Reports,* 1985, *27*(3), 24–30.

McLaughlin, J. B., and Riesman, D. *Choosing a College President: Opportunities and Constraints.* Princeton, N.J.: Carnegie Foundation for the Advancement of Teaching, 1990.

McPherson, M. S., and Shapiro, M. O. *Keeping College Affordable.* Washington, D.C.: Brookings Institution, 1991.

Marchese, T. J., and Lawrence, J. F. *The Search Committee Handbook: A Guide to Recruiting Administrators.* Washington, D.C.: American Association of Higher Education, 1987.

Marks, L. R. "Directors' Liability: What You Don't Know Can Hurt You." *Symphony Magazine,* 1987, *38*(5), 18–21, 60–61.

Mason, H. L. *College and University Government.* New Orleans, La.: Tulane University Press, 1972.

Massy, W. F. "Double Trouble." *Policy Perspectives,* 1989, *2*(1), 1–4.

Massy, W. F. "A Strategy for Productivity Improvement in College and University Academic Departments." Paper presented at the Forum for College Financing, Albuquerque, N.M., Feb. 1990.

May, W. W. *Ethics in Higher Education.* New York: American Council on Education/Macmillan, 1991.

Mayhew, L. B., Ford, P. J., and Hubbard, D. L. *The Quest for Quality: The Challenge for Undergraduate Education in the 1990s.* San Francisco: Jossey-Bass, 1990.

Millard, R. M. *Today's Myths and Tomorrow's Realities: Overcoming Obstacles to Academic Leadership in the Twenty-First Century.* San Francisco: Jossey-Bass, 1991.

Millett, J. D. "The Academic Community: An Essay on Organization." New York: Unpublished, 1962.

Millett, J. D. "Interim Report on the Minnesota Community College System, Technical Report No. 1: Report on Enrollment and Costs, Minnesota Community College System." Unpublished paper, Minnesota Higher Education Coordinating Board, 1980.

Millett, J. D. "The Staffing and Budget Needs of Small Colleges." Unpublished report, Minnesota Higher Education Coordinating Board, 1982.

Millett, J. D. *Conflict in Higher Education: State Government Coordination Versus Institutional Independence.* San Francisco: Jossey-Bass, 1984.

Mintzberg, H. "Crafting Strategy." *Harvard Business Review,* July/Aug. 1987, *65*, 66–75.

Moots, P. R. "A Fresh Look at Your Bylaws." *AGB Reports,* 1991, *33*(3), 24–28.

Mortimer, K. P., and McConnell, T. R. *Sharing Authority Effectively: Participation, Interaction, and Discretion.* San Francisco: Jossey-Bass, 1978.

Mueller, R. K. *Behind the Boardroom Door.* New York: Crown, 1984.

Munitz, B. "Reviewing Presidential Leadership." In R. T. Ingram and Associates, *Handbook of College and University Trusteeship: A Practical Guide for Trustees, Chief Executives, and Other*

Leaders Responsible for Developing Effective Governing Boards. San Francisco: Jossey-Bass, 1980.

Nason, J. W. *The Nature of Trusteeship: The Role and Responsibilities of College and University Boards.* Washington, D.C.: Association of Governing Boards of Universities and Colleges, 1982.

Nason, J. W. *Presidential Assessment: A Guide to the Periodic Review of the Performance of Chief Executives.* Washington, D.C.: Association of Governing Boards of Universities and Colleges, 1984.

Nason, J. W. *Trustee Responsibilities.* Washington, D.C.: Association of Governing Boards of Universities and Colleges, 1989.

Nason, J. W., and Axelrod, N. R. *Presidential Search: A Guide to the Process of Selecting and Appointing College and University Presidents.* Washington, D.C.: Association of Governing Boards of Universities and Colleges, 1984.

National Association of College and University Attorneys. "Delivery of Legal Services to Higher Education Institutions: A Survey." *College Law Digest,* 1984, *15,* 7–33.

National Association of College and University Business Officers. *College and University Business Administration.* (4th ed.) Washington, D.C.: National Association of College and University Business Officers, 1982.

National Center for Education Statistics. *Undergraduate Financing of Postsecondary Education: A Report of the 1987 Postsecondary Education Student Aid Study.* Washington, D.C.: U.S. Department of Education, National Center for Education Statistics, 1988.

National Center for Education Statistics. *Digest of Education Statistics, 1990.* Washington, D.C.: U.S. Department of Education, 1990.

National Center on Education and the Economy. *America's Choice: High Skills, Low Wages.* Rochester, N.Y.: National Center on Education and the Economy, 1990.

National Conference of State Legislatures. *State Issues: Priority Issues for State Legislators.* Denver: National Conference of State Legislatures, 1992.

National Research Council. *Doctoral Degrees Awarded in the U.S.* Washington, D.C.: National Academy Press, 1990.

National Research Council. *Pay for Performance: Evaluating Performance Appraisal and Merit Pay.* Washington, D.C.: National Academy Press, 1991.

Nearing, S. "Who's Who Among College Trustees." *School and Society,* 1917, *6*(141), 297–299.

Neff, C., and Leondar, B. *Presidential Search: A Guide to the Process of Selecting and Appointing College and University Presidents.* (rev. ed.) Washington, D.C.: Association of Governing Boards of Universities and Colleges, 1992.

Nevison, C. "Effects of Tenure and Retirement Policies on the College Faculty." *Journal of Higher Education,* 1980, *51*(2), 150–166.

Newman, F. *Choosing Quality: Reducing Conflict Between the State and the University.* Denver: Education Commission of the States, 1987.

Nordvall, R. C. *Evaluation and Development of Administrators.* Washington, D.C.: Association for the Study of Higher Education, 1979.

O'Keefe, M., and Timpane, M. "Closing the Disconnect in American Higher Education." A paper in the Aspen Institute's Education for a Changing Society Series. Aspen, Colo.: Aspen Institute, 1990.

Ostar, R. H. *Public Roles, Private Lives: The Representational Role of College and University Presidents.* Washington, D.C.: Association of Governing Boards of Universities and Colleges, 1991.

Paltridge, J. G. "Studying Board Effectiveness." In R. T. Ingram and Associates, *Handbook of College and University Trusteeship: A Practical Guide for Trustees, Chief Executives, and Other Leaders Responsible for Developing Effective Governing Boards.* San Francisco: Jossey-Bass, 1980.

Panas, J. *Mega Gifts: Who Gives Them, Who Gets Them.* Chicago: Pluribus Press, 1984.

Pascarella, E. T., and Terenzini, P. T. *How College Affects Students: Findings and Insights from Twenty Years of Research.* San Francisco: Jossey-Bass, 1991.

Pascarella, E. T., and Terenzini, P. T. "Designing Colleges for

Greater Learning." *Planning for Higher Education*, 1992, *20*, 1–5.

Peat, Marwick, Main & Company. *Directors' and Officers' Liability: A Crisis in the Making*. Montvale, N.J.: Peat, Marwick, Main & Company, 1987.

Peat, Marwick, Mitchell & Company. *Ratio Analysis in Higher Education*. (2nd ed.) New York: Peat, Marwick, Mitchell & Company, 1982.

Perlman, D. H. *The Role of the Board Secretary*. Washington, D.C.: Association of Governing Boards of Universities and Colleges, 1989.

Peters, T., and Austin, N. *A Passion for Excellence*. New York: Random House, 1985.

Phillips, K. *The Politics of Rich and Poor*. New York: Random House, 1990.

Pocock, J. W. "Reporting Finances." In R. T. Ingram and Associates, *Handbook of College and University Trusteeship: A Practical Guide for Trustees, Chief Executives, and Other Leaders Responsible for Developing Effective Governing Boards*. San Francisco: Jossey-Bass, 1980.

Pocock, J. W. *The Board Chair–President Relationship*. Washington, D.C.: Association of Governing Boards of Universities and College, 1989a.

Pocock, J. W. *Fund-Raising Leadership: A Guide for College and University Boards*. Washington, D.C.: Association of Governing Boards of Universities and Colleges, 1989b.

Porter, M. E. *Competitive Advantage*. New York: Free Press, 1985.

Porth, W. C. "Personal Liability of Trustees of Educational Institutions." *Journal of College and University Law*, 1975, *2*(2), 143–156.

Quatroche, J. R., "Board Secretaries: Keeping It Together." *AGB Reports*, 1985, *27*(6), 36–37.

Regents Candidate Advisory Council. *Report to the Legislature of the State of Minnesota*. Minneapolis, Minn.: Regents Candidate Advisory Council, 1991.

Reilley, T. A. (ed.). *Raising Money Through an Institutionally Related Foundation*. Washington, D.C.: Council for Advancement and Support of Education, 1985.

Richardson, R. C., Jr., and Skinner, E. F. *Achieving Quality and Diversity*. New York: American Council on Education/Macmillan, 1991.

Robert, H. M. *Robert's Rules of Order*. New York: Morrow, 1971.

Rodenhouse, M. P. (ed.). *HEP 90 Higher Education Directory*. Falls Church, Va.: Higher Education Publications, 1990.

Rudolph, F. *The American College and University*. New York: Knopf, 1965.

Savage, T. *The Cheswick Process: Seven Steps to a More Effective Board*. Belmont, Mass.: The Cheswick Center, 1982.

Scheid, C. "Remembering the Little Things." *AGB Reports*, 1989, *31*(6), 36–37.

Schmidtlein, F., and Milton, T. "College and University Planning: Perspectives from a Nation-Wide Survey." *Planning for Higher Education*, 1988–89, *17*(3), 1–19.

Schuster, J. H. "Faculty Issues in the 1990s: New Realities, New Opportunities." In L. W. Jones and F. A. Nowotny (eds.), *An Agenda for the New Decade*. New Directions for Higher Education, no. 70. San Francisco: Jossey-Bass, 1990.

Schuster, J. H., Miller L. H., and Associates. *Governing Tomorrow's Campus: Perspectives and Agendas*. New York: American Council on Education/Macmillan, 1989.

Schuster, J. H., Wheeler, D. W., and Associates. *Enhancing Faculty Careers: Strategies for Development and Renewal*. San Francisco: Jossey-Bass, 1990.

Seldin, P. *Changing Practices in Faculty Evaluation: A Critical Assessment and Recommendations for Improvement*. San Francisco: Jossey-Bass, 1984.

Seldin, P. *Evaluating and Developing Administrative Performance: A Practical Guide for Academic Leaders*. San Francisco: Jossey-Bass, 1988.

Senge, P. *The Fifth Discipline*. New York: Doubleday, 1990.

Seymour, D. *On Q: Causing Quality in Higher Education*. New York: American Council on Education/Macmillan, 1992.

Singsen, M. P. "Charity Is No Defense: The Impact of the Insurance Crisis in Non-Profit Organizations and an Examination of Alternative Insurance Mechanisms." *University of San Francisco Law Review*, 1988, *22*, 599–634.

Smotony, B. "A Secretary Is Not Necessarily a Rose." *AGB Reports,* 1986, *28*(6), 33–36.

Smotony, B. "Results of 1991 Survey of Board Secretaries." Unpublishd paper presented at the Association of Governing Boards' Seminar for Board Secretaries, San Francisco, Mar. 7, 1992.

Smotony, B., and Summers, B. "What Do Board Secretaries Do?" *AGB Reports,* 1979, *21*(2), 33–36.

Steeples, D. W. (ed.). *Successful Strategic Planning: Case Studies.* San Francisco: Jossey-Bass, 1988.

Stone, B., and North, C. *Risk Management and Insurance for Non-Profit Managers.* Madison, Wis.: Society for Non-profit Organizations, 1989.

Taylor, B. E. *Working Effectively with Trustees: Building Cooperative Campus Leadership.* ASHE-ERIC Higher Education Report No. 4. Washington, D.C.: Association for the Study of Higher Education, 1987.

Taylor, B. E., Meyerson, J. W., Morrell, L. R., and Park, D., Jr. *Strategic Analysis: Using Comparative Data to Understand Your Institution.* Washington, D.C.: Association of Governing Boards of Universities and Colleges, 1991.

Tierney, W. G. *Culture and Ideology in Higher Education.* New York: Praeger, 1991.

Trachtenberg, S. J., and Stein, R. H. *The Art of Hiring in Higher Education.* New York: Prometheus Books, 1992.

Tremper, C., and Babcock, G. *The Nonprofit Board's Role in Risk Management: More Than Buying Insurance.* Washington, D.C.: National Center for Nonprofit Boards, 1990.

Tucker, A., and Mautz, R. B. "Presidential Evaluation: An Academic Circus." *Educational Record,* 1979, *60*(3) 253–260.

Ulich, R. *Three Thousand Years of Educational Wisdom.* Cambridge, Mass.: Harvard University Press, 1959.

Undergraduate Financing of Postsecondary Education: A Report of the 1987 National Postsecondary Education Student Aid Study. Washington, D.C.: National Center for Education Statistics, 1988.

U.S. Bureau of the Census. *Statistical Abstract of the United States, 1990.* Washington, D.C.: U.S. Bureau of the Census, 1990.

U.S. Department of Education, National Commission on Excellence in Education. *A Nation at Risk.* Washington, D.C.: U.S. Department of Education, 1983.

U.S. Department of Education. *State Higher Education Profiles: 1985.* Washington, D.C.: U.S. Department of Education, 1987.

U.S. House of Representatives Select Committee on Children, Youth, and Families. *U.S. Children and Their Families: Current Conditions and Recent Trends, 1989.* Washington, D.C.: U.S. Government Printing Office, 1989.

United Way of America. *Risk Management: A Guide for Nonprofits.* Alexandria, Va.: United Way of America, 1988.

Voluntary Support of Education, Vol. 1. New York: Council for Aid to Education, 1991.

Walton, M. *The Deming Management Method.* New York: Perigree, 1986.

Washington, V., and Harvey, W. *Affirmative Rhetoric, Negative Action: African-American and Hispanic Faculty at Predominantly White Institutions.* Washington, D.C.: Association for the Study of Higher Education, 1989.

Weeks, K. M. *Trustees and Preventive Law.* Washington, D.C.: Association of Governing Boards of Universities and Colleges, 1980.

Zander, A. *Making Groups Effective.* San Francisco: Jossey-Bass, 1982.

Zirkel, P. A. "Higher Education Litigation: An Overview." *Education Law Reporter,* 1989, *56,* 705–708.

Zwingle, J. *Effective Trusteeship.* Washington, D.C.: Association of Governing Boards of Universities and Colleges, 1984.

Index